FROM ZIGGURATS
TO ALGEBRA

'I find no other delight but to learn.'

Petrarch

Francesco Petrarca (1304-74),
Italian scholar, poet and humanist

FROM ZIGGURATS TO ALGEBRA

The civilising of Western Europe

George Cornelius

To my wife Annabel, who has encouraged me in our travels to many famous sites and museums – and who took the cover photograph of a 'cyclopean' Mycenaean bridge at Arkadiko, between Nauplion and Epidaurus.

And to my erudite friend Stewart Mackie, who taught me the quotation of Horace that appears at the end of the Conclusion.

© George Cornelius 2012

First published in 2012

British Library Cataloguing in Publication Data

A catalogue record for this book is available from the British Library.

ISBN 978-0-9571135-0-3

Published by George Cornelius

Edited and designed by:
Priory Ash Publishing
2 Denford Ash Cottages
Denford
Kettering
Northamptonshire NN14 4EW

01832 734425
www.prioryash.co.uk

Printed and bound in the Czech Republic

Contents

Maps

Preface

This book tells the compelling story of our initially fragile *Naissance*, up to the fall of Rome – and of the fortuitous prelude to the *Re-naissance*, a thousand years later.

From the start of my passion for the subject, I have been increasingly aware that objective study of this fascinating story has to highlight two crucially misleading myths that have only become fully exposed in recent times. The first myth concerns the academic stance – which prevailed until the late 19th century – that sought to convey the perfect originality (or flawless birth) of Classical Greece. The second myth, which is still a sinister influence at this pivotal time in the 21st.century, is the long-perpetuated deception that the wonderful Renaissance that brought the Middle Ages to an end had a purely Western pedigree, fostered (or at least tolerated) under a (mainly Catholic) Christian aegis.

My developing interest in ancient Mediterranean history, over nearly 40 years – without any formal education in the subject – has required me to buy dozens of books, most of which are addressed to intellectuals or academics. I have had to do this in order to

- piece together the timetable of events,
- pick out some of the key turning points, and
- work out which sites in each country are the most exciting and informative.

I must confess that when – about seven years ago – I started to make notes and cut out articles for a book I might eventually try to write, I imagined it would become a series of chapters that had a fairly constant theme – and that there would be no particular conclusion. But as I became immersed in research, it became increasingly clear that there should be three distinct phases, as outlined below – and further explained in the Introduction. And there is also a quite opinionated – and no doubt controversial – conclusion!

Part I covers the period from prehistory until the coming of the Iron Age. It has a mainly archaeological theme, and devotes much space to Schliemann and Evans, who – well before Carter in Egypt – brought this new 'science' to the attention of a worldwide public.

Part II starts with the chaotic (Mediterranean) Dark Age, and ends with the collapse of Rome. In between, it dwells on the wonders of the Classical Age and the Hellenistic legacy in the Middle East, caused by Alexander the Great's spectacular exploits.

Part III takes us from the struggle of Christian Europe to survive the (European) Dark Age, through the amazing near-800-year presence of Muslim Arabs in Spain, and on to the fall of Constantinople. As my knowledge has increased, my eyes have been opened to just how great a debt we owe to the survival of the Eastern Roman Empire. Even more intriguingly, we are hugely indebted to the Muslim and Jewish scholars of Southern Spain, who enabled a priceless legacy to be bestowed on 'Western students'.

I am completely fascinated by the 'detective story' of how most of the accumulated knowledge of Greece and Rome managed to survive the collapse of the latter, and centuries of chaos and dislocation – until the Early Renaissance put Europe on the track that has led to our way of life, now taken for granted across much of the globe.

I humbly hope the book will appeal to those who lead – as I have, until recently – a typically hectic lifestyle, but who are intent on getting to grips with how it all began. You may also perhaps intend to visit a number of the fascinating sites that lie throughout this vast and complex region, stretching thousands of miles from Andalusia to Iran.

Through travel guides, occasional eye-catching discoveries, TV 'edu-doc' programmes – or (as in my peculiar case) something ticking in the brain – there must be many readers and travellers who can't/won't sit on a beach for long – or who don't walk huge distances – but who would love to learn (concisely) much more about the roots of *our* civilisation.

My very specific target has been to collate in a single volume much of all that keen readers might need – as well as would-be travellers who want to make the most of each visit to different parts of the region. Wherever you are, from year to year, hopefully reference to these chapters will quickly enable you to know where it all fits – in the chronological jigsaw of history.

Above all, I have tried to *keep the book simple* in terms of language, with as little darting backwards and forwards as possible, and a minimum number of references – although the Bibliography lists all the sources from which I have learned so much over nearly four decades.

This book is a history that can only briefly introduce the *Re-Naissance*. It is just that I could not possibly compete. The fact is that there are *hundreds* of English-language books that cover the scientific advances of the Renaissance, and go into enormous detail on spectacular churches and works of art.

What I am trying to do – in a modest way – is to draw attention firstly to the 'transfer' period of more than 2,000 years (circa 3000BC to 750BC) from the Mesopotamian cradle of knowledge to the Mediterranean, and on to the subsequent flowering of Classical Greece … and secondly to the steps that led to the late-medieval 'Rebirth', and in particular the much neglected (and tragically underrated) Arabic contribution to that phenomenon.

Finally, I hope the Time-line Chart will prove to be useful – as an at-a-glance guide to the sequence in which each civilisation rose and fell in relation to its predecessor and successor, and as to their longevity.

Introduction

To set the scene in **Chapter 1**, we start with the way in which archaeological methods have changed beyond all recognition from the earliest expeditions. Only in this way can we understand how much more we will learn about our past over the rest of the 21st.century. Then in **Chapter 2** we move on to examining prehistory, from the era of astonishing cave paintings in the West, to the miracle of wheat in the East, some 10,000 years ago. We then (**Chapter 3**) discuss the circumstances that led Mesopotamia to become the most advanced society in the world – including invention of the potter's wheel, which led to the wagon wheel, and the earliest form of writing. In **Chapter 4** we cover ancient Egypt, and the paradox that while its pyramids, tombs and museums attract so much interest today, ancient Egypt's impact on the rise of civilisation in the Mediterranean was quite modest. We then move (in **Chapter 5**) to the first tentative seaborne forays from the Levantine coast into the Eastern Mediterranean, and cover some unique aspects of the island of Cyprus.

Then we come to the astonishing discoveries of the late 19th century, and a fairly detailed examination so as to understand the two giants of modern archaeology.

Ancient Greeks took, without question, Homer's *Iliad* and *Odyssey* (both probably written down around 750BC) to be a true history of the Heroic Age, although these fabulous accounts are also interwoven with Man's relationship with the immortal Gods – and their convoluted relationships with each other. When Greece was absorbed by Rome, Strabo and Pausanias travelled throughout Greece, toured the ruins of Mycenae, and both wrote *factually* of the returning 'Achaean' heroes, and of their spectacular fortress home.

By the first half of the 19th century knowledge of Egypt, Mesopotamia and Assyria had grown extensively, mainly through the writings and sketches of intrepid travellers. Napoleon's invasion of Egypt uncovered the Rosetta Stone, which had a trilingual inscription – deciphered in 1822 by Champollion as being written in demotic

Egyptian, hieroglyphics and ancient Greek. This was a massive leap in linguistic interpretation. Yet Classical orthodoxy still clung to the notion that, despite the Near East (see Chapter 3) and Egyptian flowerings (see Chapter 4) there had been a complete absence of civilisation throughout the Mediterranean, until the near-miraculous rise of Classical Greece. Despite many tales, augmented by Dodwell's brilliant 1805 sketches, the Oxbridge 'club' forcefully promoted the concept of untrammelled classical purity, and resisted any notion of a pre-Classical age, now known as the Bronze Age.

Consider this: in the preface to his *History of Greece* (1846) the MP and historian George Grote wrote: 'I begin the history of Greece with the first recorded Olympiad, or 776BC ... nor will any man be astonished to learn that the State of Greece ... in 1400BC cannot be described to him with anything like decent evidence.' He continued: '...the fabulous incidents attached to the name of Minos were ... essentially a legend and nothing more.'

Contrast the above with the fact that – being born in 1822, and therefore already obsessed with Homer when Grote's categorical statements were being printed – Heinrich Schliemann (the 'father of Archaeology') made his most thrilling discovery at Troy, only 27 years later on 14 June 1873 (see **Chapter 9**). Naturally much of academia was outraged at Schliemann's subsequent claims, with assertions of fraud, as well as much ridicule, being heaped upon him. Nevertheless, he was welcomed in London, mainly through the open mindedness of a (sceptical) Charles Newton, Keeper of Greek and Roman Antiquities at the British Museum from 1861 to 1886.

One individual, who – from the first moment – never doubted the authenticity of Schliemann's discoveries was Arthur Evans, later to unearth the wonders of Knossos in Crete from 1900 onwards (see **Chapter 6**). He was only 25 in 1876, when details of the first year's yield from Troy were disclosed in London, in a series of lectures given by Schliemann himself.

Also in 1876, Schliemann made his even more spectacular discoveries at Mycenae, after which his words rang round the world when he stated memorably (though incorrectly): 'I have gazed upon the face of Agamemnon' (see Chapter 9).

In 1881 – after only eight tumultuous years of frantic work, in the field and at his desk – Schliemann published his monumental 800-page volume on Troy (titled *Ilios*). By then his great friend, the highly

12

respected Professor Virchow, was moved to write in his preface, only 35 years after the seemingly irrefutable statements of the unfortunate Grote, '...This excavation has opened for the studies of the archaeologist a completely new theatre – like a world by itself. Here begins an entirely new science.'

In **Chapter 7** we discuss the Minoan civilisation in some detail. (Even though Schliemann's discoveries preceded those of Evans, we deal with Knossos [and Thera] before Mycenae, because they were much the earlier civilisations.) We take the trouble to do this because the island of Crete – a vast field of continuous research – has yielded so much valuable detail in the 110 years since Evans made his first startling discoveries. Then in **Chapter 8** we move to the parallel culture on the comparatively tiny island of ancient Thera (modern Santorini) where only a 'fingernail' of rugged terrain remains after the effect of by far the greatest volcanic eruption of the past 4,000 years, anywhere in the world. Every tourist who visits the island today should be dragooned into visiting the preserved city of Akrotiri – buried by volcanic ash from 1628BC until its discovery (exactly 3,595 years later) by Spyridon Marinatos, as recently as 1967. In **Chapter 10** we cover the Mycenaean empire – based on the Peloponnese – which was the 'ancestor' civilisation to Classical Greece. Here, the massive 'cyclopean' walls of Mycenae and Tiryns still have the capacity to amaze. The first phase of our story finishes in **Chapter 11** with the crucial role of the Hittites – in their development of iron smelting and casting, which presaged the onset of the Iron Age.

Moving ahead to **Part II**, we can see (in **Chapter 12**) how recent research is constantly demonstrating that the Mediterranean Dark Age did not last as long as was earlier thought – and was by no means as densely 'black' either – with Homer's pair of epic *histories* preserved, but not yet written down. In **Chapter 13**, the brilliant achievements of the Phoenicians are displayed – especially the degree to which they exploited the central and western areas of the Mediterranean, however much their contribution was later disparaged by both Greeks and Romans.

And then, in **Chapter 14**, we study the extent to which the Greeks owed their 'miracle' *naissance* to Mycenaeans, Hittites and Phoenicians, before bestowing upon the Western world the greatest flowering of every branch of knowledge that has ever yet been seen. We also cover the spread of Greek influence through their scattered colonies ... even as chaos erupted in the birthplace of their genius, Athens, and throughout the Peloponnese – the clearest demonstration of their capacity for endless ideas, but not for maintaining stable government.

In **Chapter 15** we see how the spread of 'Hellenism' to Egypt and the Middle East – through Alexander's lightning conquests – had such momentous consequences for the later preservation of knowledge. More than that, it was the blending of Hellenistic scholarship with the Babylonian legacy that – a thousand years later – enabled the remnants of the Umayyad dynasty to bring their accumulated wisdom across North Africa into Spain.

Then, in **Chapter 16**, we cover the Etruscan origins of the spectacular rise of (arguably) the greatest empire ever seen, and the astonishing accomplishments that arose through the irresistible combination of Greek ideas and hard-headed Roman practicality. Part II finishes by touching on the inherent weaknesses of the Roman model of government, wherein the deadly combination of a spoilt population at home and the onslaught of successive waves of dynamic tribes from central Europe brought about an inevitable catastrophe.

And so, in **Part III**, we come to the European Dark Age, which started with despairing poverty-stricken communities clinging on for dear life, while heroic Christian figures kept their heads down in scattered monasteries – particularly along the Celtic fringes – preserving such priceless manuscripts as they were able to garner. But then, in **Chapter 17**, we also see how – painfully – a degree of order started to arise from the chaos, and how, while the Italian peninsula remained incredibly fragmented, elsewhere nation states started to emerge.

Then – so as to start drawing the threads together of the background to the eventual Renaissance – we have to go East, to understand just how great was the Mesopotamian legacy. We pick up this thread (**Chapter 18**) before 2000BC, with the background that led to the Babylonian supremacy. We then follow a succession of rulers, from the Assyrians right through to the Parthians, whose supremacy over this vast region lasted for nearly half a millennium, which almost exactly straddled the centuries before and after the pivotal life of Christ.

Chapter 19 takes us through the mighty 400-year Sassanid Empire to the other individual who so changed the world, the prophet Muhammad. We examine how he managed to survive the wrath of his pagan compatriots, and what he *actually* taught and achieved, in such a short space of time – including his benevolent attitude to Jew and Christian. It is important to cover in some detail the crucial 180-year period between Muhammad's birth in 570AD and the overthrowing of the Umayyad dynasty in 750, with the origins of the Sunni and Shia schism explained. Within the space of a century, the Arab surge from Mecca and Medina managed to ally their unmatchable (Muslim-inspired) vigour with the Hellenistic legacy of knowledge and administrative capability ... and create a mini-renaissance of their own, centred on one of the world's oldest cities, Damascus.

Quite early in **Chapter 20** we recount the hair-raising escape of 19-year-old Abd al-Rahman from the Abbasid massacre of his extended family in Damascus, and his dangerous flight through North Africa ... that ended with his 30 years in Spain, which initiated the great flowering of Islamic culture. We see how by 1000AD, southern Spain was a land of plenty, through adoption of irrigation techniques that had been developed in Mesopotamia nearly 5,000 years previously. The spectacular advances in living standards were matched by a continuous transfer of manuscripts from Baghdad, which (mainly) indigenous scholars studied, for generation after generation. Through various dynasties, the Moorish presence in al-Andalus lasted for nearly 800 years, only ending in 1492, the year Columbus set out to find America ... aided by the marine astrolabe guiding his terrified sailors.

In **Chapter 21** we discover the extent to which the brilliant and astute Normans started to make their indelible mark – as much in Sicily and Southern Italy as in their much-publicised modernising (and refining) of England. We catalogue the European philosophers who, in expounding their *humanist* beliefs, dared to flout Catholic doctrine. We can also see where the far more advanced thinking in Muslim Spain started to make itself felt, amongst a growing band of incredulous French, English and Italians.

Then in **Chapter 22** we begin to appreciate the full extent to which Muslim and Jewish scholars received their North European and Italian guests at the sophisticated cities of Cordoba, Seville and Toledo – giving them free access to thousands of Greek texts of which they were previously unaware – which the eager 'students' laboriously translated into Latin. It is here that the second myth starts to become exposed. For as regards *any* knowledge being recognised as emanating from a *Muslim* country, how could the all-controlling Church acknowledge (let alone bring itself to publicise) that – in the middle of the very same 200-year era during which the Crusades were being intermittently fought so bitterly in Palestine (1095-1291) – Christian scholars were beating a path to Andalusia, so as to sit at the feet of the Muslim Averroes (1126-98), the greatest Greek-speaking polymath to have existed anywhere for a thousand years?

By **Chapter 23** we have moved east again. We need to understand the origins of Constantinople and the Eastern Roman Empire. This enables us to see how that society, which survived for a thousand years after the collapse of Rome (despite being almost annihilated during the fourth crusade), never stopped learning – and seeking to interpret the works of the Classical Greeks. And so we come to the point of exposing the other half of the second myth. For with the Greek language almost lost in the West since the fall of Rome, as the rest of Europe became cut off from the influence of Muslim Spain, it was a succession of intrepid *humanist* Byzantines who ran the Ottoman blockade to reach Italy. There, in Florence and Venice, they undertook the painstaking task of teaching Greek to the Italians, so that these men (who were teachers in their own right) could get to grips with the legendary texts put into their hands.

The final chapter takes us into the Renaissance. Here we attempt to give due weight to the three factors that conspired to make us who we are: first, such learning as had survived the fall of Rome, and been protected and developed in Western Europe; second, the contribution – mainly between 1000 and 1250 – from Muslim Spain; and third, the contribution – from 1350 until well after the fall of Constantinople in 1453 – from immigrant Byzantines. To illustrate this, we examine the extent to which a number of soon-to-be-famous individuals utilised classical knowledge to influence their work. And lastly we pay tribute to the man whom many commentators today believe was the greatest polymath and philosopher of history of all – the Muslim Ibn Khaldun – whose 13th-century works were soon lost, and have only been republished during the last 150 years.

And so to the **Conclusion**. This will be highly controversial in the eyes of some readers. All that can be hoped is that only a minority will jump to reading this first – and forming their own views – before they have read the preceding arguments.

Part I

Chapter 1

The impact of modern technology

Most of those who study the subject of this book now believe that Man's early achievements date back much further than was previously thought (that is, by most expert opinion prior to c1970) *and* that Man's accomplishments were far more widespread than we are (still) able to verify.

From Schliemann's creation of archaeology as an (admittedly fairly basic) 'science' at Troy in 1873, all the vital discoveries over the next 100 years were largely conducted by 'bucket and spade' endeavour, with technological methods making only modest contributions in the latter part of this most exciting period.

However, there are many *specific* scientific techniques – nearly all developed in the past 40 years – that have greatly improved our knowledge, and interpretive capabilities. The reason why this book gives this whole area prominence at this early stage is to highlight that:

a new research is continually changing what we know about sites that were originally dug prior to 1970,
b completely new discoveries are being made on ground that has been examined in detail, or trodden superficially many years previously, and
c firm conclusions drawn in books published before about 1980 should be viewed with some caution – however erudite or famous their author may have become. The best policy is always to find latest editions, or (where available) new writings on a subject.

A predominant factor that our current generation is privileged to be associated with is that – as in the case of medicine or information technology – archaeological and pre-historical research has made more progress in the past 40 years than ever before, that is since Napoleon Bonaparte took scholars to Egypt in 1798 in a determined bid to learn as much as possible of that country's mysterious history.

A salutary yet fascinating illustration of this phenomenon concerns Fernand Braudel, widely regarded as the greatest historian of the 20th century. He wrote his book *The Mediterranean in the Ancient World* in 1969, but died in 1985 without it being published. It was finally printed in French in 1998, and translated into English by Sian Reynolds in 2001. *However*, in their preface to the French edition (and in the Notes that follow) Jean Guilaine and Pierre Rouillard – almost apologetically – had no choice but to repeatedly correct many of the earliest dates that Braudel, and previous historians, had calculated (or accepted as being reasonably accurate), *in each instance* demonstrating that the subject structures were built much earlier than had been previously supposed!

Listed below are the main scientific branches now in constant use, though there are always emerging variants or sub-divisions.

Radio carbon dating
This technique (based on the radioactive properties of Carbon-14, and used for dating objects up to 50,000 years old) has not only settled many disputes/riddles, but has engendered a whole new set of puzzles by proving that nearly all previously calculated dates are in fact *much earlier* than was supposed.

One spectacular example is to be found on the Atlantic coast of France, where Megalithic monuments have been carbon-dated to the 7th-6th millennium BC and – being a completely separate development – have therefore nothing to do with the earliest voyages (? 4th-3rd millennium BC) to fetch gold from Ireland or tin from Cornwall.

What may prove to be even more significant is the case of Sardinia, where it is now certain that traces of Palaeolithic settlement from the 13th millennium – *or even earlier* – have been identified.

Yet again, there is the Gobelki Tepe complex in south-east Turkey, first excavated as recently as 2004, but now know to date from around 9000BC.

Radiology (computerised tomography) and Magnetic Resonance Imaging (MRI)

A quite different case is the 1991 discovery of an entombed 'iceman' in the Alps, on the Austro-Italian border. Carbon-dating enabled scientists to prove that Neolithic 'Otzi' died 5,300 years ago, and – because of his excellent state of preservation – these related techniques, already utilised in the examination of Egyptian mummies, provided more information about his diet/lifestyle/cause of death than in any other Stone Age find thus far.

Deoxyribonucleic acid (DNA) analysis

Where there is enough material for a sample to be taken, in this science crucial forensic details are yielded up, for example showing:

- Neanderthal/Sapiens distinctions, plotting the demise of the former,
- analyses of animal species, and human bloodlines or sex, and
- the contents of otherwise empty ceramic containers.

A most spectacular recent application of this technique took place as to the original home of the Etruscans, who developed a most sophisticated society in Tuscany, and contributed substantially to the early rise of the Roman Empire. Speculation has been rife ever since Herodotus claimed that the Etruscans came by sea from Lydia (Western Turkey). In 2007 an Italian team took samples from people living in deep mountainous Apennine villages, where it was known (after nearly 3,000 years!) that the Etruscan heritage was strongest. Put simply, a genetic variant was identified that is only shared by people from Lydia and the nearby island of Lemnos. Incredibly, a comparative study of local cattle exhibited a similar (almost) identical match.

Satellite technology

Since, in the Afghanistan 'war on terror', pictures from space can identify newspaper headlines, by the same token archaeologists can now 'read' every hillock/wrinkle in the Earth's surface, as to whether a blemish is natural or man-made ... or is at least worthy of physical scrutiny.

The launch of the Quickbird satellite in 2001 took image resolution to a new level, but also – through colour interpretation – can (for example) identify well-watered vegetation (highlighted in red) that is not visually apparent on the ground.

Computer-aided technology

The last (Wurm) Ice Age ended some 9,000 years ago, as a result of which sea levels are known to have risen about 400 feet world-wide. Computer technology has enabled accurate maps to be redrawn that show the previous coastline of each continent.

Recent exploration has now (virtually) proved that ancient civilisations prospered miles away from the present-day shore – the most irrefutable evidence yet being off the south-east and north-west coasts of India. Both of these remarkable finds *may* soon cause a complete revolution amongst prehistorians, particularly as to the origins of the Harappan civilisation in the Indus valley – already known to be one of the oldest (and most advanced) in the Stone Age world.

Dendrochronology (tree-dating)

This technique (based on widely variable annual ring growth), which can date timber-included structures back many millennia, is partly derived from original Norwegian examination of long-fossilised trees. In the Aegean, differing research teams have pieced together overlapping evidence to effect precise dating, sometimes resulting in a most spectacular fix – witness the establishment of the date of the cataclysmic volcanic explosion on the island of Santorini (ancient Thera). (See Chapter 8)

Ice-core dating

There are many methods of applying this scientific skill, the cross-referencing of which can establish pre-historical dates within a very narrow date band. The most obvious is the counting of annual layers, but other techniques include the use of predetermined ages as markers and the radioactive dating of inclusions.

Although still controversial, precise dating of the Thera explosion has 'almost' been agreed as the same as that demonstrated through dendrochronology, as a result of very intensive Greenland ice-core analysis.

Pollen analysis (palynology)

Microscopic analysis of pollen laid down in archaeological layers can identify the crops and vegetation present at that time. Only this technique could identify that 'Otzi' (see above) lived in the South Tyrol, because – even today – only on those sunnier/warmer slopes can the Hop Hornbeam tree survive.

Ground-penetrating sonar

The same methods that can identify where earthquake victims might lie underground, or in pockets within the rubble of a collapsed block of flats, is being used to seek out space beneath the soil where a tomb may be hidden.

Ever-improving techniques have recently enabled ground to be examined up to a depth of 100 metres, so as to distinguish parent rock from accumulated debris. (See Chapter 12 on the 'Odysseus Unbound' story.)

Underwater sonar

Particularly used for locating sunken vessels, this branch of science has resulted in hundreds of recoveries. One of the most spectacular examples is amongst the earliest – the shipwreck at Uluburun (14th century BC) found off the southern coast of Turkey, and now housed in the museum at Bodrum.

As can be visualised, a combination of these scientific techniques, together with leading-edge computer software and all manner of revolutionary digital aids, is now habitually being brought to bear. Two recent underwater sites that exemplify the archaeological 'weaponry' now available are the Franco-Egyptian work on ancient submerged Alexandria, and the Anglo-Greek exploration of the submerged city off the southernmost tip of Laconia in the Peloponnese, known as Pavlopetri.

In summary, whereas in the early days of archaeology attempts to ascertain eagerly sought details resulted in the partial (or sometimes total!) destruction of the subject item, a vast array of available modern skills are now brought to bear *specifically* to preserve each artefact in its original state. By ensuring that nothing is damaged (let alone destroyed), successive specialists are able to revisit sites or skeletal remains or recovered treasure time and again, so as to reveal yet more layers of vital and fascinating information.

Chapter 2

Prehistory

Homo sapiens in the Upper Palaeolithic Age – from about 30,000 to 10,000 years ago

It was from about 30,000 years ago that Homo sapiens became widespread, dominating the much less populous Neanderthal species. The latter were not necessarily hunted down and slaughtered – today there is (admittedly controversial) DNA evidence emerging that the majority may have been absorbed through inter-breeding.

Indeed, Neanderthal man – who emerged probably as far back as 500,000 years ago – has had his 'status' progressively raised during the last century to that of Homo sapiens neandertalis (as distinct from Homo sapiens sapiens). He is credited with fixing a double-sided flint to a wooden handle, burying his dead (the existence of rituals?) and inventing artificially created fire.

From this springboard, Homo sapiens sapiens – himself a mixture of many species – developed a range of more specialised tools, most notably a spear (at the beginning of this 20,000-year span) and the bow and arrow (towards the end of same). He also worked in bone (and, less frequently, in ivory and horn) to produce key micro-tools such as needles and fish hooks.

Amazingly, art appeared throughout the western Mediterranean and the western land-mass, whereas (in contrast) all the *technical developments* were confined to the eastern half of the Mediterranean.

In art, first of all came the widespread production of female figurines – 'Venus' representations, with exaggerated breasts, thighs and bellies, clearly signifying a preoccupation with fertility. Then followed cave paintings – so fabulous that the earliest discoveries (in the late 19th century) were denounced as fakes. When one realises that their remarkable efforts took place – with primitive tools – deep inside

24

caves, with only a flickering oil-lamp for company (using lichen as a wick) we can grasp the intensity with which they must have worked. Was it to do with magic or ritual ... or just to overcome loneliness during the seemingly interminable cold winters? We do not know, but present visitor displays – most spectacularly at Lascaux in France and Altamira in Spain – are 'once seen, never forgotten'.

Global *cooling* (and warming)

The next point of discussion is the effect that sharp changes in temperature had on the precarious developments taking place. In the world of the 20th millennium BC, where the *global* population – cruelly reduced to possibly only *10,000* in the penultimate glacial maximum of around 130,000 years BC – might have clawed its way back towards 1 million, the onset of the last glacial maximum (LGM) at this time was again devastating in its consequences.

The gist of the above paragraph is taken from Steven Mithen's fascinating book *After the Ice*, and he explains that much of the LGM was precipitated by the shape, tilt and wobble of the Earth's orbit. However much these combined factors caused the phenomenon, we know that a massive ice sheet covered Scotland and the northern half of England. The benign conditions across most of Europe that had supported the woolly mammoth, disappeared (together with these huge beasts) to be replaced by a much harsher environment. These tougher circumstances supported smaller varieties of animal, and diminished human settlements, which survived by much-increased 'hunting' and much reduced 'gathering'. In the Near East, tentative settlements in the warmer/wetter low-lying areas of present-day Israel and Jordan were abandoned, as the small human groups had to revert to hunting, clinging on in higher (more forested) terrain.

Mithen shows a fascinating graph, wherein this colder/drier period lasted until 12,700BC, after which for 2,000 years there was a dramatic warming (Late Glacial Interstadial) followed by an equally dramatic cooling for more than 1,000 years – the Younger Dryas – which ended in 9600BC. These rapid switches caused havoc to human development in Northern Europe, but were much less pronounced amongst the scattered peoples of the Near East. Could it be that their faster and more sophisticated progress (which forms the catalyst for this story's beginning) was the result of a long period of *moderate* disruption and adjustment, as opposed to the more catastrophic changes to the North and West that will have caused mass migration over vast distances, if not the disappearance of the majority of peoples?

(As an aside, the switch to warm/wetter conditions reached a peak around 7500BC, from when [apart from an as yet unexplained cold/dry dip around 6200BC] it has very gently subsided up to the present time. Put another way, current rapid warming – as most believe, set to continue – has some way to go before the conditions applying 9,500/10,000 years ago are again met!)

The Mesolithic era – from about 10000 BC to about 9000BC

Now a critical change took place, *on which hinged the switch of progress from West to East.*

In the West – as the LGM receded, and warmer/wetter conditions steadily took control – at first all appeared set fair. Family groups attached themselves to the massive herds of reindeer, horse or bison, and tracked their migrating patterns. They had not only food in abundance, but all the 'spin-off' products – hides, bones and dung. From these by-products they could now (respectively) make tents or huts and sew clothes, develop sophisticated tools and weapons, and have fuel to keep warm. Indeed, the animal graveyards that have been uncovered stretch the imagination both as to variety (including bear, goat, snail and fish) as well as quantity (50,000 animals discovered on a single site!).

However, although these hunters fully exploited their skills, they could not advance – indeed (though the reasons are hotly debated) they went into a relative decline as the glaciers retreated and vast areas of pastureland disappeared for ever. Furthermore, warmer weather induced the growth and spread of forests, forcing the population ever northwards. And the wonderful art? It had died out in the LGM as mysteriously as it had arisen, leaving a (perhaps) shrinking population grimly eking out their existence by adapting to forest life in pursuit of smaller game such as boar and deer.

The Proto-neolithic (without pottery) era –
from about 9000BC to 7000BC

Meanwhile, two developments were taking place in the Middle East, namely *animal rearing* and *agriculture*, which were to change everything. However slowly it took place, a sustained (symbiotic) relationship between hunter and animal appeared, perhaps – crucially – because there was no further climatic upheaval to interrupt the move to domestication. Men and women started to realise the virtues of our buzz-word – *sustainability*. Why kill every animal in sight when it could breed offspring … and/or could produce milk – and wool?

Over time a virtuous circle was created. Man did not need to chase after wild animals, so he and his group stayed put. As their small village grew (there is evidence for upwards, as well as outwards) the pile of human and animal waste started to 'breed' seeds and berries, which eventually became recognisable vegetables, fruit and (most importantly) grain. This – initially miraculous – turn of events encouraged the inhabitants of the crude settlement to persist in this initiative, and the rest, as they say, is *quite literally* our history.

In his book Mithen refers to the work of Gordon Hillman. Perhaps *the* key moment was when – amongst the random falling of ripe wild cereal grains into the dust, to be gathered as best as possible over several weeks in each season – the harvester noticed that the odd stalk held its 'ear' of ripe grain intact. Hillman says that this incidence (a genetic mutant) might occur once or twice in every 2-4 *million* stalks. Fed up with scrambling in the dust, competing with birds and insects for grain, the day must have come when the whole of that ripened ear (holding a disproportionate percentage of the day's hard-won yield) was rubbed in the palm of the harvester's hand, stored for a time, then *sown afresh*.

Gordon Hillman and Stuart Davies have calculated that – being realistic about the crude circumstances of the time – *it may still only have taken about 200 years* from the day the 'penny dropped' to move from several millennia of garnering wild cereals to, effectively, producing a properly farmed crop.

27

The birth of Civilisation –
around 7000BC (the Neolithic era)

The first hesitant step, according to Braudel, took place when a group of human beings 'had something to pass on'. The second step, or 'confirmation', was the appearance of 'beliefs' – an 'elementary attitude towards death'.

If the insecure little group was to expand, and influence others nearby, it then had to have some kind of agriculture, which stabilised the extended family to a particular site. It is believed that at this time animals were first harnessed individually, then (possibly) yoked together.

Until about 1950 it was thought that the emergence of an agricultural settlement had to coincide with *writing* – the 'cement holding together any coherent society' – but it is now realised that communities arose throughout the Middle East/Near East/Asia Minor from as early as 9000BC, long before even the most basic form of writing emerged (between 3000 and 2500BC).

Painstaking archaeological work is being increasingly undertaken – at innumerable sites – to dig right down to the virgin soil at selected hillocks or tumuli, so as to fully plot and understand the entire sequence of layers. At Knossos (Crete) the depth between 1900AD and the 7th millennium BC is 15 metres (50 feet). Through this diligent method it has been realised that the Neolithic age did not equate to the existence of pottery, necessarily. Hence the designation 'proto-neolithic', during which agricultural groups slowly prospered without a trace of pottery to hand.

To sum up therefore, at this early stage in our story, by 7000BC the earliest civilisations used fire and water. They cultivated plants and kept domesticated animals. They lived in houses in a village or small town. They had developed artistic abilities, and they indulged in some form of cult activity, *at recognised holy places*.

These summarised developments were long thought to have only taken place in the great river valleys of first Mesopotamia, then Egypt. Braudel wrote that 'the East was the point of departure for everything else', but we now know that there were dozens of 'points of departure' across a very wide region.

We also know that long-distance exchange took place almost from the beginning. It seems that there was another virtuous circle, wherein

28

the correcting of 'imbalances' of many kinds acted as a spur to progress, which – in turn – created further (perhaps different) imbalances, which only served to galvanise the earliest entrepreneurs into even more varied trading activity.

The Fertile Crescent – three of the first 'cities'

From perhaps as early as 10,000 years BC this trading activity took place along the enormous length of a 'crescent' or arc that stretched from the Persian Gulf in a north-westerly direction up the mighty Tigris and Euphrates rivers. Swinging slightly further west, the Euphrates has a kink, from which the overland route to the Orontes River (in modern-day Syria) is only 100km, with a further 50km to the Mediterranean coast. The 'Fertile Crescent' then had a northern 'branch' into southern Anatolia (Turkey) while a southern journey took the intrepid traveller – with his precious cargo – down through modern-day Lebanon to Israel.

An outstanding example of the period – reaching back into the Mesolithic era – is the city of **Jericho**, carbon-dated to 9500BC. Nothing exceptional has been noted until 7500BC, after which water cisterns and grain silos have been excavated. There are also traces of salt and bitumen, both of which can only have been brought from the Dead Sea – whose nearest point is only 10km distant.

The evidence at Jericho shows that – contrary to thought until about 1950 – much of the activity between these two dates (though carried out in the Near/Middle East) took place other than in Egypt or in Mesopotamia. Here at Jericho there appeared brick houses (with more than one room), ramparts and a large tower. Agriculture developed with the aid of irrigation, in the unforgiving climate, and trade in minerals took place with Anatolia.

Anatolia crops up as a link in many of the known settlements at this time, a common theme being the trade in obsidian (volcanic glass), which had a multitude of uses. It could be polished as a mirror, be the point of a spear/arrow, or – in slivers – be used to shave a beard, or to skin animals.

Catal Hoyuk was at the centre of this comparatively brief Anatolian flowering. It was a town with rectangular houses – entry to which was through an opening in the flat roof, via a ladder.

Agriculture was sophisticated, with wheat and barley, together with peas and lentils. They nurtured fruit and nut trees, and produced oil, while domesticating sheep and hunting a variety of wild animals.

Their near-monopoly in the export of obsidian was balanced by imports of flint (Syria) and shells from the Mediterranean. Significantly, they used local copper, and may have exported copper ore.

Most intriguingly, apart from their skills as craftsmen they developed their unique sacred art. Many artefacts have been unearthed, including sculptures in various materials, and – perhaps – the first examples of painting on the interior of rooms. Above all, they let the bones of the dead be picked over by vultures, then buried the (clothed) skeletons, with their erstwhile belongings, under a platform in their own homes!

Jarmo lay to the east, on a tributary of the Tigris. Here, alongside huts built of clay, remains of several semi-wild cereals have been recovered, together with peas and lentils. The use of pitch was in evidence, as was domesticated goat. By around 6000BC the foundations of houses were of stone.

Jarmo was never much more than a village, and soon disappeared. Catal Hoyuk was abandoned, and Jericho declined into obscurity. But there had been enough going on in these places, and many others, to kick-start a settlement process that – despite all the setbacks and catastrophes – would (as we now know) never look back.

Surface minerals

One remarkable phenomenon (to our eyes now) was the proliferation of every conceivable type of mineral on the surface of the planet – either blasted there from outer space billions of years ago, lying in open seams, or glinting at the primitive observer from shallow river-beds. One way of visualising this last feature is to look back at the American (or Australian) gold-rush, where panning in rivers was – for a short period – a major industry.

Another perspective is to consider recent (widespread) evidence of the wealth of minerals on the oceanic floor – of every type, and of incalculable value. It is mind-blowing to imagine the scene whereby the same celestial forces that showered our deep sea-beds with such (as yet largely untouched) riches, indiscriminately embedded the same array of minerals in advance of the earliest 'gatherers' – literally

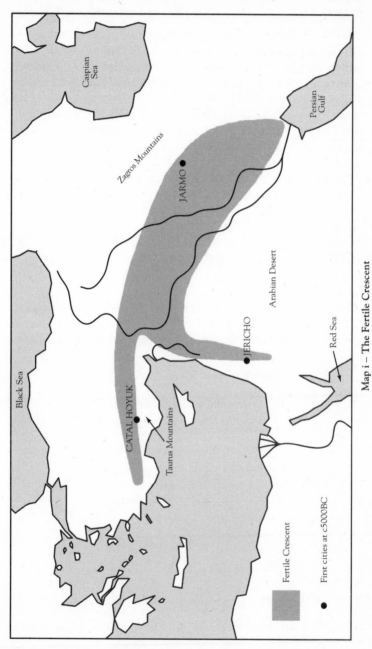

Map i – The Fertile Crescent

Fertile Crescent

First cities at c5000BC

anywhere and everywhere close to, and on top of, the Earth's land surface.

This is a crucial element of 'advantage' to bear in mind, when considering the fact that Neolithic man had access to abundant minerals – *especially* when the point was reached at which his developing intellect and skills could actually start to exploit these riches.

Chapter 3

Mesopotamia: 'first off the mark'

The quote from Braudel in the chapter title summarises – in just four words – complex developments that took place over thousands of years. Yet all the evidence points to 'civilisation' in the irrigable region of the two great rivers (in modern-day Iraq) as having preceded many of the – broadly comparable – achievements in Egypt by perhaps one millennium.

Developments in the north of the region came first. From about 6000BC primitive agriculture and animal husbandry progressed in the drier lands, between Syria to the west and the Zagros Mountains (bordering what is now Iran) to the east. In this area there is no evidence of irrigation, but pottery was widespread, and copper utilised.

In the southern region, development took place from the 5th millennium, and it his here that Sumerian immigrants started to make their lasting contribution. No certainty exists as to the origin of these ingenious people, but what sets them apart from every other stuttering communal activity was the *harnessing* of the key resources that enabled them to exploit the limitless potential of the two great untamed rivers.

Harnessing resources

This 'harnessing' took three forms, in sequence. The first was irrigation. Both rivers were comprehensively (and unpredictably) flooded each spring by melt-flows from the upstream mountainous regions, wherein the fertile alluvial mud (alongside the rivers) was swamped, resulting in stagnant pools that festered in the summer heat. Irrigation of this low-lying land – which received a very low rainfall – was instigated, so as to control the water inflow and outflow. Some

4,000 years before Archimedes, the Sumerians mastered the manufacture of a 'screw' device, which – together with canals, dams and sluices – enabled them to move water considerable distances from the main water channels, in any direction.

Building these complex structures involved much labour – recruits had to be imported – and to feed a growing population the field system needed to be expanded continually. In the now expanding acreage under control, cereals, fruit and sesame grew in abundance – hence the actuality (and subsequent legend) of a Garden of Eden. Sesame was a crucial crop, incidentally – the only bulk source of oil for many applications, until use of the olive became widespread from about 3000BC.

The second type of (literal) harnessing was of animals, as opposed to their domestication for milk, breeding and meat/clothing. Oxen were yoked so that, as still seen today, they could walk in endless circles, turning the crude 'wheel' that raised water. From the 4th millennium, the plough was developed, with oxen dragging (slowly improving) mechanisms. The ass became a pack animal, trudging up and down the riverside, carrying incredibly heavy loads.

The third aspect was harnessing the river, not for irrigation, but for travel. Fishing from the riverbank had probably encouraged the construction of simple rafts to exploit the many lakes, and the estuaries at the mouth of the Persian Gulf. Such rafts may also have been used to ferry people/goods/animals across the waters, at the narrowest points, from the dawn of history.

Subsequently, Sumerian seals from the later 4th millennium showed boats for ritual procession – reeds lashed together, and coated in pitch. The breakthrough was that these could be steered by pole downstream, and laboriously rowed back upstream. At least (from a trading point of view) that was a step on from the previous method of collapsing coracles made of skin, for them to be carried back up the riverbank by pack animal! Along the length of the two rivers, increasingly active trade saw grain/foodstuffs and reeds taken upstream to the hilly/dry country, with stone and timber for building – and livestock – for the burgeoning population going in the opposite direction to the ever more widespread arable farms and settlements.

Potter's wheel, wagon wheel, and weaving

The concepts of the stone grinding wheel and the wooden water wheel both probably came about as a means of handling the sheer volumes to be 'processed' in each case. Flattish blocks of stone or tree stump probably became rounded at the edges to make it easier for man or beast to trudge round in circles.

These crude wheels operated horizontally, with the logic of finding a method of perfecting the 'roundness' becoming obvious over time. The same tortuous development route will have taken place with pottery, where clay slapped onto a smooth horizontal surface will have been much easier to work if that surface could be made to spin round – *especially* if most of the finished objects were to be round bowls or containers of some kind. Once a means had been reached of making this stone or wooden surface revolve, ensuring that the block was rounded at the edges, and eventually a perfect circle, so that the potter could work the clay as close to his body as he chose, must quite quickly have become apparent.

As the limitations of man or beast to bear ever heavier burdens over greater distances became increasingly apparent, from the above three types of rounded 'machine' or 'wheel' – laid flat – must surely have emanated the suggestion of trying to create such a device that could stand on its edge. Solid discs of woods were stood upright, in pairs, and a method of holding them (apart – but joined together) so that they could rotate but not topple over, was painstakingly experimented with.

Thus these remarkable people made the single most crucial mechanical breakthrough yet devised, one that – its horizontal state having achieved three types of crucial advance – enabled the movement of bulk goods to take place overland, involving ever longer distances.

The plaiting of grasses and marsh-grown reeds – for roof and floor protection – may have originated as early as 9000BC, simultaneously with the twisting of fibres to create string.

Preceding clothing, the skill of basket-weaving had also become widespread – all these related skills promoting ideas of *strength* and *protection* through the acts of intertwining or looping.

The weaving of cloth was evident at Catal Hoyuk from at least 6000BC, but it was domestication of sheep, and flax-growing, that must have encouraged the farmer (often female) to clean the excess wool and start to work fibrous materials respectively – precipitating the art of weaving woollen and linen garments. The fundamental practice of warp and weft, as found on ancient cloth fragments, remains unchanged to this day.

Key raw materials – timber, copper, volcanic flow, and highly prized 'constituents'

Timber

As the most used (and most easily worked) material world-wide, it seems perverse that Mesopotamia (and Egypt) could make such rapid early progress without having any significant sources of this vital component. And yet it is that very shortage that helped kick-start what Braudel calls the trading 'turntable' – the fundamental pump-primer for any emerging economy, even in the modern era.

Syria and Lebanon had abundant forests, well able to supply the massive tree trunks required for ambitious building programmes … and so, already well-versed in orchestrating the bulk two-way river traffic, the Sumerians instigated the caravan traffic across the most westerly (overland) stretch of the Fertile Crescent. In the absence of conventional currency, trade had to be effected by barter, and thus the serious import and export business that survived for millennia along this route was born.

Copper

Use of this workable material started with the collection of raw nuggets, lying on the ground, and their subsequent hammering into shapes. This surface evidence led to the discovery of shallow copper seams. It is now considered that the high temperatures required to refine the mined material meant that – from 6000BC at Catal Hoyuk, and 4000BC in northern Iraq – special kilns and crucibles had to be created. A high level of quality could be achieved: the axe head found with 'Otzi' in the Tyrolean ice (dated to 3250BC) is 99.7% pure copper.

Volcanic flow

Neither Mesopotamia (nor Egypt itself) 'enjoyed' any volcanic activity, but extremely versatile obsidian (volcanic glass) came from Anatolia (modern Turkey) together with lava lumps, which retained heat for cooking long after a fire had died out.

Highly prized constituents

Only certain examples can be mentioned here: in the realm of long-lasting food, wild honey, almonds, dates, dried beans/pulses, wine from Shiraz (Iran), and spices from India, brought along the Indian Ocean shoreline, and up through the Persian Gulf. As to precious metals, there was gold (from Egypt) and lapis lazuli from Afghanistan by trade routes that may never be properly ascertained.

Many dyes were widely traded, including 'royal purple' – extracted from the Murex seashell from the Lebanese coastline. Huge demand caused this process to become one of the world's first industrial-scale manufacturing operations. Other traded dyes were ochre, pomegranate and henna (from Persia) and – somewhat later – Indigo from India.

The trading 'turntable'

The 'middlemen' in this burgeoning trade to the west of the Euphrates, whether goods were to be for onward shipment by sea, south to Egypt, or by land, north-west to Anatolia, were the Canaanites – forerunners of the Phoenicians – living in the Western Levant (modern-day Syria, Lebanon, Jordan and Israel).

Since no currency existed, all outward trade had to be balanced by matching inward product. Here, the Canaanite merchants honed their bargaining skills, on the one hand making a handsome living, and on the other hand having to search ever further for the 'balance' of trade – hence the demand for silver and copper ingots from Turkey, and an ever-widening range of semi-precious stones from Egypt. If – from modest beginnings – Egypt wanted to buy ever more 'Cedars of Lebanon', she had to cull or mine (from her deserts, the Blue and White Nile, and from her neighbouring African regions) bargaining product of increasing volume and value.

As trading activity steadily increased, the seeds of great civilisations to come were sown. As a result of brilliant seafaring skills, the Phoenicians (direct descendants of the Canaanites) founded an empire in the Western Mediterranean in the 1st millennium BC (see Chapter 13). And as suppliers of raw materials, the powerful Hittites created a land-based Anatolian empire in the 2nd millennium BC (see Chapter 11).

Sumerian life

Lacking timber and stone, single-storey houses were built of mud-brick, with only the wealthy citizen having two floors. Houses comprised several rooms, together with a courtyard, with discreet areas for cooking, worship and lavatories. Because of their simple structure, houses were always being demolished (perhaps coinciding with a death in the family), then rebuilt on the same spot – in this way, each settlement grew higher from the valley floor, to eventually create an artificial hummock or 'tell'. Perhaps, being descendants of immigrants from hilly or mountainous country, building up a tell was an instinctive and nostalgic practice – certainly, successive generations were afforded a view over the surrounding plains, and the benefit of any breeze in the stiflingly hot climate.

In this early Ubaid period, religion was a crucial part of daily life, with each small city having a temple. When considering the byzantine complexity of the gods of classical Greece, it is astonishing to realise that 4,000 years earlier Sumerian worship was almost equally as convoluted. The father of the gods was An, whose wife was Ki. Enlil was their son, who eventually was adopted as the supreme deity, whilst Enki was the god of water. There were gods of the sun, the moon, war – and of both agricultural and human fertility.

Couples were married, usually through family influence, and civil life operated within a carefully established legal system. It was a patriarchal society, with easy divorce for the husband – that is, if he chose not to add a second wife.

Ziggurats

Strictly speaking, monumental structures built throughout the world that, whatever the shape of their base, have triangular-shaped sides that slope towards a single cone or peak, come within the category of 'pyramid' (from the Greek 'pyramis'). The term 'ziggurat' is an Akkadian-language expression, meaning 'built on a raised area', and two of the most famous surviving examples are in fact in modern-day Iran. Of the many constructed in the 'Middle East', the oldest date from c5000BC, pre-dating the pyramids of Egypt by at least two millennia.

As the cornerstone of the well-developed Mesopotamian society,

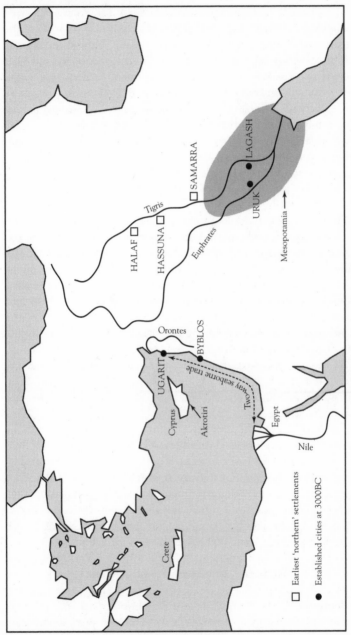

SAMARRA

Tigris

LAGASH

URUK

Mesopotamia

HALAF

HASSUNA

Euphrates

Orontes

BYBLOS

UGARIT

Two-way seaborne trade

Cyprus

Akrotiri

Egypt

Nile

Crete

☐ Earliest 'northern' settlements

● Established cities at 3000BC

Map ii – The Near East between 5000 and 3000BC

temples rapidly took the form of deliberately constructed terraced mud-brick buildings of enormous height and girth – these were the ziggurats of lasting fame, which were the link between earth and heaven. Vatican-like high priests wielded great power, and operated these temples as self-contained mini-economies. At Uruk, the largest city in Mesopotamia of the 4th millennium BC – home to Gilgamesh, the mythical hero-king of the 3rd millennium – the vast ziggurat was first seen by William Loftus in 1849, and has been under intermittent excavation for a full century, starting with the German archaeologist Julius Jordan, in 1912.

Origins of writing and law

As in so many other areas of expertise, the Sumerian language remains the earliest known. Their script was 'wedge-shaped' or cuneiform, and began as a series of pictographs. Developed towards the end of the 4th millennium, the message was first chipped into stone, and later carved into soft clay to be sun-baked. Clay 'cylinder seals' were so engraved to show ownership, and establish legal claims or rights.

Writing development was the critical mechanism for the promulgation of a quite comprehensive legal system – even (as now!) often involving arbitration, so as to prevent a case coming to court. Even if a case came to court – before a judge – the outcome needed to be 'written in stone'. Although not fully codified until the middle of the 3rd millennium, a gradual build-up of individual laws took place during the intervening 1,000 years.

Gilgamesh is considered to have reigned around 2500BC, and in the *Epic of Gilgamesh* is credited with having built the city walls of Uruk. The *Epic* is one of the earliest works in world literature, and is based on earlier Sumerian legends, interwoven with the exploits of the semi-legendary figure of Gilgamesh himself. The most complete extant version is preserved on 12 tablets from the library collection of the 7th-century Assyrian king Ashurbanipal, brought back to the British Museum by Austen Henry Layard in the mid-19th century.

Medicine, mathematics and science

Cures for ailments emerged from the realms of magic to (what we would call) homeopathic medicines and even reluctant surgery –

reluctant because a failed operation had dire implications for the unfortunate surgeon. The wide range of medicines was culled from many branches of the animal, vegetable and mineral worlds, through constant experimentation and refinement.

The Babylonian Empire – which flourished from the middle of the 2nd millennium – drew its mathematical skills directly from its Sumerian forebears. From 3000BC metrology developed, with – during the next half-millennium – multiplication, division and geometrics being committed to clay tablets (then sun-baked) for the continual amazement of modern scholars.

Similarly, Babylonian expertise in astronomy developed directly from the deep Sumerian interest and exploration of this field. In summary, despite invasion, pestilence and the overthrowing of empires there was an unbroken link from the earliest Sumerian colonisation of Mesopotamia, through to the eventual invasion of Babylon by Cyrus of Persia in 539BC. And – crucially – it was the westward spread of their unsurpassed achievements that (directly and indirectly) gave the springboard to Classical Greece, as will be recounted in succeeding chapters.

Chapter 4

Egypt

No book attempting to explain the Mediterranean *Naissance* can ignore the amazing achievements of Dynastic Egypt – that is from around 3100BC – but it is the case that exhaustive searches over the past century to catalogue proactive Egyptian influence over cultural and technological developments in that huge basin have yielded modest evidence of any such activity.

When occasionally discussing the subject of this book with friends, the most frequently asked question is, 'How many times have you been to Egypt?' And the answer (still at the time of writing) is, 'Well, none, actually, because Egypt is not central to the story of linkage and continuity that I want to tell.' This revelation may shock the reader, and viewing the incredible achievements *within* Egypt it seems so obvious that they must have dominated proceedings to the north/north-west, i.e. on the eastern rim of the Mediterranean. There are several reasons for this (seemingly illogical) anomaly, which need to be explained.

It is generally accepted that – at the start – developments in Egypt lagged behind those in Mesopotamia by perhaps a full millennium. Historians remain bewildered as to why – with society increasingly well-ordered among such an intelligent population – virtually all the keys to economic success in Mesopotamia (wheeled cart, potter's wheel, use of bronze) should have eluded Egypt for at least a full millennium. Why this should have occurred has not been fully identified, but there are a number of very strong clues. And these clues directly link to the relative isolation of Egypt, and its lack of *positive contribution* to the rest of the developing world.

Isolation and reluctance to change

First, the geographical and anthropological contrast with Mesopotamia could not have been starker. As we have seen, Mesopotamia was virtually ringed by a wide range of struggling proto-societies, with great achievements made in prehistory on virtually all sides: on or inland from the Eastern Mediterranean coastline; to the north-west (Anatolia) and to the north/north-east dryer northern Mesopotamia and the Zagros Mountains; and probably from as far away as Armenia and the Caucasus.

For millennia, prior to the Sumerian flowering, emergent trade had been flowing in many directions, and – as happens now in any entrepot – every kind of human 'cross-pollination' ensued. However hesitant initially, Braudel's trading 'turntable' knew no bounds of curiosity or of the instinct or urge to travel so as to exchange goods with near neighbours.

As to Egypt, however, although (for example) the fertile North African coastline strip is known to have once had much greater depth – extending westward from the Nile delta into what is now the Libyan desert – by the early 4th millennium the emerging civilisation was clustered around the delta itself (Lower Egypt) and along either side of the great river (Middle Egypt).

As will be seen, as well as nomadic travel across the surrounding deserts having long taken place, forays from the Nile settlements for stone, precious metals and other minerals were a significant feature of Egyptian life. However, there was no question of trying to harness the desert, and – for the most part – these vast tracts of inhospitable land remained impenetrable, to both east and west.

The seasonal flooding of the Nile was much more predictable than with the great rivers of Mesopotamia, and perhaps, by reason of a more manageable yearly agricultural cycle, the need for elaborate irrigation systems was absent. To the south – upstream – there were settlements along the narrowing (and less fertile) river into Upper Egypt, and traffic through Nubia into modern-day Sudan. Ancient Nubia held great natural wealth for which the Egyptians started to trade – gold, ivory and incense, to name only three of the most sought-after imports.

In summary, wherever the bulk of the emerging Egyptian population came from – perhaps indigenous, possibly (though unlikely) even from Mesopotamia by a circuitous route – they developed as a largely *isolationist* people. In particular, from the time Egypt became unified, and its monumental building programme was undertaken (c2700-2300BC), the state showed itself to be completely uninterested in change – see A *History of Knowledge* by Charles Van Doren. Once the kingdom had been established, successive rulers became fiercely determined to avoid progress ... a status quo they managed very capably for two whole millennia!

Seafarers from the delta?

Peoples of the Nile delta must have been aware – from earliest times – of vibrant activity in Palestine, and along the coast to Lebanon/Syria. So why did the Egyptians not become intrepid sailors?

From the start, the main preoccupation was navigation of the delta and the Lower Nile. Although having prominent prow and stern sections, the design of boats made of (waterproof) papyrus strips had no keel. These rafts (in effect), whether sailed or rowed, were ideal for ferrying goods, and for funeral journeys along the river – especially in shallow or marshy areas. Without a keel, however, no travel on the ocean – even for short distances – could be contemplated.

It is true that recent research indicates boat-building in kit form for hauling over the Sinai desert and reassembly on the Red Sea. This concept matches the c1500BC records of seafaring trips to Ethiopia on behalf of Queen Hatshepsut – and perhaps the occasional foray to the Aegean. But by this late era the 'damage was done'. Daring voyages – *by others* – throughout the eastern half of the Mediterranean had been carried out for more than 2,000 years, including the sating of Egypt's appetite for her one crucial requirement – *timber*.

Timber

Egypt had absolutely no indigenous large timber suitable for its increasingly ambitious building programme. There were limited supplies of smaller trees to be found in the Sudan, but between Khartoum and Thebes (Luxor) there were five cataracts on the Nile, which made for a tortuous journey of 1,000 miles (1,600km). The delta itself was then another 400 miles further north.

From earliest times, sailors from the Levantine coast had plucked up the courage to venture overseas. Crucially, they must have worked out over hundreds of years that, in order for man and cargo to survive, the early rafts must be watertight, have rounded sides so as not to ship water in a heavy sea, have the stability that a keel could provide, and be manoeuvrable via some kind of steering mechanism, i.e. a tiller.

Having no access to papyrus, the watertight problem was solved by one of the 'miracle' materials of early history, namely pitch. Long before, pitch from surface seepage in Mesopotamia had been used to bind mud-brick walls, and even insulate floors and roofs. Now – probably from seepage beside the Dead Sea – it was deployed by the first true boat-builders on the Lebanese/Syrian coast to caulk their timber frames. Water tests would be carried out to prove the ability of the shell (or hull) to avoid significant leakage over the planned ocean-going journeys.

Cardial pottery (from the cardium sea-shell, imprinted on wet clay) had been exported widely around the Mediterranean, from Byblos in the Lebanon, since as early as the 6th millennium. By the time Egypt was crying out for an inexhaustible supply of quality timber (3500-3000BC) intrepid sailors – employed by Canaanite merchants – were able to sail down the Palestinian coast, hugging the shore and towing massive cedar tree trunks on rafts linked together.

This distance of only 500 miles (800km) offered a far more viable proposition than any alternative – despite storm-induced disasters – *especially* since these heavily laden rafts could be untied at the mouth of the delta, then steered most of the way upstream towards their eventual destination. At this point the seafarers were only too happy to be paid for their efforts in gold, precious metals and other small-volume luxuries – which made the return leg of their journey, in their single-keeled lead-boat, much quicker and less hazardous.

Egyptian influence in the Mediterranean

The above three combining factors alone may seem inadequate to render Egypt a 'client state' of others – directly or indirectly – but perhaps the Egyptians' pharaoh-dominated culture and preoccupation with palace, pyramid and mausoleum construction took their capabilities to the limit, and served to make them an inward-looking or self-obsessed society ... one that considered itself superior to all neighbours, and was incapable of a mercantilist outlook.

Even if Egypt had wanted to compete as an outward-looking free-trading state, it would have been further inhibited by its hierarchical set-up, which was managed by an ever-growing bureaucracy that – over many centuries – became increasingly corrupt.

Because also of its seafaring inhibitions, Egypt was obliged to see all two-way trade (from the north) conducted by Mediterranean outsiders, with its requirements being initially monopolised by the Canaanites. Soon it was importing copper from Cyprus, and – later – raw materials (including timber) from Crete.

Every developing culture in the Eastern Mediterranean beat a path to Egypt with its increasingly spectacular and monumental architecture. The Minoans from Crete (see Chapter 7), who appear in Egyptian scripts as 'Keftiu', certainly borrowed building techniques, for the living and the dead, in their own island. They also adopted artistic ideas – and perhaps provided some of their own in return – but it was they who had to make all the running, and who had the seafaring skills to match.

Occasional military adventures

Egypt's greatest degree of overseas influence was at Byblos in the 3rd millennium, at a period when the commercial and cultural ties were so strong that this immensely successful Canaanite port effectively became a vassal state of the Pharaoh. Even here, however, it can be seen that Egyptian hegemony was limited to protecting its specific interests. This political bridgehead was never extended along the coast or inland.

Otherwise, for the next two millennia there were occasions when Egypt had to defend itself – often by launching pre-emptive strikes. One such instance was when Thutmose III decided to launch a vigorous campaign against the threat of Mitanni, a short-lived state that filled the vacuum left by the Hittite defeat of Kassite Babylon. In 1458 Thutmose secured a decisive victory at the battle of Megiddo in Syria, some time following which the Israelite tribe was taken in captivity to Egypt – the start of a prolonged agony that is evocatively documented in the Old Testament. However, no subsequent attempt was made to put down roots outside the Egyptian homeland – a pattern that was to occur at several such opportunities, both earlier and later in Egypt's inordinately long history.

The pottery legacy

After all that has been said above on Egypt's isolationist stance, it is supremely ironic that – mainly through Arthur Evans's genius and diligence (see Chapter 6) – it was only the Minoan links with Egypt that enabled the successive eras in that parallel culture to be accurately dated.

First, through the elaborate written records of the Pharaohs' 'civil service' we have acquired an accurate date sequence of all the Egyptian Dynasties – from c3100BC onwards. Second, we know that every society around the Mediterranean came to trade with Egypt to a greater or lesser extent. And it was during these visits over the succeeding millennia that the visitors received a mass of pottery – whether as gifts or in exchange for goods – which they took home to show off, or to utilise in everyday life.

Starting with Evans's ground-breaking research more than a century ago, the dating of Egyptian pottery – first in Crete, then at Mycenae, and later at dozens of other sites – has been a crucial tool of the modern archaeologist … a wondrous (but accidental) legacy of a people who hardly ever ventured themselves from their homeland.

Chapter 5

Migration to the West (the eastern Mediterranean)

W hy did this happen? It was one thing for seaborne trade to take place down the coast to Egypt, but it was a huge step for groups of people to consciously leave their homeland by sea, either for reasons of trade or curiosity, or to seek a better life, with all the risks and dangers implied by taking to the uncharted ocean.

Of course, as provided by pottery evidence, small parties had bravely sailed huge distances since as early as the 6th millennium. However, set out below are the main reasons why occasional trading forays turned into permanent settlement.

Population explosion

An especially severe glacial maximum occurred about 130,000 years ago, and it was around that time that Homo sapiens emerged in Africa. Despite several more excruciatingly difficult ice ages, this tiny population (of a few thousand) may have grown to a *global* population of several hundred thousand – or even perhaps to a million – by the end of the last glacial maximum, around 11,000 years ago.

Of course, not only was this number spread throughout planet Earth, but the proportion that lived in the 'Near East' was (as we have seen) congregated in the most benign regions. After a further 5,000 years of rapidly increasing activity – namely by the middle of the 4th millennium BC – the numbers living in Mesopotamia and Egypt might each have totalled some hundreds of thousands, which would have included a significant percentage of migrant workers or

48

slaves from outside the natural boundaries of these pioneering civilisations.

On the Syrian/Lebanese coast too, rapidly growing trade across the Fertile Crescent will have caused a burgeoning population. As was such a feature of the Bible, there will have been repeated famine and pestilence in between the good years, and increasingly nasty local disputes over land or livestock, which occasionally erupted into serious bloodshed.

Thus, when intrepid sailors returned with glowing stories of far-off islands, how appealing must it have seemed for hard-pressed locals – in their worst moments – to think of 'trying their luck' by making a fresh start, or at least by spending a season garnering the 'low-hanging fruit' that they had begun to realise was readily available.

Search for minerals

Did the Near East attraction to the Mediterranean islands stem from the ever-widening search for 'working' minerals? Perhaps the distribution of early pottery was a result of the temporary appearance of traders in a wide range of locations. In any event, it is worth noting the immense distances from which minerals were sourced:

Obsidian: Lipari (north of Sicily), Melos (west of Thera in the Cyclades), and perhaps from Thera itself, which did not 'lose' its volcano until the middle of the 2nd millennium.
Copper: Cyprus and – as only recently realised – the huge deposits of Laurion in Attica (close to modern-day Athens).
Silver: also mined at Laurion; no one knows how early it was obtained in ever-growing quantities from the Guadalquivir River region of southern Spain.
Tin: though mined in Iran, tin was also brought to Syria/Lebanon from Spain, and – astonishingly – from Cornwall in Britain (though how early is still hotly disputed).

Accident

Early sailors will have quickly acquired a rough knowledge of the prevailing winds, and of the sea currents that moved their little boats along in unexpected directions. They will also have been fearful of winter storms, which have always bedevilled the best efforts of even the most skilled and well-equipped seafarer.

Much modern-day research has been carried out into annual wind patterns in the Mediterranean, which – on a prevailing basis – vary considerably with the seasons. Similarly, there are now known to be established current flows that are irresistible. Recent sailing trials in the region – without the support of oars (let alone an engine!) – have conclusively established the apparently meandering or approximately 'circular' direction in which a ship would be obliged to travel some 6,000 years ago.

A graphic example is provided by the amazing range of contents in the Uluburun shipwreck. There was initial puzzlement at the sheer variety of goods, seemingly destined for every port in the Eastern Mediterranean, until the experts realised that this was indeed the case ... simply because the journey was planned to be travelled in one *circular* direction – going with the prevailing winds and currents, the combination of which should eventually have returned the (near) empty vessel to its place of origin.

At that time the ram had been invented, and therefore the use of oars to commit an act of piracy (or even fight a battle) was known. However, any ship carrying a mixture of women and children, together with worldly chattels and livestock, would not have had the means or the manpower to operate with oars. Moreover, since such sailing craft could not successfully tack into the wind, the early explorers would have tried to time their outward journeys to match the most favourable conditions ... as they would similarly if, as was likely, they intended to return to their homeland for the winter.

However, one can picture a fairly chaotic scene: many ships foundering, with all hands; many being blown onto an island or coastline, other than the intended destination – perhaps taking months or years to realise their 'mistake'; and, inevitably, a proportion that became stranded for the winter (or through a shipwreck) in a place where they had no alternative but to carve out a living ... by which time they felt they had discovered a lotus land, so that even if 'rescue' did eventually arrive, nothing would have persuaded the original castaways to leave their new home.

Tentative settlements – the example of Cyprus

To keep a sense of perspective, there were a great number of fruitful lower slopes, valleys and coastal strips to be exploited in most of the countries that comprise the Middle East today – lands of milk and honey indeed. However, nothing has changed: just as we see today, successful economies are a magnet for comparatively impoverished migrants, many of whom would have been invited to help develop the aspirations of the emerging 'state'. A more reliable diet and resourceful medication will have reduced infant mortality, and increased the adult lifespan. Thus the whole process (yet again, as now) will have repeated itself continuously … more people, more food, more space, more timber, more land, more livestock.

Most of the islands and territories covered in the ensuing chapters had been inhabited for *some of the time* since the dawn of history, but not consistently and usually by a very modest number of people. These would have arrived by accident, or been raiders or traders, who settled for a lengthy period, during which they managed to achieve a certain level of development. But their successors would then have left, been driven out (perhaps by a natural disaster) or have died out through disease or infertility. Then, perhaps half a millennium later, the process would repeat itself.

In the case of Cyprus, this stop-start situation recurred several times, and is worth a brief examination. In the first place – as in the case of some other islands – there was a substantial population of pygmy (or dwarf) hippopotami for the human intruders to kill and butcher, and a lesser number of pygmy elephants. Researchers put this dwarfism down to a limited gene pool, the fauna being so far geographically from their original source.

The earliest evidence of human settlement has been dated to around 9000BC, while it is known that there was continuous occupation from around 3000BC.

From 9000BC to circa 3500BC there were *four* distinct phases: first, the Akrotiri phase, solely on the southernmost central tip of the island; second, the Aceramic (no pottery) Neolithic period; third the Ceramic Neolithic period; and finally the Chalcolithic (Copper) Age.

The intriguing aspect of these peoples, who mainly came from northern Syria or from eastern Turkey (Anatolia), is not so much that their achievements post-dated (in each instance) those on the mainland by 1,500-2,000 years, but that there were 500-1,000-year gaps between *each* phase. This does not mean that the large island was completely deserted, but it does show that – each time – the tortuous process of developing their communities over hundreds of years was brought to an abrupt end.

What happened? Was it disease that ravaged the population? Were the inhabitants overrun by marauding invaders? Did successive generations find the comparatively isolated struggle to prosper too harsh to bear, and decide to 'go home'? Could it be that their quite well-ordered existence was rendered unsustainable because of a succession of natural disasters?

Each phase seemed to have achieved much, whether it was the wells carved through rock fissures, their mud-brick houses with clearly delineated living areas, religious activity (mainly directed towards fertility), animal husbandry, textile manufacture, later pottery skills, cereal cultivation, or the harvesting of semi-wild fruits and nuts.

Archaeologists will debate the reasons for the decline of these four distinct eras in Cyprus for decades to come, but what the above sequence clearly illustrates is the tenuous nature of early attempts to colonise such seemingly promising territories.

Islands of (irresistible) opportunity

A glance at the map will show that Cyprus was always likely to be subject to the first attempts at settlement, tucked into the north-east corner of the Mediterranean, with its own north-eastern tip being just 50 miles (80km) from both Turkey to the north and Syria to the east. But there were other enticing islands, although much further away. What was their particular appeal? Several answers can be proposed.

Climate

As discussed, there were extremely fertile stretches in the Near East, with some areas close to cooling mountains. But for most of the year the heat was stifling, and – with huge tracts of barren desert – access to fresh water was always a problem (as it still is today), with the fearful threat of severe drought never far away.

In contrast – as exampled by Cyprus – many of the islands further west (though not all) had a much more benign climate. Some were a mixture of high mountains, huge forests and incredibly fertile soil,

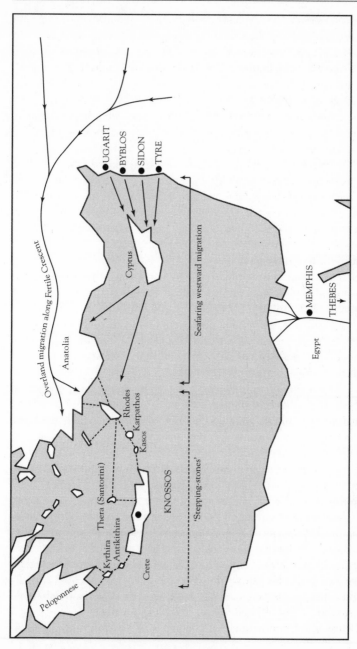

Map iii – Migration to Crete and Thera (and later the Peloponnese), c3000BC

with the winter rainfall pouring down streams that never dried up, and high water tables in the plains that enabled shallow wells to be dug. In no case was there a desert to be crossed, and the sea was never more than a short distance away, with an inexhaustible supply of fresh fish.

Variety of foodstuffs

The abundance of wild fruits, nuts and vegetable types was remarkable, with evidence of currants, raisins, figs, apricots, apples, pistachios, beans and many other types.

The grape led to wine, herbs were plentiful, but *best of all* was exploitation of the olive. In Mesopotamia sesame had been laboriously crushed to produce cooking oil, but realisation that the golden liquid could pour through the simplest press made this oil – with its many applications – and the olive itself very highly prized indeed.

The wonder of wheat

There is a sharp contrast between the harvesting of readily available food of all kinds (and the 'easy meat' provided by game and wild animals, including the prime example of deer) and the hundreds of years it took to learn to make the most of the wide range of semi-wild cereals. Nevertheless, as with finding out how to make the most of semi-domesticated animals, it is crucial that we appreciate the vital role that wheat has played over the last 5,000 years.

The three major staple cereals in the world are rice, maize and wheat, but it is wheat that *spread west from Mesopotamia* – certainly without the initial 'shippers' even beginning to understand the momentous turning point they had initiated.

Wheat (of the genus Triticum) is extremely nutritious, being 70% carbohydrate, 12% protein, 2% fat and 2% minerals. Its protein composition is more than double that of rice – 1lb (450g) of wheat yields about 1,500 calories. This fortuitous mix has given Mediterranean (European) man a physical advantage over peoples from predominantly rice- or maize-eating regions of the globe.

Being a (predictable) seasonal plant, it only requires intensive labour at sowing and harvesting times. Thus – unlike rice-growers – wheat farmers had plenty of time during which they could *crucially* grow secondary crops, clear land, hunt wild game, tend animals, build structures ... and even politicise or resort to fighting.

A drawback is that wheat depletes the soil, if sown continuously, so the early farmer had to learn the hard way how to let his land lie fallow and (eventually) operate a mixed arable and livestock 'system' … which in turn brought about an ideal diet, with which to grow strong offspring and help combat disease.

Another bonus – really an unforeseen *miracle* – was that, in trying to make bread, it was only the wheat proteins from gluten that (when mixed with water) resulted in dough. The wonder does not stop there. Gluten retains the carbon dioxide that is emitted from the yeast fermentation, resulting in the fact that a wheat loaf is lighter, finer and more digestible than any of its competitors.

Animal husbandry

We see today that drought and other catastrophes can lead to mass animal death or slaughter in Africa (and most recently Australia), as must also have been repeated time after time in the Middle East. More than 5,000 years ago, new migrants into the Mediterranean region must have gradually realised that consistent seasonal access to forage and water could encourage selective breeding, and the idea of *sustainable* practices.

Pigs (which can survive on almost anything, reproducing extremely quickly) and cattle (for milk products, horn and leather) thrived in the less harsh climate. In addition, flocks of the less destructive sheep (which need little water and provide an annual yield of precious wool) began to overtake the more voracious herds of goat, which can turn semi-arid grazing and scrubland into a virtual desert.

Chapter 6

Crete: the story of Arthur Evans

The start of modern archaeology

The *Oxford Dictionary* describes archaeology as 'the study of human history and prehistory through the excavation of sites and the analysis of objects found in them'.

This study is a very new science – quoting again from Virchow in 1881 – with Johann Joachim Winckelmann (1717-68) generally regarded as the 'prophet and founding hero'. The quite slim roll of honour includes Richard Colt Hoare (1758-1838) and, of course, Jean-Francois Champollion (1790-1832 – see the Introduction). One of the first academic institutions was the School for American Archaeology, founded in 1907 at Santa Fe.

Even today, argument rages as to whether archaeology is history, anthropology or culture- history. More recently there has been a move to promote 'New processual archaeology', and even since 1980 the 'Post-processual' movement has been promulgated by (among others) Ian Hodder, whose decades-long work at Catal Hoyuk has been widely praised.

All the above is meant to show how undeveloped the subject was when Schliemann (1822-90 – see Chapter 9) burst onto the scene in 1873. Among his London audience in 1876 was 25-year-old Arthur Evans. (The reason this book reviews the remarkable life of the younger man first is because the Minoan civilisation preceded the rise to supremacy of Mycenae by as much as a full millennium.)

We also need to study the life of Evans (as later with Schliemann) so as to obtain an impression of the dramatic way in which this pair – whose backgrounds could hardly have been more different from each other – opened up this 'entirely new science', and in so doing changed the lives of thousands of students from many disciplines in the generations that have followed.

Hopefully, these two potted life histories will show how archaeology is also an art, and that the whole process only leapt forward because a tiny handful of determined enthusiasts would not bow to convention – and had the capacity and flair for lateral thinking, or (to use the modern idiom) to think 'outside the box'.

A rebellious young life

Born on 8 July 1851 in Hemel Hempstead – into a dynasty of eminent scholars on both sides of his family – Evans was the offspring of Sir John, who had married his cousin Harriet Dickinson. Sir John made a success of everything he touched, and took over the Dickinson paper business from his father-in-law. Considering that he had seven paper mills to run, it is amazing that he had a parallel career as an eminent scholar of antiquities, with a particular emphasis on numismatics – and in later life prehistory. He collected widely (see the John Evans corner – formerly a whole room – at the wonderfully enlarged Ashmolean Museum in Oxford).

Arthur, the eldest of five children, was only six when his mother died. Although his father married twice more, the two of them got on well together, sharing many interests. Arthur's much younger half-sister Joan wrote a biography of Arthur, *Time and Chance*, not published until after his death, which was very revealing in at least one crucial respect. She wrote that he was extremely short-sighted, and that – without his glasses – he could only see small objects if they were held very close to his face, but that he could then make out the content '…in extraordinary detail, while everything else was a vague blur. Consequently the details he saw with microscopic exactitude, undistracted by the outside world, had a greater significance for him than for other men.'

He was unsuited to the normal school sports at Harrow, but he was wiry and tough, enjoyed swimming and horse-riding, and was prepared to endure physical hardship when trekking, particularly through Eastern Europe, even while still in his youth.

Arthur was always wealthy and – perhaps as a result of being known as 'little Evans, son of John Evans the great' – was a rebel in many areas

57

of his life. He was a Whig to his father's Tory, only obtained a First in History at Oxford by the skin of his teeth, and decamped to Ragusa (now Dubrovnik) between 1877 and 1882. He became deeply involved in Balkan politics – treacherous then, as until very recently – was lucky not to be shot and, after seven weeks in jail, was summarily deported by the Austrian authorities.

He married another scholar, Margaret Freeman, in 1878, and celebrated their engagement by taking her to London to see Schliemann's exhibits from Troy. Margaret travelled with him faithfully each summer, putting up with the heat, disease and primitive living conditions, but she never produced a longed-for child. Her health, which first gave way in 1880, never really recovered, and she died on yet another exhausting trip in 1893. Arthur was 42, and in that same year his father – having married for a third time – became, at the age of 69, a father to Joan.

It is worth noting that thereafter Arthur forswore a second marriage, and fostered or adopted impoverished young boys for the rest of his life. He is now regarded as probably having been homosexual.

The Ashmolean Museum

The oldest museum in the UK, the Ashmolean was founded in 1677 to house the botanical curiosities of Elias Ashmole in a building provided by Oxford University. The early collection had languished for 200 years under low-paid keepers – culminating in John Parker, a local bookseller, who was appointed in 1870. With considerable string-pulling (aided by Parker graciously stepping aside), Arthur Evans became keeper in 1884. Enlisting the support of his friend Charles Fortnum – who needed a permanent home for his private collection – Evans bullied and cajoled the authorities into building a new museum, which Fortnum then lavishly endowed.

One of Evans's towering achievements was realised when the handsome new building was opened in 1894 – by which time the Ashmolean had at last become a great institution for learning and research. Evans fought the stuffy classicists tooth and nail (notably Benjamin Jowett, vice-chancellor of the University) so as to ensure that the museum displayed exhibits from the dawn of civilisation through to the Classical Age, without separating off the latter as '...the remains of a few privileged centuries'.

From now on he and others insisted that human history be charted as a linear evolutionary process – starting with hunter/gathering, through 'Savagery' and 'Barbarism' stages to 'Civilisation', this last indicated by the use of writing. Of course, Evans and his supporters were much aided by Charles Darwin, whose sensational (and bitterly contested) *Theory of Evolution* had culminated in his publication of *On the Origin of Species* in 1859. This was followed by *The Descent of Man* in 1871.

(It is perhaps appropriate to note that the museum has just undergone a rebuilding programme at a cost of £60 million. This has doubled display space, and for the first time the museum now houses an Education Centre. Evans would surely have approved!)

Breakthrough

Like his father, Arthur was deeply interested in numismatics. For example, he recognised the tiny artists' signatures on Sicilian coins. 1893 – the year in which his wife died – proved to be a turning point. Staying in Athens, he studied many of the tiny objects that Schliemann recovered from Mycenae. Inspired, he came across small stones in an antique dealer's shop, which were engraved with minute symbols. Could what Evans saw on these seals and signet rings – with his microscopic scrutiny – be some form of writing?

'Where do the seals come from?' he asked the dealer.

'From Crete,' he was told.

In the previous year (1892) Arthur had met the Italian Federico Halbherr, who had already investigated a number of Cretan sites, and who had brought back for the Ashmolean some 'seal stones' that he knew would be of interest. Evans had already acquired a collection of 'Phoenician' seals – and was able to 'interrogate' their tiny scenes of amazing complexity. What was more, by holding them close to his eyes under an intense light, he noticed various peculiar characters. He considered that these illegible markings – as with those in Athens a year later – bore some relationship to Egyptian hieroglyphics. By this era, European scholars were quite familiar with Egyptian hieroglyphic writing, but somehow these inscriptions were different…

Puzzled at first, many years later Evans was the first to understand that these characters were among the earliest examples of a 'mid-Mediterranean' language – which he christened 'Linear B'. Though not deciphered until 1952 (by Michael Ventris and John Chadwick), Linear B proved to be a most crucial linguistic building block, dating perhaps from the late 15th century BC – until it seems to have died out in the Dark Age, c1100BC. Linear B is so called because Evans discovered an earlier form of writing – in Crete – which he christened Linear A. Dating from around 1900BC, this script has never been satisfactorily deciphered, despite monumental efforts all around the world.

Knossos – the struggle to dig

Schliemann and others had tried to negotiate with the occupying Turkish regime in Crete to allow excavation, but – partly due to extortionate demands – all their attempts had failed. In 1894 Evans made his first visit to the island, and at once became deeply attached to Venetian Heraklion, and the surrounding countryside – aided by his deep feelings for the legendary home of King Minos, his daughter Ariadne, and her hero Theseus.

He bought (only) a share of the presumed site of Knossos from a Turkish landowner. Stone walls and large pithoi – jars for grain or oil – had already been uncovered, but he could not take much further action, a saving grace being that, under Ottoman law, no one else could touch the site either. In the event, Turkey finally gave up control of the island in 1898 after a last burst of violence, and partly due to Evans having given such vocal support to the independence movement, he was almost at once given a lease to explore the place (known as the Kephala Hill).

Work actually began on 23 March 1900, and almost immediately Knossos started to yield the most wonderful objects. Only by roaming the 'Palace of King Minos', coupled with visiting the amazing museum at Heraklion, can one begin to grasp the importance of the site – a place of continuous occupation and development for more than 1,000 years, from 2500BC right through the Palace-building phase from 1950BC, until (at least) the final destruction of the Palace in 1375/50BC, from a cause that is not yet fully understood.

Knossos became (and remains) one of the most controversial archaeological sites in the Western world – due to Evans's obsessive eagerness to show off to visitors and readers alike 'his' Minoan civilisation. He invented the name 'Minoan', and wanted the culture to appear almost modern, so as to undermine his classical enemies. In reconstructing key parts of the site to his historic architectural interpretation, he eventually triggered a backlash (now considered somewhat extreme in itself) whose adherents have derided Evans for having single-handedly 'invented' the Minoan civilisation.

The 'revisionist' view – well portrayed in *Minotaur* by Alexander MacGillivray – is that, far from preceding Mycenae, and dominating the Cyclades and mainland Greece 'for a thousand years', Minoans and Mycenaeans 'shared' the Eastern Mediterranean between them, until the latter subjugated the former in c1500BC.

Perhaps a more balanced view is that while Evans rebuilt Knossos to his vivid perspective of how it appeared at its zenith, it is equally undeniable that he unearthed a unique civilisation – previously thought to have been purely mythical. Minoan culture – preceding Mycenae – *did* dominate the Eastern Mediterranean by largely peaceful means for hundreds of years, and its technical skills and artistic achievements served as a vital stepping-stone between Anatolia, the Near East (and Egypt) and the civilisation(s) of pre-Classical Greece. Furthermore, support for Evans's interpretation is reinforced by the incredible discoveries on the island of Thera (see Chapter 8), which has only been excavated since 1967.

Later life

John Evans died in 1908, living long enough to derive great satisfaction from Arthur's achievements at Knossos. When Arthur's great uncle (Dickinson) died later in the same year, he became exceptionally rich, and funded almost all activities at Knossos on his own, for many years to come. He published every scrap of information about his discoveries (including his monumental *Palace of Minos*), was made President of the Society for the Promotion of Hellenic Studies in 1911, and President of the Society of Antiquities in 1914.

During the Great War, in typical fashion he made impassioned pleas to prevent former colleagues – now official enemies – from being expelled from various learned societies. Due to ethnic turmoil in the region (which cost their Muslim assistant dearly), Evans and his chief aide Mackenzie did not return to Crete until 1923, discovering the 'House of Frescoes' during that season.

A brilliant protégé, Richard Seager, died on his way to Egypt in

1925, and Evans had to relieve an alcoholic Mackenzie of his duties as Curator in 1929. Immediately, Evans offered this position to the brilliant 24-year-old John Pendlebury, who – having made his name at Amarna in Egypt (see Chapter 19) – quickly proved less subservient towards him than the long-suffering Mackenzie had been over the preceding 30 years.

Evans visited Knossos for the last time in 1935 and, at the age of 84, was made an honorary citizen of Heraklion before a crowd of thousands. He lamented to a London public audience in 1936 his 'failure' to decipher Linear B, but the 14-year-old Michael Ventris (though not actually in the hall) was introduced afterwards to the great old man.

In the spring of 1941 Evans was mortified to learn of the German invasion of Crete and – much worse – the execution of Pendlebury (still only 36), who had unhesitatingly joined the Partisans. To add insult to injury, the German commander took up residence at the Villa Ariadne, which Evans had built 40 years earlier as his summer home/office/guest house.

(To show a glimpse of how 'life's rich pattern' – with all its thrills and tragedies – permeates the fields of history, archaeology and travel just as much as in other walks of life, one could do a lot worse than read just two chapters from *Words of Mercury* (edited by Artemis Cooper), written by a man with an exceptional love of Crete – Patrick Leigh Fermor. One episode is 'Abducting a General' – which is particularly memorable for its last half-page. The other article is titled 'John Pendlebury', a most moving account that needs no added words of this writer.)

On 8 July 1941, Evans's 90th birthday, he was visited at his home at Wooton (later demolished) outside Oxford by three long-time friends and colleagues, including Edward Leeds, then Keeper of the Ashmolean. Three day later Arthur Evans died.

Chapter 7

Crete: the sequence of events

Anatolian linkage

It is likely that many of the original settlers in Crete at around 7000BC came from Anatolia (together with raiders/traders from the Syrian/Lebanese coast), and it is important to review that region's crucial role in helping to kick-start developments further west. The Anatolian town of Catal Hoyuk, although occupied from before 7000BC, grew dramatically (on a 32-acre site) during the next 1,500 years before its sudden demise around 5600BC. There were three key reasons for this precocious development: the exceptional agricultural conditions provided on the surrounding Konga plain; mass exploitation of obsidian from nearby volcanoes, which was traded far and wide; and, most significant of all in the long term, nearby mines from which copper (and lead) objects had long been hammered into shape, even before the beginning of this period.

Age-old mastery of fire and its effect on various minerals (accidentally or intentionally) had led to primitive copper smelting at the site prior to 6000BC. As techniques improved, Catal Hoyuk's export of small tools – together with its burgeoning reputation – spread down the great rivers into Mesopotamia, with a particular legacy at Tell Halaf (near modern-day Mosul on the Tigris). Though (not surprisingly) difficult to prove conclusively, experts are convinced that, so far advanced were these coppersmiths (with seemingly near-magical capabilities), the highly sought-after craftsmen travelled throughout Mesopotamia, and along the Fertile Crescent and its various spurs. Their caravan would include raw copper (and eventually ingots of great purity), together with an extended family and auxiliary personnel.

It was inevitable – with so many natural advantages (see below) – that the roaming raiders and traders would be probing at the coastal fringes of Crete from the earliest times, and equally inevitable that skilled Anatolian migrants (though not themselves accomplished sailors) would be brought into the picture.

As regards the dangers of open-sea sailing, the high degree of risk in trying to reach Crete was somewhat tempered by what Braudel refers to as the plethora of 'stepping stones'. While Heraklion is 85 miles (135 km) from Santorini (ancient Thera), each 'step' from Turkey's south-western extremity is 25 miles (40km) or often less, to reach the eastern tip of Crete. (Thinking of later Mycenaean interaction, exactly the same maximum distance applies to the steps required to hop from the southernmost point in the Peleponnese to the north-western tip of Crete.)

Lotus land

From the sea, sailors would be impressed by the (somewhat broken) mountain chain that runs east-west (up the nearly 8,000 feet in height) as the backbone of the 150-mile-long (240km) island. The climate was wetter than now (but as mild – with the south coast sub-tropical), only becoming as we know it today (with hotter summers) about halfway through the 2nd millennium BC. As with Cyprus, pygmy elephant and hippopotami were plentiful, until (all too easily) wiped out. Wheat and barley came with the first settlers, and oats from the Early Bronze Age (EBA). Olive trees and vines proliferated, but were probably not cultivated until the EBA, which is calculated to have started in about 3200BC.

Although the island appears to be dominated by mountains from a distance, this impression masked (very much as now) a wondrous mixture of forest, hillside pasture and extremely fertile valleys and plains. It was this ideal mix that enabled agriculture to become the first great Cretan success story, and the foundation of the wealthy Minoan lifestyle. As with their immediate Near East forebears – apart from the bonus of indigenous fruits, nuts and vegetables – the colonisers quickly displayed advanced skills of animal husbandry, with cattle (and the *bull* in particular) becoming such a potent symbol over the ensuing one and a half millennia.

As we can see from the amazing art unearthed in the early 20th century, dogs were an everyday feature, and the hunting of deer, hare and game birds was obviously more of a sport than a necessity. Fishing was a serious business, both for shellfish and (for example) octopus. Bees and honey were a preoccupation, featuring – in beautiful and moving terms – in the most lovely gold jewellery.

Building materials were plentiful. As to timber, cypress provided the larger beams required, and there were many smaller-growing varieties. Stone of all kinds was available on the doorstep, a graphic example being soft gypsum (mined very close to Knossos) with which some of the palace walls were eventually lined.

Access to copper was, however, a real headache. There were small deposits on the island, but nothing like enough to sate the growing appetite for this vital metal. Mass imports came from Kythnos in the Cyclades, which was very soon alloyed into bronze by using locally occurring arsenic. Copper was also sourced from further afield, but – surprisingly – tests show no evidence of supply from Cyprus, the most obvious location of mass deposits in the eastern Mediterranean. The sources of tin have proved difficult to identify, as found in the examination of other cultures. Anatolia was a possible supplier, as was far-away Afghanistan, via Iranian and Mesopotamian trade routes.

Bronze was in huge demand, partly for ceremonial needs, and this alone was a major motivation for Minoans to become pivotal seafaring traders throughout their long period of supremacy. They traded in silver from Laurion, and from the Cyclades – perhaps from Egypt, as well as from Lebanese and Syrian ports – and in return brought gold and precious stones from Egypt, some of which will have been passed on to their neighbours in the Aegean.

The Egyptians referred to their regular seafaring visitors as 'Keftiu', for whom they had great respect, and – viewing their wonderful murals – it is almost certain that these people were indeed Minoans.

Chronology

Precision in this area has proved very difficult, partly due to the absence of an early (decipherable) language. So Evans devised a comprehensive linkage to Egyptian dynasties, based on Egyptian artefacts found at key Minoan sites.

However, this archaeological method – used universally for nearly a century – is now being contradicted by science-based techniques (see Chapter 1 for a potted menu!).

The most fiercely fought – and spectacular – debate (upon which so much else hinges) is the definitive date for the volcanic eruption on Thera. Since there is general acceptance that extensive Mediterranean-wide disruption took place at around 1450BC, an 'ideal' explanation was/still is to tie this catastrophe to the volcanic explosion that is calculated to have been 4.5 times more powerful than that at Krakatoa in the late 19th century (AD).

J. V. Luce (in *The End of Atlantis*) makes a powerful case for this coincidence. Science – namely dendrochronology (tree-ringing) and ice-core analysis – have almost settled on the much earlier date of 1628BC. J. Lesley Fitton (*Minoans*, 2002) is clearly torn, but settles pro tem for around 1525BC, even though, as she writes herself, this can be seen to be illogical since it fits with neither of the two main theories.

Sticking with Fitton's chronology, the key sequence is as follows (the dates are all BC):

Early Minoan	Prepalatial	3200-1950
Middle Minoan	Protopalatial	1950-1700
Middle to Late Minoan	Neopalatial	1700-1450
Late Minoan	Final Palatial	1450-1350
Late Minoan	Postpalatial	1350-1200

Mediterranean volcanic and earthquake activity

The reference to Thera makes it appropriate to discuss these phenomena of nature, which have had a frequently traumatic effect throughout the Mediterranean since the Earth first cooled. In the Bible, could some of the unexplained afflictions that cursed the Israelites have been caused by the eruption? We do know, from examining sea-bed cores for volcanic debris, that the prevailing wind was a west-north-westerly, depositing ash several metres thick almost as far as the Nile delta – and clipping the eastern quarter of Crete.

We have a well-documented catalogue of volcanic eruptions and earthquakes in (for example) Italy, Greece and Turkey, going back thousands of years, and it is entirely possible that – apart from clear-cut disasters such as Thera and Pompeii at a 1,700-year interval – there

66

will have been many other cases where a particular city, or whole region, was wiped out by either of these natural calamities.

On Cephallonia right now, as vividly described by Robert Bittlestone in *Odysseus Unbound*, a major exercise is taking place to establish whether the most western peninsula of Paliki was originally a separate island – the 'real' Ithaca – some 3,300 years ago, the time to which Homer was referring when writing the *Odyssey*.

Eye-witness accounts of the 1953 Cephallonia earthquake – vividly displayed in the museum at Argostoli – give dreadful testament to the destruction of half of all property, and terrible loss of life. Statistically, earthquakes in the region (above 7.0 on the Richter scale) happen every 55 years. This assessment is based on the *actual* experience since 1444AD, implying that there are likely to have been more than 60 such catastrophes since the time when legend has Odysseus struggling for 10 years to make his way home to his beloved (and long-suffering) wife Penelope.

Quite apart from being ravaged by (for example) plague – which we know caused sites to be completely deserted, in some cases for ever, in medieval England – it is almost impossible to comprehend the disruptive effect that either volcanic eruption or earthquake must have wrought periodically throughout the central swathe of the Mediterranean, since man first began to populate that region.

It may be that – because of so many man-made horrors of our own time – we are failing to realise that *natural catastrophes* have sometimes been the cause of abrupt population movement (or complete disappearance) in the distant past. The factual record that – in 1953 – 40% of the *surviving* population of Cephallonia fled abroad (mainly to the USA or Australia), despite massive medical and rebuilding aid from around the globe, gives a salutary clue as to what it must have been like, in an age when there was no question of any sort of external assistance being remotely possible!

Furthermore, the action of tectonic plates has also had the effect of tilting mainland and island alike – as the African plate continues to bore underneath the Euro-Asian plate. There are many notable features one can see in Crete or elsewhere in the region, wherein man-made structures first built in antiquity are now either submerged or elevated.

Prepalatial Crete (3200-1950BC)

At 3200BC houses were quite simple, giving no clue as to the later magnificent achievements. Already, however, great attention was being paid to burial of the dead. In the north, natural caves or rock fissures were mostly used, but in the south there are the remains of a substantial number of 'tholos' (beehive) tombs. Even at their simplest, construction was a serious business, resulting in these tombs being used many times over. Interestingly, the doorway usually faced east, with bodies laid east-west, the head facing east.

In the north-east of the island there was a clear Cycladic influence, with many artefacts either being imported or of similar design. This is not surprising, as before 7000BC the earlier Cretan settlers relied extensively on obsidian from Melos (100 miles [160km] due north from Heraklion/Knossos).

By 2500BC crop-growing and animal husbandry had become quite advanced, and – crucially from the viewpoint of future wealth – the vine and olive tree were being deliberately cultivated. Houses were more complex, with textile and pottery manufacture taking place.

At this time two particularly Minoan features appeared, the first being 'kernoi' – stones with circular depressions, probably used as gaming boards. The second ubiquitous item was the stone stamp-seal – used repeatedly to press a clay seal, probably to identify (and control) the ownership of goods – a mandatory practice during the later Palatial period.

From the later 3rd millennium graves have yielded up more jewellery, some showing the delicate use of gold leaf. Examples of more complex tomb types are best seen at the Phourni cemetery, on the outskirts of present-day Archanes, where recovered marble figurines definitely show a recurring link with the Cyclades.

It is noticeable that, at the close of the millennium, most Minoan sites appear to have been completely undefended, while turmoil is known to have affected the Cyclades – and was severe enough in mainland Greece to set back its development by several centuries.

By 2000BC the sites at Knossos, Mallia and Phaestos – though not in any way *palatial* – were enjoying continuous expansion, covering an ever larger area. From this time there is clear evidence of caves being used for 'cult' purposes, while simultaneously mountain-peak shrines were being utilised. Eventually, most religious activity was centred on the palaces, but at this stage the deities were being worshipped in the darkest and/or most desolate of places.

At this time there were the beginnings of painted pottery and the carving of many-shaped stone vases. A much wider range of bronze implements has been recovered, while ornaments and jewellery of the period were more lavish, utilising elaborate silver and gold working techniques.

Stamp-seals – as opposed to the Near East method of 'rolling' the seal – became more sophisticated (in stone or bone), with detailed animal depiction being favoured over any human imagery. Relationships with the Near East and Egypt were exemplified by the introduction of scarab seals, although these were very quickly developed into a distinctly Minoan style.

As previously referred to, the circuitous sea routes, necessitated by dint of wind and current, meant that *outward* travel to Egypt could take place directly and comparatively quickly, whereas *inward* journeys from Egypt had to be anti-clockwise – north via the Palestinian and Syrian coastal route, then west along the southern stretch of Turkey, before island-hopping back to the Cretan homeland. Of course, the bonus for this laborious route was the cumulative cargo of very saleable exotica.

From the start, Minoan palaces were of unique design, but did the increasingly well-to-do Minoans draw on the Near East or Egypt for their inspiration? Possibly they did, because (as Fitton says) while modern thinking might like to claim this dynamic island as the most south-easterly point of pre-Greek civilisation, its rapid development would have been seen very differently at the time it was taking place – and that is as the north-western extremity of a Middle Eastern phenomenon!

Protopalatial Crete (1950-1750BC)

Note! Although the palaces at Phaestos and Mallia have many fascinating aspects – as do numerous other sites – this section is mainly focussed on developments at Knossos, which (by itself) gives a clear view of the 'leading-edge' achievements of the Minoans.

Knossos – at the foot of the Kephala Hill – had ample fresh water, wood and stone for building, fertile surroundings, and was only 4 miles (6km) from the sea. It therefore had easy access to harbours, much as can be seen at Heraklion today.

Myths and legends

Before going any further into the palace design, in realising that much of the Minoan effort was devoted to worship of their gods, life and death, and ritual, we should consider how important Crete was in their Pantheon – both to the Minoans themselves in 2000BC (and, for example, to the armies at the gates of Troy in c1300BC, as recounted in Homer's *Iliad*) and to the Greeks a thousand years still later. Legend had it that the king of Knossos was Minos, son of Zeus and Europa, the Phoenician nymph. Minos married Pasiphae, daughter of Helios the sun god. There follows Pasiphae's passion for the bull (Poseidon's gift to Minos), which led to the birth of the Minotaur – a man with a bull's head.

Daedalus created the Labyrinth for Minos (the cuckolded husband), in which maze the Minotaur was imprisoned. There follows the romance between the Athenian hero Theseus and Ariadne (daughter of Minos). Having rescued her, Theseus was ordered to abandon Ariadne on the island of Naxos, where she was 'given' to Dionysus. The mythological cycle closes with the flight of Daedalus and his son Icarus from Crete, with waxen wings. Icarus flew too close to the sun, his wings melted, and he fell into the sea and was drowned. The distraught Daedalus sought refuge in Sicily, where he managed to escape pursuit from Minos, who was killed.

Back to (a kind of) reality

The above stories do not represent history, but at their core lie certain historical facts – or at least beliefs that have guided man's endeavours ever since. Ariadne became the personification of fruitful growth, which withers and dies in winter, only to be born again each spring. The mythical labyrinth *is* the palace at Knossos, with its uniquely intricate layout, while Daedalus (whose ingenuity helped Pasiphae lure the bull into mating with her) personifies the essence of Minoan architectural and technological progress. Most important of all, while Europa gave our continent its name, her son Minos epitomised to the Greeks a powerful ruler and law-giver, and sovereign of the Minoan civilisation at its peak.

To cap everything, in May 1900 D. G. Hogarth (Director of the British School of Archaeology at Athens) made an in-depth survey of the Dictean Cave high up on Mount Lasithi – the legendary birthplace of Zeus – which Evans had first explored in 1896, but who was now preoccupied with his first season of digging at Knossos. Amazingly, after blasting their way to the furthest extremity, Hogarth's nervous team of workers found many hundreds of votive offerings to the god wedged in the multitude of crevices in the limestone stalactites – knives, miniature double-axes, and ornaments – all of which, due to ancient rock fall, had lain unseen and untouched for thousands of years (see the most evocative work, *The Bull of Minos* by Leonard Cottrell, first published in 1953).

Back to the palace – and surrounding area

First, it should be said that the palace overlaid previous buildings, and was itself (in part) incorporated into the second palace. It was built around a central court, on an approximate north-south axis – as was the case with palaces elsewhere. A striking feature that greets the visitor is the amount of well-ordered space given over to storage. Huge clay jars (pithoi) had been uncovered before Evans, who in turn not only discovered more of these (reminding Cottrell of Ali Baba and the 40 Thieves!) but also large circular pits, probably for keeping grain.

There seemed to have been separate domestic quarters, and probably areas set aside for craft activities – most likely including textile manufacture. At this stage there was no use of ashlar (cut) masonry, but plenty of evidence of blocks of gypsum. The palace had several entrance points, one via the 'Stepped Portico' from the south, and another via the 'Royal Road' in the north-west corner.

(The 'Royal Road' may have served a mainly religious purpose, but by the start of the 2nd millennium BC the Minoans had established a network of durable roads between major cities. Dick Parry, in *Engineering the Ancient World*, writes: 'Some lengths of these roads compare in workmanship with those of the Romans two millennia later. One major road from Phaestos to Knossos had to pass through the Mesara Valley, before climbing over 1,500m (5,000ft) to cross the precipitous mountain spine dividing the north and south of the island. In a typical paved cross-section the Minoans carefully excavated and compacted the road base and, on this, placed a 200mm-thick (8-inch) layer of rubble and broken stones in clay to make it watertight... The Minoans knew of the need to keep water away from the subgrade and, in addition to the watertight layer immediately above ... they provided stone side drains to carry away the surplus surface water.')

From this time the palace has yielded evidence of hieroglyphic writing, in both seal and tablet form, which gives some clue as to formal administrative activity. Fitton records that, very recently, a scrap of a Linear A tablet has been recovered from just outside the palace. The term 'palace' seems to many commentators an overblown claim – with so many artisanal functions carried on, interspersed with ritual activity, and the possibility of separate quarters for a 'ruling' family or group. Nevertheless, it is perhaps churlish to quibble, since the Minoan lifestyle revolution was unique in the Mediterranean at this time, and as one set of building structures was almost continually being metamorphosed into the next stage of ever more sophisticated 'palace' style and complexity.

The surrounding Knossos town was substantial, the successive stripping of timber and stone by much later generations (which invoked Evans's scorn) not disguising the fact that the population may have reached some 10,000, with perhaps a similar number of inhabitants in the wider region, whose life's work was to keep the palace and town supplied with an immense range of food and materials.

Writing

To return to the crucial development of writing, it is perhaps best to summarise the island-wide activity. Clearly, the start of a structured society *and* (in particular) the formal storage and distribution of foodstuffs required a need for record-keeping. To know the peak stored quantities, who had been issued with what, and even some control over stock 'rotation', made the development of a *system* mandatory.

To support the separate sovereign state theory, as between the major cities, it is interesting to see (for example) that whereas in the north of the island a Cretan system of hieroglyphics held sway – quite different from the Egyptian, though transferred from the Near East – at Phaestos (on the south coast) the use of Linear A became quite widespread.

Thousands of seals have been recovered, involving hundreds of differing 'sealings'. Also, quantities of broken seals have been found, probably because keeping these was a way to count 'stock reduction'. We can also assume that the vast majority were later destroyed, since all seals were merely sun-dried, as opposed to being 'fired' for longevity.

Religion/ritual

During the Protopalatial period the earlier peak sanctuaries flourished, as did certain of the caves. The Kamares cave – which gave its name to the fine pottery of the period because a quantity of objects were found there – was linked to Phaestos, from where in fine weather it can be seen, high up on Mount Ida. While some religious activity within the palaces can only be deduced from scanty evidence, at Phaestos there are distinct rooms, one with benches and a corner drain (for animal sacrifice?) with another housing an 'offering table'.

One of the most spectacular discoveries stems from the highly praised work carried out since 1965 by the husband and wife team of J. and E. Sakellarakis, at first in the town of Archanes, south of Knossos, and later in the nearby cemetery of Phourni. In 1979 they discovered a ruined temple at a site known as Anemospilia, on the northern slopes of Mount Juktas, clearly visible from Knossos to the north, less than 4 miles (7km) away.

The astonishing feature of this discovery was that – by virtue of the four skeletons found in various postures – there was clearly a specific ritual being carried out when the temple was engulfed by overwhelming volcanic activity, and perhaps a simultaneous earthquake. The excellent Sakellarakis guidebook draws the inescapable conclusion (as other experts have later confirmed, however unpalatable to modern pro-Minoan sensibilities) that a human sacrifice to try and ward off impending disaster was actually being enacted at the very moment of widespread catastrophe.

Among many intriguing features, the bones of many animals were found, including those of bulls – the significance of which is the degree to which (subsequently) bull sacrifice came to be so frequently depicted, the most famous example being on the Ayia Triadha sarcophagus.

Pottery, jewellery, and foreign trade

The best way to appreciate just how fine Kamares ware was (and still is) would be to visit the wonderful Heraklion Museum. The decorated vases, pithoi, jugs and 'rhytons' (ritual pouring vessels) are spectacular, but – arguably – no exhibits of this period are finer than the most elegantly decorated one-handled cups, which would definitely be admired if used for serving afternoon tea nowadays. In a different vein, the large stemmed bowl (found at Knossos) with a chequerboard pattern and white lilies in relief, is equally amazing.

Spectacular examples of gold ware include the intriguing double-faceted Phaestos disc (not yet deciphered) and the Aigina treasure.

This collection – reportedly found on the island of Aigina in the Aegean, less than 50 miles from Athens – which came into the hands of the British Museum more than 100 years ago, is now known to be Minoan and dates from the Protopalatial period, although some items probably originate from the Neopalatial period that followed.

It is not surprising that, with their long-held sailing expertise, the Minoans could now 'come into their own' as exporters of high-quality goods. As Minoan influence grew, settlers from Crete started to put down roots within the Cycladic island chain – perhaps as intermediaries who facilitated supplies of all kinds to an ever-widening client base. The island stepping-stones at each extremity of Crete would become logical trade routes, and the two-way attractions of covering the 100 miles to the north to reach Thera and Melos would have encouraged these much longer (and riskier) sea-going forays. Minoan objets d'art of this period have also been found in Syria/Lebanon/Palestine, as well as in Egypt.

A particular fascination is the Tod treasure. Although unusually (for Minoan art) made of silver, this cache from Tod, near Luxor, has been dated to the reign of Amenemhat II (1922-1878BC), and has definite design linkage to the Minoan style that then applied. Cretan products have been found as far afield as Mari, on the Euphrates, and it is also true that desirable items were taken back to the palaces from all these locations.

People at the end of an era

As this 250-year-long period of sustained development drew to a close, we have a quite populous 'nation', operating in a federal or 'city-state' mode. Brimming with confidence, they erected no tangible defences against potential intruders, while securing steadily growing respect throughout the Eastern Mediterranean, and into Egypt and the Middle East.

Their life-span was short, as evidenced by examined skeletons, due partly to disease (e.g. malaria) and hard work. In contrast with the sophisticated clothing worn 1,500 years earlier by 'Otzi' in the bitterly cold high Tyrol (see Chapter 1), male clothing, as depicted on painted clay models, was simple, with a belt (of leather or rolled cloth) holding a rectangular garment or type of kilt in place.

Female figurines show full skirts and open (bare-breasted) bodices, with high collars and some kind of head-dress frequently worn. Both sexes wore a type of sandal. However, these idealised (warm-weather or processional) images should not disguise the fact that – even in ancient Crete – people would háve had to wear somewhat warmer garments in the lowland winter, and very much warmer clothing in the rain-or-sleet-prone hills and mountains.

And so, if it were not for the horrific event that devastated the whole island, the scene would have been set fair for untrammelled progress. However, some time around 1700BC widespread destruction took place, which – though it did not kill off the whole population – must certainly have been a grievous setback. What happened at Anemospilia must have been representative of the instant (literal) collapse meted out to all the palaces and towns, and the cause is almost certain to have been a sudden catastrophic eruption on Thera. We know (from the next chapter) that the Akrotiri population (on the southernmost rim of Thera) had notice of the 1628BC devastation, when the wind blew from the west-north-west, and only clipped the eastern segment of Crete.

On this occasion we can surmise that the four unfortunates killed at Anemospilia were struggling to complete their macabre offering to the gods, after preliminary warnings of volcanic eruption had been given to their fellow citizens. Perhaps the overall loss of human life was modest but, if the prevailing wind was from the north, the massive deluge of ash and rock would still have been enough to severely damage the palaces, and give the survivors no choice but to set about a major programme of recovery and reconstruction.

Neopalatial Crete (1700-1450BC)

After the disastrous setback around 1700BC, this next 250-year period was the era that saw the greatest flowering of Minoan civilisation and culture. Debate continues as to whether the Minoan apogee was before or after the next major eruption on Thera – whether this occurred in the 'scientific' year of 1628BC or in the 'archaeological' year, posited at somewhere between 1530 and 1520BC. (A terse layman's comments might be that only when the experts eventually reconcile this key date between themselves can the 'before or after Thera' argument be finally settled!)

(Note! As with the preceding Protopalatial description, this section concentrates mainly on Knossos, which was arguably the finest of the palaces, and certainly [at 135 metres square] the largest, and likely to have been the most awe-inspiring to the visitor. However, because Evans regarded the palace at Archanes as being inextricably linked to Knossos – as have the subsequent Sakellarakis researches at this site, and also at Anemospilios and Phourni – the script that follows encompasses all four locations, the furthest distance between which is less than 10 miles [15km].)

Stretching from its four extremities, the second palace at Knossos is truly labyrinthine in its complexity. Walking round the multitude of buildings (so controversially restored by Evans) is quite headache-inducing, even with a detailed map in hand. However, even in making allowance for Evans's exaggerated 'improvements', each visit leaves an indelible impression of opulence and success.

Clearly part of this complexity arises from the way in which the second palace subsumed many of the undamaged elements (at differing levels) from its predecessor, and part also arises from the bewildering variety of 'quarters' incorporated within the 5-acre site – royal/personal servants, processional/ritual, government/administrative, food storage/preparation, and art/craft or artisanal activities. And all of these diverse requirements fanned out from the massive central courtyard, which alone was 45 by 25 square metres (or 150 by 80 feet).

A feature common to all Minoan palaces is a 'West Court', and having said we are going to concentrate on Knossos, one of the finest single impressions for a visitor is actually the West Court at Phaestos. The sense of grace and style, as one walks up the shallow steps of the Grand Staircase (more than 60 feet wide), flanked by beautifully cut ashlar stone, is quite unforgettable – only matched on reaching the top by the wonderful view of the palace and its immediate surroundings.

How the frescoes vitally assist us!

Almost from the start of his excavations, Evans recovered fragments of frescoes from deep within the ruins. These fragments were beautifully decorated, but have been the source of endless controversy, mainly because Evans went 'over the top' in employing skilled artists to reconstruct complete scenes to his own idealistic interpretation of life in Knossos, more than 3,500 years ago.

In reaching quick conclusions, and employing the skilled and imaginative French artist Gillieron, half a dozen fragments from the northern area of the palace were incorporated as the 'Saffron Gatherer', showing a young man harvesting. Later research showed the lithe figure to be that of a monkey, earning scorn for the middle-aged entrepreneur – without whose vision, persistence and money, however, discovery of these vital clues would have been long deferred.

Another such find was what became known as the 'Grandstand Fresco', wherein a crowd standing in a building are watching a Courtyard ceremony. Yet another set of fragments clearly depicted possibly the most uniquely famous image of the Knossos palace – namely the tapered pillars, but *inverted*, that is with the thickest part of the column uppermost.

Whereas most purists would say that the palace ruins should only have been cleaned up and made safe – while much longer-term research was carried out – Arthur Evans did undoubtedly rush through his restoration programme far too quickly. Within 10 years the key rebuilt areas became very much as we see them today (exactly 100 years on), and certainly Evans was partly motivated by a desire to beat his existing and potential critics to the punch – that is, he wanted his image of this wonderful culture to become *the* correct and only interpretation.

Three crucial points must be made at this juncture. First, all these originally recovered scraps of evidence – after proper coolly executed 'due diligence' – do definitely guide us as to how remarkably advanced this 'second' palace phase became, particularly as regards the sheer richness of its occupants' lives, and the supreme skill of their artistry.

Second, it is wonderful to note – in comparison with the *static* representations in contemporary Egyptian painting – how much movement and exuberance the Minoan artists managed to convey, whether of humans, animals (on land and in the ocean) or foliage. This natural and fluid style is nowhere better seen to advantage than in a room of the Royal Villa at Ayia Triadha. Though badly burned at around 1450BC, this continuous fresco across three walls depicts sweeping scenes: a cat stalking a bird, leaping deer, one seated figure, and another gathering crocuses. It should also be said that – as Minoan influence spread – very typical examples of unmistakeable *Minoan* style were found as far afield as Avaris in the Nile delta, and at Tel Kabri in Israel.

Third, when we come to examine Akrotiri on Thera in the next chapter – and realise that all its artistic wonders (so closely linked to

Minoan Crete) were accomplished before its total burial in 1530BC (or, more likely, in 1628BC), one is blown away in admiration of the almost *complete* murals and frescoes. Since the peeling away of the ash covering Akrotiri only started in 1967, there was no evidence to moderate the arguments over Evans's exaggeration of the art and architecture in the restoration at Knossos for another 60 years.

A visit to Akrotiri, after touring the Knossos site, is perhaps the best way to achieve a balanced view. At the very least some of the worst insults hurled at Evans were unjustified. At best he had remarkable prescience of the supporting evidence for his theories that would eventually be revealed elsewhere, and – in his piecing together of the Minoan past – came very close to a factual representation of their culture, if Akrotiri is anything to go by.

Architectural innovation

Evans's 'wish-list' focussed on establishing Royal quarters – the separate King's and Queen's rooms – when the supporting evidence was decidedly flimsy. What cannot be gainsaid, however, is the legacy of advanced architectural thinking and engineering execution. Many of the rooms were certainly very fine, and incorporated elaborate features. Some had three external walls, constructed in a manner that enabled doors to be slid into recesses during hot weather, so that, except for supporting pillars, the space was quite open so as to catch any breeze. Elsewhere light-wells were cleverly designed, again so as to introduce fresh air, but also to relieve an otherwise gloomy interior.

Certain rooms were sunken – what Evans described as a 'lustral basin'. These mostly had a drainage outlet, leading to divided opinion as to their use: ritual (including sacrifice), washing/bathing, or lavatories. Indeed, it is worth examining aspects of Minoan ingenuity at this time, in the field of 'waste management'. The outflow requirements had the small ducts from every such room leading into a main drainage system. The system of large-diameter tapered terracotta pipes was interlocked over a considerable distance to an outflow – the tapering effect imparting a propulsion motion, so as to avoid the build-up of sediment!

The security of fresh water supplies was no less ingenious. We would expect to find evidence of deep-cut wells within the perimeter of the palace, as well as a water course from the Kephala Hill. What is astonishing is the collection system for rainwater. Leonard Cottrell was shown round the palace in 1952 by Piet de Jong (a Yorkshireman after the writer's own heart!). De Jong was the last British curator, before the whole site (and the Villa Ariadne) was handed over to the Greek state. It is worth repeating in detail the explanation of what Cottrell saw.

Along each stretch of roof were stone channels, in the same way as gutters run nowadays. However, because there were so many flights of steps, the channels (suitably sloping from one run to the next) had to abruptly turn at right-angles on the outside of each corner of the particular stairwell. Had each sloping duct had a flat bottom, the speeding water would have merely poured straight over the edge, at each corner. Quoting Cottrell:

'...the trick was to slow down its speed; and this was done most cunningly by making the bottom of the water-channels in a series of parabolic curves. The curves themselves almost exactly agree with the natural parabolas that the water falling down a slope at such an angle would make. Therefore the water reached the bottom of each flight at about half the speed it would have reached had it poured down the slope in a straight line, instead of in a series of jumps.

Nor was this all. A series of catch-pits collected the sediment on its downward course, so that when the water reached the bottom of the steps it was still pure and fit for washing purposes.'

As Evans said of these touches of genius: 'Nothing in the whole building gives such an impression of the result of long generations of intelligent experience on the part of Minoan engineers as the parabolic curves in the channels.'

While such intelligence was being displayed in the palace redevelopments, villages and luxury villas were also being built. Roads and harbours were constructed and irrigation systems perfected. An example of durability is that the present-day road, which bypasses Archanes towards the south coast of the island, has been proven to have been originally laid down in this Neopalatial period.

Another wonderful example is the Reservoir at the (Tourkoyeitonia) Archanes palace. This may originate from the Protopalatial era, and was first excavated by Evans – with J. Sakellarakis fully uncovering the whole area in 1964. The underground circular structure of poros-stone effectively surrounds a spring, and is 18 feet (5.5m) in diameter and 20 feet (6m) high. At one end there are steps that lead up to the water level. The outlet was fed into a 1 metre by 1 metre conduit or drain that supplied the palace and immediately surrounding buildings.

The people, artisanal activities, writing, ritual and burial
Palace activities would have varied widely – with great attention being paid to the recorded storage and issue of the three staple 'foodstuffs', namely wheat, wine and olive oil. In the designated areas, craftsmen would have worked in gold, ivory and semi-precious stones.

During this era hieroglyphic script faded out and was replaced by Linear A, the origins of which are still fiercely debated. Though a number of examples survive on pottery (or on stone) as well as in tablet form, this is only because they were later burned by accident.

Most pottery manufacture would have taken place further afield, mainly because of the need for adequate supplies of clay, firing kilns and storage space for finished articles, which ranged from day-to-day requirements to the highly decorated palace ware. So would the processing of huge quantities of imported bronze, being consumed in the making of practical tools, weapons (whether ceremonial or not) and even extremely large cauldrons.

Since the staggering discoveries at Anemospilia and at Phourni (both very close by), it is questionable as to how much religious and ritual activity took place within the palace confines. Perhaps the 'royal' circle involved itself in private ritual with senior 'priests', and otherwise (partly for space reasons) focussed palace ceremonial mainly on civil or administrative formalities.

In similar vein, as to 'bull-leaping' festivals, although we have fresco evidence of acrobats performing their hair-raising summersaults, as supported in pottery decoration and (in minutely accurate detail) on gold rings – see the Ashmolean Museum – it is difficult to believe that bulls could be kept within the palace labyrinth (whatever legend tells us) or that these death-defying spectacles could have been accommodated within the confines of the West Court at Knossos.

On the west side of the Knossos valley Evans found the 'Little Palace', from which was recovered one of the most iconic items – a 'rhyton' (ritual sprinkling vessel) in the shape of a bull's head. This (restored) near-black carving in steatite is remarkably lifelike, and seems to be in exact proportion to an actual modern-day animal.

One of the intriguing mysteries of the age is supplied by the evidence of goddesses performing an 'epiphany' ritual. The evidence for these 'cult' scenes is most graphically provided in the (again) startling detail cast or cut into gold rings. As one studies examples in museums for several minutes, it can be quite an eerie experience trying to work out exactly what 'ecstatic' experience is being undergone, and what it must have meant to the spellbound audience. In relation to the gold rings, expert modern craftsmen remain in awe as to how – even with a magnifying glass, held stable in perfect light – the geniuses of the day could cut such intricate designs into such tiny spaces. The wonder – in a museum – is to alternate between examining the ring through the in-situ magnifying implement, and seeing this beautiful 3,500-year-old article with the naked eye.

On the question of recovering skeletal remains, it is quite strange that – within the palace, or close by – there is precious little evidence *from this particular period*. There are a number of plain tombs, but nothing to compare with either the *preceding* or *succeeding* eras. By far the richest nearby burial area has recently been discovered in Heraklion, where – in a densely populated Neopalatial town – it is likely that evidence of hundreds of burials will eventually be revealed.

The most significant burial ground in the whole of Crete, only a few miles from Knossos, was at Phourni – from the word 'phournos' (oven) – completely unknown until excavated by J. Sakellarakis in 1964. The cemetery was in use for 1,200 years, from 2400 to 1200BC, and there is a wide pathway still preserved today that leads from the village of Kato Archanes. The partial paving of this path is very similar to the paved Minoan road within the cemetery itself.

However, sticking to the Neopalatial period, there is very little amongst the amazing wealth of discoveries that can be dated to this 250-year-long era. The majority of the most remarkable finds date from the Final and Postpalatial periods (which will be discussed later), leading one to the inescapable conclusion that the Minoan tombs and lesser graves – up to the middle of the 2nd millennium – were enlarged or 'cannibalised' to make way for the far more elaborate procedures that followed.

Art, and the 'seal' phenomenon

Small-scale sculpture, in stone, ivory and bronze, was a speciality of the age. There are wonderful examples of highly decorated stone and pottery vases and other 'specialty' products, but for whatever reason a large proportion of the immense body of work (of Neopalatial art – in all forms) was in *miniature* – but no less fascinating for that. Faience (tin-glazed) figurines of snake goddesses found at Knossos are famous examples in the field of pottery. Bronze (lost wax) casting – of, amongst other works, an acrobat leaping over a bull – testifies to the artists' skill.

Harking back to when Arthur Evans was first rummaging in antique shops in Athens, the almost *obsessive* miniaturisation category was in the field of seals. Made in every conceivable geometric shape, and in almost every conceivable type of stone, these wonderfully artistic 'jewels' handed down to us are in many ways the Minoan 'signature'. Indeed, as Evans was to find, these objects were handed down through the generations – over thousands of years – as good luck charms, and (as 'milk stones' worn around the neck) to ensure fertility.

As to gold work, one of the most beautiful pieces of jewellery is a bee pendant – from the earlier phase of the Neopalatial period – that was found in the cemetery at Mallia. But perhaps the most interesting items are the pair of cups found at Vapheio (near Sparta) in the last decade of the 19th century. Until Evans's early discoveries at Knossos, these were thought to be Mycenaean, but it was then realised that they were of Minoan design.

The intriguing aspect – which Cottrell describes in great detail – is how only the beady eye of Evans realised 20 years after they were first publicised that in the bull-trapping scene (with nets) on one cup, the surviving hunter clinging to the horns with arms and legs to avoid impalement is a *girl*. On the other cup, where it was thought that hunters were facing a pair of bulls, Evans deduced that one of the 'bulls' is in fact a decoy cow, which – with raised tail – is attracting the attention of the bull … at which point one of the wily hunters is able to throw his lasso over the bull's head!

Minoans in the wider region

During this era Minoan influence spread far and wide. Gifts from these 'Keftiu' people have been found in Egyptian tombs and there is evidence of trade along the Palestinian coast. There were links with Anatolia; plenty of evidence in the Dodecanese islands (those nearest to south-west Turkey); and – as would be expected – along the stepping-stone islands off the north-western and north-eastern tips of Crete.

The extraordinary finds in the 'royal' grave circle burials at Mycenae included a rich Minoan contribution (see Chapter 9). However, it is not surprising that – due to their proximity to Crete – the greatest Minoan influence was to be within the Cycladic islands, particularly on Melos (the major eastern Mediterranean island source of obsidian in Neolithic times) and, most of all, on Thera – see next chapter.

End of this second palace era

As some 250 years earlier, the whole island was completely devastated in around 1450BC, but archaeologists still cannot be sure of the cause. Perhaps there was a combination of events? It is almost certain that massive earthquake damage was at least partly responsible. However, a bigger question is whether the increasingly powerful Mycenaean 'empire' – jealous of long-established Minoan superiority – had already started to flex its muscles militarily, or whether it took a purely opportunistic role, in 'picking up the pieces' in a situation where Crete was in no position to defend itself, or was even only too glad to receive food and other vital supplies, and – in so doing – give up its erstwhile position of pre-eminence throughout the Aegean and beyond.

Final Palatial and Postpalatial Crete (1450-1200BC)

Although Knossos itself survived the natural and/or human-induced disasters of around 1450BC, none of the other major sites escaped. In any event, from this date until the onset of the 'Dark Age', we can be fairly sure that the whole island fell under Mycenaean control. The evidence for Mycenaean dominance is varied. One telling feature is the appearance of Linear B at this time, with the somewhat frugal legacy so far unearthed being very similar on the mainland (e.g. at Poros in the south-western Peloponnese) to the caches found on Crete. The clear implication is that – if not immediately – a language commonality slowly emerged.

The Minoan pottery style and their burial system both soon bore a distinct Mycenaean appearance. Did a Mycenaean prince take control of Knossos, or perhaps marry into the existing Minoan dynasty? Certainly, various alterations to the palace ensued, with the most famous being creation of a 'Throne Room'. The Mycenaean-style frescoes are impressive, but the unique elements are the stone high-backed throne itself and the gypsum benches that spread along the wall on either side. The griffins on either side of the throne may *possibly* be based on the pair of animals guarding the main entrance to the fortified citadel at Mycenae. Known as the Lion Gate, these (long-since headless) animals were so named by Schliemann ... but this was 25 years before Evans discovered the throne room at Knossos! Other preserved frescoes are the 'Cup Bearer' (though the detail of the restoration is somewhat disputed) and the 'Dancing Girl', whose movement causes her skirt to billow – yet another example of the Minoan artist's ability to convey life-like movement.

Another changed aspect of life on Crete was the influx of sheep, with herds spread around the island, and wool being sent to the palace. This coincided with an upsurge in textile manufacture, as testified by the quantities of loom weights recovered from both palace sites and burial chambers.

Changes in burial practice

An earlier section of this chapter touched on the cemetery at Phourni, and it is these last phases of Minoan culture that show the true wonder of the site – and impart to the visitor so many aspects to consider – from a period when the whole area had already been in use for well over 1,000 years. The Mycenaean Grave Enclosure contains seven graves from the 14th century BC – unique up this time in Crete. All had been disturbed, but one shaft still contained four impressive bronze objects, another an exquisitely decorated ivory comb, and yet another three lentoid (lens-shaped) seals in differing stone and each beautifully designed.

The 'Tholos' (beehive) Tomb A was the first funerary building to be excavated at Phourni in 1965. A hut had always been there, used as a shelter/hiding place, with a door facing east towards the north-south road. Over time the tholos and its 'Dromos' (long downward-sloping walled entrance) had filled up – to the height of the original lintel. This had been the threshold of an upper entrance punched into the above-ground part of the beehive space – probably forced by the original Minoan grave robbers, or even by Roman thieves well over a thousand years later!

The ground plan is virtually identical to the 'Treasury of Atreus' at Mycenae, although on a much smaller scale. However, the main chamber (14 feet [4.3m] in diameter), which had a shallow pit in the floor, seemed to yield very few finds initially. But, first of all between this pit and one wall – adjacent to what turned out to be a side chamber – was discovered (under rubble) the complete skeleton of a six-year-old horse, which had been dismembered with the greatest care, leaving all the flesh attached. This was clearly a sacrifice in honour of the deceased.

When the apparent blockage to a possible chamber started to be dismantled, the skull of a bull was found to be wedged into the stonework – clearly also involved in a ritual sacrifice. Scholars had long been puzzled as to why a bull sacrifice had been depicted on one side of the famous Ayia Triadha 'larnax' (closed coffin). Now they had definitive proof as to the reason.

Then, seeking access to the hoped-for second chamber, it was apparent that an outer wall lay behind the aforementioned rubble. Since this was fundamental to the stability of the whole tholos tomb, the Sakellarakis team had no choice but to dig down from above. Their nervous anticipation can only be imagined as they slowly revealed, 16 feet (5m) down, a rock-cut trapezoidal chamber of only 33 square feet (3.7sq m) containing a single clay larnax – one of the largest found to date in Crete. The untouched larnax had remained sealed for more than 3,300 years, and the skeletal remains (sex initially unknown) showed that the body had been laid to rest in the foetal position. Excitingly, within the coffin were numerous necklaces and ornaments (many in gold) together with gold signet rings – one a brilliant cult scene – seal stones and several other personal objects.

Outside the larnax there were ten bronze vases – seven of which were neatly piled to save space. There were many other bronze objects, iron beads (extremely rare for this date) and three miniature figure-of-eight ivory shields, which together with other ivory items formed the front panel of a now-disintegrated footstool. The *crucial* aspect of this wonderful discovery – which, on full analysis, must have been a princess's burial – is the light it throws on the Minoan-Mycenaean relationship at a date of around 1350BC. No wonder that the Sakellarakis couple have been so honoured for their brilliantly painstaking and informative research!

Continued exploration at Phourni revealed many finds, but – in the space we have – just one more exquisite revelation will briefly be recounted. In Tholos Tomb D, an undisturbed rich female burial was uncovered. The body was resting on a wooden 'stretcher' and, despite subsequent rock fall, the skeleton's position and layout of offerings and jewellery were unaltered. The dead woman held a bronze mirror with her left hand, in front of her face (so that she could still 'see' her reflection in the afterlife). On her head she wore a single gold diadem, made up of 37 rectangular pieces, and she was adorned with three beautiful necklaces. There was a wealth of other jewellery about her person, some of it decorative, but other items of a strictly practical use, such as the pair of glass paste pins that held her gown at each shoulder. Away from the body was a sealed 'pyxis' (cosmetic or jewellery container), which revealed yet more stunning personal belongings. All in all, the best impression one can obtain of the moving scene is to study the wonderfully colourful and detailed reconstruction of the burial.

The end of Minoan Crete, onset of the Dark Age – and the degree of Greek debt

As we move from the Final Palatial to the Postpalatial phase, the increasing signs of Mycenaean dominance become unmistakeable. Linear B tablets show the gods being worshipped as a mix of the *Minoan* with the *Olympian*. Even so, many of the key features of the famous Ayia Triadha sarcophagus, which dates from between 1400BC and 1375BC, bear an extremely close relationship to those revealed at the purely Minoan site of Anemospilia.

The fall of Knossos is dated to between 1375BC and 1350BC. Even so, at this time Crete continued to maintain many of its traditional burial procedures, albeit in Mycenaean-style chambers – witness the number of wonderful clay 'larnakes' (coffins) found at Armenoi, near Rethymnon, which is dated to just later than the above find in Tholos Tomb D.

In a nutshell, it seems – as so often has been a feature in modern times – that although day-to-day living bore the Mycenaean stamp, adherence to *Minoan* deeply held religious convictions and practices continued for a very long time. Perhaps this crucial feature in the lives of the population was perpetuated mostly in the peak sanctuaries, or at other mountain settlements, but it is striking that Evans discovered a shrine of the 'double axes' in the ruined palace at Knossos, which dates from around the middle of the 13th century BC. And so, in the upheavals that disrupted every region of the Eastern Mediterranean – and heralded the Dark Age – all the coastal sites in Crete were abandoned. There is no doubt that Minoans will have eked out an existence in their impenetrable mountain chain for hundreds of years – indeed there might be solid DNA linkage between their generations and the modern Cretan (as with today's citizens in Tuscany and Western Turkey).

In the Introduction to this book, the 19th-century argument was posed, between those who believed that there was only 'barbarism' before 800/750BC, and those who believed that the Greeks owed Minoan Crete (as well as Mycenae) a huge debt. That argument still rages. What is irrefutable is that Crete featured very significantly in ancient Greek mythology, as outlined earlier in this chapter. The *Iliad* tells of Idomeneus, grandson of Minos, leading a contributing Cretan force at Troy. We also know (as Fitton has described) that Thucydides wrote of the 'thalassocracy' – sea-based empire – of Minos, and that he 'organised the first navy, stamping out piracy'. Evidence of the detail in Minoan warships is sketchy, but one day we may find out what elements of their design were incorporated in the Athenian fleet that defeated the Persians at Salamis in 480BC – some 1,000 years later!

Part of the problem is Evans's legacy. His unreasonably idealistic vision of the 'Minoans' living not just a prosperous life, but one that was (as he wished it to have been) intelligent, peaceful and comfortable, has provoked a fierce backlash. How, say some critics, can his 'perfect' vision be squared with a preoccupation for sacrifice – even, as at Anemospilia, human sacrifice? One of the most vocal critics was the historian Robert Collingwood (1889-1943), who contrasted the 'barbarously utilitarian' Cretan artists with 'Hellenically Classical' Greece.

Collingwood was positively vitriolic about what he saw at the palaces, complaining of artisanal architecture, wherein (as in art too) the Greeks owed nothing to the Minoans in their 'spirit of order and symmetry and proportion'. Of course, in his lavish restoration work – of buildings and wall-paintings – Evans did his cause no favours by leaving himself wide open to accusations of invention, and even falsification. These issues were made much worse when it became clear – years later – that he (or his artist) had plainly made interpretive mistakes.

However, Collingwood died a quarter of a century before Marinatos first revealed the wonders of Akrotiri. Here, the cameras of the world recorded an uncovered town, which appeared exactly as it was when suddenly deserted 3,500 years previously. As we shall see in the next chapter, the buildings only required to be made safe, and whole wall paintings hardly needed more than protection from exposure to the atmosphere.

To what extent, if any, would a close examination of Akrotiri have modified any of Collingwood's dismissive opinions?

And what about Minoan jewellery? Surely it would be perverse not to attribute any Minoan legacy to the Greeks from the beautiful array of totally authenticated jewellery recovered by Sakellerakis from tholos tombs at Phourni (again some 25 years after Collingwood's death)?

Finally, what cannot be denied is the link of language. The still undeciphered Minoan Linear A script (evidence of which has virtually never been discovered in the Peloponnese) definitely begat the Linear B script (deciphered in 1952 by Ventris and Chadwick), which was comparatively widespread in both locations. And there is no doubt at all that the ancient Greek language comprised elements of Linear B – otherwise known as Mycenaean Greek – in combination with the attributes derived from the Phoenicians (see Chapter 13).

Chapter 8

Thera, and the role of Spyridon Marinatos

This community had a glittering Bronze Age history that paralleled that of Crete but, unlike other islands in the Cyclades archipelago, the golden age on Thera was brought to a tragic end through a cataclysmic volcanic eruption – this catastrophe being dated to 1628BC scientifically, and approximately to 1530BC archaeologically. Thera warrants its own chapter, partly because there is an extraordinary story to tell, and partly because its wonderful preserved city of Akrotiri was only discovered as recently as 1967.

Thera today

Traditionally known as 'Strongyle' (round island), Thera – modern Santorini – is today a mini-archipelago of three islands, together with the two new actively volcanic islets of Nea Kameni and Palea Kameni at its centre. The former, still active, has been created over the past 300 years, while the latter first appeared in 197BC. When the complete middle of the round island blew up – and the sea rushed in to fill the huge space, all that was left was the main island of Thera, somewhat crescent-shaped from north to south, protruding to the east, the much smaller Therasia to the north-west, and the tiny Aspronsi to the south-west.

Lying over the same African/Eurasian fault-line as does Cephallonia, Thera was entirely created by volcanic activity in the first place. Therefore, quite apart from the terrible events of 3,600 years ago, it has been bedevilled by repeated volcanic (and tectonic) activity over the ensuing millennia. The latest cruel outburst was in 1956, when huge earthquake damage occurred and – as on

Cephallonia in 1953 – many villages were destroyed, and half the population emigrated to seek a better future elsewhere.

Consequently, the overwhelming feature that strikes any visitor is layer upon layer of successive volcanic debris that constitutes the spectacular walls of the 'caldera'. This debris is mainly comprised of 'pozzolana' (fine ash) and pumice (aerated lava), and its thickness across the three islands – from the event of 3,600 years ago alone – is up to 40 metres! The volcanically originated soil on Thera is very fertile, and grows excellent wine, and it is only an acute lack of water that limits the amount of produce that can be grown annually.

Although the island only made a slow economic recovery from the 1956 disaster, the picture today is quite different. First, the inherent beauty of this unique place has made it a magnet for holidaymakers over the last 30 years – and the Mediterranean's No 1 spot as a wedding venue! Second, excavated Akrotiri, the new museum at Phira, and other sites from antiquity have added an unmissable set of archaeological attractions.

Ferdinand de Lesseps and the Suez Canal

From the middle of the 19th century a modest amount of archaeological investigation started but, alongside the curiosity of a range of individuals, de Lesseps realised that the inexhaustible supply of consolidated pozzolana was exactly what he was looking for (see also Chapter 16). Pozzolana is a 'miracle' material, in that – when mixed with water – it solidifies into cement. De Lesseps, in cutting the Suez Canal (for 11 years, until it opened in 1869) needed to line the sides and bottom of the 120-mile (195km) waterway, and one can still clearly see today the cliffs on Therasia from which the immense volume of material was taken over the decade-long period of construction – as well as the remnants of the dock and gantries, way below at the water's edge.

Incredibly, as the blocks of pozzolana were removed, and the parent rock (as at 1628BC) was revealed, several enlightened gentlemen collected samples of flora – flattened at that very moment so long ago, and unseen for nearly 3,500 years – some examples of which are beautifully displayed in the Phira museum. Today, as a continuing legacy of this 2nd millennium disaster – on top of all those that occurred previously – one of the major industries on the island is the annual export of 2 million tonnes of quarried volcanic debris, for use elsewhere in Greece.

Comparison of the 1628BC eruption
with that of Krakatoa in 1883AD

To grasp why Thera has been claimed as the 'Lost City of Atlantis', and why the eruption's aftermath has been postulated as the cause of cataclysmic events in the Bible, it is necessary to have an understanding of just how globally devastating that fateful catastrophe was. And one of the best ways to do this is by comparing what happened with *known* latter-day events.

The most violent – and well documented – eruption in recent times was that at Mount St Helens (Washington State, USA) in May 1980. This was not as violent as the result of the largest nuclear device ever exploded, by the USSR in October 1961, measured at 50 megatons (MT) of TNT. However, the violence at Krakatoa, between Java and Sumatra, on 26-27 August 1883 was equivalent to 200MT, and left its mark around the globe.

What is so relevant to the major catastrophe on Thera, is what scientists recorded in the immediate aftermath of Krakatoa. The explosions were so violent that they were heard more than 3,000 miles away; ash was propelled to a height of 50 miles (80km); pumice floated across the oceans for years afterwards; loss of life was huge, with bodies/skeletons appearing off the African coast a year later; and, *most crucial of all*, average global temperatures – in the ensuing year – fell by 1.2°C, with weather patterns taking five years to return to normal.

Attempts have been made to measure the explosive force at Thera for many years, and the most recent scientific tests show that the overwhelming force at Thera was nearly *four times* that of Krakatoa, with a TNT equivalent of an astonishing 750 megatons! No wonder that Thera is the favourite choice as the lost city of Atlantis! No wonder that theories abound that the subsequent devastation was at the root of the succession of Old Testament disasters!

It was a miracle for Minoan Crete that the wind ensured most of the ash column fell 'harmlessly' into the Mediterranean between Thera and the Nile delta, with only the eastern quarter of the island being caught – as detailed by J. V. Luce in his fascinating book *The End of*

91

Atlantis. However, no one has yet managed to assess the effect of one or more giant tsunamis, though it seems almost certain that huge loss of life and material damage would have been wrought throughout the entire Mediterranean rim.

Spyridon Marinatos (1901-74)

One of the foremost Greek archaeologists of his time, Marinatos was involved practically in the subject from an early age – unlike Schliemann, or even Evans. He was Director of the Heraklion Museum by the age of 27, where he met Evans, and he excavated Amnisos – the Bronze Age port for Knossos, just along the coast – in 1932. His most spectacular finds in this phase of his life were at Vathypetro, a Minoan villa just south of Archanes, where he discovered a kiln, an olive press, and a wine press. By 1937 he was based in Athens and turned his attention to the Mycenaean sites in the Peloponnese. However, for another 30 years the notion that there were spectacular discoveries to be made on Thera – coupled with a burning desire to prove that the mid-2nd-millennium volcanic eruption was the cataclysmic event that ended Minoan civilisation – kept bringing him back to the island.

In 1967, following minor discoveries by others (as the island slowly recovered from the 1956 trauma) and local stories of donkeys suddenly falling into crevices in the ground, he had the inspiration to judge that a 'lost city' might lie under the ash deposit on the southernmost point of the semi-circular rim – the closest point of the island to Crete.

And so commenced another fabled chapter of discovery – on the most remarkable scale – of the town of Akrotiri. From 1967 until his sudden death at the site in 1974, Marinatos progressively revealed the town, although 40 years later the majority of the whole site is considered to be still unexcavated. Until his death he was convinced that the eruption must have been the cause of Minoan collapse, but virtually all experts now agree – as outlined earlier – that, depending on which school one belongs to, the abrupt demise of Akrotiri/Thera *preceded* the collapse of Knossos by either 200 or 100 years. The precise relationship between Akrotiri and Knossos – in relation to the degree of autonomy – may never be established but, while not in any way 'palatial', the uncovered (and unembellished) town gives the visitor a graphic insight into the Minoan-style way of life.

Moreover, the intact full-size wall paintings go some way to bolstering Evans's interpretive credibility as to the details of Minoan life.

Introduction to the town of Akrotiri

A first point to note is that – as with Pompeii – what the visitor sees today is the unearthed streets and houses, frozen at a moment in time some 3,600 years ago. At Knossos (and at Troy) the number of settlements built one upon another reaches well into double figures. And whereas at Knossos – as we know from the previous chapter – one now sees a complex mix of original structures and reconstruction, the only restorative work to date in Akrotiri town has been (for example) the delineation of original door and window apertures.

A second point is as regards dating accuracy. While the earliest date of any settlement is always difficult to determine, there can be no confusion about the date when the Theran world was so brutally terminated. This cut-off cannot be later than 1530BC, and – as we have discussed in previous chapters – it could be as early as 1630BC. This is important when comparing the achievements at Akrotiri, up to that 'deadline', with those of the second palace era at Knossos and other Cretan sites, which ran until c1450BC.

The third point is that – in complete contrast to what happened at Pompeii – the population must have had one or more warnings of volcanic activity, because – apart from the trace of a single pig – no other evidence of any humans or animals being overwhelmed (as can be seen so vividly at Pompeii) has to date been found. The entire population, together with all personal possessions (particularly anything portable – seal stones, figurines, jewellery) must have escaped its initial fate by dint of a large fleet.

What may never be established is whether the fleeing inhabitants made good their escape (to Crete?) or were overwhelmed by a tidal wave at sea. It is also conceivable that isolated groups of individuals, perhaps from outlying villages, were buried under ash and pumice elsewhere on the island, but to date no such traces have been found.

The houses
One of the attractions of modern-day Santorini is the nature of higgledy-piggledy housing clusters, encompassed by winding streets.

Far from being in any way palatial, that is exactly what one sees at the first glimpse of Akrotiri. Each house – up to three storeys in height, with mainly stone staircases – had a drainage system made up of clay pipes, which were linked to under-street sewers. Walls were mostly made of rough stone, mud and straw, reinforced with timber – with ashlar masonry only for doors and windows. It is clear to see by the degree of fine-cut stone, and whether the floors were of earth or paved with stone slabs, which were the houses of the wealthy. All roofs were flat, and – as still seen today on the island – covered in earth, which helped keep dwellings warm in winter and cool in summer.

Although the size and shape of every house was different, there seem always to have been a number of common features, indicating self-sufficiency: cellar space where food could be kept cool; ground-floor workshops, storage, and grain milling; sanitary features; and large upstairs windows in the residential rooms, usually with evidence of a loom. Walls were generally plastered and – without exception – at least one upper room was painted throughout in varied base colours, then embellished with a fine wall painting.

Wandering through the narrow streets is a remarkable experience: seeing a collapsed stone staircase; the neatly stacked pithoi (often highly decorated) with small measuring vessels alongside; and huge boulders from the volcanic eruption, lying where they fell. With no great leap of the imagination, one can almost feel the bustle of day-to-day activity – with the intermingling of everyday living, craftsmanship, and wide-ranging trade.

Other aspects of life
Details recovered from Akrotiri give a vivid insight into the seemingly comfortable Theran lifestyle, which – even despite their sailing exploits – must have involved an almost total reliance on self-sufficiency. Stored residues show a very wide agricultural spread in the daily diet, aside from the products of domestic milling. The evidence includes grapes, sesame, olives and honey (from clay beehives). Fishing, by various methods, was clearly a major activity, as evidenced in the wall paintings, as was weaving and dyeing – in almost every household.

A difference from Crete was the widespread (continued) use of stone. Successive eruptions had covered the island with every conceivable type of stone and rock, so the softer materials could easily

94

be worked into a wide variety of containers. The hardest materials made ideal hammers and other construction tools, while the immense range of coloured stones could be fashioned for decorative purposes.

One is also left with a clear impression of artisanal skills, when walking the streets of what must have been a prosperous and well-managed community. Apart from the obvious, glimpses of the exceptional are provided – for example the (replica) wooden and hide bed, deduced from a plaster cast poured into a hollow space, a method pioneered at Pompeii. Some wall paintings vividly display Theran ship-building capabilities, with long-distant commercial travel probably combining Theran imports/exports with cargoes being moved on behalf of other island clients.

Pottery

As mentioned above, all recovered pottery items are sizeable, and there are many beautiful examples. Birds seem to have had a special place in art at Akrotiri, and this decoration is nowhere better displayed than on a lovely ewer with a buff background throughout. There are many vases and jugs to be seen (in the Phira and Athens museums) one of the latter – a nippled version, with an amazing painted swallow in mid-flight – being particularly admirable.

Among other treasures are a magnificent imported Minoan 'rhyton' (ritual pouring vessel) and wonderfully decorated oblong round-ended containers, which have never found anywhere else, and whose use is uncertain.

Wall paintings

These are Akrotiri's *pièces de résistance*. The best pictures in a book simply cannot convey anything of the startling impression that the visitor derives from a face-to-face viewing.

Before examining any individual painting, there are a number of themes to catalogue: first, all walls were plastered, then, while still wet, were rubbed with pebbles to make them smooth (hundreds of worn pebbles have been retrieved from the ruins); then there is the fact that the artist made full use of the wall-space available, adjusting his subject matter as to whether he was dealing with (for example) the narrow space between two doors, or had a whole wall at his disposal.

Then again, there seem to be no rules, with the artist seemingly quite free as regards design, colour choice, subject matter, and movement. Furthermore, the depiction of life in the animal kingdom, as between the hunter and the hunted, is just so redolent of what we see and learn of today. Finally, the subtlety and diversity of each imaginative storyline seems to know no limit. One simply does not expect to find more and more to wonder at and think about, the longer one walks backwards and forwards along the length of each room, and gazes repeatedly from floor to ceiling.

A detailed account of so many individual paintings cannot be listed here. Instead, there follows a list of some of the most striking images, in an attempt to whet the appetite of the reader:

- lilies in rocky terrain, while swallows dart around above
- a cat stalking a bird at the water's edge
- a spread of crocuses, with swallow chicks awaiting food, and blue monkeys – one with a sword in hand, another with a harp!
- two fishermen, each with his impressive catch
- two well-coiffed ladies against a starry background
- antelopes
- child boxers, both with a gloved right hand
- immensely detailed 'miniatures' from the West House
- a fleet sailing from harbour to harbour – a most informative frieze

The above is just a sample of this unique collection, which – through Akrotiri's final agony – has been miraculously preserved for our appreciation. What is impossible to determine is just how unique these Theran skills were in the region at that time. Were Theran artists out in front of their peers? Or is it the case – as glimpsed at Knossos – that comparable skills were widespread in the Aegean, but that nowhere else were the sparkling results protected (by an overwhelming disaster) for generations to pore over, 3,600 years later?

Going back again to the acerbic Robert Collingwood (see the previous chapter) I cannot believe that if he had been able to visit Akrotiri – and seen the wonderful displays in both the museum at Phira and the Archaeological Museum in Athens – he would not have modified his well-publicised criticism (as recounted by Fitton) that the Classical Greek '…spirit she in no way owes to Bronze Age Crete, where it is wholly lacking, and whose entire life is, to use the Greek term, barbarous.'

Chapter 9

Troy and Mycenae: the story of Heinrich Schliemann

As an introduction to this fascinating tale, a 'health warning' needs to be issued as to the veracity of certain aspects of the life and career of Heinrich Schliemann. There is no doubt that he embellished the story of his early life, and was economical with the truth in relation to the precise details of his discoveries at Troy. Even so, exhaustive research (sometimes, but not always, by academics and writers set on diminishing his achievements) have not substantially altered the view of Professor Virchow in 1880, that Schliemann's heroic efforts had created 'an entirely new science'.

As followed by Evans at Knossos – the other 'maverick' digger at the end of the 19th century – prior to circa 1870 there were no professionally trained archaeologists, anywhere in the world. The vast majority of classicists were not interested in moving outside their comfort zones, and no kind of funding mechanism had begun to be considered – certainly not for any expedition outside the known Classical World.

Today there are thousands of well-trained archaeologists and historians – with the massive benefit of hindsight, and a welter of sophisticated weaponry at their disposal – operating within a formal 100-year-old profession. They are much aided by easy travel, grants or sponsorship, the best health protection, and little threat from local bandits. Not only that, but the front-man (or woman) often heads up a bewildering array of specialists, including geologists and anthropologists – indeed, scientists from a wide range of disciplines.

It is easy, therefore, to criticise the motives, methods and exaggerations of the handful of pioneers in this field. The truth is that without the obsessive drive and wealth of one or two very remarkable characters – which must include Howard Carter and Lord Carnarvon in Egypt early in the 20th century – some key discoveries in this 'new science' might never have been made, or would at the very least have kept their spectacular revelations secret for many more decades.

Schliemann as a youth

Even those elements of Schliemann's first 25 years that have been verified are the stuff of a far-fetched novel, and the description that follows owes quite a lot to the romanticised story as recounted by Leonard Cottrell. Young Heinrich was born in January 1822, in Northern Germany, one of six children of an impoverished pastor and a mother who died when he was nine. His father had regaled him with stories of Homer's *Odyssey*, and at the age of eight his Christmas present was a copy of Jerrer's weighty *Illustrated History of the World.*

Before he saw the book, the boy had come to believe that every word of Homer was true and, on seeing an engraving of the monumental walls of burning Troy, he vowed that one day he would discover for himself what remained. He was also inspired by his father recounting his own good fortune at having seen both Pompeii and Herculaneum. Unfortunately, even though he had taught him Latin, Heinrich's father was a waster, and at the age of 14 the boy had no choice but to become apprenticed in a grocer's shop, even though he continued to read voraciously at every available opportunity. A poignant consolation in this dreary job was a visit one evening by a drunken former pastor called Neiderhoffer. This man, now a miller, had at least not forgotten Homer – and was persuaded by young Heinrich to recount hundreds of lines, even though the besotted listener understood not a word of Greek at that time. This fortuitous meeting only served to fire his imagination for ancient Troy even more fervently.

After enduring this strictly non-academic job for five years, Schliemann travelled to Hamburg in 1841, and became a cabin boy on a steamer, bound for Venezuela. After only 12 days at sea, the ship foundered in a gale. It was a miracle that he and several companions survived, being washed up on the Dutch coast. From there he made his way to Amsterdam, and gained employment as a bookkeeper. Due to his diligence, he learned everything he possibly could about commerce, and in 1844 managed to secure a better position with an import/export company, B. H. Schroder & Co. There he soon became valued, and was sent in 1846 (aged 24) to act as the company's General Agent in St Petersburg.

The businessman

He had long decided that an aid to future prosperity was the acquisition of languages, and in this endeavour he was exceptionally talented – creating his own system for accelerated learning, which he deployed repeatedly. Throughout this phase, Schliemann never lost his obsession with Homer, and always knew that one day he would pursue his boyhood dream. Over the course of his life he became fluent enough in some 15 languages to be able to keep a diary in most countries he visited, which he wrote up in that particular tongue. He learned Russian, English and French early on, and later Arabic, and both Ancient and Modern Greek.

In Russia he became a senior employee of B. H. Schroder, specialising in the indigo trade, then eventually started acting on his own behalf. He readily obtained access to working capital, and began to amass a small fortune. In his new-found position, he sought marriage with his childhood sweetheart, Minna, whom he had not seen for 14 years, and was devastated to learn that she had only just become married to someone else.

Plunged into despair he worked even harder, and following the success of his (newly deceased) brother as a speculator in the California goldfields, he travelled there in 1850, aged 28, ostensibly to settle his sibling's affairs – but ended up starting a bank in Sacramento that traded in gold dust, and promptly made another fortune! He only stayed in California long enough to publish an account of the San Francisco fire of 1851, before returning to a gentlemanly life in Russia.

He had been introduced to the niece of one of his friends, and married Ekaterina Lyschin in 1852. Though they had three children, this was never to be a happy marriage. He had a desire to be always on the move, while she wanted him to settle down and become even richer. His wife also had no interest whatsoever in his romantic notion of travels to the East, let alone the question of serious exploration/excavation. At first he bowed to Ekaterina's wishes, making another killing as a supplier to the Russian Army of materials for the Crimean War (1854-56).

The travels start

Some time around 1860 Schliemann became semi-retired, pledged himself to discovering Troy, and set his travel plans in motion. He made an extensive tour of the Middle East, and travelled to Mecca in disguise – having been circumcised as a precaution! Details of the ensuing years are hazy, but it is known that he visited America again in 1868, returning to attempt yet another reconciliation with his now-estranged wife, a feature of which was to buy her a magnificent house in Paris. Also in 1868 – perhaps inspired by the first excavations made on Santorini by Ferdinand Fouque in 1862 – he made his first visit to the Troad, in the extreme north-western corner of the Turkish mainland. He also knew of Frank Calvert, who had been conducting exploratory work there for 20 years on the Hissarlik Hill, part of which he had acquired. In the same year, Schliemann had explored the island of Ithaca (seeking the palace of Odysseus) and had comprehensively toured the Peloponnese.

Schliemann researched alternative sites for Troy, which others had proposed in the recent past. In particular, he was intrigued by the location of the 'two lovely springs', one always hot and the other cold, as described by Homer in the *Iliad*. There are two springs, with a modest temperature difference, near the village of Bounarbashi, but he was not persuaded that the nearby rocky hill of Bali Dagh held the secrets he was looking to uncover.

He had an incredibly busy season, but still found time to publish a paper that sought to demonstrate that Calvert was digging in the right place – to back this up, he agreed to partner Calvert in his quest, finally accepting the irresistible challenge to spare no effort to unearth ancient Troy. His long-doomed marriage was now an inhibiting factor, and, still in the year 1868, and using his American citizenship acquired nearly 20 years earlier, he took steps to divorce Ekaterina in a rather dubious legal process.

A remarkable union

This story then has another remarkable twist, arising from Schliemann's long-held desire to have a loyal wife, who would live and work alongside him, in the arduous period that lay ahead. Ever resourceful, while still in America awaiting his divorce to become a reality, he advertised the position (!) in an Athens newspaper, and a friend of his – no less than the Archbishop of Athens – suggested that his 16-year-old niece (Sophia Engastromenos) might be the ideal choice, sending him a splendid photograph of the beautiful young girl.

In 1869 the 47-year-old businessman finally secured a divorce, and rushed to Athens to 'interview' his prospective bride, who was even better-looking in the flesh. This took the form of asking her to answer searching questions on Homer! The young lady (now 17) passed the test, and this most unlikely couple were married in October of that year. Sophia quickly produced two children, who, of course, were given 'Mycenaean' first names!

The Trojan dig

Having established a permanent home in Athens, Heinrich and Sophia started to work in earnest at the Hissarlik site in 1871. Due to issues with the Turkish authorities, work did not begin until November, with 80 men driving a trench 33 feet (10m) into the slope. Crucially, never thinking that there could be older cultures than the Trojan dynasty – then dated to c1200BC, but now calculated at 1300BC – and being impatient as always, Schliemann cut straight through to the lowest strata, ignoring every upper level, and creating a massive heap of unexamined spoil.

Winter soon intervened, and returning afresh in 1872 he continued with the crude methods that were to shock later *trained* archaeologists. He fell out with Calvert, but continued relentlessly towards removing this enormous wedge of ground, which has been likened to a giant 'slice of cake'. Schliemann contracted malaria, and both he and Sophia endured terrible heat, flies and snakes. When they returned again in 1873, they still had little to show for their efforts from the previous year, pottery shards not proving to be of any assistance, since at that time no comparative dating system had been evolved. Schliemann believed there to be seven layers of civilisation, and in 1872 had uncovered a pair of massive walls at a depth of 46 feet (14m), which he named the 'Great Tower'. Redoubling his efforts in March 1873, more definable structures came into view, together with a mass of burnt debris. He then came across two large gateways, and very unwisely announced to the world that he had discovered the Scaen Gate and the Palace of Priam.

Many scholars, particularly German, opposed his work. Deep in their study chairs they had theorised for a century as to the site of Troy – but never ventured out into the field. And now there was this totally unqualified businessman using the crudest of methods … then having the audacity to make quite outrageous claims. What is more, he was pinning everything on his long-held intuition that Homer had recorded actual *history* – and had not just written down a series of wonderful epic *stories*!

A miracle is revealed

Fate now intervened, in that Schliemann (in a letter sent to his brother in May) had decided to end his three-year investigations at Troy on 15 June, and pay off his workforce – as we shall quickly see, a decision with an uncanny resemblance to Carter's sixth and 'final' season in the Valley of the Kings. On 14 June he had noticed a large copper object embedded in the ruins … and behind it something that gleamed brightly in the sunlight. Sure that his workmen had noticed nothing, he calmly asked Sophia to announce a rest break, telling her to say that it was his birthday! When the men had disappeared, he dug out from the hard-packed earth item after item of shining gold or dull silver. At some risk of the overhang he was creating, he pressed on feverishly, laying out each object in Sophia's shawl, so that when he thought he had retrieved the whole cache the pair of them could walk nonchalantly back to their hut on top of the hill, and lock the door.

As they sifted through their finds, the loveliest items were two magnificent gold diadems, one of which turned out to have no fewer than 16,353 separate gold pieces. There were six gold bracelets, and a gold goblet weighing 21oz (600g). A large silver vessel – in which the diadems were found – also contained 60 gold earrings, 8,700 small gold rings, and dozens of other items. The 'copper' item that Schliemann had first noticed turned out to be a bronze chisel, alongside which had been silver and bronze vases, and bronze weapons.

Quite one of the most astounding images of the age, which reached all corners of Europe and America, was the picture of 21-year-old Sophia wearing these wonderful treasures – on her head, ear-lobes, neck and shoulders – a fantastic array that any 19th-century queen would have been proud to wear. And yet Heinrich believed his remarkable find to be no less than 3,200 years old.

The aftermath

Because of lax Turkish supervision, and his horror at the prospect that his treasures would not be appreciated, Schliemann (with the help of a reconciled Calvert) easily smuggled his horde out of the country to Athens. But then what? He confided in a few responsible people, so as to try and ensure the authenticity of his find, but he must have known that the astonishing story would leak out, and a storm of protest ensue. And so it did! The Greek authorities – anxious not to upset Turkey – searched his premises, but found nothing. They denounced him as a smuggler, and even cast doubt on the authenticity of his claims.

So began a three-year struggle by Schliemann, on the one hand to obtain approval to dig at Mycenae, and on the other hand to avoid having to hand over the treasures to Greece, all the time joined by the Turkish Government 'jumping up and down on the touchline'. Eventually, after paying (voluntarily) five times the fine imposed in a lawsuit brought by Turkey, in 1876 a compromise was reached with the Greeks that allowed him to dig at Mycenae under strict supervision, with all his finds being handed over.

The first year at Mycenae

What – above all else – distinguished Mycenae from Knossos and Troy in the 19th century was the fact that the citadel had never become 'lost'. It was known to Homer in the 9th century BC, to Aeschylus in the 5th century BC, and to the Greek historian Pausanias in the 2nd century AD. Its cyclopean walls (so named because only Cyclops could have lifted the immense stones into position) had always loomed over the valley, through which the north-south road ran from Corinth to Argos (and on to present-day Nauplion). By the time that Schliemann arrived on the scene, the site had lain in ruins for three millennia, together with nearby Argos and Tiryns, although the massive 'Lion Gate' was plainly visible.

And what distinguished Heinrich Schliemann from all his peers was first his encyclopaedic knowledge of every scrap that had been written about Mycenae, and second that he interpreted each phrase as being

103

the literal truth. Thus he noticed that, whenever Homer mentioned Mycenae, he always referred to it being 'opulent' and 'rich in gold'. And Pausanias wrote that 'they say … Clytemnestra and Aegisthus were buried a little outside the wall, for they were not deemed worthy of burial within it, where Agamemnon lies and those who were murdered with him.' As Cottrell says, this 'was the crux of Schliemann's triumph at Mycenae'. He worked out that, unlike Lords Elgin and Sligo (who had dug briefly at Mycenae before him), he needed to work in the restricted and seemingly barren area *inside* the cyclopean walls, and not – as they and a Turkish gentleman had done – in the much larger area outside, which has a number of tholos tombs nearby. Maybe that is why the Greek authorities – even though they appointed an 'ephor' (supervisor) to keep an eye on his every move – were fairly relaxed about his proposal – he wouldn't find anything!

Lightning strikes twice!

For the reader to obtain a detailed account of the progress made by Heinrich and Sophia during the blazing summer heat of 1876, there are many wonderful books that have a devoted step-by-step narrative, with the level of excitement rising to a crescendo. Schliemann took more care than at Troy, partly due to the near-hysterical complaints of the poor ephor, whom both he and Sophia managed to run rings round! After a few short weeks, working within a circle of upright slabs that he had exposed, Schliemann discovered a vertical shaft 87 feet (26m) in diameter. Working their way across the circle, the team found a total of six rectangular graves. Nothing can better describe the heart-stopping moments, as these were gently exposed, than the words of Professor Wace in his *Mycenae*:

> 'On the faces of the men lay golden masks and on their chests golden breast plates. Two women wore golden frontlets and one magnificent diadem. The two children were wrapped in sheet-gold. By the men lay their swords, daggers, drinking cups of gold and silver and other equipment. The women had their toilet boxes of gold and dress pins of various precious metals and their clothes were decked with gold discs ornamented with bees, cuttlefish, rosettes, and spirals… This was indeed one of the richest archaeological discoveries ever made.'

Can one imagine how Schliemann felt at those moments? Never mind his numerous contemporary critics, whom he was about to demolish! What about the five conquering 'regimes' who had trampled – unknowingly – over (as he saw it) such hallowed ground: Dorians, Romans, Goths, Venetians, and Turks? Mycenae had kept its uniquely remarkable secrets for – as Schliemann calculated – well over 3,000 years.

(What was later proven was that the Trojan War – if it did indeed ever take place – would have had to have been around 1250BC, and not 1200/1150BC as Schliemann and others supposed. Even then, we also now know that these graves were from a much earlier period – around 1600BC – as was also the case with the treasures Schliemann found at Troy. Also at Troy, recent systematic excavation shows that there were probably 13 levels of occupation, with the treasures being from level VI, and the legendary War having taken place at the time of level VIIa.)

In the fifth grave, removing the mask of the third warrior, Schliemann was astonished to find a fleshed-out rounded face, unlike the skeletal appearance of the first two skulls in the pit, which crumbled away. He kissed the mask, and that evening wrote a telegram to the King of Greece, in which (romantically but incorrectly) he made his most famous declaration: 'I have gazed on the face of Agamemnon.'

Unparalleled fame

Much more was uncovered that season, and – as will be covered in the next chapter – ensuing expeditions would continue to reveal marvellous finds, covering the half-millennium from 1600BC to the onset of the Dark Age in circa 1100BC. But for Schliemann, the high point of the next year (1877) would be his reception in England. Despite a great deal of scepticism throughout Europe about his revelations at Troy in 1873 – somewhat mollified by his *verified* discoveries at Mycenae – he was invited to London by no fewer than 30 societies, and renewed his acquaintance with Prime Minister Gladstone, whom he had first met in 1875. He even persuaded Gladstone to write the preface to the book he was writing on his excavations at Mycenae.

Schliemann spent several weeks in England, where Sophia travelled to join him. Their crowning moment was before a thousand guests at the Royal Society, where each was presented with a special diploma. They both spoke in English, and Sophia held the audience riveted as she told the honoured guests of how she had been beside her husband for 25 days at Mycenae, as they lifted the treasures – one at a time – from the earth. For Schliemann the warmth of their reception was tinged with bitterness at the continued abuse to which he was subjected by his own country, which was only slowly moderated in the ensuing years.

The later years

In 1878 Schliemann commissioned the construction of his magnificent new Athens home, on what became University Street. No expense was spared in this palatial building, with its marble staircases and friezes everywhere depicting scenes from antiquity, intermingled with those of Schliemann's archaeological life. Inscriptions from ancient Greek authors abounded, none more amusing than – above his study door – Pythagoras's immortal words 'All who do not study geometry, remain outside'! On the ground floor were displayed with great pride the (erroneously named) 'Treasures of Priam' – the result of Schliemann's first 'breakthrough' at Troy in 1873. So fabulous was this property (designed more like a public building than a family home), and so devoted did Athens become to its adopted son, that – with the gracious cooperation of Sophia – today this 'Iliou Melathron' (Palace of Ilios) is the Athens Numismatic Museum.

For the next 12 years Schliemann kept up a relentless pace. Having mended his fences with Turkey, he was back at Troy in 1879, and by virtue of his far-sighted invitation to a German national – despite continued vilification from his own country – was blessed by the arrival of the most distinguished scientist Professor Rudolph Virchow. Because Heinrich respected him so much, Virchow was able to have a beneficial effect on all his work during the last decade of Schliemann's life. Most importantly, Virchow restrained the older man's impetuosity, and – together with a small group of other academics – they evolved an increasingly *systematic* method of working. In readdressing the conundrum of the hot and cold springs, and (on Mount Ida) locating the source of the River Scaramanda, the two became such close friends that the former buccaneer had no difficulty in persuading the

106

independent-minded intellectual to write the preface to his forthcoming 800-page *Ilios*.

In 1881 Virchow negotiated for Schliemann the Freedom of Berlin, in exchange for the city being presented with the entire collection of his 1873 discoveries from Troy.

(For this astonishing cache there is only the most macabre sequel. Looted from Berlin in 1945 by the conquering Soviet Army, the dazzling array disappeared, and was only acknowledged to be held in Russia in 1990 – the centenary year of Schliemann's death – after the collapse of Communism. A promise was eventually made by the Russian Government to return the collection to the unified German state. However, to date that eagerly awaited event is thwarted by the Museum Director in St Petersburg, on the grounds that Germany has never made adequate reparation for the death and destruction caused to the Soviet empire. To say that this 65-year-long tragedy would have Schliemann turning in his grave must be a monumental understatement!)

Through the early 1880s, aided now by his brilliant young assistant Wilhelm Dorpfeld, Schliemann wrestled with the strata issues at Troy – if the lowest layer did not belong to Homer's Priam, whose generation did it belong to? And which layer did then relate to Priam? Frustrated by his still prickly relationship with the Turkish authorities, he came tantalisingly close to unravelling this conundrum – a problem that Dorpfeld (who founded the German School at Athens in 1896) did not finally master until after Schliemann's death.

The pair turned their attention to Tiryns in 1884, discovering cyclopean walls similar to those at Mycenae, a wonderfully corbel-roofed gallery, and the foundations of a 'megaron', or hall, very similar to that found at Troy by Dorpfeld. Slowly it dawned upon them that the common thread at these sites – and being revealed elsewhere by other newcomers to the field of archaeology – was the *fact* of a hitherto unknown pre-Greek civilisation. The pronouncement of Grote in 1846 was profoundly contradicted, and the *reality* of Homer's history lesson became (as we shall see in Chapter 12) more and more apparent.

In 1886, Schliemann, now aged 64, turned his attention to Crete, and the archaeological prospect of the Kephala Hill (Knossos). However, with the island still under Turkish control, he again became mired in endless disputes as to ownership and licences. He felt that he still had so much to do in his remaining years, and vented his frustration at the delaying tactics and obfuscation of the authorities. And indeed, time for Schliemann was running out.

An untimely death

After a fourth expedition to Troy with Dorpfeld in 1888-90, Schliemann – who had long been troubled with ear infections – travelled to Germany in August 1890 for an operation. Though not fully recovered, and ever-impatient, he resumed his travels to various capital cities, planning to return to Athens in time for Christmas. The pain in one ear troubled him on his train journey south through Italy, and became so bad that he had to stay in Naples to try and obtain relief. Having cabled Sophia that he would be late for the family celebrations, and having seen a doctor, he visited Pompeii on Christmas Eve. But on Christmas Day he collapsed in the street, and having no identification about his person – and being unable to speak – was refused admission to hospital. Eventually, through a paper in his pocket, the doctor he was attempting to visit was located. But it was too late. Alone in a hotel room where he had been taken – and while a surgeon debated what possible action could be taken – Heinrich Schliemann died on Boxing Day, 26 December 1890.

His body was taken to Athens, and interred in the First Cemetery – in a mausoleum shaped like a miniature Greek temple, designed by Ernst Ziller. Arthur Evans had met Schliemann at the latter's home in Athens in 1882, and wrote many years later:

'I still remember the echoes of his visits to England, which were his greatest scenes of triumph … and I have myself an almost uncanny memory of the spare, slightly built man … wearing spectacles of foreign make, through which – so fancy took me – he had looked deep into the ground.'

Epilogue

For more than a century argument has raged over the authenticity of the 'Treasures of Priam', with even accusations that Schliemann himself put together the collection, from various dubious sources. In this matter, the only good to have come out of the St Petersburg

Museum in the past two decades is the knowledge that, when a team of experts was allowed to examine the artefacts in depth, this unique and quite wonderful collection was shown to be unquestionably genuine.

Chapter 10

Peleponnese: the Mycenaean supremacy

As was outlined in the previous chapter, early enthusiasts for the existence of a 'Bronze Age' civilisation were hugely outnumbered by (irrationally) prejudiced Classicists. Thankfully, the calming influence of Charles Newton ensured that Schliemann received a fair hearing when he first presented his findings to a sceptical audience in London, in 1886. However, the underlying reason as to why Newton (still somewhat sceptical himself) faced down hostile critics lay in his fascination with a batch of objects entrusted to his care at the British Museum in 1868 – as described by J. Lesley Fitton in her *Discovery of the Greek Bronze Age*. In that year, the enthusiastic amateurs Salzmann and Biliotti started to excavate a series of tombs at Ialysos on the island of Rhodes. Since their initial discoveries were clearly from the Classical period, these subsequent finds were deemed to be somewhat 'earlier', but difficult to classify.

The key moment was when, eight years later, the open-minded Newton was able to draw a number of comparisons between the Ialysos finds and the Schliemann discoveries at Troy and Mycenae. It was clear to him that – with the three discoveries at a considerable distance from each other, all broadly bordering the Aegean Sea – there was enough evidence of a distinct culture that preceded the Classical period by hundreds of years.

How early was this newly discovered culture? Despite artefacts within the finds that linked to Egypt at around 1400BC, and that pointed to the correct dating, Newton (abetted by Schliemann's obsession with the Trojan heroes, whom he placed at around 1200BC) mistakenly pronounced that the evidence pointed to 1200-1100BC. He also fell into the trap (unsurprising, in view of the surrounding hostility) of considering the artistic achievements of these people – who had inconveniently appeared in 'Greek' territory – as being primitive and crude. It is cringe-making to our modern ears to read that their efforts (in his words) could not be rated higher than 'the work of New Zealanders and other savages'!

Nevertheless, Newton (well before any discoveries on Crete had emerged) did more than any other academic in the closing years of the 19th century to promote the reality of a Mycenaean civilisation, and such errors as he committed must be seen in the light of many faltering steps that were made in the early days of this 'new science'.

Were the Mycenaeans Greek?

Despite the mounting evidence of a powerful civilisation, the 20th century opened with an academic majority adamant that such a 'crude' people could not possibly be early Greeks. Arthur Evans had discovered Linear A tablets at Knossos and elsewhere in Crete, but – even to this day – all attempts to interpret this language have failed. He also discovered Linear B on the island, from the Final Palatial and Postpalatial periods, but this remained indecipherable for another half-century. Then, crucially, the American archaeologist Carl Blegen – in unearthing Nestor's palace on a hill just north of 'sandy' Pylos (in the south-western Peloponnese) in 1939 – came across hundreds of clay tablets that were inscribed with an identical form of writing to that which Evans had named as Linear B. But then the Second World War intervened.

After the war, archaeological digs resumed throughout the region, and Linear B tablets were found at Mycenae itself, and at Tiryns. Eventually this language was deciphered in 1952 by Michael Ventris and John Chadwick. Fifty years of fierce debate were brought to a close when Ventris announced (on the radio) in June of that year:

'During the last few weeks, I have come to the conclusion that the Knossos and Pylos tablets must, after all, be written in Greek – a difficult and archaic Greek seeing that it is 500 years older than Homer and written in a rather abbreviated form, but Greek nevertheless.'

Whence and when did the Mycenaeans arrive?
As discussed by Louise Schofield in her book *The Mycenaeans*, ever

since the pronouncement by Ventris (who was tragically killed in a car crash in 1956, aged still only 34) archaeologists have searched for clear evidence of an early Greek invasion and settlement of the Peloponnese. The one significant disruption occurred around 2300BC, when the seemingly settled and progressive environment was shattered at many identified sites, which were clearly burned to the ground. The strongly fortified site of Lerna in the Argolid, with its famous House of Tiles, conforms to this pattern, as does the violent destruction at Tiryns, and (for example) at Asine. It is interesting that there are elements of Linear B that philologists have identified as being demonstrably not Indo-European, and many of the characteristics of the peoples that settled the land after the 2300BC traumas – including some of their objects and technology – bear comparison with what has been found in Anatolia from the same period.

However, most current opinion is that the Mycenaean Greek population at the beginning of the 2nd millennium is highly unlikely to have been derived from a single wave of migrants. It is much more likely to be the case that – with comparatively easy overland access, allied to short-distance island-hopping – the inherent attractions of the Peloponnese drew an intermittent flow of eager immigrants over many centuries. Certainly, after the setback towards the end of the 3rd millennium, cultural progress was very slow. The proposition put forward by some that Mycenae and Knossos developed in parallel between 2000 and 1700/1600BC is simply not sustainable, there being no comparison between the modest lifestyle in the Peloponnese and the burgeoning palace culture on Crete – especially when considering the dominant fleet and far-flung trading exploits of the Minoans.

During this period trade between these peoples was mainly confined to meeting the huge Minoan demand for lead and silver from the mining complex at Laurion (near Athens). Otherwise trade seems to have been concentrated on the island of Aigina, and with various of the Cycladic islands – most notably the island of Melos, for its inexhaustible supply of obsidian – extending a continuous trading pattern with the mainland, which had existed since Mesolithic times. Towards 1600BC can be detected a growing population, larger and more sophisticated settlements, and the onset of warrior burials. It is difficult to pinpoint the triggers for this rapid development, but the most likely reason was the collective urge to emulate the standard set by the Minoans – at sea, in palace sophistication, in engineering capability, and artistically.

Since the Mycenaean traders with Melos will also have visited nearby Thera – and been amazed at the inhabitants' dynamic lifestyle – a further intriguing possibility can be considered. We have already seen that excavations at Akrotiri have not led to a single skeleton being found amongst the ruins – nor even an imprint of a corpse in the ash, as has been revealed many times at Pompeii. It may be generally assumed that – given advance warning of the impending tragedy – the entire population had the time to sail in their fleet to Crete, the 'master' society of the whole region.

But maybe not. The nearest point on Crete was a daunting 85 miles from Thera, with no island 'stepping-stones' in between at which a huge fleet could regroup, whereas the small but vibrant community on Melos was only half that distance – with many islands northward providing a network of stepping-stones to the mainland. Could it be – in the aftermath of the 1628BC volcanic catastrophe – that the awakening civilisation in the Peloponnese absorbed some proportion of the hapless Theran exiles, whose skill in so many disciplines then gave their economic and cultural ambitions an enormous boost?

The 'grave circles': a guide to growing prosperity

Since the early Greeks (as with the Minoans) revered their deceased rulers/warrior chieftains – together their wives and offspring – the remarkable 'grave circle' finds at Mycenae provide a very clear insight into the growing level of Mycenaean wealth and sophistication. Confusingly, the 'shaft graves' in Circle A (mostly discovered by Schliemann in 1876 within the fortified wall of the citadel) mainly relate to the early phase of the Late Bronze Age (1600-1450BC), whereas the shaft graves in Circle B (discovered in 1951/52 *outside* the monumental wall) mainly relate to the late phase of the Middle Bronze Age (c1700-1600BC).

Whole books have been written on the implications of these discoveries, which are so crucial to our understanding of the rise of Mycenae as a dominant power in the region, but it is only possible to provide a limited summary here of the progression during the above 250-year period. Dealing with Grave Circle B first, the older finds (from close to 1700BC) are quite simple, comprising modest pottery items and the occasional weapon. Some 50 years later, gold ornaments and amber trinkets appear. By the end of the Late Bronze Age – getting closer to the quality of the earliest grave goods of Circle A – a much richer variety of objects was recovered, the jewellery and personal items of some of the women being particularly fine. One had a bronze crown with gold leaves, and another a diadem of gold bands, together with beautifully composed necklaces.

As to Circle A, the first point to note is that – initially placed outside the settlement – the six graves were encompassed within the massive wall constructed in the 13th century BC. The Circle was surrounded by slabs, which effectively created a continuous bench with a diameter of 90 feet (27.5m). Never built over throughout its history – and with Pausanias being told in the 2nd century AD that Agamemnon was buried 'within the walls of Mycenae' – all the literal-minded Schliemann had to do (as he said himself) was to start digging! It now seems incredible that no previous individual (ancient or modern) had the wit – over the intervening millennia – to beat him to the punch!

The stelai marking the graves were carved with militaristic scenes, and the rectangular pits lay underneath 10 feet (3m) of spoil, below which was excavated a further 16 feet (5m) of soft rock. Above the bodies, ledges were cut into the rock to support wooden beams – and on these were laid beds of tree branches, which were then back-filled with earth and stone. None of the burials had ever been disturbed, and some of the wonders found by Schliemann have already been referred to in the previous chapter. The appeal of the gold face masks is indescribable, as is the women's breathtaking jewellery and the sheet-gold wrapping for a small child or baby – not to mention the gold-inlaid dagger, and the gold 'rhyton' (drinking vessel) designed as a lion's head.

All in all, though many recent books carry very detailed descriptions and beautiful photographs, no such impressions of the finds can match the remarkable displays at the (elaborately restored) Archaeological Museum in Athens, although the copies to be seen at the new museum at Mycenae itself hugely whet the visitors' appetite.

The 'shaft grave' era: burial fixation

What does the wealth of grave goods from Circle A tell us about the level of Mycenaean civilisation, culture and military prowess at this time – i.e. between 1600 and 1450BC? It seems that, although some of the items had been worn by their owners, this did not mean that the ruling class lived a lavish lifestyle, certainly not in terms of palaces or magnificent houses. It is apparent that – while recovered artefacts from across the region show the degree of exchange that must have taken place between the emerging 'city' communities – nearly all opulent behaviour was vested in complex burial chambers, as well as in the lavish contents thereof.

It is accurate to say that throughout the expanding Mycenaean world, those in authority were obsessed with the quality of the 'send-off' they could provide for their predecessors and family members. The vast number of known chamber tombs comprised a 'dromos' (entrance passage) cut into a steep slope to a circular chamber cut deep into the rock. After burial, the entrance was blocked by a wall of stones. The relative handful of 'higher-class' burials took place in 'tholos' (beehive) tombs, wherein the dromos led to an ashlar (cut) stone-built entrance. This was topped by a massive lintel, above which was constructed a further triangular stone aperture. Even this impressive sight is dwarfed by the beehive-shaped tomb itself, built of dry-walled stone in a corbelled (inward-sloping) fashion, culminating in the uppermost layers carefully ensuring that the whole entity was locked securely in place – for 3,500 years!

Tholos tombs also had a 'secret' side chamber. The whole edifice was extremely labour-intensive, especially as the entire structure was usually covered with spoil and (eventually) grassed over. This type of tomb grew in sophistication over several hundred years – the apogee being the so-called 'Treasury of Atreus' at Mycenae, built around 1250BC, wherein the single stone lintel above the doorway to the tomb (and curved on two faces) is calculated to weigh no less than 127 tonnes! With an internal height of 44 feet (13.5m) and diameter of 47 feet (14.5m), this smooth-sided dome was the largest in the ancient world, until construction of the Pantheon in Rome 1,000 years later.

Although Mycenae itself was becoming the dominant force in the Peloponnese, burgeoning settlements were springing up throughout the region. In the Argolid (south-east), Tiryns and Argos were beginning to flourish. In Laconia (south) we have the artefacts recovered from the tholos tomb of a Spartan chieftain at Vapheio – here we see signs of imports from Crete, perhaps including one of the two beautiful Vapheio Cups, depicting the capture of a bull. In Messenia (south-west), there were developing towns and villages in

115

the fertile Pylos area on the coast, below the later site of Nestor's palace. Away from the Peloponnese, expanding activity was taking place in Attica, at Athens and Marathon, as well as on the island of Aigina, and at Volos (Thessaly) and Thebes (Boeotia). At all these sites an emerging theme was the evidence of imported grave goods, nowhere more so than from Minoan Crete.

The 'shaft grave' era: trading patterns

As we have seen, the mainland had become a major exporter of precious materials, mainly to Crete, and probably to Thera. It is then quite interesting to make a comparison with modern China over the past 30 years – in exchange for raw materials, an inward flow of 'finished' goods starts to accelerate (utilising the client's shipping in both directions), then the developing nation (Mycenae) starts to copy and manufacture, in an ever more sophisticated manner. In the next stage it develops its own designs (today's 'intellectual property') and acquires its own fleet. Coming right up to China in 2011, the powerful newcomer quickly acquires overseas influence, with an amazing ability to capitalise on the weaknesses of the previously omnipotent superpower (for the USA substitute Minoan Crete).

Although repeated many times throughout history, this might be an uncanny account of the rapid acceleration enjoyed by Mycenae, and it only took 150 years – in comparative terms probably even faster than the Chinese example, as viewed from Crete and the Cyclades. In piggy-backing on the trading networks steadily built up by the Minoans over a thousand years, the evidence shows that Mycenae gained access to artefacts from the Anatolian coast, the Near East, and Egypt, the last being particularly treasured for its supplies of gold and semi-precious stones. Furthermore – in an ominous harbinger of future hegemony – before being buried under a mountain of volcanic ash, one miniature frieze from Akrotiri (see Chapter 8) clearly depicts Mycenaean warriors with their unique style of boar-tusk helmets and oxhide shields.

The changing of the guard:
Minoan collapse and Mycenaean supremacy

As we have failed to firmly identify in Chapters 7 and 8, the reasons for the collapse of the Minoan palace era at around 1450BC – and the

116

preceding destruction of Thera – are still subject matters of seething debate. The main problem is that continuing archaeological finds keep moving the 'definitive' date for the Theran eruption backwards and forwards. The experts who separately argue with 'forensic' evidence for 1630BC, or 1540BC, or 1450BC cannot all be right – or can they? Perhaps a pointer to repeated devastation lies in the recent tragic example in the Indian Ocean, wherein an *underwater event* caused an immense tsunami to bring massive loss of life and material damage to coastlines a vast distance away, and in almost every direction. Could the scenario in the Mediterranean have been that

a the middle of Thera did indeed blow out in 1628BC – leaving, apart from ash deposits, a mass of pumice floating for years afterwards as per Krakatoa, but that

b subsequent tsunamis from underwater activity then ruined the coastline of Crete at least once, in support of the evidence found by Marinatos, thereby progressively weakening Minoan resistance to the much more militaristic and fast-rising Mycenaean power.

The catastrophes around 1450BC – which proved terminal for Minoan suzerainty over the whole Aegean – do not seem to have coincided with aggressive Mycenaean colonisation of Crete at this juncture. It was around 1400BC that the latter started to construct their 'palaces' at Tiryns and Pylos, this development coinciding with the first Mycenaean settlements on islands such as Rhodes and Kos, and their adoption of Minoan trade routes. As to the date when Knossos palace life collapsed, another argument rages as to whether this was as early as the originally calculated date of around 1375BC, or much later, perhaps coinciding with the chaos in the whole Mediterranean region after 1200BC; a large part of the continuing debate focuses on the date and implication of the cache of Linear B tablets found amongst the ruins.

Mycenaean confidence: their palaces

Just as the flowering of the Minoans was reflected in their palace statements, so – throughout the 14th century BC – did the Mycenaeans instigate an equivalent building programme. Many sites were developed, some of which have only recently been discovered

117

(see Chapter 12), with others almost certainly yet to be located. Here we will concentrate on Tiryns in the Argolid – close to the sea and modern-day Nauplion), Mycenae itself, and Pylos in the south-west of the Peloponnese.

Referring to **Tiryns** first – because the start of its monumental construction preceded that of Mycenae – there were three building phases between 1400 and 1200BC. It seems that each time there was earthquake damage, the scale of reconstruction became even more spectacular. Eventually the walls were so massive – at differing widths of up to 10 metres – that the amazing corbelled galleries we see today (the finest in the Mycenaean world) were actually built *within* them.

At **Mycenae** it seems that early settlement on the rocky hill had been unfortified for hundreds of years, until the first stout walls were erected at around 1350BC. Following the pattern of Tiryns – and similar earthquake devastation – the walls (extending to a similar thickness) progressively encompassed a larger area. In 1250BC the rebuilding was stretched to bring Grave Circle A within the massively fortified area, and we are still uncertain today as to whether the closely fitting 'cyclopean' stonework was strictly necessary for defensive purposes – or was constructed so formidably to impress visitors and nearby communities. It was around 1250BC that the famous 'Lion Gate' was incorporated, still a most impressive sight. The massive wooden gates were set into the wall at each side, where one can still see how they were cleverly hinged. Above the lintel were set the pair of carved lions (or griffins? – as their heads were lost long ago) whose majestic presence must have given an unmatchable aura of power to all who passed underneath them.

The palace lay at the highest point, with a commanding view over the surrounding countryside, and the main north/south route to the west. Perhaps the most remarkable feature of all – in the eastern corner of the triangular site – is the cistern well, cut down an extremely hazardous set of steps, with no natural light. Built around 1200BC, it is amazing to visualise how the inhabitants worked out, in such undulating terrain, that their efforts would lead to securing an *external* water supply, with guaranteed access from *within* the (extended) fortress walls.

In a sign of the more fraught times approaching, this siege mentality was reflected in parallel water cisterns being constructed at both Tiryns and Athens. Learning the art of fresco painting from the Minoans, the palace was decorated in bright colours. Ashlar masonry and wooden beams were incorporated, with the long-standing Minoan obsession with the bull demonstrated in many features. The wealth of detail inside and outside the citadel – including all the tombs and burial areas that have been revealed – testifies to the pre-eminence of the whole site, and also to its longevity.

As mentioned earlier, Homer had written of Nestor's Palace at 'sandy' **Pylos**, and Blegen's discovery of an impressive settlement on the Epano Englianos hill, to the north of the modern town, was another triumph. Symbolically, at the mid-point in the 140-year history of modern archaeology, 70 years ago – and a further 70 years after Schliemann first started digging for Troy on the Hissarlik Hill (in the extreme north-west of the Turkish mainland) – this crucial find in the south-west of the Peloponnese was not widely known until well after the Second World War. Nevertheless, the Linear B discovery and decipherment was perhaps the tipping point at which countless scholars and archaeologists redoubled their efforts to understand better their copies of the *Iliad* and the *Odyssey* (see Chapter 12).

Whether or not the original port was a Minoan trading post, fragments from the 14th-century-BC buildings (which took the place of the 'shaft grave' settlement) certainly exhibit their traits – particularly the colourful detail of a bull-leaper. Crucial to our detailed study, the succeeding 13th-century-BC palace was destroyed around 1200BC, and – unlike Mycenae – was never subsequently built over, thus enabling us to obtain a much better idea as to how it functioned. The approach to the 'megaron' (great hall) had painted stucco floors, and walls that were covered in frescoes. In the centre of the megaron the large hearth is still perfectly preserved, alongside which stood the throne. As detailed by Louise Schofield, the lavishness of the decor that applied throughout must have dazzled all visitors to the wise old king Nestor. The megaron was surrounded by many types of room: a bathroom with a fine terracotta tub, which even included a soap dish; two rooms that contained 33 large pithoi and Linear B tablets, all concerned with olive oil and perfumes; rooms with wine jars and related Linear B tablets; areas that were set aside for religious purposes; and others that were workshops.

With a nod to Chapter 1, whereas it was thought for more than half a century that the palace was not fortified, a recent geophysical survey has demonstrated that the overall site is huge, that the palace lay at the

119

heart of a significant town, and that thick walls protected at least part of the whole community. There is also evidence that – as at Tiryns and (most impressively) at Gla in Boeotia – the inhabitants possessed the skills to level areas of land, divert water courses, and create reservoirs. The greatest claim to fame of Pylos is undoubtedly the comparatively large cache of Linear B tablets recovered. Originally, the tablets of soft clay were not fired, but – with their soft surface being smoothed – they could be used repeatedly to reflect (for example) current stock levels of palace resources. It is therefore ironic that the fire that destroyed the palace in around 1200BC accidentally also 'fired' the extant stock of inscribed tablets, and preserved for Blegen to find 3,200 years later the crucial linguistic link between the Mycenaean and Minoan civilisations.

Mycenaeans in Greece, and the wider world

As Minoan influence throughout the western Mediterranean subsided, the burgeoning mini-kingdoms and principalities of Mycenae increasingly exploited their long-established trading patterns. Whereas Crete had laboriously built up a network of outposts, and learned the seasonal sailing 'best practice' around the Mediterranean (for more than a millennium), the lengthy period of two-way trade with Mycenae meant that for many aspects of the import/export requirements – in all manner of goods – the fast-growing 'federation' did not have to 'reinvent the wheel'. It is in seeking to examine the details of their two-way trading exploits that the meticulous detail (and sheer volume of information) inscribed on Linear B tablets makes such an outstanding contribution to our understanding. Our insight into the Mycenaean world grows continually, propelled by ever more discoveries (through the use of 'every trick in the book' as per Chapter 1) exemplified by the recent find at Thebes in Boeotia, the main bonuses to our comprehension being:

- the extent to which (Greek) Mycenaean centres took and received hospitality from, and traded with, each other – through the naming at one site of the peoples from another;
- the richness and amazing variety of furnishings and artefacts within the palaces, together with raw materials used – through meticulous stock-taking by the appointed 'administrator';

- the court and political structure, together with the extent of territorial sway – as explained or alluded to, with repeated references, in tablets from Pylos;
- most interestingly, the naming of their gods – which shows that they were the same as those worshipped in Classical times – together with certain religious sites and cult practices; and
- the identification of precious materials imported and exported, together with trading outposts, Mycenaean settlements away from the Greek mainland, and overseas nation states with whom trade took place.

Turning to areas of control within the Peloponnese, continual research shows that each 'kingdom' controlled the surrounding *productive* area, with individual towns/villages providing food, wine and materials for palace/fortress use. Territorial boundaries were mainly natural – usually comprising mountain ranges or rocky escarpments. Road systems were well developed, and many Mycenaean bridges are still perfectly intact – some still in constant use. Several wonderful examples of bridges of 'cyclopean' masonry (with a corbelled arch to handle the river in spate) lie a few feet away from the main road from Nauplion/Tiryns to Epidaurus, near the village of Arkadiko – they are most evocative sights, being so massive but simple, and having nobly withstood all traffic, innumerable earthquakes, and invasions over the intervening 3,300 years.

Dealing with raw material requirements, imports of 'oxhide'-shaped copper ingots came from Cyprus (as witness 10 tonnes found in the 1300BC Uluburun shipwreck, which also held 1 tonne of tin). Despite every effort, to date it has not been possible to identify a Cornish tin content in Mycenaean artefacts. The evidence of Spain as a source is much more compelling, as is the case for Afghanistan, which also supplied – almost exclusively – the semi-precious (and highly prized) lapis lazuli. Other exotic materials, previously supplied mainly to Crete, came from Egypt, and amber – overland and by river – from the Baltic.

As to exports, many beautiful examples of Mycenaean pottery have been found in the Near East, and there is evidence of textiles and perfumed oils finding their way overseas. Other shipwrecks have indicated a vibrant two-way trade taking place along the Turkish coast, with Cyprus, and with Lebanon and Syria. We have already discussed the appearance of Minoans (known as 'Keftiu') in Egyptian records as visitors, and it seems likely (again from Linear B texts) that Egyptian emissaries visited the Greek mainland. As valued 'stepping-stones', strong Mycenaean colonies were established on Kos and Rhodes – and probably on Cyprus. To the west, Mycenaean pottery has been found as far afield as southern Italy, the Po valley, Sicily and eastern Spain. There may also have been trade with Sardinia. Mycenaean exports also permeated the whole of both modern-day Greece and Albania.

Aspects of Mycenaean living

It might be thought fanciful, but development of the Minoan/ Mycenaean relationship – during the 600-year period from 1950 to 1350BC – bears some comparison with the way in which Britain's relationship with the USA has developed in modern times, since 1600AD:

- the early years, when the New is hugely influenced by the Old, as to exploitation of its mineral wealth, the establishment of trading posts, and many aspects of lifestyle;
- the middle years, when the fast-learning Newcomer asserts its independence, as its confidence grows and its worldwide trade overtakes that of the Old; and
- the later years, when – speaking the same language, with the same religion, and with many inherited arts and crafts – the New (in many respects) effectively colonises the Old, in any event becoming an awesome technical and military super-power.

The analogy can be continued, in that – as in the Britain/USA example – prolonged warfare between the two principals may have been comparatively limited. It is likely that – just as the USA benefited from the awful debilitation suffered by Britain in two World Wars – Mycenae stepped into the Mediterranean power vacuum, which *probably* arose from the horrendous volcanic/earthquake damage on Crete between 1450 and 1375BC. It follows that, especially since Chapter 7 contains some detail on Minoan life, it is only necessary here to focus on particular highlights or differences (apart from the marked warfare contrast below) rather than effectively repeating (to the non-academic reader) a series of similar descriptions.

In religion, the 'shaft grave' era replication on the mainland did diverge from 1450BC onwards. First there is the 'warrior-goddess', as evidenced by the boar-tusk-helmeted female found on fresco fragments in the excavated Cult Centre at Mycenae. She holds aloft a (fictional) griffin figure, this being a 'companion' originated in Minoan deific art. Overall, the huge body of research to date (particularly gleaned from Mycenae itself) suggests that female deities were much more important than has been identified on Crete. As mentioned earlier, Linear B tablets point to many of the gods worshipped by Mycenaeans as being not only the same deities as (from hundreds of years before) on Crete, but also identifiable as the same as those who dominated the lives of all in Classical Greece – starting some 400 years later, after the onset of the Dark Age. Sacrificial offerings of produce and animals (though humans have never yet been discerned) were prevalent, with the bull being the highest form – reflected in the Mycenaean sarcophagus at Ayia Triadha on Crete, and in the habitual use of head-shaped 'rhytons' (drinking vessels).

It should also be emphasised that, though found on Crete (when under Mycenaean suzerainty) the 'tholos' (beehive) tombs that proliferate throughout mainland Greece were a specific Mycenaean development, whereas the earlier 'shaft grave' method of interment was inherited from the Minoans. One can only presume that, as with all empire-builders, the Mycenaeans thought they were invincible, and therefore – far from hiding their chief or warrior burials – glorified in these ostentatious, beautifully adorned, and highly visible structures.

Apart from their role in religion – whether as goddesses or priests – it seems clear from Linear B texts that women (though prominent in civilian life) did not appear as rulers, or achieve queenly status. However, judging by fresco evidence from the excavated palaces, no effort was spared in the lavishness of their attire, or in the immensely wide range of beautifully worked jewellery worn by the ladies of the court. The quality of female clothing, including attention to detail, must have involved hundreds of seamstress hours per garment, while every known kind of precious metal and semi-precious stone was used to produce necklaces, bracelets, ear and finger rings, diadems and hair clips. At the height of Mycenaean prosperity (Louise Schofield records) a breakthrough took place wherein moulds were used to mass-produce glass jewellery for the 'middle-class' market; these steatite moulds were carved in a wide array of designs, the resulting beads sometimes being sheathed in gold, so as to give – for example – a necklace the appearance (much as is the case today) of solid gold!

A militaristic people

Whereas on Crete the evidence of fortifications and a standing army is scant, the picture in the Peloponnese could not be more different. Whether the contrast in attitude basically stemmed from the former being an island – quite geographically separate from all but the smallest of neighbours – while the Mycenaeans may themselves have had aggressive antecedents, and were increasingly on guard against potential invaders, may never be proven. Certainly, the evidence of their warlike attire – oxhide-shaped shields and boar-tusk helmets – appeared in miniature frescoes at Akrotiri as early as the middle of the 16th century BC, if not before.

No palace within the Peloponnese has yielded up fresco fragments without these depicting a wide variety of warrior images – armed for conflict, duelling, with horse-drawn chariots, or fighting pitched battles against unknown enemies. The warrior-chief helmet itself could only be created after acts of conspicuous bravery, namely the killing of several mature boars so as to produce up to 60 tusks. Proper battle armour – as opposed to fine decorative ceremonial comparisons – is exemplified by the full-body bronze suiting, known as the Dendra Panoply, after the small settlement east of Tiryns where it was found.

Finally, any doubts at attaining/retaining military superiority are removed by a brief study of Homer's *Iliad*, and the importance that was attached to the variety and quality of their weapons. Apart from those of the beautifully decorated ceremonial variety, every conceivable type of bronze heavy sword and rapier, spearhead, arrowhead and dagger has been recovered, all of which were graphically shown in Mycenaean art and decorative pottery. As in most militant societies, when not in actual combat the most popular form of part training/part hobby – namely hunting – was a major preoccupation. Boar were not just hunted for their tusks, but for the thrill of the chase (with dogs very much involved) and as a showcase for the courage and daring of the participants. Boar and deer were the prime sources of feasting meat, and one hunting scene shows figures carrying large tripod cauldrons – these being highly symbolic in Mycenaean society.

Mycenaean decline, from around 1200BC

The next chapter tries to analyse the causes of the Dark Age catastrophe throughout the known world, and dwells on the near-miracle of Homer's ability to write (in c800BC) of events that we now know took place well before this decline started. However, since the main casualty in our attempt to trace the (tenuous) continuity of Mediterranean civilisation was the demise of the Mycenaean 'empire', we must here try to evaluate its particular situation.

It should first be said that the fundamental problem with any attempt to discover how civilisation in the region suffered such a set-back over a 200-300-year period is the disappearance of writing, which – as far as has been 'unearthed' to date – ceased abruptly when the (growing) caches of Linear B tablets uncovered in the 20th century were burned and/or buried as each major centre was destroyed. If no written record equals no 'history', then it can be no surprise to read in *The Aegean from Bronze Age to Iron Age* by Oliver Dickinson that the life-long efforts of hundreds of scholars have simply not been able to reach any firm conclusions – even though many contradictory theories have been put forward or resurrected over the past 60 years.

Certainly, at around 1200BC Mycenae and Tiryns made their wall fortifications even more massive, with both being extended so that a secure (secret) water supply could be accessed from within – a strong clue to impending siege? Tablets at Pylos hint at both rationing of food and raw materials (famine?) and of soldiers being delegated to watch over a lengthy stretch of coastline (a threat of invasion from the sea?).

What we can do is list here the theories that can be particularly applied to the Mycenaean decline, most of which will be examined in more detail in Chapter 12 – in the context of the onset of the Dark Age throughout the whole Mediterranean and Near East regions:

- Climate change: did a pronged period of cold weather drastically reduce food production throughout the previously abundant Greek peninsula, causing devastating famines?
- Earthquake (and fire) devastation: as shown in Chapter 7, the Greek region has suffered approximately two major earthquakes each century since time immemorial. Resultant damage is in evidence at most major sites, but was the catastrophe so severe (as on Crete c1450BC) as to bring the well-ordered civilisation to its knees?

- Invasion from the north: several theories have been expounded including an early 'Dorian' invasion, but although there is modest evidence of migration from the north – through a handful of artefacts, variations in Linear B inscriptions, or language dialect differences – there is no weight of archaeological evidence to support a mass influx of an aggressive people.
- Invasion by the 'Sea Peoples': again, there is a lack of evidence, and it is too simplistic to transfer the very real effect of such havoc as was wrought on the Levantine coast and in Egypt to a parallel occurrence in the Aegean.
- Internal strife: could war have been waged between rival dynasties? This would have been unlikely to result in the near-simultaneous destruction at each centre. Could the oppressed underclass (including a large slave population) have risen up from within? In which case, would the severity of their assaults (at each site) have resulted in fires so severe that cyclopean stones themselves would have become distorted, and have even melted?
- Pestilence: as graphically alluded to in the Old Testament, could a prolonged period of disease and pestilence – perhaps following chronic crop failures – have so weakened the indigenous population so as to allow a chaotic dismantling of the carefully created systems of government, and have consequently destroyed the ability of each debilitated centre to withstand the incursion of envious aliens, perhaps from widely differing sources?

This writer thinks that, while aggressive invasion (from sea or land) may have 'finished off' the palace cultures, the most likely explanation for their initial collapse is one or more catastrophically severe earthquakes, of which there is firm evidence at Mycenae, Tiryns and Midea. As is known from tragic examples in the 20th century, earthquakes very high on the Richter scale can set off a sequence of 'society destroying' events: the initial quake that destroys all property, sets off fires, and ruins sources of potable water; then (apart from those killed, maimed or immediately fleeing abroad – about 40% in the 1953AD Cephallonia disaster) the remaining population takes to the countryside; aftershocks (over weeks or months) prevent population return, so crops remain untended and animal flocks disperse/die; effective government ceases to exist, and manufacturing/processing industries – particularly of basic foodstuffs and clothing – collapse.

126

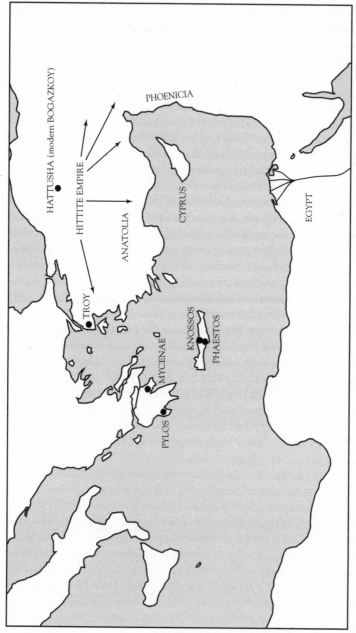

Map iv – The eastern Mediterranean, c1500BC

Since this apocalyptic scenario has been monitored many times in living memory, it is not difficult to see how 3,200 years ago – with no kind of relief agencies rushing to help from all corners – the fairly well-ordered societies of the day could have been destroyed.

The century after 1200BC

As has been subsequently observed in devastated regions in modern times, a visitor to the Peloponnese decades after the disaster, who had known the fabled cities in their prime, would have been shocked and appalled to have seen large sections of the reduced population living as refugees in the countryside – but the evidence shows that, while Pylos never recovered, occupancy at Mycenae and Tiryns did continue. What is more, all the available evidence points to the (albeit much reduced) population as being entirely Mycenaean. As in the 1953 example, some previously minor Mycenaean settlements benefited from an influx of desperate immigrants. Lefkandi (on the island of Euboia), Ialysos (on Rhodes) and Cephallonia all prospered as a result.

A summary would be that while the Linear B palace records systems became redundant and disappeared, most aspects of living continued, but at a more modest level. This meant that the construction of impressive buildings and tombs ceased, as did virtually all demand for the import and/or manufacture of luxury items. There is no trace of frescoes being painted, and very little stone carving, with the one industry that seemed to have succeeded over a wide geographical area being pottery manufacture. Overall, even though the outlying settlements mentioned above received a cultural boost initially, the 12th century BC saw more suffering in the form of recurring earthquakes, and evidence of fresh fire damage.

At least the way in which the Minoan civilisation came to an end was through being subsumed by the rising power in the region, with many of its stellar achievements being enthusiastically adopted by this rapidly developing Mycenaean Empire (or loose federation). However, this dynamic society itself could take no reflected glory in turn, through the envious grasp of an eager successor. Its remarkably fiery 500-year cultural era simply petered out, with just a few barely glowing embers surviving the ensuing Dark Age, to be rekindled some 400-500 years later at the very beginning of the Archaic (pre-Classical) Greek flowering.

Chapter 11

The Hittites: the start of the Iron Age

Because this book has the overall objective of tracing the chronological and geographical spread of knowledge, Chapter 4 explained that Ancient Egypt cannot feature more prominently because of its near-isolationist nature during three millennia of fabulous history – that is, until its conquest by Alexander the Great. There are many other fascinating 'stand-alone' cultures (with minimal records) to which we could devote considerable space, but, although remarkable in themselves, they will not feature in detail, since there is little or nothing to link their distinctive achievements with prior or successor communities elsewhere.

In the Mediterranean, a good illustration of the above 'non-qualification' is the early Bronze Age Tarxien temple and cemetery culture on Malta. This applies also to the mysterious megalithic art displayed along the Atlantic fringe – in Iberia, Brittany and Ireland – and the Skara Brae settlement in Orkney (in the north of Scotland). In the fast-moving world of scientific archaeology, wondrous discoveries such as 'Otzi' in the High Tyrol (see Chapters 1 and 7) may also eventually lead to the discovery of a hidden culture in northern Italy with strong links to those we are discussing – but not yet. However, the still quite enigmatic Hittites warrant their own chapter for two fundamental reasons – first because, before their demise at the onset of the Dark Age, they 'founded' the Iron Age, and second because, even during that chaotic period, descendants migrating westwards from central Anatolia to Turkey's Aegean coastline, or to the Greek mainland, *most probably* became part of the (presently still unexplained) ethnic mix from which the subsequent Greek genius emerged.

129

Almost at the start of this book – in Chapter 2 – we have a brief mention of the Neolithic town of Catal Hoyuk, in south-central Anatolia (modern Turkey). An excellent account of this unique site is provided by Michael Balter in *The Goddess and the Bull*, from the original excavations by the controversial James Mellaart (in 1958) to the incredibly detailed research then carried out into the 21st century under the leadership of Ian Hodder. These remarkable men have proved that the town – covering a 32-acre site – dates back to nearly 10,000 years BC.

One of the twin secrets of Catal Hoyuk's success lies in the fertility of the adjacent land, which (now called the Konya plain) was – in Neolithic times – a drying-out lake that attracted a wide variety of animals for meat, and subsequent husbandry. The other factor was its proximity to still-active volcanoes, which were an abundant source of obsidian. We have seen in earlier chapters how this vital material was a key driver of trade in the Middle East, and there is every reason to suppose that the Anatolian obsidian 'fields' were major suppliers to Mesopotamia from the outset of its spectacular rise to prosperity.

In his book *The Hittites*, J. G. Macqueen states that there is evidence for obsidian being exported from eastern Anatolia (close to the source of the Euphrates) to the Zagros Mountains bordering Iran and Iraq as early as 30,000 years BC, and it is in this region that rich copper mines were being exploited by 7000BC. While much of the raw copper will have found its way eastwards to Mesopotamia across the Fertile Crescent, Catal Hoyuk's importance ensured that supplies reached it via a tortuous journey westwards of some 300 miles (500km) – and we know that by 6000BC local smiths had developed a technique for smelting, so as to be able to shape small copper (and lead) decorative items.

(Anyone being introduced to archaeology might wonder at the intense scrutiny habitually applied to pottery, when many metals were known to have been simultaneously worked, in any given era. The paradox is caused by the 'quirk' of fired clay being non recyclable – and therefore surviving for millennia, whether intact or as shards, so as to provide us with a dating 'fix' – whereas the originally acquired metals could be used over and over again, particularly once a seam or mine was exhausted or hard times had eroded a community's purchasing power.)

From Catal Hoyuk to the first Hittite 'kingdom'

The earlier chapters on the Minoans and Mycenaeans provide a comparatively full picture of developments in Crete and Greece, from c3000BC until the onset of the Dark Age in c1180BC. A major factor in the wealth of detail available is that – with interruptions caused by two World Wars – archaeological work has been intensive in these areas since 1900 in the case of Crete, and since c1850 in the case of Greece, although scholarly 'tourists' had been visiting Athens and the Peloponnese since Roman times.

Unfortunately, widespread study and excavation in Turkey over a vast and complex land surface has only achieved a real head of steam since the Second World War, save for repeated forays to the Troad – ever since Schliemann's spectacular discoveries in the 1870s. Macqueen provides clues to the speed with which our knowledge of the Hittite era is gaining ground, when one reads the 'addendum' to the 1996 paperback version of *The Hittites*, 10 years after the original hardback was published. It is almost certain that in 50 years' time our understanding of the Hittite contribution to the flow of ancient knowledge will be vastly greater than it is at present.

5600BC has been fixed as the date when occupation of Catal Hoyuk ceased, in favour of a number of more northerly sites that were closer to rich metal deposits. One of the most interesting points to note is that, whereas settlements developed around temples in Mesopotamia, even at this early date Anatolian villages showed signs of primitive citadels being their main focus.

Over the ensuing millennia, it seems that scores of self-contained city states grew up throughout Anatolia, with identifiable 'castles' that housed each ruling family. And it is most noticeable that, whereas agriculture always provided a basic livelihood, the source of real wealth – in case after case – was derived from either the mining of metal deposits and/or the manufacture of metal objects. Many sites have yielded spectacular *metal* treasures, the most outstanding of which were discovered by Schliemann at Troy (Chapter 9). When Schliemann photographed his young wife Sophia festooned with diadems and necklaces, he shouted to the world that these were Helen's jewels, and dated the Trojan War to c1200BC. We now know that in the course of recent research in St Petersburg (see Chapter 9), this amazing treasure was dated to having been actually produced a full millennium earlier, c2300BC.

Schliemann repeated this error three years later at Mycenae, with his even more remarkable finds. They were much too old to belong to Agamemnon's family, and were *most likely* to have been manufactured in Anatolia. It may also be the case that the fabulous treasures at Ur travelled from an Anatolian source. We should also note that, while all early archaeology placed these wonders much too late, it is not surprising since there were few age comparisons that could then be made, dating methods were crude, and – most of all – the intrepid explorers of that era simply could not believe that such exquisite workmanship could have been executed so early in what became known as the Bronze Age.

If we accept that the results of highly prized central-Anatolian workmanship travelled huge distances to the east and west, the whole question of trading patterns becomes crucial in advance of the actual Hittite dynasties. As was discussed much earlier, Canaanite seafarers probed to the west throughout the early Bronze Age, and there is strong evidence to suggest that – with or without Cyprus as a staging post – the dozens of natural harbours along the entire Turkish coastline were a vital means whereby a wide range of goods could be moved from the Levant to Crete and Greece, with much-sought-after materials and products travelling in the opposite direction. This burgeoning seaborne trade should also be compared with the extraordinarily difficult alternative of overland caravans through Turkey by man and donkey.

At the same time, Macqueen states that trade with Assyria – centred on the Upper Tigris, and bordering eastern Anatolia – became so important from c2500BC onwards that Assyrian merchants journeyed through the rugged terrain to establish trading 'colonies' in central Anatolia, intermarrying with the indigenous population. He goes on to state that Assyria needed silver, gold and copper, and – in return – supplied woollen cloth and clothing. Until recently, it was felt that the Hittite forebears also imported much-needed tin (for bronze-working) from the Assyrians, but research in the Taurus Mountains has now shown that native supplies of this crucial material existed locally – as did a tin-working industry.

This mutually advantageous trading partnership continued for hundreds of years, but came to an abrupt halt around 1800BC. From sketchy records it appears that the Hurrians (about whom we know little) interposed themselves between the Assyrians and the Anatolians, and severed the trading relationship that was so important to these two peoples, with disastrous consequences.

While Assyria became severely weakened and was shortly subsumed into the Babylonian empire, Anatolia – in losing its trade routes – also became threatened by the Hurrians. At this point the tenuous documentary evidence fails. We know that there were father and son 'kings' (respectively Pithanas and Anittas), but after the latter's death in c1750BC a chaotic period ensued for more that a century, until a ruler emerged who established his capital at Hattusas (near modern Bogazkoy), and enthusiastically changed his own name to Hattusilis.

Emergence of the Hittites

Despite the assertion, earlier in this chapter, that (outside the Troad) only limited excavations took place in the first half of the 20th century, it is the case that before the First World War thousands of tablets – in a *cuneiform* script – were recovered from Bogazkoy. These tallied with a pair of tablets, covering diplomatic correspondence, found at the start of the century at El Amarna in Egypt, the site where John Pendlebury first made his name. This language – named Arzawan – seemed to emanate from western Turkey, possibly from Lydia.

Up to the late 19th century our only knowledge of 'Hittites' had come from the Bible and from Egyptian records. So the picture became very confused when hundreds of rock-carvings – in a *hieroglyphic* script – were also found in the years before the First World War throughout Asia Minor, and in Syria, a script that was clearly the work of Hittites. It has taken most of the subsequent century for careful research to enable a majority of scholars to agree that these two Hittite languages are related variants of Arzawan.

We now come to the even more vexed question of how the Hittites came to be in Turkey, in which there are competing theories for the origins and migration of all Indo-European peoples. This volume does not have the scope to examine these alternative views, which are known as

- the Palaeolithic Continuity theory,
- the Anatolian hypothesis,
- the Black Sea deluge theory, and
- the Kurgan hypothesis.

The last of these was first proposed by Marija Gimbutas in 1956 and, although hotly disputed in the early years, has gradually gained ground as the most likely explanation as to the *direction* from which a significant enough number of migrants moved *east* across the Hellespont, such as would later develop the power to dominate central Anatolia. The Kurgan culture was originally spread widely through southern Russia and the Ukraine, and – in the Bronze Age – made its presence felt in Romania, Bulgaria and Macedonia. The time-span over which this culture held sway – as evidenced by the elaborate way in which lives of the deceased were celebrated – lasted from late-Neolithic times, through the Bronze and Iron Ages, and even (in distinct regions) through the Classical era.

The Kurgan burial method involved vast earthen mounds, initially with separate timber chambers, which later became more sophisticated stone-reinforced structures. Remarkable numbers have been excavated over this huge geographical area, revealing wonderful artefacts – including the magnificent tomb of Philip II (northern Greece – Chapter 15) and that of King Midas (in Phrygia, north-western Anatolia, which lay to the east of Troy). Although the evidence of Kurgan-like behaviour (for example, the use of hill-forts) in Anatolia is scanty, there are hints of their occupation of Troy (on which site we are now aware of some 20 different levels between c2900 and 1200BC). We have reasons to believe that by c2500BC these determined people had penetrated east towards central Anatolia, and had established (seaborne?) trading links with the coastal region of Cilicia, which lay at the eastern end of Anatolia, not far from the thriving entrepots 'round the corner' of the Mediterranean, in Syria and modern-day Lebanon.

Although a complicated picture, it seems from Macqueen – mainly through pottery similarities – that the main drive towards the establishment of Hattusas came northwards before the turn of the second millennium, from Cilicia via the important settlement of Kultepe, where a large building with a 'western-style' 'megaron' (otherwise alien to central Anatolia) has been revealed. Throughout the period preceding the Hittite ruler Hattusilis, there is also – confusingly – the appearance of the Hattians, though there is presently no clarity as to whether these people *preceded* or *followed* the Hittites into Anatolia.

Another intriguing possibility – again according to Macqueen – is that early Greek-speakers from the north also followed the Hittites, and came to populate north-west Turkey, and in particular the Troad. Could it be that the Trojan War (c1300BC) was not fought between Hittite and Greek, but between the Troad 'Greeks' and their invading Greek 'cousins'?

(In examining the Hittite 'kingdom' from 1650 to c1220BC there is no space here for a detailed examination of more than 400 years of immense complexity. As throughout this book, we will try to select the major ways in which Hittite Anatolia contributed to the transfer of knowledge and technology across the Mediterranean region.)

Continuous autocracy

This long period of more than 400 years saw an almost unbroken succession of identifiable rulers – from the emergence of Hattusilis I to the death of Tudhalyas IV – although the creation of 'empire' was only achieved with the inevitable series of wars, alliances and internal strife. At its greatest extent, under Mursili II (c1321-1295BC) the empire covered virtually the whole of modern-day Turkey (with the exception of what can be simply described as the 'greater Troad'), together with the whole of Syria, including Damascus, except for its forbidding desert region. At the eastern border lay the formidable Assyrians, in what is today Kurdish Iraq. Also, what are today the countries of Lebanon and Israel constituted a southern buffer-zone between the highly prized Syrian coastal cities – at the western extremity of the Fertile Crescent – and the might of Egypt.

Offensive military capability

To gain, and then hold, such a huge swathe of territory, the Hittites developed a most formidable military machine, the centrepiece of which was their three-man chariot – a remarkable combination of engineering skill, both extremely light and manoeuvrable. These vehicles, which sowed terror among less sophisticated adversaries, were produced by the thousand, and reached a peak performance in one of the most famous (and closely studied) battles of early history. The Battle of Kadesh (Quadesh) on the Orontes River in Syria took place in the summer of 1274, between the massed forces of Hittites under Muwattalli II and the equally vast Egyptian army of Rameses II.

135

The latter, an unusually expansionist pharaoh who at that time controlled the coastal strip all the way from Egypt, met his match in this titanic battle, and though each side claimed victory the actual result was indecisive.

Defensive strategy

We have touched on the 'Greek' Troad, and in studying defensive fortifications exhaustive researches at Troy show clear similarities – in the middle of the 2nd millennium – between its massive structures and those in the (Mycenaean) Peloponnese to the west, and at Bogazkoy to the east. In all cases, selection of the best natural sites and the skill in creating walls of massive width and height continue to amaze the modern visitor. In addition – although not fully proven in relation to sustaining the huge population – there is evidence at Bogazkoy of deep-cut water cisterns with stairway access, just as at Mycenae and at Troy. However, a legacy of unique Hittite thinking at Bogazkoy is a remarkable 83-metre-long sloping tunnel (of corbelled stone construction) that served as a link between deep inside the fortified site and the outside world – above which was placed a huge earthen mound, with a section of the defensive wall running at a right-angle on top.

Hittite life: industry, art and religion

Rural life and agriculture

The capital city of Bogazkoy (ancient Hattusas) extended to some 400 acres (160 hectares), with population estimates still varying widely between 20,000 and 40,000 people. From evidence now available, the range of rural activities was as widespread as anywhere else in the Bronze Age Mediterranean world, with the peasant lifestyle in that era remarkably unchanged until very recently. Feeding the city population as well as themselves, farmers were involved in every kind of grown crop, domesticated animal, wild animal for meat, orchards and bee-keeping – all ensuring a varied diet. The firm impression is given of a thriving and vigorous community, such as would promote a dynamic domestic economy and parallel relationship with the wider world.

Industry and international trade

Painstaking research in the city has revealed a (mid-2nd millennium) hive of activity in almost every conceivable trade that would have been needed to service the needs of such a large population – ranging from building tradesmen, through cloth-making to shopkeepers. Into our 21st century, archaeologists are continually revealing not only more evidence of smelting sites, but the existence of a considerable number of ore mines – ever more demonstrating that the Hittite regime was not solely dependant on imported copper, tin and lead. Of course, this is not to deny the fabulous discoveries of Bronze Age shipwrecks, and their most illuminating contents. The breadth of items recovered clearly shows that the harbours on the southern coast acted both as stopping points for two-way trade between the Levant and Crete/Mycenae, *and* as the vital stations for Hittite imports/exports.

Stone carving

Though the sheer weights involved would have largely precluded exports, we can tell that elaborate semi-finished sculptures were transported huge distances within Anatolia, to be finished once they were in situ. The evidence for this practice is best seen at Yesemek in the far south-east, where hundreds of semi-finished statues awaiting shipment still lie. (This late-2nd-millennium practice – and the circumstances under which the quarry was abandoned – is eerily reminiscent of what can still be movingly observed at Cave di Cusa near Selinunte on the southern Sicilian coast, where 1,000 years later (2,500 years ago) work was abruptly halted due to a Phoenician invasion, with the freshness of the monumental cut stone columns looking as though they were being worked on only yesterday!)

Seals

Showing an intriguing linkage with simultaneous developments on Crete and in the Peloponnese, we have many examples of seals, though mainly stamp-seals, wherein increasingly sophisticated decoration and cuneiform or hieroglyphic symbols occur, as the Hittite dynasty unfolds. Occasionally we see cylinder seals, and, very exceptionally, a gold signet ring – of the exact same type that so excited and motivated Arthur Evans in his fascination for Crete, after he first stumbled upon examples of these in Athens antique shops (see Chapter 6).

Art

Superficially the Hittite artistic legacy does not compare with those of Egypt, Crete or Mycenae, but perhaps time will tell the extent to which great skill ever existed, but became lost through the turbulence of the ensuing three millennia. Currently the most important aspect for us is the degree to which links must have existed with the great contemporary cultures: the Lion Gate at Bogazkoy, in relation to that guarding the entrance to Mycenae; the Sphinx Gate at nearby Alaca, in relation to the pervasive presence of this phenomenon in Egypt; and the ritual bull-vases found at Bogazkoy, compared with the Minoan obsession with this dominant creature.

Literature

In this area the linkage with Mesopotamia is clear – first in the way the training of scribes developed, with an identified school at Hattusas (Bogazkoy), and second, the Gilgamesh epic was preserved in the Bogazkoy archive, not only in the original Akkadian, but also in Hurrian and Hittite languages. To add to this – although only fragments remain – we have text that relates to the god Kumarbi and his blood-thirsty 'kingship' struggle with his rival Teshub. Tantalisingly, a few fragments also exist of what was probably a soldier's song.

Pottery

The Hittite pottery of central Anatolia is not particularly remarkable, save for the animal features incorporated into different types of vessel – most frequently water birds and bulls. Fine examples of the latter are the abovementioned pair of ritual bull-vases, standing 3 feet (90cm) high. In western Anatolia, the pottery is of a much finer quality, a wide range of clean and elegant shapes – found in profusion at Troy – being finished in burnished grey (known as Grey Minyan). Unsurprisingly, on the western and south-western coasts there is evidence of Mycenaean influence, with a smattering of actual Mycenaean manufactured imports.

Religion

The picture here is almost bound to be complex, when considering the successive waves of immigrants, as set out earlier in the chapter. As found at Catal Hoyuk (in common with most other Mediterranean

138

sites), up to the 3rd millennium the dominant figure was the earth mother-goddess, with her male partner holding an inferior position. Only perhaps as temporal man assumed an increasingly militant role did the male god counterpart – maybe based on an imported 'Zeus' – elbow aside the mother figure in importance.

The great temple at Bogazkoy sat in a rectangular complex that extended to nearly 2 acres (0.75 hectare), and the complexity of the buildings delineated by researchers is testament to the importance that worship played in the lives of the Hittite citizens. As to burial practices, there is linkage between the Hittite tradition and those of Mycenae/Troy, and – as more recently ascertained – clear evidence of cremation being adopted throughout the Anatolian mainland.

Demise and aftermath

Aspects of the Hittite world summarised in this chapter show that diligent research has revealed a people who, while not being a primary catalyst for changing history, formed for several centuries a crucial bridge between the Middle Eastern and Aegean worlds. The unique Hittite contribution was their initiation of the Iron Age – founded on the Anatolian genius for smelting metal, which had been developed over a span of at least five millennia.

The Hittite empire collapsed quickly after 1200BC, chaos in Anatolia coinciding with turmoil throughout the Mediterranean region, caused perhaps by the havoc wrought by the mysterious 'Sea Peoples'. But the precious iron-working techniques survived through the ensuing Dark Age. Another 50 or 100 years of research may tell us more about the extent of the Hittite contribution to the 'DNA' of the subsequent Greek flowering – but their 'fingerprints' are definitely there to be seen in the miraculous genetic composition that caused the spectacular Classical Naissance.

Part II

Chapter 12

Homer, Odysseus's Ithaca, and the Mediterranean Dark Age

Of the 'barely glowing embers' that survived this Dark Age, we will describe the eventual rekindling of those we can identify, in Chapter 14, with the exception of the one that glowed the brightest of all in Classical Greece – and which has provided us with the two most enduring literary works in Western history – namely Homer.

(There have been thousands of translations of Homer's works of genius, but here we will refer to the work of the American Robert Fagles (1933-2008), who – with the benefit of all previous academic research and archaeological interpretation at his disposal – published his highly acclaimed versions of the *Iliad* in 1990, and of the *Odyssey* in 1996. It is the latter that Robert Bittlestone has relied upon in his *Odysseus Unbound*, referred to later in this chapter.)

Before discussing any detail of Homer, it must be said that we are very lucky to have anything more than a shadowy knowledge of his existence at all, since many Greek Classical texts only reached Florence from Byzantium shortly before the latter's seizure by the Ottoman Empire in the 15th century AD (see Chapter 23). Following this piece of good fortune, the first printed edition of Homer (still in Greek) was circulated in Florence in 1488. Many more interpretations in Greek followed, but Fagles particularly focussed on a two-volume Greek text published in 1908 (edited by David Monro and Thomas Allen), which was based on the elegant hand-writing of the brilliant – but erratic – Cambridge scholar Richard Porson (1759-1808). Porson's work, which appeared in 1801, was in turn based on Italian manuscripts from the Harleian Collection. (The Medieval and

Renaissance collection of the Harley family was purchased by the British Government for £10,000 in 1753, and formed a key part of the original British Museum Library – since 1973 the British Library.)

Controversy raged in Classical times as to who Homer was, where he was born, and when he lived. Argument continued throughout the near-1,000-year existence of ancient Alexandria as capital of Egypt, from its founding in c331BC by Alexander the Great to its conquest in 641AD by the burgeoning Muslim empire. And academic dissent has continued on these issues from the Renaissance to the present day. It is to be hoped, therefore, that the reader will not be disappointed when no attempt is made here to be categorical on any aspect of this most intriguing of historical figures!

The best summary that can be mustered in these pages is that Homer – perhaps a wandering bard/minstrel – probably lived around 850/800BC; 'he' may have been more than one person, each of whom contributed sections of his most famous works; he may or may not have been blind, and he probably lived too early to write (because writing had disappeared with the demise of the Mycenaean era, and did not reappear until about 750/700BC, as judged by widespread pottery finds in the Mediterranean); he therefore could only recite to his listeners; and consequently his works were probably committed to 'paper' by learned scribes some 100 years after his lifetime.

A key issue that has always exercised academia has been the accuracy of Homer's memory, and – since the events that he is recalling *probably* date to 1300-1150BC – the memory of dozens of intermediaries, upon whose very specific recollections he himself was relying. Only in the last 70-80 years has intense scientific study of oral traditions around the world revealed the incredible accuracy with which even the most minute details can be handed down over many hundreds of years, bringing the Homer 'gap' straddling a total of up to 500 years well within the scope of generations of 'photographic' recollection.

The reason that this issue is crucial is that (allied to archaeological progress) it is now clear that – inter-woven among the actions of the gods – the *Iliad* and the *Odyssey* contain, within their wonderfully colourful stories, a wealth of historical and geographical detail. As every decade brings fresh discoveries – helping particularly to fill in the location jigsaw puzzle – archaeologists/historians (and non-academics) are poring over hundreds of paragraphs, searching for wherever a nuance of meaning might provide a vital hitherto-overlooked clue.

In the next section of this chapter we will examine one of the most recent such exercises, but a brief summary of the sequence of major archaeological finds paints an amazingly *factual* picture of what – until 1870 – was considered to be just a fascinating pair of ancient *stories*:

1873 Schliemann discovers Troy (home to Priam and Hector)
1876 Schliemann discovers Troy (home to Agamemnon)
1900 Evans discovers Knossos (home to Minos)
1939 Blegen discovers Pylos (home to Nestor)
1967 Marinatos discovers Akrotiri on Thera (modern Santorini)
2001 Yannos Lolos unearths a 'palace' on Salamis (home of Ajax?)
2005 Robert Bittlestone publishes *Odysseus Unbound* – the 'real' Ithaca

Going back to the aftermath of 1873, in his majestic 800-page tome *Ilios* Schliemann starts to change long-held perceptions by demonstrating the pin-point accuracy with which Homer describes the location of Troy, its relationship to surrounding rivers, mountains and the sea, weapons carried by participants (heroes) in the 10-year siege, details of body armour, shields and even a boar-tusk helmet, and many other varied artefacts recovered from the site. This breadth of comparison has been repeated at almost every subsequently excavated site. In certain cases the details of painted frescoes exactly match Homer's description, and there are accurate portrayals of the burial techniques and rituals for heroes (and their families), details of sacrificial animals and the sports at funeral games, not to mention his precise descriptions of gold jewellery worn by living queens and other royal personages.

Odysseus Unbound: the search for the 'real' Ithaca

At a time when Virchow's 'whole new science' did not exist (before Schliemann's discovery of Troy and Mycenae in the 1880s), one can see that this new field of activity was wide open to entry by deep-thinking individuals from a non-scientific and/or non-academic background. But even 120 years later it has taken an energetic holidaymaking businessman to demonstrate that modern Ithaca is almost certainly not ancient Ithaca, while the modern-day westernmost 'finger' of Cephallonia may well have been the real island home of Odysseus. What follows is taken from the remarkable book *Odysseus Unbound: The search for Homer's Ithaca* by Robert Bittlestone with James Diggle and John Underhill (2005). And there *are* faint (and faintly amusing) comparisons to be made with Schliemann: Bittlestone had a formal education in Classics, while Schliemann's introduction to the subject was most graphically informal (see Chapter 9); both men pursed careers in fields far removed from their boyhood fascination; crucially, both men worked on the assumption that Homer's geographical descriptions were *accurate*; and – far from conducting armchair research – both tested their particular theory by tramping backwards and forwards over their selected terrain, Homer's text in hand!

Ever since Schliemann's early triumphs, Bittlestone and a host of famous archaeologists have tried to prove the whereabouts of ancient Ithaca, with only a small proportion convinced that the home of Odysseus was indeed the island that we know today as Ithaca. Ridiculous as it may appear to the reader, theories have placed the island all around the Mediterranean, and way beyond the Pillars of Hercules (Strait of Gibraltar), wherein the 10-year wanderings of Odysseus are even postulated as being as far afield as Brazil! However, with his feet firmly on the ground, Bittlestone's first conviction – while holidaying with his family on modern Ithaca in 1998 – was that modern and ancient Ithaca could not possibly be one and the same island. Fagles's newly published (1996) translation clearly spoke of *four* islands in a group, whereas today there are only *three*. Homer emphatically quoted Odysseus as saying of his home: '...around are many islands, close to each other, Douchlion (modern Ithaca?) and Same (definitely Cephallonia) and wooded Zacynthos (no change). Ithaca itself lies low, *furthest to sea towards dusk*; the rest, apart, face dawn and sun.' So, questioned Bittlestone, where is the *fourth* island in the group?

His prime theory is that the Paliki peninsula of Cephallonia is the real Ithaca; that it was a separate island 3,300 years ago; and that repeated catastrophic earthquake activity (in the Mediterranean's worst 'hot-spot') has filled in the narrow channel that once separated 'Ithaca' from 'Same'. The central proposition is that once the Paliki peninsula is regarded as having been a separate island, every single physical attribute seen today 'fits like a glove' with Homer's brilliantly detailed descriptions. To my mind – and to thousands of other readers

146

worldwide – *Odysseus Unbound* is an un-put-downable detective story, and since every paragraph makes a specific contribution towards proving Bittlestone's case, there is no meaningful way in which one could make a potted summary that is better than that available on the author's web pages. In the book he diligently examines (with the aid of his academic colleagues) – on a sentence-by-sentence basis – every one of Homer's geographical references, and the relationship between dozens of different locations.

Another (21st-century) aspect is that – both in researching for their book, and in the following years of fieldwork so as to prove their theory – the 'Real Ithaca' team have used virtually every scientific technique listed in Chapter 1, as well as the array of leading-edge methods perfected by their Dutch world-leading geological survey partner FUGRO. Having studied science at an early stage (as well as classics), and having then read economics at Cambridge – as well as embracing all learned contributions – it seems to the writer that Bittlestone has given his core team the best possible chance of success. As of late 2010 the team has shown (through underwater research) that there is clear evidence of a channel having existed at the northern end of the (projected) steep-sided waterway. The presumed level of 'infill' rises to some 600 feet (180m) near the southern 'exit', and they have also demonstrated that – down to some 300 feet (90m) – there exists no parent rock, only consolidated spoil/rubble. Because of the above maximum height and the present limitations of the new technology, the expanding team is now engaged in creating a series of deep bore-holes, drilled in a conventional manner.

It must be remembered that Fagles's translation did not set out to suit a particular theory or island. Instead Bittlestone, in rereading a story familiar to him, had the staggering experience of plotting perfect fit after perfect fit, on a section of Cephallonia that neither he nor anyone else had ever examined in depth before. If, therefore, it is eventually proved that Paliki was once a separate island, such a discovery will be of monumental importance – no more so than in establishing (once and for all) that Homer was a remarkable *geographer*, as well as historian and fabulous story-teller ... then, of course, the definitive search for Odysseus's palace can begin! And what if, in the end, a navigable channel cannot be found to have existed? In this case Bittlestone (and his team) will have promoted the unique works of Homer to a worldwide audience, and demonstrated

147

that – with ever more sophisticated weaponry at their disposal – archaeologists with whatever background can look forward to another century of unimaginable surprises!

The Mediterranean Dark Age

Attempting to explain satisfactorily exactly when and why a 'collapse' in ordered society took place has so far eluded all scholarship, and trying to account in detail as to how successive generations lived through several centuries has also so far proved almost as difficult. Any reader who believes that the above sentence is merely trying to gloss over the not particularly eventful end to the prehistorical period is invited to read – line by line! – the 20-page conclusion of *The Aegean from Bronze Age to Iron Age* by Oliver Dickinson (2006). Dr Dickinson – a highly respected academic – starts his conclusion by acknowledging that, since 1970, there is vastly increased data for specialists to digest, but admits that all this added information has not made it any easier to answer a number of basic questions. Set out below is an attempt to address just five of these questions, though the impatient reader is perhaps unlikely to be satisfied with a series of 'politician's' responses!

What caused the Dark Age to be such a widespread feature throughout the Eastern Mediterranean?

As the Mycenaean dominance in the Peloponnese faded, the first casualty was the demise of Linear B – thus there are no written on-the-spot records. We are, therefore, fortunate that both Egyptian scripts refer frequently to the invasions of the 'Sea Peoples', as does the Old Testament of the Bible in graphically relating their epic struggles against invaders that they termed 'Philistines'. We know that Gaza was destroyed, and (in Turkey) that the Hittite Empire was devastated. Piracy in the Mediterranean had been a feature ever since sailing the 'wine dark sea' had become commonplace, and the most plausible cause of the Dark Age onset may well have been the conjunction of aggressive seaborne invaders together with plague and famine across the whole region. After all, we know that the bubonic plague was brought by sea to medieval England, and caused death to nearly half the population, having previously ravaged mainland Europe (see Chapter 21). Then again, while piracy, plague and famine may have devastated the Near East, a more likely *initial* cause in the Aegean could have been earthquake damage, as postulated in the previous chapter.

In the Aegean, when did this era start?

Records show that Egypt may well have been invaded in c1225BC, and again in c1185BC. These dates tie in with the probable timing of destruction at Troy and Gaza, and the Mycenaean palace era is deemed to have suffered irreversible decline from around 1200BC. However, as Dickinson and Schofield both point out, although new building work fizzled out in c1200BC, the Mycenaean 'kingdoms' and civic structures probably stayed intact for about another 100 years – until (it is generally agreed) about 1080BC.

At least one can now confirm that an earlier generalisation of this Dark Age lasting for 400 years, starting in 1200BC, is no longer valid. (This is a quite crucial judgement, tentatively giving support to the notion – as deduced by exhaustive research into the aftermath of the fall of Rome – that neither 'Dark Age' lasted as long as was at first thought, nor were in all likelihood as deep or bleak.)

How did the Dark Age affect society and the way the population lived?

As the well-ordered palace-centric structures fractured – probably coinciding with a sharp fall in population – the evidence is that (with one or two exceptions) urban living declined. With the palaces deserted and eventually destroyed, small groups became spread around the countryside – effectively living a village existence, mainly dependant on locally produced food. Palace-driven mass production of clothing, pottery, olive oil and domestic tools would have ground to a halt, replaced – over time – by a myriad of cottage industries. We must also assume that seaborne trade in luxury goods – a trade with the whole of the Eastern Mediterranean that had been built up over at least a thousand years – came to a fairly decisive halt.

There were a few exceptions to this rapid descent to a peasant lifestyle. For unexplained reasons, a group of sites in central Greece survived intact long after the Mycenaean collapse, with some being continuously occupied through to the start of the Archaic period. The most notable of these was Lefkandi, a coastal village on the island of Euboea, close to which the Heroon mound revealed the grave of a 'hero' in 1980. Even more intriguingly, the monumental building constructed around 950BC (50 metres long and nearly 14 metres wide) was clearly a precursor of the temple architecture that started to appear c750BC.

What, if any, were the notable technology advances during this period?

Significant developments were few and far between, but there was a notable mark of progress with the start of the proto-geometric style of pottery c1050BC. A faster potter's wheel was developed, which ensured symmetrical shapes, as well as the use of a compass so as to achieve perfect circles and semi-circles. In addition, higher firing temperatures resulted in a better quality of glaze.

However, the most remarkable step-change was the transition from Bronze Age to Iron Age. It may seem incongruous that this should take place when the whole region was in turmoil and deep economic depression, but since c1500BC easily won supplies of tin and copper ores (for bronze – mainly weapons) had become increasingly difficult to find. Indeed, there were piratical activities throughout the region dedicated to seizing copper and tin ingots.

From perhaps 1800BC the Hittites had mastered iron-smelting techniques – producing a sword whose edges could be made razor sharp (unlike bronze), which had greatly aided their military expansion in Turkey. Initially iron nuggets from meteorite deposits had been used, then, when this supply was exhausted in Anatolia, ore seams close to the surface were exploited. This led to Cyprus – from c1500BC – becoming a major producer, since it held readily available supplies of ore deposits, and by c1200BC this new industry was making its mark in the Aegean.

This activity – using native ore deposits previously ignored by the Mycenaeans – grew rapidly from c1050BC as a cottage industry, and by 900BC almost all grave-goods weaponry had been switched from bronze to iron.

In the Aegean, when was the point at which the Dark Age ended, and the Archaic Greek era began?

A theme of this book is the remarkable amount of additional information that is being unearthed each decade – discoveries that alternately correct a previously held view, or open an entirely new avenue, or start to bridge a gap in time with invaluable detail. Referring to the oft-stated 1200-800BC 'envelope', Dickinson states that '…these terms are gradually going out of use, since the former lack of archaeological evidence in a period that was mute in its lack of inscriptions has been shown to be an accident of discovery rather than a fact of history.'

As we have seen above, the start of this Dark Age can now be said to have been delayed until 1100 – or perhaps 1080 – BC. So it is with the end of the Dark Age, and the emergence of Archaic Greece. It is now clear that vibrancy throughout the period at Lefkandi and other central Greek locations was far more significant than was thought (say) 50 years ago. Their cultural and trade links with the Levant coast blossomed from about 900BC, as did their involvement with Cyprus, which resulted in a notable migration to that island.

All in all, a summary of this most puzzling phase – for specialists in Egypt, and throughout the Eastern Mediterranean – is that the picture was distinctly 'grey' between 1200 and 1100BC, and again from 900 to 800BC, but that the 'true' Dark Age only prevailed between 1100 and 900BC – that is, as experts see it today. In another 50 years the picture – which, with all the tools available, can only move in a more revealing direction – may have changed yet again!

Chapter 13

The Phoenician diaspora to the Western Mediterranean

Just as the 'dawn' of the Archaic era was becoming detectable, the Phoenician migration achieved a huge momentum and, by the time Classical Greece was a reality, these interlopers had established an iron grip over the western third of the Mediterranean. For 700 years – from c850BC until Carthage was burned to the ground by Scipio Aemilianus in 146BC – these very different people were a constant thorn in the flesh of Greece and Rome, and yet brought with them the most valuable gift of all – the alphabet – from which both Ancient Greek and Latin was derived. As previously described, from early prehistory there had been an inexorable east to west migration. Archaeologists and historians are mostly uncertain as to where successive waves of immigrants originated, though – as in the case of the Etruscans – future DNA analysis of ever-greater sophistication may eventually solve these problems.

However, the Phoenician homeland and their diaspora (dispersal) to the Western Mediterranean are comparatively well documented, first by Biblical and Assyrian records, and second by classical historians – although we now have many disparities between 'historical' dates (written down centuries after the event) and recently assessed archaeological dating. Argument has raged in many areas: Phoenician influence in – and relationship to – the Tartessian culture in Andalusia; the Greek and Roman view of Phoenicians as being no more than cunning pirates; and the view that they brought nothing to the world in the way of art. What is indisputable (which both Greek and Roman writers may have found particularly difficult to swallow!) was their legacy of a *written* language.

(Regarding terminology, **Canaan/Canaanites** is the name given by the inhabitants to their homeland and to themselves, and which historians have used within a Bronze Age concept, up to c1200BC. **Phoenicia/Phoenician**, though their origin is unknown, are the terms used within Classical Greece, and which historians have used (in a Mediterranean-wide and Iron Age context) from 1200BC onwards. **Carthaginian** covers the period from the 6th century BC, when the city of Carthage (in modern-day Tunisia) dominated the Western Mediterranean. **Punic** is the term used for the Carthaginians by the Romans, throughout their 150 years of mutual conflict.)

The Canaanites (forerunners of the Phoenicians) in the Bronze Age

We have mentioned the Canaanites in the chapter on Egypt, their mercantile role at the western edge of the Fertile Crescent, and their seafaring prowess in managing the trade down the Palestinian coast to the Nile delta. Indeed, throughout the Bronze Age the Canaan coastal territory stretched from almost as far north as the mouth of the Orontes River, through Palestine and down to the Egyptian border in the south – a distance of some 300 miles (500km).

Canaanite mercantilism dominated trade, with vibrant coastal cities exploiting every requirement: of Mesopotamia via the Fertile Crescent; of the flourishing Syrian city states; and of Egypt via the coastline to the Nile delta. So closely interwoven was the link with Egypt that the early pharaohs held great sway over Canaanite activities, with their agents and emissaries assuming almost colonial influence.

The city of Byblos was pre-eminent in the 3rd millennium BC, but Tyre – whose 3rd-millennium origins were doubted by historians until fairly recently – quickly became almost as important. Around 2000BC there was a crisis caused by invading Semitic groups, but the key cities of Byblos, Tyre, Sidon and Ugarit soon recovered – again coming under marked Egyptian influence. Trading with Crete was established, which was augmented in the Late Bronze Age (1550-1200BC) by links with Mycenae. We know of a wealth of correspondence from this period between Byblos and the pharaohs, written in Akkadian cuneiform (wedge-shaped) script, often emphasising the loyalty of the former to the latter.

The rise of Phoenicia
(modern-day Lebanon and the southern coast of Syria)

The coastal sprawl of the Canaanites had existed throughout the Bronze Age, but at the onset of the Iron Age around 1200BC the delineation of Phoenicia was crystallised by a series of crises, as graphically recounted in the Old Testament of the Bible. Three almost simultaneous events effectively corralled the Canaanites into a small area: the Philistine occupation of the Palestinian coast to the south; the (somewhat tenuous) Israelite grip on the mountainous terrain to the south/south-east; and the Aramean emergence as the controlling power of what has become Syria to the north.

The confinement of the Canaanites into the much-diminished coast-facing 'wedge' of Phoenicia – in simple terms corresponding to modern-day Lebanon – must have been the catalyst for these enterprising people to address themselves to a *maritime* future. Phoenician prosperity now depended on their modest inland acreage of very fertile soil, dense forests for timber and game, fishing and fish processing, and continuation of their antecedents' cloth and purple-dyeing (from the Murex mollusc) industries. The now quite dense population continued to benefit from its huge trading volumes with Egypt and (indirectly) with Mesopotamia, but seafaring further afield – with naval supremacy assured – was to become the vital ingredient for continued success.

The fortified ports – brilliantly sited to the north (Arvad) and the south (Tyre) – included Byblos and Sidon. Acting competitively with each other for trade ensured that Iron Age Phoenicia developed as a loose federation of city states, never as a homogeneous nation state. Following the disruptive 'squeeze(s)' around 1200BC, these cities bounced back to great prosperity in only 50 years, and were to dominate all coastal activity in the region throughout the early Iron Age – i.e. until c900BC. During this 250-year period it is doubtful that embryonic Phoenician colonies were being established in the Western Mediterranean – as was originally proposed by earlier historians – if only because the Philistines and other 'Sea Peoples' (pirates) would have ruptured any attempt to establish and nurture such long-distance lines of communication.

Tyre expansion and seafaring: constant probing to the Pillars of Hercules and beyond

Seafaring freedom only became 'normalised' following two key events: David's victory over the Philistines in 975BC, and the pre-eminence of Tyre within Phoenicia from the moment King Hiram (969-936BC) became its ruler. From then on the blossoming of Phoenicia became synonymous with Tyre becoming the most influential port-city in the Mediterranean. Today a peninsula, Tyre was *the* prototype Phoenician port-city that was later exported to the Western Mediterranean: a fortified offshore island, with two opposing harbours that were developed for maximum shelter and security, and which had an interconnecting canal.

Hiram I, while depending on the adjacent fertile plain for food for the burgeoning population, developed a (cistern-fed) water supply for the island. He caused at least three major temples to be built to the gods Melqart (Hercules), Baal and Astarte, and the few bas-reliefs handed down to us show the mighty towers and walls that fortified the island city. While recent archaeology shows almost continuous occupation since the early Bronze Age, the most fascinating revelations (dated to 750-700BC) show a pottery style identical to that of the Phoenician settlements in Andalusia of the same period. This is not so surprising, as the date of these finds lies in the middle of Tyre's golden age (900-550BC).

The combination of circumstances that led to the city's Mediterranean pre-eminence were David's victory over the Philistines, the decline in Egypt's power, a lengthy static phase of the Assyrian Empire, and the fractious situation amongst the main Syrian city kingdoms. Thus the golden scenario of its non-reliance on others, and a surrounding power vacuum, gave Tyre an unrivalled opportunity to exploit both its naval and commercial potential to the full.

An early example of 'seizing the moment' was Hiram I's 'technology transfer' agreement with King Solomon (960-930BC). This led to their joint shipbuilding programme on the Red Sea, which in turn led to 'oriental' forays (manned by Phoenicians) as far afield as the Indian Ocean. Then, throughout the 9th century BC Tyre expanded its commercial grip eastwards, into Asia. It also spread its trading tentacles into Turkey, and (as early as 820BC) towards establishing a colony on Cyprus at Kition, near Larnaka. (When Jezebel, daughter of

155

Tyre's King Ithobaal I [887-856BC] married King Ahab of Israel (874-853BC), it was her introduction of the worship of Baal that led to the religious tensions described in the Old Testament.)

As had the Minoans well over a thousand years earlier, the Phoenicians (formerly Canaanites) had long ago learned about the prevailing winds throughout the Mediterranean, their seasonal changes, and the dangers of winter storms that prejudiced their ability to sail 'home'. In addition, they had inherited a sound knowledge of astronomy, for sailing at night, as recounted by Homer in the *Odyssey*. Though still hotly debated as to the earliest dates, Phoenician sailors had been making exploratory and trading forays to the middle, then western, coastline of the Mediterranean from well before the 1st millennium BC.

At some point they had intrepidly sailed through the Pillars of Hercules (Strait of Gibraltar) and brought back wondrous artefacts from the coastal villages of present-day Morocco. Most significant of all, they had become famous for their purchase and shipment of vast quantities of silver, mined and traded by the Tartessians in south-eastern Spain.

Assyrian pressure leads to westward migration

With King Asurnasirpal II (883-859BC) the Assyrian Empire started to 'squeeze' the Phoenician cities, initially forcing the payment of tribute – in various exotic forms – in return for being left alone. Gradually, however, these cities were too prosperous, influential and strategically important to be left alone. In the second half of the 8th century BC this 'tribute' phase turned into Assyrian domination of the Tyre-controlled hinterland – but not into a siege of the island city itself, presumably because Tyre's commercial supremacy (similar to that of Hong Kong in recent times) worked in the Assyrians' favour. Early in the 7th century BC, however, the city was repeatedly blockaded, leading the 'street-wise' Phoenicians to press ahead ever more vigorously with the rapid expansion of their strategic outpost Carthage, and a myriad of other key sites in the Western Mediterranean. Tyre itself managed to survive into the 6th century BC, but the ascendancy of Babylon – whose King Nebuchadnezzar laid siege for 13 years (585-572BC) – heralded its eventual demise, and to the eventual recovery of Sidon as the Levant's pre-eminent trading entrepot, a situation that lasted until the latter was conquered by Alexander the Great 300 years later.

The establishment of Carthage and satellite enclaves (control of 'stepping stones')

There are two areas of unrelenting debate, one as to the date when settlements in the Western Mediterranean first took place, and the second as to whether it was Assyrian pressure that forced the Phoenicians westward (to search for precious metals as tribute) or whether – predominantly – the Phoenicians were acting of their own accord. At present authors on each of these issues lie in two distinct (unreconciled!) camps. As to when Cadiz (in southern Spain, just into the Atlantic) and Utica (just north-west of Carthage) were founded, whatever the ancients wrote about much earlier dates, the fact is that no archaeological record has been unearthed in either case before the 8th century BC.

On the question of their being forced westwards or not, the opinion expressed here, which has a lot to do with *The Phoenicians and the West* by Maria Eugenia Aubet (2nd edition, 2001) is that – as each new decade reveals ever more detail about the plethora of Phoenician colonies in the western third of the Mediterranean – they must have planned their expansion, for three main reasons. The first would have been population pressure, since this has always been a factor when a dynamic nation that is confined geographically creates a high standard of living (through its manufacturing or mercantile success) over many generations. The second reason would have been the drier agricultural conditions in the Levant from c1200BC. Indeed, there is a view that the disruption at this time throughout the Central and Eastern Mediterranean – which enabled the 'Sea Peoples' to 'make hay' – was largely or partly caused by near-drought conditions. And the third reason was the relentless search for raw materials – ranging from the diminishing sources of copper and tin, through its replacement by iron ore, to silver and gold – in order to feed the array of manufacturing industries in Phoenicia.

To cap these three reasons, the Phoenicians may have rightly perceived that their long-term future in the west was set to benefit from the vacuum created by the collapse of the palace-based economies, and the ensuing fragmentation. Mycenaeans, Hittites and

157

Egyptians had conducted very formalised (mainly two-way) trade, with meticulous record-keeping. As the Dark Age turmoil subsided, the inviting potential of the whole Mediterranean sea was wide open to these expert sailors, with their commercial flair and no rigid hierarchy. Perhaps the nearest 'recent' comparison would be the Elizabethan buccaneering spirit, followed by the remarkable maritime-led achievements of the free-trading English and Dutch (two very small countries) in the ensuing centuries.

Strategy for control of the Western Mediterranean

In the early phase the Phoenicians did not have everything their own way. While by the middle of the 7th century BC they were well established along the south-eastern coast of Spain, on Ibiza, and in Sardinia (as well as most of western Sicily), they could not prevent the Phoceans (Greeks from the western coast of Turkey) from making forays across the Ligurian Sea to found Massalia (now Marseilles) and Emporion in Catalonia (now Empuries). Carthaginian defeat (at sea) around 600BC prompted an alliance with the Etruscans, which eventually resulted in this combination trouncing the Phoceans off their base Alalia (Corsica) in 535BC, thus putting to an end their ambitions on this island and on Sardinia.

Nevertheless, to sum up the particular skills that the Phoenicians had been honing for centuries, these were seafaring, with state-of-the-art warships, expert visualisation of key coastal sites to be adapted for their needs, commercial entrepreneurship, and manufacturing skills. If their seafaring skills are 'given', their commercial and manufacturing ambitions pivoted on their ability to obtain absolute security of the far-west of the known world, and – as Greeks and Romans would later discover the hard way – the drive for security was achieved by a series of supremely clever defensive measures.

The fortified harbour cities

The Phoenicians put into practice repeatedly all their accumulated experience from Tyre. They chose the most defensible *natural* harbours, then engaged in massive engineering works to *modify* the chosen site to their exacting requirements. Ms Aubet devotes several fascinating pages to a detailed examination of the *probable* natural topography of the Cadiz archipelago, and how they fashioned the area to meet their exacting standards. As with Tyre, an immediately available and secure source of plentiful fresh water was also always a prerequisite.

The 'instant' fleet, everywhere

In the specially built museum at Marsala lies a reconstructed Punic warship, found in the harbour in very shallow water, by the legendary marine archaeologist Honor Frost in 1969. This miracle of preservation – the oldest warship yet found – is thought to have been sunk in c250BC, during the first Punic War with Rome, and was carefully lifted from the seabed by Frost's archaeological team in 1971. It has taught us some crucial lessons about the way in which the Phoenicians (by that time Punics) had cleverly bolstered their matchless defensive armoury during the preceding 500 years (see *Motya: Unearthing a lost civilisation* by Gaia Servadio [1988]). The Greek historian Polybius (203-120BC) wrote in detail of the third Punic War and alleged that the Punics could assemble ships 'overnight' from kits supplied by Carthage, but nobody believed him. Pliny also said that they could build a fleet of 100 ships in two months! Now, after an interval of two millennia, the Punic secret was confirmed when Honor Frost discovered the unmistakable matched lettering on joined timbers, which had instructed the builders as to the required method of assembly! Not only that, but we now know that each Punic colony had a strategically positioned dry dock (a 'cothon') abutting the sea, in which the ship could be placed; the cothon was then flooded, and the vessel floated into the sea through a narrow opening, before the dock was drained so that the process could be repeated (see the intact cothon on Motya).

The 'stepping-stone' barrage

The distance between Cape Bon – the tip of Tunisia just east of both Utica and Carthage – and the tiny island of Motya just off the western coast of Sicily (near Marsala) is less than 100 miles (150km). By also occupying the island of Pantelleria, halfway between these two major settlements, the Phoenicians could effectively prevent any seaborne incursion to the west from taking place. In addition, they had a 'forward position' at Malta, and could also use the tiny island of Lampedusa.

(The Messina Strait between Sicily and the southern tip of Italy

159

gave the only other possibility of access, but was notorious in legend, and extremely hazardous in reality. As illustrated above, however, Greek settlements originating from directly across the Aegean became permanent colonies on either side of this waterway [in eastern Sicily and the southern half of Italy]. They remained a constant presence, as will be seen in the next chapter.)

The Phoenicians were invaders in the west, bringing a migrant population that was thinly spread around a comparatively vast area. Their religion, diet and other ways of life were quite alien to the indigenous populace of a wide number of countries. Yet, with tenuous lines of communication to their far-off homeland – unlike Greek colonists in Italy and eastern Sicily, who were always close to 'home' – they forged an effective maritime empire that survived for hundreds of years – with a never-ending struggle against the Greeks for control of Sicily. And it then took 150 years for them to be obliterated after three epic wars with Rome, all this due, in great measure, to the above remarkable – and unique – triple method of defence.

The Phoenician language, and its Greek and Latin derivations

Reference has been made earlier to the Akkadian cuneiform script, but the only scripts ever found in the Aegean are Linear A (still indecipherable today) and Linear B, which died in 1200-1100BC, with the demise of Mycenae. In the western Mediterranean no trace of any 2nd-millennium-BC language has ever been found. In total contrast there had been a developing array of languages in what today is termed the 'Middle East', as well as in Egypt, and (in the middle Bronze Age) a Hittite language in modern Turkey. To summarise these worlds apart, in stark terms that would have made George Grote shudder in 1850AD, written languages were second nature throughout the 'civilised' Middle East *continuously* from c3000BC, whereas the 'barbarian' far west of the known world remained completely mute in this crucial respect until c750BC.

Around 1500BC – during the Bronze Age phase when Canaanites occupied the entire Palestinian coastal strip – they adopted from West Semitics a proto-Sinaitic script that had spread northwards. From this was developed (c1400BC) a proto-Canaanite (north-west Semitic) alphabet, and this in turn was progressively transformed into the

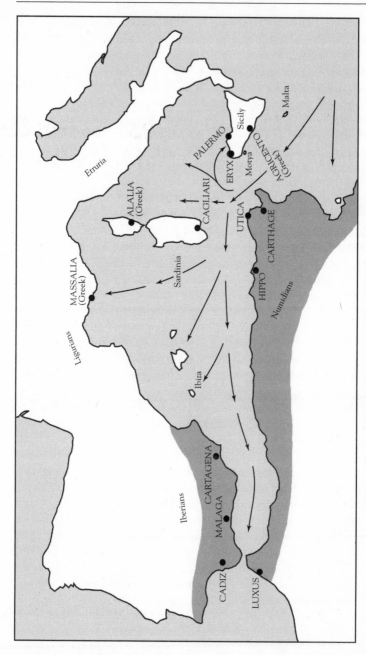

Map v – Phoenician colonisation of the western Mediterranean, c800-300BC

Phoenician alphabet over the next 200 years or so, appearing in an engraved epitaph on the sarcophagus of King Ahiram (c1200BC).

This alphabet – unlike cuneiform and Egyptian hieroglyphs – was *phonetic*, and by the 9th century BC had been reduced to 22 consonants, but with no vowels. It was this unique combination that the Phoenicians took with them to the Western Mediterranean – a combination that enabled the alphabet to be later utilised not only by differing peoples in a number of languages, but also by a much wider section of the populace, thereby diminishing one of the most powerful previously held weapons of the governing elites.

The long decline: versus Greece (500-300BC) and Rome (300-146BC)

As the Greek city states expanded rapidly, with dynamic colonies blossoming in mainland Italy and eastern Sicily, early trading relationships with Carthage (and its colonies) were bound to turn to conflict sooner or later. In particular – as many books have detailed – Sicily (the largest island in the Mediterranean) became an intermittent battleground. With Greek dominance in the east, and the Carthaginians' long-established position in the west – each side refuelled from their respective 'headquarters' – successive wars raged over a 200-year period, without any realistic possibility that either side would comprehensively defeat the other.

Then, when the whole region of Greek influence was absorbed into the rapidly emerging Roman Empire, it was inevitable that a 'fight to the finish' would ensue. As with the Greeks, Roman propaganda demonised the 'alien' Punics (with dreadful tales of child sacrifice), whom both nations considered to be 'oriental' impostors, not interested in their own ideas of high civilisation, let alone cultural brilliance. Thus, in 264BC, began the first of three Punic Wars – epic contests comprising 33 years of actual fighting spread across a 120-year period. Every schoolboy used to pay rapt attention to the heroic figure of Hannibal, who crossed the Alps with his elephants at the start of the second war, and – following crushing victories at Lake Trasimene in 217BC, and at Cannae in 216 – came tantalisingly close to capturing the city of Rome itself.

After such a close call, Rome rallied and thought it had sufficiently crushed the Punics by 201BC – in North Africa – that they would never again be a threat. However, turmoil ensued for the next half-century, with Gaul a provocative ally of Carthage. Finally, the Romans could stand the persistent threat to their 'global' ambitions no longer, and in 149BC launched a final assault, with the express intent of raising Carthage to the ground.

Many satellite cities of Carthage had long realised 'which way the wind was blowing', and pledged their neutrality, or active support of Roman intentions. But Carthage itself vowed to resist to the last. The cunningly fortified city proved immensely difficult to capture, with the Romans having to gain ground house by house. Even then, Carthaginian men, women and children – if they could not die fighting – preferred to commit suicide or die in the flaming ruins. Even the battle-hardened Roman generals were taken aback by these thousands of acts of self-sacrifice, but – under the leadership of Scipio Aemilianus, who was made Consul in 147BC, and was under the strictest mandate from Rome – the city (with its fortified harbours) was first levelled to the ground. Then the fires of battle were deliberately encouraged (probably aided by the copious use of pitch as a roof sealant) until the whole wider city area was completely destroyed.

Finally, as a last act that reflected Roman paranoia that somehow Carthage might rise from the ashes, instructions were given to 'sow' the whole area liberally with salt – including the surrounding countryside – so that no crops could ever flourish in the region again.

Chapter 14

Classical Greece and the colonial heritage

A t this momentous point in our story (the birth of arguably the greatest civilisation in the western hemisphere), it is perhaps appropriate to recap on the exponential archaeological progress that has been made since 1870, if for only two reasons: we still don't know the tribal/ethnic composition of the 'Classical' Greeks, and – partly as a result – we have no satisfactory explanation as to how these people displayed such 'cleverness' in every field from the start.

We have explored earlier how field archaeology made comparatively slow progress in its first century from 1870 to 1970, and, in Chapter 1, how the rapid development of a dozen new techniques has changed everything in the past 40 years. To this ever-increasing pace, we must add another phenomenon, if – as most experts believe – *some* part of the origins of this wondrous 'happening' lies to the north, in the modern-day Balkans, Bulgaria and Romania. There is evidence, not only of the Etruscans having migrated (probably by island-hopping) from Lydia in south-west Turkey to Tuscany, but also of Hittite refugees drifting westwards at the onset of the Dark Age, from Turkey into the north-west corner of Greece. The most fascinating conundrum, however, is what the amazing finds taking place currently – to the north of Greece – will eventually disclose. For it must be remembered that all those countries that lie there were only freed from Communism 20 years ago. More than that, as evidenced by Arthur Evans's travels c1880 this whole region has suffered almost continuous turmoil up to the present day, rendering to even the most devoted archaeologists a desperate (and poorly financed) environment in which to persist with their field research until very recently.

There must, therefore, be every chance that during the next 30-50 years of continuous endeavour amongst Greece's northern neighbours, vital clues will be revealed that give us at least partial answers to the two crucial, long-fought-over – questions:

1 Who exactly were the 'Classical Greeks'?
2 What 'chemistry' in their composition enabled them, so soon after the Dark Age drew to a close, to show such a remarkable capability in so many practical and intellectual disciplines?

Currently, the majority view is that the 'Dorian invasion' (from where did *they* originate?) was a modest affair, and that – like in so much of the world, even today – Greece was mostly the recipient along its porous borders of intermittent migrant 'seepage' from the north and east, resulting in a healthy increase from the low point of its Dark Age population, a population that had (from all our evidence) shrunk drastically from its Mycenaean zenith some 500 years previously.

Mycenaean-Homeric/Dark Age/Phoenician legacies

In the past 400 years we have the example of North America, where from only a tiny indigenous population in relation to the size of territory, but with fabulous natural resources, successive waves of mainly European immigrants created the most powerful nation on earth (the USA) and an extremely prosperous neighbour (Canada). It should not be thought, either, that most of these millions were the cream of European industry, commerce, or academia – the vast majority were the desperate (often persecuted) poor, prepared to work phenomenally hard to secure a better future in their adopted homeland. In Greece of the 9th and 8th centuries BC, while answers to the above questions can only – presently – be speculative, we can set out the *main* 'tools' that the polyglot (Greek for 'many-tongued') communities scattered across the mainland and countless islands inherited from their forebears in Greece, and from the surrounding region. We need to keep in mind that the fairly skimpy list that follows must have been augmented by the myriad aids to their rapid development that had survived the Dark Age, as a result of all the civilising and cultural activities of the past throughout the Peloponnese, the wider Mediterranean basin, and from even much further afield.

The Mycenaean-Homeric legacy

In his introduction to the 1996 edition of *The Greek Myths* by Robert Graves, the editor, Kenneth McLeish, writes:

'From earliest times, Greek myth not only validated the daily lives of the people who created and maintained it, but irradiated their imaginations. The myths offered precedents for, and examples of, everything: what beauty was; the difference between bravery and cowardice; how to be sly, proud, noble, faithful, long-suffering, a hero, a fraud, a nuisance. The characters and incidents of myth were so multifarious that they were not so much lateral to life as the continuum of life itself, and every variety of human experience and behaviour seemed to be contained in them.'

He continues:

'This richness ... dominated "high" artistic endeavour of every kind. Greek "imaginative" literature depended almost entirely on myth for themes... Public art, from the sculptures used to decorate buildings to wall-paintings and pottery in private houses, depicted myth's gods, monsters and heroes...'

He also (crucially) writes that 'Greek myth ... was also invasion-proof, ready (as the Roman poet Horace later put it) to "conquer the conquerors", and live on in cultures alien to those where it began.'

McLeish's hardback edition of Robert Graves's book is 666 pages of tightly packed script that includes only a handful of illustrations. It deals with hundreds of mythical figures, and – as we have read earlier – it was Homer who (after centuries in which memorised details had been passed by word of mouth from generation to generation) first wrote down, in the *Iliad* and the *Odyssey*, details of all the main 'characters' in these most convoluted epic tales.

The Dark Age legacy

While in terms of peasant and artisanal living many of the Mycenaean skills acquired many centuries ago would have been carried on in a humdrum fashion, as we have also read, earlier clear-cut advances in pottery techniques were made that – from the springboard of the geometric period – soon blossomed into the most beautiful range of designs. Most important of all, by 900-850BC the Iron Age was all-pervasive, including the period when use of this material for luxury items only became superseded by the manipulation of iron for a wide range of burial, military, domestic and manufacturing uses.

The Phoenician legacy

From the previous chapter we know that the Phoenician alphabet was adopted by the Greeks in their 'homeland', and in each of their growing number of colonies. However, to the 22 acquired consonants they added four vowels – probably (though not certainly) utilising 'defunct' or surplus Phoenician letters. As we can imagine – especially if we try momentarily to speak without vowels! – this inclusion enabled the developing language to flow much more smoothly. Initially the adopted language was spoken in a wide variety of dialects, but there eventually developed the unified Ancient Greek that we know today.

It is also of *great* note that the Greeks adopted a decimalised system of numerals directly from the Phoenician method – a type of 'shorthand' known as 'positional notation' – and this was the key building block for their remarkable arithmetical and subsequent sophisticated mathematical skills.

The other priceless asset – which did not come to the Greeks by a kind of osmosis (another Greek word, meaning 'push'!) – was ship construction, particularly 'state of the art' warship design. It is most likely that Persians (in the east) and later Romans (to the west) adopted Phoenician design technology, but – after a series of defeats in their early conflicts – the Greeks realised where their disadvantage lay, and deliberately *stole* the key Phoenician design features. These were the features by means of which, for centuries, Carthaginian designers and craftsman had given their naval brethren unmatched superiority – in manoeuvrability, in speed, in a reinforced prow for ramming purposes, and in the 'knock-down' componentry for instant volume assembly at any port within their control that had a 'cothon' (dry dock).

To match the Phoenicians at sea was one thing, but it is at least arguable that without such a deliberate policy of design improvement the Greeks would never have turned the tables on the mighty Persians at Salamis in 480BC – let alone have been able to soundly defeat them at Plataea the following year, thus putting an end to the long-held Persian ambition to conquer the Greek mainland.

Any near-academic who has troubled to read this book so far will deem it to be only a potted history, which, of course, is what it is meant to be! The same individual will think this chapter – together with Chapters 15 on Alexander and his legacy, and 16 on Rome – are 'super-potted'. Any attempt here to write in detail on these two pre-eminent eras would take up hundreds of pages, and in any case the discerning reader has dozens of specialist tomes to turn to, if he or she so wishes. This trio of chapters, therefore, does not focus on military exploits, but instead tries to give a flavour of the breadth and depth of Greek and Roman civil and cultural achievements.

The Early Archaic 'moment' is considered to have lasted 200 years. This was followed by the Archaic 'moment', and a century later by the Classical 'moment'. From 600BC until long after Alexander's death, ancient Greek history represented as convoluted a story of colonisation overseas, invasion at home, civil war, political upheaval, the search for and exploitation of resources, and economic fluctuation, as has been seen anywhere before or since. However, although the above complexities made the Greeks 'what they were', we are most interested in their truly unique legacy, as tortuously passed down to the Early Renaissance more than 1,500 years later. Therefore the rest of this chapter will only make occasional reference to these 'habitual' aspects of history, and will instead try to highlight the individuals (together with magnificent sites and inimitable works of art) whose contributions were eventually to change the nature of European civilisation and culture for ever.

Early Archaic: from 800BC

Even as the Phoenicians were migrating to the far west, so did the Greeks – to eastern Sicily, southern Italy, and the south of France. But they also spread east, into Western Turkey, and even as far afield as a trading station (Al Mina) at the mouth of the Orontes River (in modern-day Syria). As a result of their eastern exploits, one remarkable feature was that Greek artistic expression took on an *eastern* style, a startling transformation from the previous geometric designs. This *oriental* influence permeated art, in all forms, whether this was in the *rectangular* structures that started to appear, or on monumental pottery, later emerging in carving, all types of building, and human sculptures. Whether by continued immigration, or through an indigenous phenomenon, population increase gathered momentum throughout the (now definitely) Greek world, especially in the fast-growing cities. And a particular feature in Athens was the rise of dominant families, who claimed ancient (even Mycenaean) ancestry. They emphasised their self-bestowed special status by elaborate worship of their dead, and even by utilising long-neglected Mycenaean tombs. It was at this time that the main cities were ruled by successive 'tyrannies' (from the Greek 'turannos').

By the beginning of the 7th century BC the Greek alphabet became firmly established, perhaps initiated by the firm Phoenician links with Crete. This theory derives from the early Cretan dialect of the Archaic period having a distinctly Phoenician edge to it. Of course, Homer's works were firmly established, but his (almost) contemporary Hesiod also made his lasting mark. Whereas Homer's works were seen from the standpoint of the nobility, Hesiod's most famous 800-verse poem *Works and Days* expressed the views of the peasant farmer, although he is also an important source for astronomy and time-keeping, as well as mythology. To keep abreast of developments in the rest of the known world, although we covered the Phoenician consolidation in the Western Mediterranean in the previous chapter, this era saw other fundamental shifts: the height of the Hallstadt Iron Age culture (in modern-day Austria); the weakening of the Assyrian Empire from its height at around 1000BC (Middle East and Levant coast); and – most significant of all in the long term – the foundation of Rome.

High Archaic: 600BC

The zenith of Archaic flowering was marked by a 'knowledge explosion' and an ever-widening range of achievements. As Van Doren notes, '...it could be claimed that the ancient Greek investigators understood at least as well as we do what can and cannot be reasonably said about human nature and a good life'. He also states that '...the Greek knowledge explosion may even seem to be the more widely influential of the two' (meaning as compared with 'our' explosion dating from the early Renaissance). Of course, just like today the Greeks made many mistakes, some with disastrous consequences. They were the first people to lucidly identify the concept of *arrogance*, devising the 'sin' of 'hubris', which was invariably punished by the goddess Nemesis.

The 6th century BC also covered the lives of several brilliant men.

Thales

Thales was born at the key city of Miletus in Ionia, the Greek coastal region of western Turkey in around 625BC. He is widely regarded as being the first philosopher, and the first scientist. He believed there to be a 'cosmos' – a universe or world 'order' – he was sure that water held the key to life, and he crystallised a series of fundamental geometric principles. Thales may have inherited some of his polymathic skills (Greek 'polumathes' – 'having learned much') from predecessors but, because none of the many works he is alleged to have written until his death in c546BC, have come down to us, we will never have an answer to this question.

This was the age in which coinage became established. Millennia of exchange by barter had become augmented by certain 'standard' bargaining 'chips' in key materials. Initially the most notable item was obsidian (in various forms), succeeded by copper, then bronze ingots. Probably originating in Turkey, electrum coins started to take the place of the latest material (iron 'bars') and quickly spread throughout the region, mainly in the form of pure silver. The importance of cities escalated, with the stirrings of democracy in Athens being counterbalanced by the rise of the martial city state of Sparta in the south-central region of the Peloponnese. This era also saw the pronounced influence of 'black' figured pottery, most art being exemplified by its most beautiful simplicity.

In addition to Thales, three other men – each in their field – helped to pave the way for the spectacular achievements of the 5th century BC onwards. Here there can only be the briefest summary of the key attributes of each.

Solon

A native Athenian, living from 638 to 558BC, he was a statesman, lawmaker and poet. Crucially – in a tyrannical era – he was so appalled by what he saw as a decline in standards at Athens that he attempted to legislate against political, economic and moral decline. Though

170

meeting with only marginal success, he is nevertheless credited with having laid the foundation of Athenian democracy.

Pythagoras

Born on Samos, and living from c580 to c500BC, he was – and is still – regarded as the father of mathematics. He had a dissident and arrogant personality, in which his disciples were thoroughly inculcated. Following in the footsteps of Thales, his 'team' propounded many theories, of which every schoolboy used to know (!) the most famous – pi. This 16th letter of the alphabet is also the numerical value of the relationship of the circumference of a circle to its diameter (22 divided by 7). The Pythagoreans – tormented by what they saw as 'irrational' numbers that were 'dangerous' – were constantly hounded from city to city, to such an extent that their movement was eventually driven to extinction.

Xenophanes

Born at Kolophon (north-west of Ephesus) and living from 570 to 480BC, he was the first of the philosopher-poets who explicitly wrote for future generations, one of his surviving fragments claiming 'fame that will reach all Greece, and never die while the Greek kind of song survives'. He was also a social and religious commentator, who was a pioneer in rejecting the notion of the gods taking a human form, and suggested one deity above all others, thereby being an early proponent of monotheism.

Other 6th century BC landmarks

The 6th century BC also saw a significant rise in *religious* activity. In particular, the prestige of Delphi, Olympia, Mount Olympus, and – perhaps most of all – Eleusis started to become ingrained in the Greek psyche. Demeter – subject of the Homeric hymn, of which we have a written record – was the goddess of grain. The temple to her at Eleusis, situated in the mainland bay north of Salamis – which celebrated the cycle of resurrection and rebirth, in all its aspects – was linked to Athens by a 12-mile (20km) 'sacred way'.

The Athens Acropolis – 'akron' (summit), 'polis' (city) – is a flat-topped hill that stands 490 feet (150m) above sea level. Occupied since Neolithic times, there is still speculation as to whether a Mycenaean palace stood on the site, but it was the Mycenaeans who definitely constructed a typically cyclopean perimeter wall, and secured a deep well at the north-eastern corner of the site. In the early Archaic period, this spring, the Clepsydra, was protected within a new walled fortification. A temple was built to the goddess Athena in the mid-7th century BC, and another to the same goddess in the latter part of the century. It is from this time (c625BC) that the elegant Peplos Kore dates, one of many fine sculptures of young females (and males), the exact religious purpose of which has not been clearly established.

In the fields of architecture, pottery, sculpture and metalwork, the century saw many other staggering achievements, of which just a few examples may be described: at the very outset (c620BC), from Melos, a monumental amphora, vividly showing the 'orientalising' style of vase painting; found at Olympia, a lovely gold Corinthian offering bowl from about 600BC; a wonderful helmet from Archanes (south of Knossos, Crete) also dates from c600BC; the 'Francois' vase from c570BC, now in the Etruscan Museum at Florence, was an early masterwork of Greek narrative drawing; and from the island of Siphnos, beautiful marble decorations of the Treasury from c530BC.

However, perhaps the most intriguing find of all is the enormous bronze Spartan 'krater' (wine container) found at Vix, at the foot of Mont Lassois in the middle of France. Discovered in 1953 within the grave complex of a Gaulish princess, this remarkable artefact – at a crucial trading crossroads – dates from c500BC, at the height of the Celtic La Tene dynasty, whose centre was at Hallein in Austria. The vessel stands 5ft 5in (1.64m) high and weighs one-fifth of a tonne. It had a capacity of 270 gallons (1,200 litres) and – since the beaten body is only 1mm thick in places – it begs the question: did the object or the craftsman travel from either the Greek mainland, or even from a Greek colony in Italy? Considered to be one of the finest (if not *the* finest) examples of Laconian (Spartan) art, this masterpiece is – not surprisingly – the focus of the charming little museum at Chatillon-sur-Seine. In 2006 further crucial finds were made at the site (6km to the north), demonstrating that this extremely tall princess (whose beautiful funeral chariot has been reconstructed) resided in a Celtic palace, the only one to have been located in the whole of modern-day France.

At the same time as Darius was conquering a moribund Egypt, and creating his huge empire, we now know (from a 19th-century discovery) that at Gortyn, in southern Crete, a legal code was being promulgated; it was being inscribed in more than 600 lines, on stone masonry, at some point in the 6th century BC. In Athens and other cities, the tug-of-war between law-based democratic tendencies and aggressive control by tyrants ebbed and flowed. Meanwhile, while most embryonic city states were not imbued with militaristic instincts – certainly not as compared with the Carthaginians or Persians – the one perennial exception was Sparta in the south-central Peloponnese, which glorified its warriors, and whose capacity for mischief was limitless. Ironically, it was Spartan expansion through most of the Peloponnese, and eastwards past Corinth towards Athens – directly or via their allies – that set the scene for their intervention in the overthrow of the last tyrant of Athens, paving the way for the introduction of democracy.

On a completely different note, the Greek interest in athletic sports had been developing since the early Archaic age, with the stadium at Olympia being the 'headquarters'. Over time, a considerable array of events developed, ranging from 'foot races' to throwing events, jumping, wrestling, all-in fighting and horse-racing. Meticulous records were kept – for example, the origin of foot-race winners over several centuries, with individuals hailing from every corner of the Greek realm. Sporting activities were deemed to be excellent military training, and great prestige was attached to individual winners in all disciplines, as well as to their families. Finally, as 500BC approached, apart from the specific regions of actual or impending colonisation, the geographical reach of the Greeks was now vastly greater than the very limited world known to Homer. Apart from their own journeys east to the Hindu Kush, via the first 'Suez Canal' built by Darius, they had become aware of the incredible Phoenician explorations around Africa, and (past Spain and France) around the British Isles, which even extended to travels up the near-Arctic coast of Norway.

The Classical Age: 500 to 330BC

The springboard for arguably the greatest flowering of knowledge the world has known – at least until the Early Renaissance 1,700 years later – was the emergence of *democracy* in Athens. Indeed, Van Doren states that '...the Greeks probably carried philosophy, especially ethical philosophy, farther than we have been able to.' The comparatively small triangular peninsula of Attica had been (mostly)

173

united for centuries, and the Athenians took pride in their continuity from Mycenaean times. Attica was rugged and not very fertile, but had the (literally) priceless advantage of the deep silver mines at Laurion, as well as inexhaustible supplies of fine marble from Mount Pentelikon, and it was these materials, and the 'empire' that was now created, that combined to make Athens rich.

The advent of democracy

Although Solon's reforms in the mid-6th century BC succumbed to a further rule by tyrants, the last of these was overthrown at the end of the century by a combination of (external) Spartan pressure and (internal) aristocratic determination. It was then that **Kleisthenes** (dates uncertain) carried through far-reaching reforms of such thoroughness (and complexity) that, as stated in *Atlas of the Greek World* by Peter Levi (1991):

> '...the Athenians invented the social basis of democracy. That is why many people are more interested in them than they are for example in the Egyptians... If another reason exists, then it must be the startling literature of the Greeks...'

Whereas earlier tyrants thrived on regional conflict, Kleisthenes set up a format designed to put an end to interminable disputes. He redrew the tribal map of Attica, specifically so as to make democracy possible. The new map effectively created 10 new tribes from the 30 differing sections ('trittyes') of Attica, wherein men with a common bond could fight a common enemy (as necessary), and wherein 50 representatives from each of the new tribes – only some of whom were from influential or famous families – were elected to the 'Boule' (Athenian council). Council members started to be returned to the Boule from remote villages ('demes'), thereby giving voice to local concerns that were far removed from Athenian politics. This patchwork tribal system proved its staying power by surviving not only the period of democracy, but even lasting into the Roman era! After Kleisthenes, **Kimon** (510-450) was the next major democratic figure in a turbulent world. After the close call against the Persians in 480-479BC, Kimon played a major role in building up the Athenian navy, and was responsible for defeating another Persian challenge (at the Eurymedon River) in 466. However, only five years later – after an unsuccessful expedition in

174

support of Sparta – he was ostracised (a democratic Athenian mechanism for a disgraced citizen, involving 10-year exile!), but then brought back in 451BC to broker a peace with Sparta. Kimon always opposed the democratic (anti-aristocratic) revolution of Ephialtes, but lost out to him and his most famous deputy, Pericles.

Pericles (c495-429) was the most famous Athenian leader, who presided over affairs during the benign 'golden' period between the Persian and Peloponnesian wars. Pericles had such an impact on Athenian society that the historian Thucydides claimed him to be 'the first citizen of Athens'. He promoted the arts and literature, and was a driving force behind 'development' of the Acropolis. Most of all, however, Pericles was an out-and-out *democrat*, such that he was damned as a 'populist' by his frustrated opponents. In the baleful atmosphere that followed the catastrophic defeat by Sparta, *democratic* Athens had no choice but to submit to an oligarchic regime. The glory of Athens was never quite recaptured, although famous statesmen and orators could still emerge.

A century after Pericles, one such luminary was **Demosthenes** (384-322BC), who rose to prominence in (vain) opposition to Philip of Macedon, and his son Alexander the Great.

Colonies to the east

Mycenaeans had all but colonised Cyprus as long ago as the late 13th century BC, and as early as the 9th century BC Greeks had firmly established themselves along the whole of the west coast of Turkey, apart from the north-westerly Troad (Troy) region. This area, together with the rest of the northern Aegean coastal strip, and the Black Sea, Levantine coast, Nile delta and (via Crete) the Libyan coast (Cyrenaica), had all come under Greek influence (if not outright control) by the early 6th century BC. Particularly in western Turkey, several cities – including Miletus and Ephesus – were famed throughout the Mediterranean, but the westward ambitions of the Persians quickly curbed Greek hegemony. First (around 600BC) they captured the Levantine coast. More critically, by 500BC they had occupied the whole of Turkey and the eastern Aegean islands, whence many famous refugees arrived in Athens, and were to have enormous *oriental* influence there – these included Pythagoras (from Samos) and Xenophanes (from Kolophon, north of Ephesus).

Colonies to the west

During the 6th century BC Greek colonies blossomed throughout the heel of Italy, the Aeolian Islands, and the whole of south-eastern Sicily. They created outposts along coastal Etruria, and, in the teeth of (long-established) Phoenician/Carthaginian opposition, at Massalia (Marseilles) and at Emporion (north-east Spain). Architecturally, several of the western city states outshone Athens by 500BC, one glittering example being the temples we see today at the small colony of Poseidonia (Roman Paestum, south of Naples). An even more brilliant history was that of Akragas (Agricento, on the south coast of Sicily), where their early temples were unsurpassed in beauty at that time. A modern-day working example is also to be found in Sicily at Syracuse, where the (slightly worn!) pillars of a vast Doric temple from c500BC still project from the walls (as aisles) in the cathedral.

Taking Peter Levi's above words about 'startling literature', and since so many characters in our illustrious catalogue are distinguished by having been truly polymathic, they have been segregated – with difficulty! – by virtue of the *pre-eminent* talents for which their lives will always remain so justly renowned. The categories that follow are philosophy and poetry; history; play-writing; mathematics; architecture; sculpture; engineering; decorative arts; and music – each chronologically. Although later some colonies, most notably Syracuse, developed an extremely assertive independence, it is especially significant that, from the 5th century BC onwards, brilliant men from all corners of the Greek 'empire' came under the influence of Athens, in most cases leaving their homeland to live there. At the same time, however, each in turn provided that city (the centre of the Western world) with a unique contribution that was in part derived from their colonial background, providing an unmatched stimulus from generation to generation.

Philosophy and poetry

Herakleitos (c525-456BC), born at Ephesus, claimed to be self-educated, though he may have been influenced by his predecessor born nearby, Xenophanes. Herakleitos hated Ephesus and Athens in equal measure for – as he saw it – all their failings. He was a loner who believed that the only constant was constant change, generally disliked humankind, and talked in riddles. To use the modern idiom, he seemed 'to carry the world on his shoulders', but it is clear that his enigmatic behaviour made a deep impression on the next generation.

Socrates (469-399BC) was a native Athenian and was another enigmatic figure; none of his writings survived beyond his lifetime. His ethical philosophy has only come down to us through his devotees Xenophon and Plato, and – much later – through the writing 'licence' taken by Aristophanes in his plays (see all three below). The Socratic Method lives with us still, being a tool used in wide-ranging discussions, whereby the questions asked do not only provoke specific answers, but also encourage a deeper insight from those present into the issues 'on the table'. Socrates lived through the Athenian trauma of losing the Peloponnesian war to Sparta, he criticised the 'new politics' at a very sensitive time, and Plato described him as a 'gadfly', repeatedly stinging the authorities into action.

Fed up with Socrates's influence over the young, the powers-that-be accused him of corruption. He could quite easily have acquired a mild punishment, but so tormented his prosecutors that he was sentenced to death by poisoning. Even then he could have escaped through his rich friend Crito's bribery of his guards, but believed that no philosopher could show fear of death, and also that he had betrayed his own principle of never to seriously harm the state. He died by taking hemlock, in calm discussion with Crito to the last.

Plato (c.429-347BC), also Athenian by birth, was Socrates's most devoted follower, though they disagreed on many issues. After Socrates's death he and other 'disciples' left Athens, and spent many years in other areas of Greece. At about the age of 40 Plato returned to Athens and founded a school for the systematic conduct of research in philosophy and mathematics. The school was located on land previously owned by one Academus (hence 'academy'), and Plato devoted the rest of his life to this cause. The Academy became so entrenched in the fabric of Athens that it continued to function until AD529, when it was closed by Justinian I (Emperor of the Eastern Empire), who judged that it threatened the propagation of Christianity.

Plato (like Socrates) was deeply concerned about political and moral issues, both men – remarkably for their time – treating the importance of man's influence on happiness or misery, including women, foreigners and perhaps even slaves! As Levi writes: 'In Plato's great dialogue about justice, *The Republic*, he had defended the thesis that rulers only deserve to rule if they have undergone an intensive and far-reaching education, so as to have become philosophers!'

'Until philosophers are kings, or the kings and princes of this world have the spirit and power of philosophy, and political greatness and wisdom meet in one, and those commoner natures who pursue either to the exclusion of the other are compelled to stand aside, cities will never have rest from their evils – no, nor the human race, as I believe.'

With all the suffering that mankind has inflicted on itself ever since, who could today improve on this remarkable credo, 2,350 years after it was written?

Aristotle (384-322BC), was born at Stageira in Chalkidiki (in ancient times part of Thrace, but now in south-east Macedonia), and was sent to Athens at the age of 17 to study at the Academy, becoming Plato's most famous – and most argumentative – pupil. On Plato's death, he travelled for more than a decade, founding a number of academies in several cities. Returning to Macedonia, he spent three years tutoring Alexander, the son of King Philip, then (in 335BC) opened the Lyceum in Athens. This school, in contrast to the Academy, was solely devoted to scientific work, but when Alexander died in 323BC a movement hostile to him arose, and Aristotle – declaring that it ill-behoved the Athenians to kill a second philosopher – retired to Chalcis (on the island of Euboea), where he died only a year later.

Aristotle wrote on an incredible array of subjects, most of which – very fortuitously (see Chapters 22 and 23) – have come down to us through his having had a profound influence on Renaissance thinking. He taught us how to reason, and invented the science of logic. He also invented the idea of dividing the sciences into different fields that were distinguished by both subject matter and methodology. Several of his theories were only corrected or modified by Newton, while not until the 19th century were some of his observations finally confirmed. Curiously enough, one sharp divergence between Socrates and Plato was Aristotle's unswerving belief in the superiority of the *Greek male*. Women and slaves were inherently inferior in his view – it was even risky to teach non-Greeks, to which end he cautioned Alexander to prohibit his aides 'from intermarrying with barbarians, lest the virus of inferiority infect the superior [Greek] race'.

178

Epicurus (341-270BC), born in Samos of Athenian-born parents, went back to Athens for his military service, but then decided to join his family after their politically motivated expulsion to Colophon, on the Turkish coast. Eventually returning to Athens in 306BC, he founded his school – the 'Garden' (because of its location) – specifically to promote his views that philosophy's purpose was to achieve a happy and peaceful life, 'ataraxia' (though not to be taken to excess), with the term 'aponia' denoting freedom from fear, hence the modern term 'Epicureanism'.

History

The conflict with Persia between 490 and 479BC galvanised the fractious Greek 'statelets' into united action. They boasted that while they were *voluntarily* defending their freedom – meaning their unique ability, as they saw it, to live as *free individuals* – much of the Persian army (and navy) was conscripted. It was the afterglow of this heroic stance against the most powerful empire in the Western world at that time that inspired Herodotus and Thucydides to invent the new science and literary form of 'history'. It is supremely ironic that Thucydides's attention was largely diverted from the wider aspects of this subject towards narrow analysis of the immensely damaging Peloponnesian wars, wherein Athens and Sparta fought each other (almost) to a standstill intermittently through the last 70 years of the 5th century BC. The fleeting 'Athenian Empire' collapsed, with Persia – via the bribery of allies to each side – gaining consolation for its humiliating defeats earlier in the century, and (in controlling central Turkey) considerable influence through the 4th century BC.

Herodotus (c425-c484BC) was born at Halicarnassus (modern Bodrum, on the southern coast of Turkey). He was an inveterate traveller who made copious notes of all he met, saw and heard. For his background to the war with Athens, he had the intellect to research most assiduously the origins of both the Persian Empire and the Egyptian dynasties. All in all, it is only just to give Herodotus enormous credit for his attempts to cross-check his facts and assemble his journal correctly – his extensive writings showed expertise in both (what we now call) ethnicity and anthropology.

Until the science of archaeology took root, many historians were highly critical of the historical accuracy in his writings, some even claiming that Herodotus merely made up what he did not know.

However, his credibility has been largely restored in recent times, two of the spectacular sites of which he wrote, and now rediscovered, being the ruins of ancient Gelonus in Scythia (located in 1975), and the (long-submerged) ruins of Heraklion, Egypt's main port near Alexandria (pinpointed in 2000). His death occurred before he could make any sense of the tragedy of the Peloponnesian War.

Thucydides (c460-c404BC), an Athenian, came from a wealthy family and was well educated. He joined the army during the Peloponnesian War and, because his family may have owned gold mines in Thrace, was stationed (as a general) at Thasos. Summoned to assist in the defence of Amphipolis against the Spartans in the winter of 424BC, Thucydides arrived too late to avoid the resident commander suing for peace. This city of strategic importance was thus lost to Spartan control, and – in a nutshell – Thucydides, in becoming the victim of Athenian consternation and scorn, was forced into an exile that lasted for 20 years until his death. Taking this blow with great equanimity – and being able to travel amongst the Peloponnesian allies – Thucydides dedicated himself to understanding the causes of this suicidal conflict, as seen from every standpoint. During this 20-year period of continuous conflict he wrote a very thorough history, which – because of its length – was divided into eight books after his death. But, within a welter of detail, the aspect for which Thucydides gained everlasting fame and controversy in equal measure was his invention of a device, namely (quoting Van Doren) '...the insertion into the narrative of speeches by important war figures, which, for their eloquence and apparent verisimilitude, are almost unique in history.'

He could not of course have been present as these speeches were being made, but he defended himself by stating that he investigated the facts surrounding each instance as carefully as possible. In any event, the legacy we have of (for example) the funeral oration given by Pericles (c495-429BC), who was the Athenian leader during the early years of the war, can rarely have been surpassed as a tribute by a leader to the courage of his fellow citizens. Thucydides watched with growing horror the pointlessness of the bitter conflict, with the democratically minded Athenians having recourse to the terrorising methods of their enemies. By implication, Thucydides had to conclude – not long before his sad death – that, in exchange for the chance of victory (which never came), Athens was tragically surrendering her soul.

Xenophon (c431-354BC) was born near Athens into a wealthy family, and became a professional soldier who – in 401BC – became involved in Cyrus the Younger's doomed attempt to wage war with his elder brother Artaxerxes II. The convoluted sequence of events led to the main body of defeated Greek mercenaries (the 'Ten Thousand') being stranded in hostile territory in western Mesopotamia. New leaders were elected (including Xenophon) and an epic march north-east took place – fighting off successive enemies – until the battered army reached the Black Sea. From there they made their way west to Greece, where they were immediately recruited by the Spartans, so as to overthrow the King of Thrace!

The key aspect in all this was that Xenophon (like Thucydides exiled by Athens) used his incredible experiences to write a complete history of the expedition – *Anabasis* – which has come down to us intact. He also wrote *Hellenica*, which covered the last years of the Peloponnesian Wars, from the time of Thucydides's death. Crucially, having been a pupil of Socrates – who disapproved of his joining Cyrus – Xenophon's Socratic writings (preserved complete) are, together with those of Plato, the best of the 'Socratikoi logoi' genre of which we are aware.

Mathematics

Little is known of Greek mathematics until the work of Thales in the High Archaic age, though the findings of its most famous practitioners may well owe a debt to Minoan and Mycenaean civilisations. It is thought that his inquisitive mind led Thales to travel to both Babylon and Egypt. Most famously, he developed the 'Theorem of Thales', which asserts that an angle inscribed in a semi-circle is a right-angle. We have also briefly covered the life of Pythagoras in the same era. In the Classical era there was one individual who shone above all others, much of whose work is still as valid today as it was in his lifetime.

Euclid's most influential life is shrouded in mystery, so much so that we only know that he was working in Alexandria during the reign of Ptolemy I (323-283BC). Via his *Elements* he contributed more of substance than any other historical individual has managed to bring to this subject, particularly in the field of geometry. Not widely disseminated until the 19th century, his principles still serve as the backbone of modern teaching in many areas. We know that he wrote other works, not all of which survive. Those that do contain other theories of Euclid – nearly all of which have stood the test of time.

Playwriting

From the Archaic period, major festivals had 'theatrical' events wherein an individual representing a god or ancient hero would declaim from a 'stage', and interact with a chosen chorus that represented the people. All this changed early in the 5th century BC.

Aeschylus (c525-c465BC) is believed to have been born at Eleusis, the famous religious centre, only 12 miles (20km) from Athens. He made the (then) startling move of placing a second 'actor' on the stage, and the infinite possibilities of drama leapt into human consciousness. For a time, the chorus remained important, but quite soon a full troupe of actors took to the centre-stage. As with the great historians, Aeschylus had been a soldier who fought against Persia at the Battle of Marathon. He may also have been involved at Salamis and Plataea; his gravestone, recording his fame as a soldier, is silent on his (everlasting) achievements as a dramatist. Only six (possibly seven) of his many works survive; we know this from his reputed 13 first prizes at the annual 'City Dionysia' competition.

Aeschylus's most famous works are contained in his majestic trilogy *The Orestia*, about the hero Agamemnon, his murderous wife Clytemnestra, and his vengeful son Orestes. His central theme is that *hubris* was Agamemnon's downfall, and that the angry gods exacted their revenge on his descendants. As true today as ever, it is *justice*, says Aeschylus, that 'is the smoke of common men's houses', with *arrogance* bringing great men down, due to the fury of the gods.

Sophocles (c496-406BC) was born just outside Athens. In his long life he wrote more than 100 plays, winning the 'City Dionysia' competition perhaps as many as 20 times. He wrote from his teenage years and, being aged 30 when Aeschylus died, took further the examination of tragedy, namely that all men are caught in an inevitable trap. His proposition was that all men felt compelled to claim a confident understanding of their future, but that – since none actually *knew* what 'was around the corner' – they could not fail to commit dreadful errors that brought about their (inevitable) downfall.

Sophocles's verses are held on the one hand to be unsurpassed in their grace and appeal, but on the other to display to the audience the true horror of man's wretched pattern of life. In *Oedipus at Colonus* he shows that we cannot countenance 'not to be born', but that having 'seen the light' (of day) we wish we could 'go back quickly whence we came'. More of his works survive than is the case with Aeschylus, the two other most famous examples being *Oedipus the King* and *Antigone*. Sophocles lived out his life in Athens, spurning invitations to travel elsewhere – unlike Aeschylus, who died in Sicily, or Euripides, who lived his last year (and died) in Macedonia. As was the custom, he favoured adolescent boys, was involved in more than one recorded 'incident', and (according to Plato) was quite relieved by old-age impotence, finally to be free of his 'raging and savage beast of a master'.

Euripides (c486-406BC) was born in Salamis, and was the last of the great 5th century BC triumvirate of dramatists. Though he did not outshine his illustrious predecessors, he had a modern outlook, treating the gods as mortals (with all the accompanying flaws) and ranging from tragic to comic real-life situations. Far more than Aeschylus or Sophocles, he portrayed women – as well as slaves – in everyday stories, with the many issues that confronted all Athenian citizens. Euripides, who 'only' won four 'City Dionysia' competitions, left a considerable body of work, thanks partly to the discovery of a manuscript that lay in a monastery for 800 years, in which his plays were set out in alphabetic order. Among the most famous of his works are *Alcestis, Medea, Trojan Women* and *The Bacchae*.

Unlike Aeschylus, both Sophocles and Euripides endured the Peloponnesian War from its beginning until (dying within months of each other) two years before its end. Both dramatists filled their later plays with anguished cries to the gods against the prolonged physical and mental suffering caused by the seemingly endless struggle, and the way in which Greek overconfidence after her victory against the Persians earlier in the century had ultimately caused her bankruptcy, in the pursuit of a pointless and cruel war.

Aristophanes (c446-386BC) was another Athenian, who was aged 40 when his two great predecessors died, Aristophanes wrote in complete contrast to the three peerless tragedians, his unmistakeable style being comedy. Only a quarter of his plays survive, but they display great powers of ridicule, and merciless caricatures of such luminaries as Cleon, a demagogue (naked populist) during the early stages of the Peloponnesian War. Plato blamed Aristophanes's play *The Clouds* for constituting a slander on Socrates, claiming that this was a catalyst for the latter's subsequent trial and execution.

However, that such a poet and playwright – 'sailing so close to the wind' – could survive throughout such a turbulent period probably indicated that Aristophanes himself always steered well clear of any political ambitions or involvement.

Architecture

While even the Greek literature we have fortuitously been bequeathed – and cursorily explored above – is only known (in any depth) within the world of academia, and most ancient artefacts can only be seen in museums around the world, the one aspect that is vividly imprinted on the minds of countless millions is Classical Greek architecture. Whether seen in the flesh or in holiday brochures, the proliferation of breathtaking achievements from 2,500 years ago is reinforced in our minds by the 'copycat' approach first adopted by the Romans, then (after an interval of another millennium) in virtually every country of the world since the Renaissance. However much had been achieved in the Archaic era – and however wonderful are the standing Greek temples that can be seen through much of the Mediterranean – we shall concentrate here on the Athenian structures that represent the acme of perfection achieved in the Classical Age, and the earliest of the fabulous theatres.

The **Acropolis**, the outstanding rock that overlooks the flat city of Athens, was first enclosed as a fortress and sanctuary by the Mycenaeans in the 13th century BC, with typically massive walls and precipitous access to a secure water supply, at great depth. After the Persians sacked the city in 480BC, their fleeting control was overturned in that year at Salamis, and at Plataea in 479, and immediately thereafter celebrations of the astounding turn of events were crystallised by an intensive period of rebuilding, firstly under the governance of Kimon, then under one of Athens's most famous sons, Pericles.

The **Temple of Hephaestus** (known as the 'Hephaisteion' or 'Theseion') was not built on the Acropolis, but within the Agora (the original marketplace). While Hephaestus was the god of metal-working, the name Theseion was based on the supposition that the temple housed the remains of Theseus, the legendary founder-king of Athens who had reputedly been buried on the island of Skyros. This first great building of the reconstruction period, which is the most complete example of a Doric hexastyle (six-columns-wide) temple, was started in 449BC, but not finished until 415. On the Acropolis, the Propylaia (state entrance) was designed by Mneskiles, and built between 437 and 432BC. It has always been the only entrance onto the broadly flat surface of the rock. The beautiful **Temple of Wingless Victory** was constructed after the death of Pericles, perhaps as a monument to victory over the Persians, and was the last (perfect) major Classical building on the revered site. Also built after Pericles's death, between 421 and 407BC – on the site of the original Mycenaean palace – was the **Erechtheion**, possibly also designed by Mneskiles and directly overlooking the sacred road to Eleusis.

However, prior to this fine pair of edifices – and built between 447 and 438BC – it is the **Parthenon** that outshines all others. Under the direction of Pheidias – and with the sculptures designed by Polykleitos – the sheer size, richness and power conveyed by the temple has never been surpassed. Many have tried to copy the Parthenon, but none have ever matched the accuracy with which it was (almost) miraculously put together. On 11 November 1992 *The Times* carried an article by the eminent Marcus Binney, which described the mammoth restoration task being led by Manolis Korres, who calculated that the original temple comprised 13,700 pieces. It is worth quoting Binney verbatim:

'The abiding fascination of the Parthenon is that it was more beautifully made, and was fitted together with greater precision, than any human structure before or since. Not a teaspoon of mortar or cement was used. Many joints are estimated to be less than 1/100th of a millimetre wide. "Not a breath of air could pass between the solid blocks of masonry," Korres says. The drums of the columns were calibrated, like the parts of a jet engine, to achieve a perfect fit. Korres has found that the drums were honed against matching pairs of stone plates, so that each stone exactly complemented those above and below...

'It is well known that the base, or stylobate, of the Parthenon was gently curved to counteract the natural distortions of the eye. Korres has calculated that similar differences applied to the walls. "We can measure these curvatures, using instruments which can pick up a difference of one-tenth of a millimetre," he says. "Also the corners of the stones are not quite at 90 degrees, but a little acute."'

Binney finishes by saying, 'The fruits of [all this] research are displayed in the Centre for Acropolis Studies... Within a few years the Greeks have brought the Acropolis alive in a way that a century of classic textbooks never came near to doing.'

As to theatres, dozens of differently sized copies of the handful of 5th-century-BC originals were built in the Hellenistic Age that followed, and by Rome, many virtually indistinguishable from the original concept, but whose date of construction was recorded at the time. Even at Athens, the theatre in its present shape was only built by Lykourgos between about 338 and 326BC. However, theatres dating from the late 5th/early 4th century BC include Corinth, Delphi, Lemnos and Syracuse.

The best-preserved of all, though dated to no earlier than the mid-4th century BC, is the magnificently sited theatre at Epidaurus. Built (as was always the practice) into a carefully selected hillside, the design of the first 34 tiers at Epidaurus is attributed (by Pausanias) to the same Polykleitos who masterminded the fabulous sculptures of the Parthenon. Two hundred years later the Romans added a further 21 tiers, but – in clearly being able to 'see the join' – one can easily visualise the spectacular impression made by the theatre in its original form.

Sculpture

As with the above paragraphs on architecture, one need look no further than the other spectacular Parthenon achievement, namely the sculptural decoration – including, of course, the major proportion that Lord Elgin brought to London. The immense (gilded) statues and astonishing friezes were both a tribute to the goddess Athene and a vital part of the 'perpetual' celebration of the defeat of the Persians.

Commissioned by Pericles and designed by Pheidias – the team primarily responsible for the temple itself – this remarkable undertaking involved skilled specialists from all over the Greek world, with the funding provided by levies from Athens's allies, in gratitude for being saved from Persian domination. The near-miracle of employing skills from far and wide was the *uniformity* of style achieved throughout, with hundreds of different figures showing off the *humanist* artistry of the Classical period at its 'apogee' (Greek for 'distance from the earth').

Engineering

While in Chapter 16 we will praise Roman practicality in masterminding astonishing infrastructure projects, we should not overlook Greek skills and ingenuity in this area. A wonderful example – long before any influence from Rome – was the tunnel on the island of Samos (close to the Turkish mainland, and birthplace of many famous Greeks, including Pythagoras), commissioned c525BC by Policrates and built by Eupalinus. There lay a highly productive spring on the far side (from Samos city) of Mount Kastro, but instead of routing a channel around the mountainside, Policrates wanted to ensure a pure supply that was also proof against any enemy action.

Eupalinus caused a half-mile (1km) tunnel to be driven from each end, through the mountain, and although these did not quite meet initially, a kink was incorporated to overcome this shortcoming. The tunnel was 6 feet (1.8m) square, at one corner of which was sunk a continuous trench. Into this were laid terracotta pipes, at a gradient of less than 0.5% throughout, over which rubble was back-filled. A reservoir collected the spring water, settling tanks were incorporated, and a cistern built at the city end – presumably to facilitate distribution.

Second only in age to Hezekiah's Jerusalem tunnel (built before 700BC), the much-visited Samos tunnel is now part of the Pythagoreion UNESCO World Heritage Site, which also incorporates the much older Heraion temple complex.

Decorative arts

In the vast range of Greek artistic achievement – made more complex by wide regional differences – we can only refer here to a number of underlying themes, the first of which is the lively application of *geometry*. This characteristic must have been prompted by Athenian fascination with mathematics and the emerging sciences. Whereas in many forms of art, geometric influence is visibly obvious, it was also used in early designs of statue, so as to secure accurate proportions.

Another uniquely Classical aspect was the breakthrough as regards *perspective* drawing, which we know was developed for life-sized or miniature application, from the art of large-scale theatrical painting, the first transfer to a domestic requirement being executed by Alkibiades. The best-known surviving examples in a more formal setting are sarcophagus paintings at Paestum (Poseidonia) on the Italian coast south of Naples (within arguably the best preserved temple complex to be found anywhere). The 'diving boy' is justly famous, but – in reflection – it is notable that these paintings (c480BC) are not *so* remarkably superior to some of the scenes painted at Knossos and Akrotiri (Thera) some 1,000-1,200 years earlier!

Another streak (towards which Peter Levi draws our attention) is '...from the late 5th century onward the burlesque treatment of heroic stories ... no doubt sometimes under the influence of Athenian comedy ... there seem to have been elements of caricature in the work of the subtlest painters at the end of the century, among them Zeuxis.' Levi goes on to describe several artistic advances by this painter (or someone from his school at Heraklia, on the Italian 'instep'), wherein a sketch of the famous ambush scene in the *Iliad* – by Odysseus and Diomedes of Dolon – depicts not only the use of perspective, but several humorous or positively gleeful scenes that are both ornamental and highly realistic.

Music

Music permeated Greek society at all levels and, even though early instruments were a legacy from the north (Thrace) and east (Turkey), it was the emerging scientific community that enabled spectacular progress to be made. Once again turning to Peter Levi, it is worth quoting a major contribution made by Pythagoras:

> 'Greek philosophers put the highest value on theory, which ... led to the development of a single-stringed measuring instrument known as the monochord. With this "acoustic potentiometer" Greek mathematicians, notably Pythagoras, were able to calculate the numerical relationships between different pitches. A single string, stretched between two points and spanning a hollow sounding box, when plucked, sounds a note. Dividing this string into two equal parts produces a note an octave higher...'

A wide range of instruments were developed. Levi continues:

> 'The pipe – made of hardwood or bone – was jointed, cylindrical (as the clarinet) and voiced by a bivalve reed (as in the oboe) so that it sounded perhaps not unlike a "krummhorn". Multiple boring and the invention of a rotary metal sleeve improved its range and ability to switch from mode to mode (polyphonia).'

The lyre was very widely taught, perhaps a descendant of the legendary design wherein Hermes killed and gutted a tortoise, so that he could use the hard shell as the basis of the 'lovely toy' that he then cleverly manufactured. We also have vase decorations of trumpeters, whose instrument '…capable of two or three notes only, had a good repertoire of signalling rhythms'.

A sophisticated later achievement (again worth describing in detail) was the 'hydraulis' or water organ:

'This instrument was invented c250 by the Greek engineer Ktesibios who worked in Alexandria as a barber with his father. When making a counterbalance system for a mirror in his father's shop, he had observed how air, being forced through a small tube and aperture, had produced a clear and musical sound. He exploited the principle and, with the aid of water to pressurise the air, was able to produce even louder sounds which could be varied in pitch by using pipes of different lengths. These were subsequently arranged on a wind-chest and valves were designed, coupled to a series of levers, enabling air to be admitted to the individual pipes as required. This allowed a simple melody to be played. This instrument, the predecessor to the pipe organ, was used widely by the Romans and Byzantines.'

Democritus

Classical Greece produced an almost infinite number of remarkable men, many of whom could not be grouped with their peers, due to their supremely *individualistic* talents. One such, whose unique life serves to illustrate the limitless intellectual thinking of this unmatchable era, is Democritus. Born around 460BC in Abdera (Thrace), he had a privileged upbringing, and – when his father died, leaving to his three sons land, property and money – chose to take the last of these, so as to fund his intense desire to travel. He visited Egypt, Persia and the Indian sub-continent, absorbing everything he saw and learned – and on his return seemingly developed a mutual dislike of Athens.

Living to an old age, and – because of his outlook on life – being nicknamed the 'Laughing Philosopher', Democritus wrote dozens of books, not one of which has survived. As a true polymath, he wrote on almost every imaginable subject, but his most remarkable contribution that has come down to us (as recounted by Van Doren) was his belief that everything material was comprised of millions of particles, which he described as 'atoms'. He explained that, while there were an *infinite*

number of atoms, there were a *finite* number of *kinds* of atom, noting –
for example – that the type that made up water was completely
different from that which made up a particular metal.

Democritus went on to discuss the universe, and speculate about it
containing other worlds like our own. While his complex thinking has
been accepted or rejected in equal measure by post-Renaissance
philosophers during the past 300 years, no one has doubted that the
main tenets of his 'atomism' were astonishingly modern – perhaps this
is why Plato wanted all Democritus's writings destroyed, which – by
one means or another – was eventually the outcome.

The Greek military machine

As Levi suggests, in among the many wonderful aspects of this glorious
culture, discussion of Greek military methods – though necessary
because it brought about such high and low points – definitely brings
us down to earth, especially since, in this respect, the competing city
states or mini-empires displayed all the awful mistakes and
incompetence that went before, and to which we have been witness all
over the world ever since.

Lightly armed soldiers were drilled to fight in a tightly formed
'phalanx', their main weapon being long spears, the first five rows of
which protruded ahead of the actual troops. Training – at least
theoretically – ensured that the phalanx could be presented to the
enemy in differing formats, to suit the circumstances. Up to the 5th
century BC most soldiers belonged to the city or state for which they
were fighting, but the practice thereafter of using mercenaries grew in
ever-increasing importance.

Greek fortresses were developed from Mycenaean precedents –
indeed, the Acropolis still had such walls when it fell to the Persians
in 480BC. As can be visualised, Greek ingenuity was brought to bear
to 'furnish' walled fortifications with ever more sophisticated *defensive*
devices or gadgetry (e.g. catapults and semi-automatic 'crossbow'
machines) while simultaneously coming up with *offensive* siege
techniques of varying reliability, e.g. types of battering ram.

Route to disaster

As presaged by internecine conflict in the Peloponnesian War, the
trouble with *all* Greeks was that – despite (or because of) being
intensely proud of their mutual heritage – they could not avoid

repeated actions against each other – and Persia, after its defeat in 479BC, was only too glad to cause dissent among the warring factions throughout most of the next century. No sooner had Sparta defeated Athens than it became involved in bitter continuing strife against (mainly) Thebes, with a severely weakened and embittered Athens intermittently taking sides.

Any independent observers at the time would have seen the only possible outcome as the whole of Greece becoming so weakened as to fall prey to final defeat by the Persians, who had continued to stay entrenched in most of modern-day Turkey. The fact that, against all odds, a completely different outcome emerged (with comparative speed) in the second half of 4th century BC is the story to be told in the next chapter.

The story of 'Greece' did not finish with the rise of Alexander – indeed, Greek influence spread more rapidly than before, particularly to the east – but from now on such increasing influence would take place within the hegemony of first Macedonia, then Rome. Indeed, for 2,200 years (from 330BC until at least the middle of the 19th century AD) – except when Byzantium had a degree of latitude following the fall of the Western Roman Empire, before the long 'squeeze' by the Ottoman Empire began – the proselytising of the truly unique Greek contribution to the world has had to be undertaken (ironically and sadly) by almost everyone else except Greeks themselves.

Chapter 15

Alexander the Great and his Hellenistic legacy

As has been referred to earlier, and will be referred to later, a crucial factor that lay behind the preservation of Greek knowledge (down to the Early Renaissance) was the expansion *eastwards* of Greek influence – and, in particular, the creation of Alexandria, still arguably the greatest seat of learning the world has ever known. But Alexandria would never have arisen at the mouth of the Egyptian (Nile) delta had it not been for Alexander the Great. And Alexander – for our eternal good fortune – was inspired to his amazing achievements by his teacher Aristotle, who tutored him over three years in his late teens.

Hundreds of years earlier, Homer had written of Odysseus that '…many were the men whose minds he learned…' Then, in the century before Alexander, Sophocles had said in Antigone, 'He can always help himself. He faces no future helpless. There is only one death he cannot escape from… Clever beyond all dreams the inventive craft that he has which may drive him one time or another to well or ill.'

Now the world was to witness, in Alexander, a man whose spectacular achievements – in so short a time – outshone all previous efforts. And this very young man put himself at Aristotle's disposal, as Van Doren says, '…sending back reports to his old teacher, together with zoological and botanical samples for the master to analyse and categorise.'

Thales and his successors made knowledge available to all who could read. Then came the new big thing, which the Greeks called 'epistome', and we call science. The search for truth took off, with the chance for all to participate – nowhere in the first place more than in the field of mathematics. When the Greeks overran Egypt, these new rulers upset millennia of *static* teaching. There was nothing that could not be questioned – no traditions, and no rules – which set in motion the pre-eminence of Alexandrian scholarship for nearly a thousand years.

Philip II of Macedon

As yet another example of spectacular archaeological detective work since 1970, the brilliant Greek expert Manolis Andronikos discovered – on 8 November 1977 – a completely intact tomb at Vergina, adjacent to the ancient royal capital of Aigai in north-eastern Greece, on a site that had previously been conjectured in 1968 by the long-lived N. G. L. 'Nick' Hammond. As a young man Hammond had been an SOE operative in Greece, and a close associate of John Pendlebury right up to the latter's tragic death on Crete in 1941.

To quote Peter Levi again:

'The contents of the tomb [which almost certainly was that of Philip himself] are extraordinary, the most glorious treasure any Greek was ever buried with, and somehow much more moving than that phrase might lead one to expect. The tombs themselves were finely decorated and made of marble. They lay under an enormous mound of earth which effectively protected them.'

Manolis Andronikos died in 1992, Peter Levi in 2000, and Nick Hammond in 2001. All three would have burst with pride (as would Arthur Evans!) if they could have seen the beautifully laid-out exhibition of remarkable artefacts from the tumuli at Aigai, which ran in the magnificent new extension of the Ashmolean Museum from April to August 2011.

If events moved quite swiftly in Athens, Sparta and Thebes, the northern Greek state of Macedonia was bedevilled by endless strife – internally and externally – which made its southern neighbours seem models of stability and tranquillity. On the other hand, the Temenid Macedonian monarchy – founded c650BC – managed to survive until defeat by Rome at the Battle of Pydna in 167BC.

Philip was the youngest of three sons of King Amnytas III, who managed to live into old age, dying in 370BC. The eldest son, Alexander II, was assassinated at the instigation of his brother-in-law,

Ptolemy of Aloros, in 368. The middle son, Perdiccas III, clung on for nearly a decade but was cut down in 359, in a disastrous defeat by the aggressive Balkan-based Illyrians. Therefore at the age of 23 Philip inherited a desperate situation, besieged by not only Illyrians but also by Thrace and Athens. He bribed the first two to desist, then defeated the Athenian expeditionary force. Having earned a brief respite, he – crucially – cemented his power base and greatly strengthened his army, developing the 'phalanx' infantry formation and the 'sarissa' (long spear) armament.

The next 23 years of Philip's life were spent in consolidating his position further, within Macedonia, then in succession he so totally defeated the Illyrians that they were never again a serious threat, conquered Thessaly to the south-east, overran Molossia to the south-west (opposite Corfu), and secured an enormous swathe of Thrace – to the north and to the north-east as far as Byzantium, a city that he unsuccessfully besieged, being a tortuous 300 miles (500km) distant from his royal capital Aigai.

Philip had (at least) seven wives, his accumulation of in-laws only further complicating the scope for intrigue and mischief. In adult life he gained enormous prestige, but many enemies also, and – whether through political or sexual jealousy – was assassinated by Pausanias of Orestis (one of his seven bodyguards) when entering the theatre at Aigai unarmed for the celebration of the marriage of his daughter – Cleopatra, the full sister of Alexander the Great.

Alexander's mother Olympias was the daughter of a Molossian king, and his father's fourth wife. Her relationship with Philip was fraught, matters coming to a head when Philip married his fifth wife in 337BC. Olympias was banished to Epirus, accompanied by Alexander, and there is at least circumstantial evidence that she was complicit in Philip's assassination a year later, with endless conjecture as to Alexander's knowledge of the dastardly scheme that was afoot. This (only too frequently repeated) gruesome act took place in October 336. Philip was only 46, but his untimely death unleashed a one-man 'whirlwind' that has arguably never been surpassed.

Alexander the Great: early life

Both Alexander's conception and his birth (in 356BC) were surrounded by extraordinary parental dreams and strange occurrences, some of these phenomena being publicised long before the boy displayed any special characteristics. One such example was the unexplained destruction by fire of the Temple of Artemis at Ephesus on the very day of his birth, either 20 or 21 July.

Great care was taken as to Alexander's tutelage, and he showed very early signs of precocity as well as remarkable courage. When only 10 he tamed a horse that had defeated all adult attempts. He was allowed to keep this bold steed, with his father allegedly saying, 'My boy, you must find a kingdom big enough for your ambitions. Macedon is too small for you.' Alexander named the animal Bucephalus, and rode the horse everywhere on his exploits. Bucephalus died in the Himalayan foothills in modern-day Pakistan after yet another battle, at the ripe old age of 30.

At the age of 13 various scholars were interviewed, but Philip chose Aristotle to further Alexander's education. This took place – together with several of Alexander's peers, who would be his loyal friends and become his future generals – at the Temple of the Nymphs at Mieza. So appreciative was Philip of Aristotle's role that he rebuilt and repopulated his home town of Stageira, which he had previously destroyed. Effectively the location at Mieza was a boarding school, where the most brilliant man of his age taught his pupils every conceivable subject. It was then that Alexander developed his passion for Homer and the *Iliad*; Aristotle gave him the annotated copy, which he subsequently took with him everywhere on his travels.

At the age of 16 (in 340BC) Philip made Alexander regent, to cover for his absence on military campaigns. This period was swiftly followed by Alexander joining his father in battle. Together – in 338 – they ended up routing the Theban and Athenian armies, and were welcomed by all cities (except Sparta) as they marched into the Peloponnese. Soon after this high point in their relationship, however, Philip fell for Cleopatra Euridice, a niece of his general Attalus. Matters took a distinct turn for the worse at their subsequent wedding, to the extent that Alexander thought it prudent to accompany his mother into exile.

A lifetime of conquest

After his father's death, Alexander returned to Macedon, and with his mother's active support quickly put to death any potential rival, whether for royal position or military supremacy. Sensing weakness, most of the territories conquered in the previous 20 years immediately rebelled, but they fatally underestimated Alexander's military genius.

While this chapter is principally concerned with Alexander's 'Hellenistic' legacy throughout the Mediterranean and the Near/Middle East – and will not dwell in detail on his seamless conquests that took place over more than a decade – it is crucial to have an understanding of just how he could conceivably have created an (almost) instantaneous empire in the first place, in which the Greek language, civilisation and culture could then flourish over such a wide (and disparate) area of the known world.

Alexander's military genius has been studied and admired throughout the ages, right down to the modern era. Hannibal described him as the best (or second best!) commander in history; Julius Caesar once wept when recounting his brilliance; Napoleon greatly admired him; and military academies around the world still pore over his tactical master-strokes.

In summary, Alexander:

- ensured all his troops were highly trained and motivated,
- surrounded himself with intensely loyal, and capable, generals,
- had the intellect to size up each and every challenge posed,
- devised or improved the best formations and known weaponry,
- surveyed – wherever possible – the terrain for best advantage,
- held pre-battle clarifying and morale-boosting sessions,
- deployed incredible speed for maximum surprise and terror, and
- while never suicidally rash, effectively 'led from the front'.

Set out below is a sequential schedule of battles won, nations subjugated, and territories gained in the decade between 336 and 326BC, in many cases achieved in the most inhospitable terrain, and often against seemingly overwhelming odds. Carried out almost entirely overland, at his death Alexander's empire covered an area of approaching 3,000 miles (5,000km) in latitude, and nearly 1,500 miles (2,500km) at each 'corner' of longitude.

It is important to realise that – unlike many aggressors before and since – Alexander was determined to *govern* each conquered territory to the advantage of *everyone*, utilising 'best practice' (much of which followed the policies of his Persian predecessors), as the list of his lasting achievements will later make clear.

335BC Thrace again subjugated – with the Celts gained as allies. Thebes makes the mistake of rebelling against Macedon.

334 Invasion of Turkey (Persian Empire), where Alexander pays homage at Troy en route to thrashing a huge Persian army on the River Granikos. He appoints a Macedonian governor for Asia Minor, leaving alone the administrative infrastructure established by the Persians. It is thought that his respect for their methods derived from Aristotle's comparative teaching of Greek and 'barbarian' systems of government.

In the same year he liberates all the Adriatic-facing Greek cities of Turkey that had been under Persian control for nearly 150 years, and restores their democratic rights while emphatically forbidding reprisals.

333 Continuing down the south-west coast of Turkey, he is checked briefly at Miletos. Capturing this city, and – not even attempting to challenge the immensely powerful Persian fleet – he frustrates the legendary Darius III by occupying every fortified harbour along the south coast. He then catches the huge Persian army unawares in a narrow coastal strip, with their losses being (allegedly) more than 100,000 men against a few hundred dead Macedonians.

332 Moving against Syria and Phoenicia, it takes eight months for Tyre, the most defensible city in the known world, to fall. It is then the turn of Gaza, then Egypt (Battle of Issos), where Alexander is proclaimed king, celebrated with Greek games at Memphis, and founds the city of Alexandria at the edge of the Nile delta.

331 Expanding his army continuously, Alexander throws no fewer than 400,000 infantry and 7,000 cavalry at what is now Iraq. He wins an immensely complicated (and much studied) battle of Gaugamela against Darius, which prompts the surrender of Babylon.

330 With the Persian Empire in a state of collapse, his vast army moves on Persepolis, exploring as it goes. In a reprise of how the Spartans were undone by the Persians at Thermopylae in 480BC (and where the Phoceans had denied Philip II early in his reign), Alexander finds a precipitous route that circumvents the heavily barricaded pass, and annihilates the powerful force of defenders. The unbelievable treasure of

Persepolis is systematically loaded onto hundreds of mules, to be carried away, while the palace is devastated and burned.

329-8   Alexander becomes obsessed with all things Persian, adopting certain of their customs and respecting the people.

327   He marries a Persian noblewoman, Roxane, and – having already penetrated with great difficulty into Afghanistan – lays his plans to conquer central Asia and India.

326   With his army ravaged by disease, and constantly requiring new recruits, he invades India, and crosses the Indus River. This incredible reach – more than 3,000 miles from home – marks the end of Alexander's expansionary exploits. His generals start to rebel, and all complain that they want to see their homeland again; thus begins the weary trek back to Babylon.

325-3   Alexander himself cannot bear to leave the centre of his huge empire. He spends these years consolidating his governance of this vast region, and scheming to build a massive fleet (which, unlike Darius, he has never possessed) so as to extend his control to the western half of the Mediterranean.

Decline and death

Alexander's ruthlessness, increasing paranoia and belief that he was a direct descendant of the gods, must have tried the patience of even his most loyal supporters, an atmosphere made worse by the terrible privations to which they had been subjected for so long. Coupled with Alexander himself becoming exhausted, it could be said that his 'Empirical' project finally ran out of steam. Whether it was a fever that finally caught up with him – or whether he was poisoned – Alexander died at a ridiculously young age, on 10 or 11 June 323BC, just six weeks short of his 33rd birthday.

Chaos at home

Alexander's father had died as a result of the internecine nature of the Macedonian state, and – having been absent for more than a decade by the time of his death – the rivalry and bloodletting that took place in his aftermath was of immense complexity, and of horrifying viciousness.

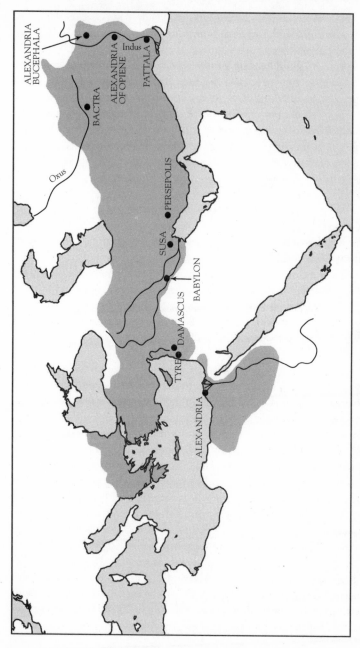

Map vi – Alexander the Great's empire at its maximum extent, 323BC

Simply put, this endless cycle of violent claim – and counterclaim – to rule continued with only the briefest intermissions until the Romans finally stamped their authority over the whole of 'greater' Greece 125 years later. Athens became a shadow of its former power, although the schools that the great philosophers had established continued to guarantee the city's position at the centre of the intellectual world – thus the 'Greekness' of this mid-Mediterranean region was never in doubt. What we are concerned at this stage in our story, however, is the degree to which all things Greek could/would become established over the vast, but disparate, territories to the east that Alexander had only very recently conquered.

Partition in the east

Immediately after Alexander's death, Perdiccas, the senior general amongst the 'Diadochi' (successors), persuaded his colleagues to let him act as regent, pending the birth of Alexander's unborn child by his marriage to Roxane. Perdiccas was intolerant of any rivals and – as was typical – had the infantry commander Meleager murdered. Then, to try and prevent a rival general – Ptolemy – from securing control of Egypt, he set out to attack him, but was killed by his own men close to the Nile, in either 321 or 320BC.

Previously Perdiccas had appointed fellow generals as 'satraps' (Persian for 'governor') of the major colonial territories at the Partition of Babylon in 323BC. With Ptolemy turning down their offer of the overall regency in favour of ruling Egypt, this group met at a Greek settlement near the source of the Orontes in Syria and, in 321BC, agreed to the Partition of Triparadisus. Unrealistically, satraps of varying stature were appointed over some 20 territories, but (apart from Ptolemy) only two other dominant rulers emerged over the next 20 years. These were Seleucus, who ruthlessly established himself over the whole of Babylonia (to which he attached all the lands to the east), and Antigonos, who accumulated most of what are the modern states of Turkey, Syria, Lebanon, Israel and western Jordan.

Despite all the ensuing turmoil and uncertainty, it is a remarkable fact that in these early post-Alexander years there were no *native* uprisings to speak of in any of these vast 'colonial' territories. For more than two millennia historians have been puzzled to account for this acquiescent behaviour, but perhaps it derived from a combination of factors: an innate respect for Alexander's god-like status; a universal admiration for the 'Greek' way; and the perception that the legacy of Alexander's governance could bring a better lifestyle and greater security than hitherto.

Whatever the reasons, it is a *crucial* fact that the key elements of 'Hellenism' that were being promulgated with great energy during Alexander's meteoric but short-lived supremacy became thoroughly *embedded* throughout this enormous eastern region after his death – a way of life that lasted for centuries, with, as we shall see later, ultimately incalculable benefits to our western world.

Legacy in the east (apart from Egypt)

The most visible legacy is the wealth of Hellenistic architecture – still identifiable at differing levels of magnificence, and widely dispersed throughout Alexander's eastern 'empire'. Quite apart from numerous wonderful examples in western Turkey (Miletos and Pergamon, for example), set out below are descriptions of sites that are spread across a vast distance. Many of the great cities were founded during the reign of Seleucus (358-281BC), who, having been forced to flee Babylon in 310 by his erstwhile colleague Antigonus, gained his revenge at the Battle of Ipsus (in Phrygia, south-west Anatolia) in 301. Three of the most famous sites – all founded by Seleucus before 300BC – are Antioch, Seleucia and Ay Khanoum, stretching nearly 2,000 miles (3,000km) eastwards from the north-eastern corner of the Mediterranean. Only Rome and Alexandria were greater cities than Antioch and Seleucia at the peak of their prosperity.

Antioch
One of four sister cities founded in (then) Syria, Antioch, on the Orontes River adjacent to the modern city of Antakia, in the small southern protrusion of Turkey, grew rapidly. An initial immigrant population of Macedonians, Athenians and Jews, amounting to perhaps 20,000, reached its peak of about 500,000 in Christ's lifetime, later becoming a safe haven for gentile Jews, much referred to in the New Testament. In 240BC Antioch became the undisputed capital of the Seleucid Empire, shifting the centre of gravity westwards and directly leading to the foundation of Pergamon, some 500 miles (800km) to the west, in the centre of the Adriatic Turkish coastline.

201

Seleucia

Not to be confused with Seleucia Pieria, a Syrian seaport visited by St Paul, Seleucia was laid out in 305BC at the confluence of the Tigris and the canal dug from the Euphrates at its closest point, and was initially populated by Macedonians, other Greeks, Jews and Syrians. Seleucus (then already aged 55) made this strategic site the eastern capital of his empire. The city grew rapidly to become one of the great Hellenistic centres and, even when captured by the Parthians in 141BC, became the *western* capital of *their* empire, retaining its status for at least another century.

Ay Khanoum (Ai Khanum)

Perhaps the most remarkable example of the eastern 'reach' of pure Hellenism, the remnants of this 'outpost' city were only discovered some 50 years ago – according to Peter Levi, during a shooting expedition of the last King of Afghanistan! The site is a full 2,500 miles (4,000km) east of Macedon, on the borders of Russia and Afghanistan (not far from China) and due south from Tashkent. It lies at the junction of the Oxus River, as it flows north-west to the Aral Sea, and the Kokcha, which flows down to the Oxus from the mountains once rich in lapis lazuli, gold and precious stones, and very close to the east-west silk route.

Excavation work has been fraught, due to successive wars, and – tragically – the site was virtually destroyed during the Soviet-Afghan war. Nevertheless it is clear that Ay Khanoum was a 'complete' Hellenistic city, with encompassing ramparts (with fortified towers) 2 miles in length, a palace, several temples, a theatre, a gymnasium, fine houses and beautiful mosaics. There are remains of a number of beautiful statues, a silver plaque featuring the goddess Kybele, and – most evocative of all – a Greek inscription in stone, recording that Klearchos (a pupil of Aristotle) had copied out certain Delphic maxims. Only one has survived, which reminds the Greeks at Ay Khanoum of 'the various virtues proper to the different ages of human life ... As children, learn good manners / As young men, learn to control passions / In middle age, be just / In old age, give good advice / Then die, without regret.' Levi records that the same advice from Delphi was inscribed at Miletopolis in Anatolia – and has any wise person come up with a better prescription in the succeeding 23 centuries?

There is much more fascinating detail that could be described, but the crucial point is that this discovery put paid to those who doubted the substance of a Greco-Bactrian kingdom – the eastern offshoot of the Seleucid Empire. The fact that all the evidence points to the city being destroyed by nomadic invaders, not long after the death of King Eucratides in c145BC, does nothing to diminish its brilliance over its c175-year existence, nor its significance as evidence of the extent to which Alexander's intention to promulgate Hellenism was so scrupulously executed – a world away from Greece, in a geographic sense only. (In the spring of 2011, the Afghan display at the British Museum told a heroic tale of the preservation of wonderful artefacts from destruction and/or thieves. This exhibition was to circle the globe until it was safe to be returned to Kabul – to begin to show the Afghans themselves their remarkable heritage.)

Listed below are four glimpses of long-lasting Hellenistic influence – each exhibiting the 'Hellenistic baroque' style developed in Alexandria over several hundred years after Alexander himself, but in which legendary city no significant examples have survived. All are spread in an arc around the Mediterranean and, though distant from each other, in no case were they established more than 125 miles (200km) from its shores.

Jerash

The ancient Gerasa was the site of a Bronze Age settlement. Situated now in the north-west corner of Jordan, Jerash became part of the province of Syria following the Roman conquest in 63BC. Increasingly important as a trading centre in the 1st century AD – and becoming part of the province of Arabia in 90AD – Jerash joined Philadelphia (modern Amman) as one of the 'Decapolis' cities. However, it was not until the early 2nd century that the great buildings we see today were constructed under the orders of first Trajan, then Hadrian, and it is these that make this wonderful site second only (in Jordan) to Petra as an unforgettable place to visit.

Massadah

Lying in eastern Israel – and more famous now for the Roman siege of Jewish rebels in 72-73AD, and their mass suicide rather than face capture – Masada was identified in 1842, but not excavated until

1963-65. It now exhibits the remains of the fortifications, beautiful palaces and baths that were built by Herod the Great (74-4BC).

Petra

Situated in southern Jordan, not far from the Israeli border, and rediscovered in 1812 by Burckhardt, this 'rose red city half as old as time' was nominated in 2007 as one of the New Seven Wonders of the World. Also nominated by the BBC as 'one of the 40 places you have to see before you die', Petra includes the 'Treasury', which is a *still complete* example of Hellenistic baroque architecture. Settled since around 1500BC, the city was created in the 6th century BC by the Nabateans, who mastered the flash floods in the Wadi Musa gorge by creating a system of dams, cisterns and water conduits. Though not possible to date with certainty, it is likely that the Treasury, as well as the Theatre and Monastery, all date from the 2nd/1st centuries BC. They are designed in a pure Greek way that owes nothing to native architecture, during an era when the (otherwise influential) Seleucid and Ptolemaic empires were in a weakened state.

Ptolemais

Obviously developed within the empire of the Ptolemies, the ruins of this city lie some 500 miles (800km) to the east of Alexandria, in Libya, between the modern cities of Benghazi and Cyrene. Though the dating of the Hellenistic buildings is not certain, the beautiful remains lay well-preserved beneath the sands until as recently as 2001, when excavation work was started by the archaeological department of Warsaw University.

Fascinating as the above examples remain, Levi describes the best preserved examples of the 'full blossoming' of Greek baroque architecture as those found in the wall paintings of Pompeii. He writes:

'The paintings confirm our normal instinct that the most attractive buildings were not always the grandest. There is ... a friendly-looking statue, with columned buildings lightly sketched in the background. This could almost be an 18th-century sketch, almost a piece of Chinoiserie. It is lightly executed, with the momentary quality that can give life to monuments and ruins. The view is informal ... this is not a grand religious ceremony, but an everyday piety of the Greeks of southern Italy in their long and on the whole happy decline.'

Ptolemaic Egypt

The main reason that Ptolemy passed up the chance to rule over most of Alexander's conquered territory was that – as Alexander's successor in Egypt, having been a 'somatophylax' (one of his seven dedicated bodyguards/generals) – he was readily accepted by the populace as the successor ruler to the Pharaonic dynasty. Declaring himself King Ptolemy I in 305BC, and later acquiring the title of 'Soter' (saviour), he and his descendants ruled Egypt in an unbroken sequence until the Roman conquest in 30BC. It was under this comparatively stable regime that the city of Alexandria flourished so mightily, becoming the largest city in the known world until eventually overtaken by Rome. Despite many vicissitudes, the city remained capital of Egypt for nearly a thousand years, from its creation by Alexander in 331BC* until the Muslim conquest in 641AD, and within which developed the most famous library – and centre of scholarship or research – in the ancient world.

Library of Alexandria

Ptolemy I Soter (c367-283BC) actively sponsored the creation of the library very early in his reign, under the guiding hand of Demetrius of Phaleron, a student of Aristotle. Initially, its creation may have been to house a (royal) collection of books, for which the Greek term is 'bibliotheke'.

In the final part of this chapter we will deal with the pervasive way in which Greek became the 'lingua franca' throughout the Near and Middle East. So far this book has included many references to Greek words, and the extent to which we have come to rely on this language, and the reader will be reminded of several more while we now survey quite briefly the remarkable scope of the library's activities over the many centuries that followed its inception.

---

* Alexander's masterstroke – perhaps borrowed from the Canaanite/Phoenician genius for creating supremely defensible double-harbours at both ends of the Mediterranean – was to join the island of Pharos (on which was located the lighthouse, one of the ancient Seven Wonders of the World) to the mainland by a mole nearly a mile (1.5km) long, so as to be able to construct a pair of first-class back-to-back harbours.

Built in the royal quarter of the city, the library was modelled on Aristotle's Lyceum and operated in tandem with its neighbouring institution, the Musaeum. The library had a layout that many university campuses follow to this day, including reading and meeting rooms, and lecture halls and dining facilities; it had gardens and walkways known as Peripatos (from which we derive the term 'peripatetic'; it even had acquisitions and cataloguing departments; and of course it had acres of shelving for the storing and identification of *hundreds of thousands* of papyrus scrolls. Its unique policy (at that time) of collecting books from outside Egypt – so as to gather 'all' available knowledge – involved experts being sent to book fairs held by Rhodes and Athens, with ample (royal) financial muscle. Of course, the rapid development of the library had the knock-on effect of making Alexandria a major trading port – starting with books (mainly copies!) and papyrus, but later extending to all manner of goods.

Again well-patronised by the Ptolemies, the library actively encouraged the residence of dozens of 'international' scholars, paying for their travel and giving financial support to them and their families. As the resulting research blossomed, the library shelves became crammed with works on mathematics, astronomy, physics and many other subjects. At the same time (about 50 years after Alexander's death) as an Alexandrian merchant vessel was shipwrecked off the coast of Anglesey, North Wales, a group of scientists in the sailors' home city were already trying to work out the earth's magnitude. On any subject, theories propounded by a nucleus of experts would be examined – through demonstration or in print – by a peer group. Only when criticism was exhausted (and any modifications incorporated) would a 'master' edition of the particular work be prepared, from which copies would be laboriously written out for circulation to other scholars and royalty, and for distribution (in a strictly commercial manner) throughout the rest of the known world.

In the early days there were no limits as to the scope of research, and the same was true with experimental styles of poetry, but after several generations of thrilling developments the level of accomplishment had, as Levi states, '…become something dustier, a scholarship of scholarships, a compilation of compilations, rather like second-rate literary scholarship today'!

Enduring Hellenistic influence,
including the Greek language

Greek influence throughout the Near and Middle East, as well as in Egypt (and its adjacent territories), was at its most profound from Alexander's decade of sweeping conquests to just before the birth of Christ, when all but the most easterly regions came under the control of Rome. The Greek mainland was conquered by Rome in 146BC, but (partly because Rome admired all things Greek) this barely caused a ripple in the east. Only when Rome expanded further east, finally absorbing Egypt into the empire in 30AD, did Hellenistic influence start to wane, while still remaining an integral feature throughout the world further east.

From the outset, Greek colonists from every corner of their homeland had 'followed the flag' and spread themselves widely. In abandoning the Aristotelian view (Aristotle only died in 322BC, a year after Alexander) that any non-Greek was a 'barbarian', they adopted a pragmatic attitude to the widely differing peoples they encountered. In this context 'pragmatic' means exporting Greek culture and language to be adopted by the senior and/or educated locals, while allowing the bulk of each population to continue with everyday life much as before – and a focal point of this parallel approach was the founding of 'Alexandrian' cities throughout the empire. It was of course the case that the spread of the Greek language (and literature) among the upper echelons of local administration and society helped to embed its use in the very areas where it was most likely to become a fixture. A crucial picture of this aspect is provided by well-preserved Jewish records.

So far in this book, Jews have not featured at all, simply because – although they battled for hundreds of years to secure a 'kingdom' of their own in the region that approximates to modern-day Israel – they were subject to endless vicissitudes, as so graphically recorded in the Old Testament. One of the supreme paradoxes throughout at least 2,500 years of our history is that – though never holding suzerainty over a large swathe of land – the Jewish influence everywhere in the world (since long before Christ) has been completely disproportionate to their physical grip over territory.

When considering the 'Jewish diaspora', most attention is paid to the ruthless expulsion of Jews from Israel in the 1st century AD, when

FROM ZIGGURATS TO ALGEBRA

Roman patience with this rebellious monotheistic nation finally snapped. However, the reality is that this infamous dispersion was the 'umpteenth' such upheaval that took place over an 800-year period. In 722BC the Assyrian conquest of Israel resulted in Jews being taken to Persia, where (in modern-day Iran) there is still a residual presence; in 588BC a large proportion of the population was taken in captivity to Babylon, and again until very recently there was a vibrant Jewish community in what is now Iraq, centred on Baghdad; Jews reached India (and probably even China) long before Christ; and in the 2nd century BC there were large Jewish communities in Greece itself, Antioch, Damascus, Cyprus and Anatolia. However, the Jewish proportion of the Egyptian peoples – perhaps 10% of a total of 8 million (with Alexandria featuring most prominently) – was the most significant of all. (The magnificent Jewish Museum, Raymond Burton House, in Camden, London, has recently been expanded, and gives an excellent insight into Jewish history over the millennia.)

Once more referring to Peter Levi, he records that the later historical books of the Old Testament were composed in Greek, as were the works of Philo (c30BC-c45AD) on religious philosophy, and Josephus (37-c100AD) wrote most of his histories in Greek, not Aramaic.

'Jewish settlements in Asia, in Greece and in Alexandria – the centre of Hellenistic Judaic literature – ... retained their identity and their religion; but they came to speak Greek, politically their existence was tenuous, and it is clear enough from many kinds of evidence ... that they absorbed from the Greeks before the birth of Christ more than the Greeks absorbed from them.'

As we shall see in the following chapters, the fact of not only the language itself but also the unique wealth of Greek history, mythology, poetry, plays, philosophy, mathematics and scientific endeavour being recorded, copied and treasured in key locations throughout the eastern world for some 1,500 years after Alexander's 33-year life, proved to be a most crucial element in the survival of knowledge, right through to the Early Renaissance in Western Europe.

Chapter 16

The Etruscans and the Roman Empire

From the early chapters in this book we have seen that – apart from the very beginnings of man starting to harness the natural world in the Middle East – no subsequent civilisation spectacularly arose through any kind of 'spontaneous combustion'. Every regional development arose out of either progress made previously in that geographical area, or what could be learned from progress made nearby, or the impetus provided by a wave of immigrants, or the impact of trade in goods, services, and acquired knowledge or skills.

So it was with Rome. The plethora (Latin!) of fractious tribes in the middle of the long boot-shaped peninsula that has become Italy saw all around them the amazing developments taking place, and must have viewed with growing envy the sheer *richness* of the lives being lived by other peoples in the central Mediterranean. By the middle of the 5th century BC, two faraway *seafaring* powers – Greece and the Phoenicians – were pre-eminent, and locked in a seemingly endless battle for supremacy in Sicily. While Greece had well-established coastal colonies in southern Italy, as well as in Sardinia, the Balearic islands and the southern coast of France, the Phoenicians (or Carthaginians/Punics) were well entrenched in Spain and North Africa, as well as holding an iron grip over the island 'stepping-stones' between Tunis and Motya (western Sicily). However, nowhere would these disparate groups in central Italy have had a starker example of what might be – if only they could become united – than in their immediate *land-based* neighbours to the north – the Etruscans.

The Etruscans

There are a number of obstacles that have frustrated our understanding of these remarkable people. One is language – although we have the benefit of several thousand inscriptions, in similar fashion to Carthage no lengthy texts have survived, and attempts to confirm the origins of the Etruscan alphabet (possibly a variation of Greek) have so far been less than emphatic. Another is their tombs – in the field of archaeology it is an almost unparalleled tragedy that (particularly in the 18th century) a veritable industry grew up that raided hundreds of tombs with the object of selling off the priceless artefacts and laying waste to all 'fixtures', especially the priceless wall-paintings. In addition, the very origin of the Etruscans has been the subject of speculation for 2,500 years, but – as described in the DNA section of Chapter 1 – we now know that Herodotus (writing in the 5th century BC at the height of the Etruscan era) was correct in that, at a period when, after a sharp growth in population, times were hard, they emigrated (almost certainly by boat) from Lydia in south-western Turkey.

Herodotus states – and after his 'story' has at last been vindicated, who should doubt him now? – that due to famine in Lydia a large group under the leadership of the king's son Tyrrhenos built a fleet at Smyrna, and reached Italy in the 9th century BC. For many years archaeologists have noted the similarities between the Lydians and Etruscans, and – since the DNA breakthrough in 2007 – it is certain now that redoubled efforts will be made to learn more about the Etruscans from their comparatively well-documented forebears. The Lydian origin explains much about the Etruscans, in that Lydia had an advanced culture: it was the most powerful of a number of principalities in western Turkey, and by the 7th century BC had created a miniature empire, with its capital at Sardis. Ruled at its height by Croesus, the region fell to Cyrus in 546BC, but not before it had established itself as a strong agricultural, mining, manufacturing and trading centre, with an advanced political system, and well-developed religious practices. Just recently, therefore, we have secured a much firmer footing on which to build a better picture of the resources that the Etruscans brought to bear in quickly establishing their superiority over the northern half of Italy, providing an object lesson to their backward southerly neighbours on the Tiber.

Etruscan development: the league of city states

At a time when sophisticated 'Etruscan' groups were establishing themselves in what we now call Tuscany, the rest of Italy – not just around Rome – was occupied by myriad tribes. ('Myriad' is from the Greek word 'murias', from 'murioi', literally meaning '10,000'!) The length of mainland Italy, virtually cut off from the rest of mainland Europe by the Alps/Dolomites, and divided vertically by the Apennines, meant that dozens of separate communities had occupied remote valleys for millennia, with craggy hills and fast-flowing rivers keeping them apart, and ensuring only slow development, certainly as compared with the tremendous changes being wrought further afield.

It is not difficult to see how the waves of immigrants from an advanced Lydian society were able to colonise the Tuscan hill country, which they chose well for its fertility and benign climate. These new 'Etruscans' had a history of contact with Greece, whose colonists were themselves well entrenched (by the 7th century BC) in eastern Sicily, the Bay of Naples and – south of Naples – at the city of Poseidonia (Paestum). Etruria's trump cards, so as to promote trade rather than conflict, were surplus food, copper and iron – and they had a powerful fleet with which to execute their policies. In a 'halfway house' between the unified nation they left behind, and the fragmented village communities they found in Italy, the Etruscans established a dozen 'statelets', each with a well-fortified capital. In this loose federation – bound by a common language, faith and culture – there were bound to be tensions. Nevertheless, each city sent representatives to attend the annual feast at the shrine of their senior god Voltumna.

In their pantheon of gods (Greek 'pan' [all] and 'theion' [holy]) some appear to be of Greek origin, and some from further east, including Gilgamesh from ancient Sumeria (Mesopotamia). The delineation of each city boundary would be created in a ceremony wherein the appropriate god would guide the plough, which was lifted to mark each gate. Then the inner town would be meticulously planned, with clever builders and civil engineers providing an amazing level of sophistication – underfloor heating, running water, and mains drainage.

Despite being subjected to such terrible vandalism, Etruscan tombs have still given us a clear idea of how they saw their afterlife – once again the remnants of wonderful paintings effectively pointing out the gulf between an eternal 'heaven' and 'hell'. In another link with further east, thoughts of Knossos and Mycenae are invoked by the Etruscan treatment of their dead, in either tumuli or rock-cut graves. However, in shocking contrast to Greek practice, all the evidence from statues points to women having equal status with men, both in married life and in public. The graves also show us the foreign influences on art and jewellery, not only emanating from Greece, but also from Egypt and Persia, and, in the opposite direction, from Gaul and from the Celts (centred on Hallstadt, in modern Austria).

The Etruscans and Rome

Whereas in c750BC Etruria's city states were confined to the area west of the northern Apennines, approximating to modern Tuscany, by 500BC the federation controlled all of modern north-east Italy and Corsica, and had probed down the west coast to (and beyond) Rome. Already under the influence of nearby Etruscan cities (the nearest two being Cerveteri and Veii), Rome – in the region of Latium – was coveted because it was the gateway to the fertile lands of Campagna further south, and a key to the lucrative salt trade. Already joined with other communities to create the 'Sepontium' (seven hills), the town had clearly benefited from Etruscan technology by the early 6th century BC in having the 'Cloaca Maxima' (major sewage system) constructed through the middle of it, and the Forum area drained.

Thereafter, the building programme accelerated, mainly because of the man who took the development of Rome by the 'scruff of the neck'. Tarquinius Priscus (Tarquin the Elder) had been denied the succession of his father as ruler of Cerveteri, and – at the suggestion of his wife – moved to Rome. He ingratiated himself with the then king (Ancus Marcius) to the extent that he was first appointed guardian to the royal sons, then successor to the crown. Upon becoming the fifth King of Rome, Tarquinius – who reigned from 616 to 579BC – expanded the city considerably, starting with the Triad temple on the Capitoline Hill in honour of three (Etruscan-inspired) gods, Jupiter, Juno and Minerva, and later the Circus Maximus.

In the course of his 37-year reign, Tarquinius crushed the Latins, fended off the Sabines, and defeated an alliance of several Etruscan cities, which feared his growing threat. He cleverly made peace with many of the surrounding territories, continually expanding the control being exercised by the emerging power of Rome. Tarquinius had initially secured the loyalty of many Roman families by increasing the

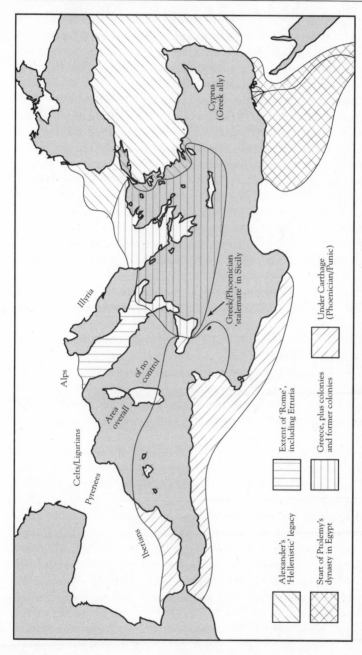

Map vii – Control of the Mediterranean at 300BC – the 'tipping point'

numbers appointed to the (long-established) Senate to 100 – the number grew to 900, and eventually to 1,800. Later in life, as evidence of his political skill he avoided assassination initiated by the adult sons of his predecessor, and appointed his son-in-law (the Latin) Servius Tullius as his successor.

In a nutshell, although Rome acted as a member of the loose Etruscan federation for the next century, its formula of centralised government provided a far more secure future than the Etruscan model. Of course, as has happened so often before and since, later Romans began to make the fabulous era of their 'mentors' disappear – certainly any debt was quite soon forgotten. The historian Diodorus stated that Etruria became soft because it was too successful in too many areas – particularly in farming and food production – and Livy blamed its demise on its only waging war for plunder and short-term gain, relying almost entirely on an army of foreign conscripts.

Rome, on the other hand, had been shocked by the ease with which the Gauls had swept south, almost unopposed, in the late 5th century BC. In response it created a highly disciplined citizen army – totally loyal to the burgeoning state – and soon after began incursions into long-held Etruscan territories. After a further century of gaining the upper hand, Rome finally destroyed the weakened Etruscan army of conscripts in 308BC at Lake Vadimon. And so – hand in hand with absorbing more and more of Etruria into its nascent empire – Rome began a process of defamation, wherein (for example) the alleged decadence of the Etruscan lifestyle was vilified, simultaneously with, in complete contrast, the beginning of the never-ending 'love affair' with Greek culture.

As the Roman Empire grew, ever more strident attempts were made to deny any debt to the Etruscans, but it is important for the balance of history that due recognition is given to the legacy passed on to the one-time upstart tribe on the Tiber. In the early days of their relationship, the Romans were eager to adopt elements of Etruscan religion, their calendar, and their alphabet. The spectacular Roman structures that are still in excellent condition – bridges, aqueducts, roads, theatres, amphitheatres, temples, and the layout of towns with all the associated engineering requirements – all had (at least in part) an Etruscan heritage, which itself emanated from the Near East, and whose pedigree can be directly or indirectly traced all the way back to ancient Mesopotamia. These inherited skills crucially encompassed advanced agricultural methods, whose prerequisite was water management – divination, drainage and irrigation. A major element in the immensely successful Roman 'business model' was to develop a professional system of agriculture, storage, processing and distribution – it should certainly be remembered that Diodorus's dismissive comments on this aspect of Etruscan life belied the astute way in which Rome adopted the very same techniques.

Expansion of Rome

As set out in the previous chapter, there follows only a brief summary of the spread of Rome around the whole Mediterranean, and the timing of the developments in its type of government.

To put it succinctly, most of our focus will thereafter be on – as summarised by Charles Van Doren – 'what the Romans knew' *themselves*, as distinct from 'what the Romans learned or copied from the Greeks'!

c280BC	The Tarentines – from the Greek colony of Tarentum, in the 'instep' at the bottom of the peninsula – enlisted King Pyrrhus (of Epirus in northern Greece) to fight Rome, which itself was supported by a Carthaginian fleet. The 'pyrrhic' victories were followed by a disillusioned Pyrrhus retiring to eastern Sicily.
272	Rome controlled the whole of the peninsula, up to the River Arno in the north.
264-241	The first Punic War took place, in which the antagonists (a word of Greek origin) fought each other to a standstill. However, one prize that fell to Rome was Sicily, her first acquisition outside mainland Italy.
218-201	Hannibal almost defeated Rome in the early stages of the second Punic War, but – eventually – Scipio (Africanus) turned the tables at the Battle of Zama (202) and Carthage had to sue for a demeaning peace.
c190	The rest of North Africa (but not Egypt) became absorbed, through the defeat of the Numidians.
146-143	Fanatical Carthage could not accept vassal status, and was finally crushed after a blockade, with the city being burned to the ground. Rome assumed control over Spain.

146	The Greek peninsula (including Macedonia) became a Roman province after the Battle of Corinth. In 88 an Athenian uprising was crushed by Sulla.
200-70	Rome extended its reach through Turkey and Syria.
63	Invasion and colonisation of Israel.
50	Julius Caesar finally subjugated Gaul, after the final defeat and capture of Vercingetorix, at the Battle of Alesia, in 52.
30	Egypt was annexed after Octavian (later Emperor Augustus) defeated Mark Antony, and deposed Queen Cleopatra.
70AD	Jewish rebellion was crushed, with the temple of Jerusalem destroyed, and subsequent mass deportation of Jews.
80	Following an initial invasion by Julius Caesar in 55BC, the whole of England and Wales was finally subjugated after the uprising of Boudicca in 61 had been brutally suppressed.
101-106	Dacia (north of Macedon and east of the Danube) was defeated by Trajan.
	There were continuous wars of attrition – Rome waged an endless struggle against German tribes, and against Parthia in (what is now) eastern Turkey and northern Iraq, with the winning of vast tracts of land that were never able to be secured permanently.
117	Under Trajan, the Empire reached its maximum extent.
Up to 285	The Empire steadily came under increased pressure, as the erosion of territory combined with increasing chaos at home took their toll.
285	Diocletian split the shrunken Empire into West and East, with the dividing line (north of the Mediterranean) roughly being between the Balkans and Greece, and in North Africa halfway along the coast of modern-day Libya.
476	After escalating loss of territory, renewed chaos in Rome, and remorseless pressure from the Visigoths, the Western Empire collapsed, with the last emperor (Romulus Augustus) being deposed.
476-1453	The Eastern Empire continued for nearly a thousand

years, its vast territory being shrunk by relentless aggression, only to enjoy several periods of renewed expansion, then again followed by further decline. After a final siege of Constantinople, the end came with the death of Constantine XI, and capture by the Ottoman Turks.

Government of Rome

Kingdom

579BC   The death of Tarquin the Elder (Priscus), as discussed earlier in the chapter.

579-535   Servius Tullius (son-in-law of Tarquin the Elder), while causing the seven hills to be fully encircled by a wall, instituted several reforms in his long reign. His most notable 'political' achievements were to further develop citizen categories so as to provide differing voting rights, and to institute a census. He favoured the poor (plebeians) over the elite, in an attempt to gain support, and was eventually assassinated through the actions of his daughter, Tullia, and her husband.

535-510   Tarquinius Superbus – husband of Tullia, and son of Priscus, and therefore Etruscan by birth – ruled Rome at a time when Etruscan power was at its zenith, and showed severe brutality in maintaining control. It seems that Superbus so inflamed the citizens of Rome by encouraging his son, Sextus, to commit the 'Rape of Lucretia' that this final straw motivated the Senate to expel him as King of Rome. The Etruscan hold of Rome and the Latium region became severely weakened, paving the way for a new form of government.

Republic

509BC   This period, in lasting nearly half a millennium, went through an extraordinary series of twists and turns, set alongside huge territorial gains, which were interspersed with severe military setbacks and recurrent social crises. In essence, the inaugural constitution contained a number of checks and balances, which, however, never

217

successfully overcame the tension between the aristocracy (patricians) and other able citizens of humbler birth (plebeians). This 480-year span saw several distinct phases:

509-367   The patrician era saw the king replaced by a pair of consuls who 'kept an eye on each other' and were elected annually. Very early on, however, the plebeians rebelled, which resulted in their being allowed to appoint a pair of tribunes with limited powers.

367-287   The Conflict of the Orders saw the consuls and tribunes initially working more closely together, for their common interest. However, despite increased poverty among the people they were supposed to represent, the increasing number of plebeian senators effectively acquired 'patrician' status as 'new nobility', progressively wresting greater authority from the old aristocracy.

287-133   The supremacy of the new nobility was given effect by the passing (in 287) of the Hortensian Law whereby the (patrician) consuls could no longer prevent legislation put forward by the (plebeian) tribunes from being debated. Once this great political question had been settled, there was a period of stability, but the hard-won improvement was undermined in later years by the consequences of small farmers being conscripted to fight, which caused their land to fall into disrepair. Laid open to their derelict farms being bought cheaply by rich patricians, hordes of plebeians began flooding into Rome, causing severe political upheaval.

133-49   The period from the Gracchi to Caesar began with the election of Tiberius Gracchus to the position of tribune, from which he tried to initiate democratic moves, much to the fury of patricians. In summary, this 84-year span degenerated into a series of internecine power struggles, with repeated conspiracies and power blocs being created, challenged and re-formed. Early in the 1st century the struggle between the democratic 'populares' party and the aristocratic 'optimates' party reached its height, with Sulla finally gaining the upper hand, only to die in 78. Now saw the rise of Pompey and Julius Caesar, who – with

Crassus – went on to form the First Triumvirate, only for this to collapse, and Caesar to seize power for himself.

49-29 The period of transition began with Caesar crossing the Rubicon (in north-east Italy), causing Pompey to abandon Rome for Greece. Caesar rapidly accumulated power in his own hands, which – in short – resulted in his assassination in 44BC. Thereupon Mark Antony, Gaius Octavian (Caesar's adopted son and great-nephew) and Marcus Lepidus formed an uneasy Second Triumvirate, ruling in a similarly dictatorial fashion. This alliance did not survive long, and eventually Mark Antony was defeated by Octavian at the battle of Actium in 31BC, committing suicide with Cleopatra. In 29BC Octavian returned to Rome in triumph and unchallenged, later accepting the title Augustus – 'exalted one'.

Empire

This vast swathe of time covers almost exactly 500 years in the West, and nearly 1,500 years in the East, mere dots along the path of overall human existence, but of greater longevity than any comparatively transient empire subsequently. As with the Republic, these immense passages of time can be considered in several distinct phases.

27BC-14AD Augustus, even ahead of his return to Rome, was awarded the title of Proconsular Imperium, which gave him overall military authority. He reorganised the army, creating the 'special forces' dedicated to securing the state (the Praetorian Guard). He made an offer to hand back his inherited powers to the Senate, but this was refused. He also devoted much time to choosing his successor, settling on his stepson, Tiberius.

14-235AD Tiberius (paranoid) succeeded Augustus, then followed Caligula (insane), Claudius (quite steady) and Nero, who – reasonably successful as a tyrant – committing suicide in 68AD. The Empire remained *just* under control, mainly due to the way in which most Proconsuls (military governors) obtained total loyalty from the respective legions under their permanent command.

219

This characteristic was vitally demonstrated during the year ('of the four emperors') when civil war raged intermittently. Only the accession of the strong Vespasian in 69AD brought this chaos to a close; his main achievements were to put the economy on a sound footing, and thereby finance the start of the Colosseum. He was succeeded by Titus, whose misfortune was to witness the destruction of Pompeii and Herculaneum by the eruption of Vesuvius in 79. Followed by his brother, who had a very poor relationship with the Senate, an unhappy passage was brought to an end by Domitian being assassinated in 96.

There followed a century of the 'five good emperors': Nerva, who restored fiscal responsibility and a good working relationship with the Senate; Trajan, who extended the Empire to its greatest extent; Hadrian, who consolidated Trajan's expansion, mainly by peaceful means; Antoninus Pius; Marcus Aurelius; and Lucius Verus. This lengthy period – the Pax Romana – declined with the murder of Commodus in 192. Successors swiftly came and went, with Severus – unable to control the military – also being assassinated in 235.

235-395 Between 235 and 284 the 3rd-century 'crisis' became acute: there were no fewer than 25 emperors in just under 50 years, grave military political and economic problems, and the effect of the catastrophic 251 Plague of Cyprian (probably smallpox), which almost rendered the Empire indefensible. The accession of Diocletian in 284 brought 20 years of respite; in restoring stability, however, he came to the view that the huge Empire was ungovernable as a single entity, and divided it in half, with two equal emperors – in effect signalling the eventual split between West and East.

Diocletian's death in 305 invoked a burst of civil war, only brought to an abrupt end by the accession of Constantine the Great in 306. He promptly reunited the Empire, and legalised Christianity in 313 through the Edict of Milan. After his death in 337, the next 60 years saw a return to internal strife with competing individuals striving to retain control over one half of the Empire, or both.

395-476 The decline of the Western Empire: the next 80 years continued in much the same vein as the preceding 60, with the exception that – in the West – successive emperors became increasingly titular, with military strongmen holding the actual reins of power. Modern historians do not completely agree that the Empire ended in 476, but this is the year in which dissatisfied Germanic mercenaries (*from within the Roman army*), stationed in Italy and led by Odoacer, rebelled and overthrew the last Western Emperor Romulus Augustus. It is quite important to realise that Rome – which had become increasingly 'germanised' over several decades – only then fell to the Ostrogoths, when their king Theodoric the Great overran Italy, after Odoacer had tried to seize Dalmatia.

476-1453 The Eastern Empire: since repeated assaults by waves of Germanic tribes had been (and would continue to be) aimed mainly at the Western arc of Britain, Gaul, Spain, the Alpine regions and Italy itself, the severing of the umbilical cord with the Western Empire initially allowed the (much wealthier) Eastern Empire to concentrate on its own – comparatively peaceful – affairs. Indeed, as it metamorphosed into what became known as the Byzantine Empire, these later additions to the original Roman Empire continued as a united entity – and even managed to regain territory in the West during the 6th century.

What the Romans copied from Greece

It would be crude to suggest that Rome developed as it did entirely on the back of other civilisations and culture. However, we have already glimpsed the extent to which early Rome absorbed so much from the Etruscans – with their own Greek-related heritage – then quickly adopted a posture of 'denial'. It is also true to say that there is archaeological evidence of Greek influence even in the native *Italian* (pre-Etruscan) communities on the Tiber.

The Romans copied the Macedonian order of battle, and Spartan weaponry. They superimposed the Greek alphabet onto the one they had inherited from Etruria (itself Greek-related in its origins), which – with the alterations they made – is the one we use today. All children of Rome, in the upper and middle classes, automatically learned Greek as their second language. If one visits any museum around the world, in moving from the Classical Greek rooms to the Roman section the startling similarity in works of art is immediately obvious.

The Romans studied Greek poetry and drama very intensively, and did their best to master the bewildering strands of Greek philosophy, without perhaps grasping all its subtle nuances. Most wealthy Romans pursued a domestic Greek lifestyle, the insides of their homes and their gardens being furnished with statuettes and vases that were Greek copies. It is indeed true to say that, in most aspects of 'culture' (defined as relating to the arts and intellectual achievements), the Romans burnished all these things they inherited from the Greeks, but hardly produced any evidence of their own originality.

Fundamental differences between Rome and Greece

Before examining – as Van Doren puts it – 'what the Romans knew', it is useful to consider the areas in which these two Mediterranean titans of antiquity differed so markedly. Cato the Censor (234-149BC) lived through the life-or-death struggle with Carthage, and saw the military erosion of Greek power in the Western Mediterranean, his 85-year span ending just three years before (in 146) Carthage was laid waste and the Peloponnese finally overrun. But he could see the 'way the wind was blowing' and railed against the headlong rush to copy all things Greek – believing that Greek influence undermined ancient Roman customs and morality. He was convinced that the Greeks' immorality and luxurious lifestyle in particular had led to their being outflanked by disciplined Roman might, and that the imminent fate of Greece to be totally dominated by Rome would – if Rome did not 'pull itself together' – become its own fate at the hands of 'barbarians'.

Van Doren reminds us that 'ambivalence' – from the Latin 'ambi' (on both sides) and 'valere' (be worth) – is a characteristic redolent throughout history. He quotes a prime example of the English fascination for all things French throughout the 18th century, even when the countries were fighting each other most of the time, and the admiration of the German upper class for the English 'gentleman' in the short Edwardian era that ended with the First World War. Nevertheless, there were initially – and so it remained for the duration of the Empire – fundamental differences between these two peoples that have influenced our lives ever since. First – as so vividly brought to us by Homer's account of the meandering 'Odyssey' of Odysseus – the Greeks were wanderers. They travelled, and settled, in every direction, with each colony soon becoming vibrantly independent of (and sometimes antagonistic towards) its mother city state. On the other hand – as depicted by Virgil (70-19BC) – his hero Aeneas, when forced to flee from Troy and search for a new home, never stopped bemoaning his exile. The Romans had a homing instinct and a loyalty towards Rome.

Next – which relates to the above – the Romans, having seen at close hand the divisiveness of the Etruscan city model, and knowing all about the internecine wars in the Peloponnese, not to mention the fierce independence of Syracuse, deliberately focussed on creating a homogeneous regime from the earliest days. 'Homogeneousness' – from the Greek 'homos' (same) and 'genos' (race, kind) – was epitomised by their motto 'Senatus Populusque Romanus', 'the Senate and the People of Rome', the abbreviation of which (SPQR) can still to this day be seen everywhere in Rome. This leads to another key point of difference, in that whereas the Greeks (prior to Alexander the Great) treated all foreigners as 'barbarians', when Rome expanded across the Mediterranean she urged on each conquered territory the virtues of the Roman way, and (effectively, as some empires have practiced since) established a method of qualification for Roman citizenship. Countless numbers, from widely different ethnic backgrounds – most of whom never actually visited Rome – seized their opportunity and came to bask in the highly prized declaration: 'Civis Romanus Sum' ('I am a Roman citizen').

Turning to the question of ideas versus practicality, the Romans were lucky in being in a position to absorb everything that the Greeks knew, then add their own particular capabilities. 'Iconoclasm' is derived from the Greek 'eikon' (image) and 'klan' (to break) and, as Van Doren describes it, the Greeks – while never very practical – had this characteristic in abundance:

'...in love with risk taking, they had feverishly sought novelty in all things, discarding the old simply because it was old and not necessarily because it was bad. The Romans, on the contrary, were consistently and habitually practical. Their practicality was manifested in many ways. They watered down the great Greek philosophies, in the process making them much more palatable to the multitudes...

'Underlying all these changes was one very important belief that the Romans embraced but the Greeks did not: A grand idea that does not work is less valuable than a smaller one that does. On this principle the Romans constructed a city-empire that endured for a thousand years.'

But then – as now – civilisations could develop in a surprising and unpredictable manner. On the one hand, the Romans promoted throughout the Empire a Greek educational curriculum, sending Greek teachers to every corner. Greek know-how in many fields (such as ceramics and metallurgy) was widely disseminated. On the other hand, there was hardly any *Roman* scientific advance on the vast body of knowledge they had inherited. At the height of the Empire, in the 1st century AD, Rome controlled the whole Mediterranean 'lake' and had the known world at its feet. Yet, even when the Romans had every resource at their disposal, they did not build on the Greek legacy. There is good reason for believing that many inventions were spurned, a prime example being the amazing prototypes developed by Hero of Alexandria, a brilliant mathematician and engineer in the purest Hellenic tradition of scholarship. His most famous machine (of several) was a kind of steam engine, known as an 'aeolipile', which was never put to any practical use. (It is only through their preservation in Arab manuscripts that we know of his remarkable 'machines', the like of which had to wait nearly two millennia before utterly transforming our modern world.)

Another remarkable anomaly in the Roman world concerned the distribution of food, but only in their home city. However 'hit and miss' the levels of efficient marketing and distribution were, a workable system operated reasonably well in the cultures that preceded Rome for providing burgeoning city populations with all manner of food from the surrounding farming communities. However, while a carefully planned supply-and-demand system worked well in most of the Empire, the population of Rome enjoyed an ancient right to *free* food, paid for by the State. Over time, no politician dared to 'bite the bullet' and change this dangerous situation, wherein up to half a million people (many drifting in from the countryside to form the mob) had this increasingly untenable benefit, while not being involved in proper employment. Therein (in the late 3rd/early 4th century) lay the seeds of ultimate disaster, with an increasingly uncontrollable mob responding to the bribery of one politician after another, while producing a crippling burden for the Treasury.

'What the Romans (*did*) know'

Roman law
While Greek philosophers continuously debated standards of justice, and the actual set of laws in place differed between city states, Rome attached enormous importance to its legal system, regarding its laws (and customs) as fundamental to the running of the state. The first codification took place in c449BC, with – following the work of a special committee – the appearance of the 'Twelve Tables'. Carved into wood (and later cast in bronze), these were displayed in the Forum, for every citizen to follow and promulgate. Copies of the Tables were taken to every captured territory, so that the locals could see what was expected from them.

Although many individual pieces of legislation were enacted in the next 150 years, the next significant step was the 'Lex Aquilia' of 286BC, wherein the roots of modern tort law were established. Moreover, a crucial contribution to what we enjoy today was the emergence of professional jurists ('jurisprudentes') together with the concept of legal science. In terms of the advance in law-making, the era between c200 and 27BC (when the Republic became an Empire) is known as the Pre-Classical period. The most notable achievement during this span was when the Civil Law practised by magistrates was merged with the code practised by 'praetors' (specially appointed individuals) to form the 'Corpus Juris Civilis', the Body of Civil Law.

In the period up to about 250AD there followed what we know as the Classical period of Roman law, during which such eminent jurists as Gaius streamlined many areas of the law – including inheritance, contracts, property and citizenship – into codes that ultimately became widely used for hundreds of years. From then, however, until the collapse of the Empire in the West (476AD) the primacy of the legal system clashed with increasingly totalitarian emperors, with dictatorial and corrupt behaviour demeaning the remarkable achievements of earlier centuries.

It was left to the Emperor Justinian, who controlled the Eastern Empire from Constantinople (517-565AD) and objected to the complexity of the legal system he had inherited, to promulgate the famous 'Codex Constitutionium' in 529, which thereafter became the chief source and authority of Roman law. This code remained in effect for a thousand years in its complete form, and is still the legal basis throughout most of Europe, and far beyond.

Roman roads, arches, aqueducts and buildings

With the prime exception of Alexander making use of the Persian road system, Rome's predecessors Greece and Carthage had accessed most territories by sea, and had never driven roads far inland. In total contrast – as 'every schoolboy' used to know – the extent and durability of Roman roads became legendary. As their geographical reach grew, the Romans immediately realised that a secure direct route across any terrain was the key to being able to govern, which included the quickest possible movement of foodstuffs and other goods, as well as armies.

It is calculated that the Empire had 250,000 miles (400,000km) of road, of which at least 20% was fully paved. So crucial was this aspect of Roman life that the 'Twelve Tables' even included a set of specifications. There were three grades of road, the most sophisticated type (the 'Via Munita') being the one that has – in countless locations – survived to the present day. This very carefully designed method has five strata, from the levelled/rammed earth at the base through to a crowned surface made up of polygonal blocks of the very best local stone available. Water drained to the sides, which were buttressed by cut stone edging, so as to stop the road spreading over time. Two famous examples are the Via Appia (Appian Way), which linked Rome with modern Brindisi, the first section of which dates from 312BC, and the streets of Pompeii, which can be seen to bear the wheel-ruts of 2,000-year-old traffic.

Despite the impressiveness of their road-building record, even more spectacular – and equally long-lasting – structures were afforded by the discovery of 'pozzolana', a volcanic ash first discovered near Vesuvius, at Pozzuoli. Over time the Romans realised that this ash had cement-like properties, since when mixed with lime and water it set as a type of concrete. The Pantheon temple in Rome, built in its current form around 126AD, still today exists as incorporating the largest *unreinforced* concrete dome in the world. A church since the 7th century, this perfectly preserved building, with a spectacular central 'oculus' (opening) to the sky at the centre of the dome, renders many first-time visitors almost speechless. Any tourist who wishes to obtain an understanding of the scale and variety of Roman building capabilities in (say) two energetic days of travel, can do no better – apart from Rome itself – than to visit 'Roman' Provence, and take in Le Pont Julien near Apt, the Theatre at Orange, the amphitheatres at Arles and Nimes, the Maison Carree temple at Nimes, and – perhaps most spectacular of all – the Pont du Gard aqueduct, which was built to bring water along a route from the Cevennes hills to Nimes, over a 25-mile (40km) stretch of tortuous terrain, with a fall of only 8 feet (2.5m) over its whole length!

Le Pont Julien is but one example of a perfectly preserved bridge from around the Empire. Three other wonderful examples, which Parry describes in detail, are the Pons Milvio across the Tiber, built in 109BC, which 'during World War II, carried the entire military traffic of the Italian, German and Allied armies'; the Ponte di Augusto at Rimini (20BC), so beloved by Palladio in the 16th century, with its beautifully cut semi-circular voussoir arches; and in Spain the majestic Alcantara (Arabic for 'The Bridge') Bridge, built in 104AD, the deck of which 'soars 50m (165 feet) above the river-bed on perfectly proportioned piers, 9m (30 feet) thick, pointed upstream and squared downstream'. Parry records that the engineer left an aptly prophetic inscription in Latin saying: 'I have left a bridge that shall remain forever.'

There are many other examples of Roman technological expertise, all of which were described by Pliny the Elder in great detail (see below). Included in his wide-ranging survey are: gold mining, including the use of fire, water and hydraulics; gold manipulation, including his description of how 1 ounce could be beaten into 750 leaves, each 4 inches square; and brick-making, perfected in the 1st century AD, of which a most spectacular example (still in an unblemished state) is the Constantine Basilica, built at Trier in Germany at the beginning of the 4th century, and now a World Heritage Site.

Roman authors

During the 555-year span between Rome securing the whole of mainland Italy (c270BC) and Diocletian splitting the Empire in two in an attempt to better handle an increasingly ungovernable state (285AD), we know that there were hundreds of distinguished Roman men of letters, all of whom have been studied in differing degrees during our modern era. It is perhaps no coincidence, however, that the most important writers who still feature so widely in today's scholarship all lived within the 200-year span of Rome at its most secure and prosperous – that is between 80BC, when Cicero (born 106BC) first shot to prominence, and the death of Tacitus in 117AD. To keep this account within reasonable bounds, we will briefly recount the lives and legacy of just ten of these illustrious men, who – in all cases – contributed greatly to our knowledge of Roman history. It is to these few, who were able to interpret and develop aspects of Greek philosophy to allow a better understanding by a wider audience, that we will pay particular attention. There follows a sequence by date of death, on the basis that the works of each mature contributor would have been comprehensively studied by his successors.

Lucretius (Titus Lucretius Carus, c94-c55BC) was a man about whose life we know very little, and whose only known work was *De rerum natura* (*On the Nature of Things*). This poem shows that he was a devoted follower of both Epicurus (see Chapter 14) and Zeno (the Stoic, c335-c263BC). The 'strange ... beautiful' poem is not remembered for the 'science' it describes, but for the author's 'profound wisdom about human life'. Van Doren continues that Lucretius '...combined Stoicism and Epicureanism in a way that made sense two thousand years ago and still does to many readers... He wanted ordinary people, like himself as he claimed, to understand and appreciate philosophical thought.' Today, Lucretius '...is loved for his humanity ... able to do what is, strangely, so difficult for many persons ... able to forgive themselves, as a wise man once said, for being human. That is, knowing that life is hard and virtue rare, they keep the ancient faith that it is better to love than to hate, to live fully even if imperfectly.'

Cicero wrote to his brother in 54BC: 'The poems of Lucretius are as you write: they exhibit many flashes of genius, and yet show great mastership.' And Virgil, referring to Lucretius, wrote: 'Happy is he who has discovered the causes of things and has cast beneath his feet all fears, unavoidable fate, and the din of the devouring Underworld.'

Cicero (Marcus Tullius Cicero, 106-43BC) was – in complete contrast to Lucretius – someone about whom we know a great deal. He was born a member of a rich 'equestrian' family ('equestrian' status was the equivalent of our 'knight', where ancestry was supposed to involve recruitment into the cavalry, then, as until very recently, considered to be a superior branch of the military!). He was very well educated, becoming an impressive combination of lawyer/philosopher/politician/orator, though now best remembered for the wealth of his correspondence and the quality of his prose. In his first career as a lawyer he trod a dangerous path (as a relative unknown) in his 80BC defence of one accused of 'parricide', by in turn accusing a favourite of the dictator Lucius Cornelius Sulla of murdering the individuals concerned, and managing to secure his client's acquittal. It has to be said that – in his favourite role as a politician – Cicero always 'chanced his arm' in the vicious era in which he lived. He got away with supporting Pompey against Julius Caesar, but sided against Mark Antony and, when the Second Triumvirate was formed, was hunted down as an enemy of the state and murdered.

A good proportion of Cicero's work has come down to us, and in his last book *On Duties* he dealt with a range of personal dilemmas, as summarised by Van Doren:

'How honest did a businessman have to be? Did shortcuts exist that could honestly be taken? How should a good man respond to the unjust demands of a tyrant? Was it all right to be silent, or should a person always speak up, even if to do so would be dangerous? How should a man treat his inferiors, even his slaves? Did inferiors have rights that ought to be respected? Cicero wrestles with these issues, urging us to always do the "right thing". "Admit it!" he exclaimed. "We do know when we are doing right and when we are doing wrong."'

Cicero's *theories* could not compare with the ideas expressed by Socrates, Plato or Aristotle, but he put forward practical suggestions on the issue of how man could have peace (no more wars) and liberty (freedom for every man to live as he pleases) *simultaneously*. In addressing himself to the threat to the (Roman) Republic, he fervently believed that a government of *laws* could take the place of a government of *men* and, despite all the pitfalls of such a proposition, his hand is to be very clearly seen in the Constitution promulgated by the Founding Fathers of the American republic. John Adams said of him, paraphrasing the immortal lines in Plato's *Republic*: 'As all the ages of the world have not produced a greater statesman and philosopher united than Cicero, his authority should have great weight.'

Virgil (Publius Vergilius Maro, 70-19BC) was born in northern Italy and, though there is debate as to his parental wealth and status, he certainly acquired a wide education. His three major works were the *Eclogues*, the *Georgics*, and – written in the last decade of his life, the poem that would give him lasting fame – the *Aeneid*. This epic poem – probably commissioned by the Emperor Augustus – consists of 12 books, written in hexameter verse, in which Virgil describes the story of the Trojan prince Aeneas, who has to flee his beloved Troy, which is in flames after being sacked by the Achaeans (Greeks), during which his wife was killed. On his shoulders he carries his aged father, he leads his son in one hand, and carries figurines of the gods in the other. He wanders the Mediterranean searching for a new home, spurns the amorous Dido (Queen of Carthage) and eventually settles in Italy, where in finding a new wife (Lavinia, daughter of King Latinus) he is forced to defeat her erstwhile suitor, Turnus. Finally settled, Aeneas occupies the site that will eventually become the city of Rome.

From the outset of their publication, Virgil's works became standard reading in the Roman educational system, and were subsequently utilised by later poets such as Ovid. Later, because his works found favour in Christian Rome – due mainly to an interpretation that he prophesied the Coming of Jesus Christ – his fame spread far and wide. For example, after the collapse of the Western Empire bishop Gregory of Tours not only read Virgil (and other Roman poets) but often quoted him in his writings, though cautioning that 'we ought not to relate their lying fables, lest we fall under sentence of eternal death'. Much later, in Dante's most famous work *The Divine Comedy*, Virgil features as the guide to Hell and Purgatory.

Horace (Quintus Horatius Flaccus, 65BC-8AD) was the son of a freed slave who owned a small farm near Venusia, in southern Italy, and managed to spend a considerable sum on his son's education. He moved to Rome as a young man, acting as a middleman ('coactor') at auctions, before suffering the vicissitudes of a defeated soldier, having joined the army under Brutus following the death of Julius Caesar. Returning to find his father dead (and his property confiscated), Horace later paid his father a moving tribute in his work *Satires*:

> 'If my character is flawed by a few minor faults, but is otherwise decent and moral, if you can point out only a few scattered blemishes on an otherwise immaculate surface, if no one can accuse me of greed, or of prurience, or of profligacy, if I live a virtuous life, free of defilement (pardon, for a moment, my self-praise) and if I am to my friends a good friend, my father deserves all the credit... As it is now, he deserves from me unstinting gratitude and praise. I could never be ashamed of such a father, nor do I feel any need, as many people do, to apologise for being a freedman's son.'

Living just between Virgil and Ovid, Horace was one of the great triumvirate of Augustan poets. He coined many phrases that we have in frequent use, two examples being 'carpe diem' (literally 'pluck the day', or, as we say, 'seize the day') and 'dulce et decorum est pro patria mori', which translates as 'it is sweet and fitting to die for one's country'. Most famously, Horace was one of Rome's great satirists, gentler and less vitriolic than Juvenal, who lived much later. He criticised social vices with light-hearted humour, identifying human failings as folly rather than evil. So revered did Horace become that he was given an estate (near modern Tivoli) in later life by one of Augustus's confidantes, and, dying without heirs, left this to the emperor for his pleasure.

Livy (Titus Livius, 59BC-17AD) was said to have been born in Padua, but very little is known about his early life, with snippets only being deduced from the records of later writers. However, it appears that he made his way to Rome as a young man, and probably started writing his monumental history of Rome at the same time as the Republic ended, with Augustus becoming emperor in 27BC, when Livy was aged 32. Writing this massive work – *Ab Urbe Condita Libri* (*Chapters from the Foundations of Rome*), which has attracted an intense degree of scholarly attention since the Middle Ages, took Livy the rest of his working life. From the start of the book he sang the praises of the Republic and, although it was very well received by the emperor and his entourage, Livy had run a huge risk since such a stance had cost many other republican sympathisers their lives.

In fact, Livy's relationship with Augustus is put into perspective some time later by Tacitus, who describes a reference by the beleaguered Cordus at his trial for his republican views, in front of a hostile Emperor Tiberius: 'I am said to have praised Brutus and Cassius, whose careers many have described and no one mentioned without eulogy. Titus Livius, pre-eminently famous for eloquence and truthfulness, extolled Cneius Pompeius in such a panegyric [from the Greek word 'paneguricos', 'of public assembly'] that Augustus called him Pompeianus, and yet this was no obstacle to their friendship.' Cordus committed suicide rather face an adverse verdict, which may explain why Livy retired to Padua after the death of Augustus – and thereby avoided any confrontation with a paranoid and vengeful Tiberius.

Ovid (Publius Ovidius Naso, 43BC-17/18AD) was born east of Rome to an equestrian family. He was educated in Rome, and his father encouraged him to study rhetoric, with a view to a legal career. This life did not suit the young Ovid, and in his late teens he travelled to Greece, Turkey and Sicily, taking up junior positions in the public service. We know so much about his life because – starting to write poetry at the age of about 20 – he told much about himself, and miraculously most of his works have survived. Ovid was extremely prolific, most of his early works – the most famous of which were *Heroides*, *Amores* and *Ars Amatoria* – being partially autobiographical; certainly he lived his heterosexual life to the full, being married three times by the age of 30, with his poems making frequent reference to his mistresses. In this phase of his life he was hugely popular, becoming as famous as his (older) poetic contemporaries Virgil and Horace.

By 8AD Ovid had finished his most ambitious – and most popular – work, the *Metamorphoses* (*Transformations*), a 15-book catalogue in the hexameter style. Entirely concerned with the 'transformations' in Greek and Roman mythology, Ovid assembles a vast body of material, and covers no fewer than 250 myths that are linked by geography, themes and contrasts. In travelling from the creation of the cosmos to the deification of Julius Caesar, he gives us an almost unparalleled insight into the world of the gods that the Greeks and Romans alike so revered. In the same year, Ovid was exiled to Tomis on the Black Sea (Constantza in modern Romania) on the direct orders of Augustus.

Endless speculation as to the reason has never produced a satisfactory answer, the most likely being that Augustus considered his racy poems to be morally subversive.

Until his death in 18AD, Ovid wrote in a much more emotive style, often recounting his despair at having to live in exile, during which his most famous work was *Fasti*, a detailed account of the background to the Roman calendar; only the six chapters covering January to June survive. Today, Romania claims Ovid as her 'first poet', many children are named 'Ovidiu', and the statue to his memory in Constantza has a Latin inscription that translates as:

'Here I lie, who played with tender loves,
Naso the poet, killed by my own talent.
O passer-by, if you've ever been in love, let it not be too much for you to say: May the bones of Naso lie gently.'

Seneca (Lucius Annaeus Seneca, 4BC-65AD) was a sickly son of a famous father whose deep interest in Hellenism may have been fired by several years of living in Egypt as a young man. He is believed to have returned to Rome in 31AD, and to have clashed with Caligula when the latter became emperor in 38, his life being spared only because Caligula assumed that his poor health would cause his imminent death. It seems that Seneca always lived dangerously, being banished by Claudius to Corsica in 41, then being brought back to Rome in 49 for the dubious task of tutoring the young Nero. Following the death of Claudius in 54, Seneca had great power as a key advisor to Nero until 62, but his star was in decline from the moment he was complicit in the murder of Nero's mother Agrippina in 59. Though supposed to have retired in 62 to concentrate on writing, he was accused (probably falsely) of plotting to assassinate Nero in 65, and was forced to commit suicide.

Seneca's reputation has ebbed and flowed over the two millennia since he lived his complex and varied life, but he comes down to us as a fine example of a multi-talented, though flawed, individual, perilously weaving his way through the most cut-throat Roman period:

• as a scholar in the Stoic tradition, whose adherence to the principles laid down was compromised by his habit of having scandalous affairs with notable married women,

233

- as a writer of the *Consolations*, wherein letters addressed to individual sufferers in bereavement turn out to be cool essays on Stoicism aimed at a wider audience,
- as tutor to Nero, the heir to an empire, he made a determined – though eventually fruitless – attempt to guide the mad young man in how to govern the known world, and
- as the writer of (as we see it today) a series of quite unnecessarily bloodthirsty tragedies, who nevertheless strove, as Van Doren writes, 'to keep alive the great tradition of his Greek predecessors in philosophy and drama.'

Pliny the Elder (Gaius Plinius Secundus, 23AD-25 August 79AD) was born in the 'new' town of Como, established with an imported population 80 years earlier by Julius Caesar (including hundreds of upper-class Greeks) as a buttress against the Alpine tribes to the north. From an equestrian family, he was educated in Rome, and trained as a lawyer. He recorded many incidents, with other anecdotes coming down to us through his nephew (see below). Joining the army at the age of 23 – as many children of equestrian families were wont to do – he spent most of his military career in Germany, but also served in Tunisia and Spain. Pliny was a polymath who, despite his busy career, spent all his spare time studying and writing a long-missing *History of the German Wars*, various biographies, and 'safe' tomes on rhetoric and grammar during the turbulent years of Caligula and Nero; he also became a confidante of the Emperor Vespasian, who made him 'praefect' of the navy, and garnered mountains of information on the natural world.

Being finally allowed to return to Rome in c75AD (aged over 50), Pliny – who never married – set to work on his one surviving masterpiece, *Naturalis Historia*, a 37-book encyclopaedia that was dedicated to the Emperor Titus, son of Vespasian. Not only is this publication one of the most comprehensive Roman works to have come down to us, but it also set a marker for all subsequent encyclopaedias, through its range of subject matter, contents pages and indices, together with detailed references to original sources and other authors.

In 79 Pliny was stationed with the fleet at Misenum in the Gulf of Naples, and in popular imagination is best remembered for his fascination with the nearby volcanic eruption of Vesuvius. In seeking a closer look, and in attempting to rescue friends desperate to escape, his 'fast-sailing cutter' was trapped against the shore by the adverse wind, and the famous man succumbed – perhaps overcome by asphyxiation – on 25 August.

Pliny the Younger (Gaius Plinius Caecilius Secundus, 61-c112AD) was also born in Como, the nephew of a famous uncle. However, we are indebted to the younger man for the hundreds of his letters that survive, and for his graphic account of his uncle's demise. Involved in the legal system from an early age, he was still in his 20s when promoted to the rank of 'quaestor' (public official). He was involved (on both sides) in the prosecution of several public figures, and managed to survive the internecine struggles of successive emperors while steadily being promoted throughout his life. He started writing as a teenager, though his poetry is lost; as an adherent of Cicero, he became a notable orator, the only surviving text of which is a tribute to the Emperor Trajan, which was read out in the Senate in 100AD.

Pliny's correspondence (the *Epistulae*) was addressed to many notables, including Trajan and his friend Tacitus, and provides us with a unique insight into the administration of the Empire at the end of the 1st century AD. One of his most famous letters was a detailed description of the violent eruption of Vesuvius in 79, and the consequent death of his uncle. So meticulous was his account of the volcano's pattern of activity – and the violence of the major eruption – that today's vulcanologists utilise the term 'Plinian' in their technical vocabulary. Another of Pliny's best known letters was one in which he asked the emperor for instructions regarding official policy towards a new – and troublesome – human phenomenon (from the Greek word 'phainomenon', 'thing appearing to view'), namely the Christians.

Tacitus (Publius Cornelius Tacitus, 56-117AD) was probably born in southern Gaul, of Celtic origin, and went to Rome as a young man to study law and politics. When 21 or 22 he married the daughter of a famous general, Agricola, who was responsible for conquering most of Britain. While making his way professionally alongside his friend Pliny the Younger – in particular through the dreadful tyranny of Domitian, who ruled from 81 to 96 – he wrote virtually nothing. However, with the accession of Trajan in 98, and confident of a more stable era, the 42-year-old Tacitus had the confidence to make his debut as a historian (and biographer), for which we are eternally grateful.

In that year he published *Agricola*, a biography of his father-in-law, who had died in 94 (much of which concerns the native Britons) and an essay on the array of Germanic tribes – *Germania* – who were a constant thorn in the flesh of Rome. In both cases the most striking feature is the sympathetic portrait he paints of the indigenous populace, contrasting their simple virtues with the brutality, vices and complacency of Rome, and prophesying the demise of Rome unless she mended her ways.

Despite eventually rising to the position of Consul, he continued to write prodigiously for the rest of his life, and it is our particular misfortune that we only know excerpts from his two most famous works. First he produced *Histories*, written c100-c110AD, which covered the period from the 'year of the four emperors' (68-69) to the death of Domitian in 96. Second, not long before his death, he published *Annals*, which went back to the death of Augustus in 14AD, and tracked events up to the point of Nero's suicide in 68. Tacitus wrote in a most graphic style, on the one hand appalling the reader with the brutality displayed (including his contemptuous view of Christians), while on the other hand gripping the reader with a fast-paced story that is difficult to put down.

With the death of Domitian, Rome entered a golden age of good governance (the 'Antonine dynasty') wherein just and virtuous rule lasted for nearly a century. In his introduction to *Histories*, Tacitus describes the start of this benign era in typically robust terms, as per Van Doren:

'I have reserved as an employment for my old age, should my life be long enough, a subject (History) at once more fruitful and less anxious in the reign of the Divine Nerva and the empire of Trajan, enjoying the rare happiness of times, when we may think what we please, and express what we think.'

How many times – around most of the globe, during the 20th century – did savagely oppressed writers yearn to be able to repeat these eloquent words? In *Agricola* Tacitus makes a further memorable comment, when describing how a Roman commander – after ruthlessly suppressing a barbarian uprising – stated that he had brought 'peace' to the region: 'Faciunt solitudinem et pacem appellant,' the trenchant historian writes ('They make a wilderness, and call it

236

peace'). Again, how often in the recent past has that disdainful remark been echoed?

The spread of Christianity to the west

We have seen that both Pliny the Younger and Tacitus referred to Christians in disparaging terms, with the latter recording that Nero blamed their small community for the Great Fire in 64AD. However, though both St Peter and St Paul are reputed to have been put to death in Rome – in c67 – towards the end of Nero's reign there is no historical record of these particular events. During the next 250 years, despite appalling persecution on – as we would see it now – the flimsiest excuses, Christian apostles established a patchwork of communities in every corner of the Mediterranean, with a strong presence in nearly all major cities.

The breakthrough came with Constantine – through the influence of his devoted mother Helena – following up the edict issued by Galerius in 311, which put a stop to the persecution promoted by his predecessor Diocletian. Constantine then secured the throne by defeating his brother-in-law at the Milvian Bridge, near Rome. That this battle has become one of the most famous in history is due to the dream Constantine had the night before, wherein an angel held a cross over him, saying: 'In hoc signo vinces' ('In this sign thou shalt conquer'). On waking, he ordered his troops to paint the Christian cross on their shields, and from then on he lived as a committed Christian. After this victory, Constantine was able to consolidate his power, and in 313 he and his rival Licinius issued the Edict of Milan, proclaiming religious tolerance throughout the Empire. Thereafter, consolidation of the new religion continued apace through the Western Empire, becoming adopted everywhere by the time the Empire collapsed.

Decline of the Western Empire, and the retreat of knowledge

The period of stable government – of which Tacitus wrote so glowingly – ceased at the end of the 2nd century AD, and earlier in this chapter we have plotted the unsteady decline, towards the desperate measure of splitting the Empire in two, and the eventual collapse in the west in 476.

It had long been the case that Greek had become the first language of the (educated) populations – from Greece itself to the Levant in the east, and Egypt in the south – whereas Latin had become predominant from Italy, through Gaul to the north and Spain to the west. With increasing turmoil at Rome and throughout the Western Empire, the nurturing of Greek language, literature, philosophy and every branch of science – which had reached its zenith between 100BC and 100AD – started to fade in this half of the Empire, in parallel with the military and civil decline.

One element, among hundreds of examples, where the precipitous disintegration can be visualised, is to consider the municipality of Baelo Claudia – situated in the dunes just behind a spectacular beach near Tarifa (west of the Strait of Gibraltar). Prospering in the two centuries before and after Christ, one can see the beautiful remains of this small city, whose status was secured by the industrial-scale harvesting, processing, packaging and distribution throughout the empire of garum – salted anchovy products – derived from the massive shoals of fish netted offshore. All evidence of the numerous (vertically integrated) factories that were sited on the sandy beach, and which employed hundreds of workmen, have long since disappeared.

The death of the Ostrogoth king Theodoric in 526 snuffed out any residual stability in the crumbling state now ruled from Ravenna. As the Vandals swept though Italy, it was not only the Greek language that became lost. The administrative and legal system collapsed, as did the infrastructure, with the whole array of Roman technology being burnt or buried. No wonder that study of Pliny's *Natural History* had learned translators (e.g. Robert of Cricklade, who presented an abbreviated version to Henry II of England in the late 12th century) completely bowled over by the remarkable extent of knowledge that was revealed!

So much destruction took place in the 4th and 5th centuries AD – with many priceless texts lost for ever – that we must now piece together how the *fragile* threads of accumulated scholarship were nurtured in *key* locations, and the means whereby this vital body of knowledge was eventually able to resurface in Western Europe, ahead of the Renaissance.

Part III

Chapter 17

Christendom: the European Dark Age and Early Middle Age to 1066

At this stage, it may be useful to define what is generally meant by the terms 'Dark Age' and 'Middle Age' (the Medieval era). As with the Mediterranean Dark Age – which is now considered to have 'only' lasted for about 250 years, from c1150 to c900BC – the European Dark Age was not so 'dark', or as long, as was originally seen. The *really* Dark era can now be said to have also lasted for about 250 years – that is (for our purpose, as will be explained later) from c480 to 730AD. The turning of this Dark Age into the Early Middle Age seemed to start at an almost glacial pace, which slowly gathered momentum. This era spanned almost another 350 years, from 730 to 1066, the end date being specific, and not only for the obvious reason that every British schoolchild might suppose!

In arable northern Europe, every field of wheat used to include patches of a colourful poppy (Papaver rhoeas, a relation of the opium variant, so valued 6,000 years ago by the Sumerians for oil) until heavy crop-spraying put paid to this evocative sight each summer. Then, a few years ago, farmers were encouraged towards organic methods, and suddenly – after disappearing for decades – poppies immediately resurfaced! How could this be? The answer is that indestructible seed pods in the ground, so small as to be almost invisible to the naked eye, can lie dormant for as long as it takes, before once again having the right conditions for germination and rapid growth towards flowering in a riot of colour.

This apparent 'miracle' is somewhat analogous to the story of how some 'transportable' knowledge (i.e. that which was committed to memory, or to print – nearly all in Latin) managed to survive amidst the chaos and dislocation that had been threatening Rome in the 4th century, and which finally engulfed the whole of Western Europe towards the end of the 5th century. At the end of the previous chapter we scheduled the debilitating *internal* factors that combined to bring about the eventual collapse. Now, before identifying where and how the 'seeds' of learning lay practically dormant, we should briefly catalogue how the nominal date (for the Fall) of 476 in no way brought to an end the destruction, death and privations endured by indigenous communities everywhere – and in quick succession – at the hands of their assorted conquerors.

The 'barbarian' surge to the west

The Great Wall of China was built to keep out marauding nomadic tribes (the Hsiung-nu), but even after its completion in c220BC the swarms of nomads were a constant threat, and were only finally dispersed in the 1st century AD, after an epic struggle with the Han empire. The Hsiung-nu were never farmers and builders, but developed as brilliant horsemen, who moved their cattle and goats huge distances around seasonal pastures in an annual cycle, carrying out devastating raids on unprotected settlements wherever they came across them in the vast steppe of 'Greater Mongolia'.

Over the next century the Chinese managed to force the westward drift of these nomads (to become known as Huns) across central Asia, and it was the migration of these natural aggressors that compelled the Goths and Vandals to move westward, which – in turn – saw the Germanic peoples driven southwards.

We have already seen how, after the bitter struggles between Rome and the Germanic tribes (roughly along the western and southern edges of present-day Germany and Austria) during the century before and after Christ, Rome started to recruit German mercenaries, to the point whereby from the beginning of the 4th century ethnic Germans formed the backbone of the Roman military machine. Then we noted that dynamic German leaders overthrew the weak Roman politicians, only to themselves face the Gothic hordes, who first sacked Rome in 410. In an increasingly confusing melee, one fairly clear-cut outcome was the demise of the Huns themselves, who never recovered from the defeat of Attila in 451 at the hands of a combined Roman and Visigoth army, at the Battle of Chalons-en-Champagne (Attila died the following year).

However, we should study briefly the rapid sweep west and south through the Empire of the main branches of massed 'barbarians', whom the Huns had originally ousted from central Asia:

- from Denmark and northern Germany: Jutes, Angles and Saxons to England
- from northern Germany: Franks to northern France
- from eastern Germany: Vandals south-east towards the Hun capital, but then east all the way across Germany and France, and south through Spain into North Africa, later fanning north to every island in the western Mediterranean, the Peloponnese and – most significantly – to Rome itself, which they sacked in 455.
- from Scandinavia: Goths south-east across the Baltic towards the Black Sea
- from near the Black Sea: Goths, splitting into the Visigoth tribes moving south, devastating a Roman army at Adrianople (sited in the 'European' wedge of modern-day Turkey) in 378, before in turn overrunning Greece and Italy, and devastating all before them across the south of France, en route to Spain; and the Ostrogoths, some venturing south-east into what is now eastern Turkey, while others went west, across Austria and Switzerland, also joining in the plundering of Italy.

Conversion to Christianity

An absolutely fundamental – and most *fortunate* – element in this part of our story is the way in which the Goths and Vandals had been converted to Christianity *before* they swept west and south, even though they then caused such physical devastation and human suffering. After several clashes between Rome and Germanic tribes in modern-day Romania and Bulgaria early in the 3rd century, a combined Gothic and Vandal force defeated (and killed) the Roman Emperor Decius in 251. In so doing they took many female captives, most of whom were Christian, and swiftly assimilated them into their society. This aspect, and the fact that the victors (at that time in awe of Roman values) respected the increasingly widespread Roman adoption of Christianity, led to a quite rapid conversion taking place, though not without setbacks.

Gothic raids in this region continued through the latter part of the 3rd century, and a prime result of the 'spoils of war' is exemplified by the life of Wulfila (c310-383), the grandson of a female Christian who had been captured in Cappadocia (east-central Turkey). At the age of 31 (in 341) Wulfila became Bishop of the Goths, though – under persecution by one of the remaining Gothic kings – he and other Gothic Christians fled to the Danube region of Moesia in 348. He then devoted most of his life to translating the Bible from Greek into the Gothic language.

The Vandal apogee, and rapid decline

The meteoric rise and fall of the Vandals as a Mediterranean power is almost exactly represented by the astonishing life and reign of Genseric (born at Lake Balaton in Hungary), who lived a remarkable 88 years (c389-477) and was their king for almost half a century, from 428. By that year the Vandal tribe – now centred on southern Spain – was in danger of being overwhelmed by the far more numerous Visigoths. Genseric, having started to build a fleet before becoming king, immediately – in 429 – moved the whole populace (of no more than 80,000) to North Africa. Very quickly taking control of most of Morocco and Algeria from the divided and weakened Romans, he captured Hippo Regius in 431, after a long siege during which Augustine (see below) died, making it the new Vandal capital.

Carthage was captured in 439, and so overpowering did the Vandal fleet become that Genseric was able to dominate the whole of the western Mediterranean, including Sicily, culminating in a further sacking of Rome in 455. Returning to the Christian aspect, it is the case that any persecution perpetrated by Genseric on victim states or cities resulted from the fact that Gothic/Vandal Christianity had adopted the teachings of Arius (c250-336), a Christian leader in Alexandria. The 'heresy' of Arius was at odds with the version of Christianity that was by then embedded within the Western Empire; Arianism (within which there are variations) believes that Jesus the Son of God was 'created', and is therefore an 'inferior' being to God, as distinct from Trinitarianism, the original teaching wherein the

'Trinity' are of equal status. Another myth can therefore be dispelled, in that Goths and Vandals were by this time *no longer* heathens – instead, they owed their savage characteristics to their harsh and uncompromising background.

Late in life the remorseless Genseric overreached himself when waging war in the Peloponnese, part of the Eastern Empire. Moreover, at the time of his death his North African mini-empire became riven with feuding between Arian Vandals and their Trinitarian (or Catholic) subjects. Weakening at the centre caused losses of Mediterranean territory, but terminal decline was initiated through a declaration of war by Byzantine Emperor Justinian in 533. The Vandals were no match for the brilliant general Belisarius, who invaded Tunisia, captured Hippo and secured a final surrender in 534. North Africa reverted to provincial status, but – apart from those Vandals who fled to join their Gothic 'cousins' in Spain – many entered service with the Empire.

Interestingly, their last king (Gelimer) was given a large estate in Galatia (Anatolia) and was even offered the rank of patrician – but had to refuse this generosity, on the grounds that he would not renounce his Arian beliefs.

Key Christian figures in the European preservation of knowledge

St Augustine (354-430)

Augustine was born to a pagan father and Catholic mother (Monica) in present-day Algeria. Although well educated, he led a somewhat hedonistic lifestyle, refusing his mother's pleas to convert, while being a follower of Manichaeism (a Persian Gnostic doctrine) and fathering a son by his mistress. Having taught rhetoric at Carthage for several years, he became disillusioned and moved to Rome, where – through his introduction to the prefect of the city, Symmachus – he obtained, at the age of 30, the highly prestigious professorship of rhetoric to the imperial court at Milan.

There his life changed completely – he became as disappointed in Manichaeism as he became enthused by Ambrose, the Catholic bishop of the city. The culmination of his soul-searching, with his epiphany the result of reading verse 13:13 of St Paul's Epistle to the Romans, was his conversion to Christianity by Ambrose, together with his son, in

245

386, after which he vowed to become celibate, give up his teaching post, and devote the rest of his life to God and the priesthood.

On his return journey to North Africa he suffered the trauma of his mother dying, followed not long afterwards by his son; desolate, he turned his family home into a small monastery, was accepted as a priest in 391, and later became the Bishop of Hippo. Towards the end of the century he wrote *Confessions* – his autobiography in 13 books – which is still regarded as a classic of both theology and world literature. He wrote much else, but his most famous work was his 22-volume *Of the City of God*, wherein – responding to the collapse of Christian morale that had followed the sacking of Rome in 410 – he expanded on Jesus's words to Peter not to confuse what belonged to Caesar with what belonged to God. The City of God, he averred, was not an earthly city. It was carried around with all true believers, and could never be 'captured' by any earthly power. Augustine died an old man when the Vandals were besieging Hippo, but in the course of burning the city they left Augustine's cathedral and library untouched.

Boethius (c480-c525)

Born in Rome to a wealthy family, Boethius was a senator by the age of 25, and – following in his father's footsteps – a consul at the age of 30. Crucially, he had been educated in Greek, which was becoming a rarity in the west, and made clear his intention to translate all of Aristotle's and Plato's works from their original Greek texts into Latin. Sadly, we do not know if he ever started on Plato, but as to Aristotle he managed only to translate the *Organon*, the great philosopher's works on logic. Even so, these translations were used in schools for hundreds of years. Boethius also wished to pass on other key aspects of Greco-Roman learning, in the fields of music, astronomy and geometry. In particular, his *De institutione musica* survived into the Renaissance, greatly aiding students to understand Greek music.

While Boethius wrote in every spare moment, his political career continued to progress; he became a close advisor to King Theodoric (an Arian believer), and by 522 reached the highest office of 'magister officiorum', the same year in which his two sons were appointed joint consuls. However, in perhaps overreaching himself in the delicate area of religious differences, he sought to achieve reconciliation between Rome and Orthodox Constantinople, and was arrested on Theodoric's instructions on a charge of treason. While in gaol awaiting almost certain execution, Boethius produced his most famous work, *De Consolatio Philosophiae* (*Consolation of Philosophy*), wherein an imaginary dialogue is conducted between Boethius and Philosophy, the latter personified by a woman. The book argues that worldly inequalities are overcome by a higher power, and everything is secondary to that divine Providence. One of the more famous extracts runs:

'O, happy was that lost age
Content with nature's faithful fruits…
Men did not plunder all the world
And cut a path across the seas
With merchandise for foreign shores.'

According to Colin Wells in *Sailing from Byzantium* (to which we will refer much more in Chapter 23), this masterpiece was second only to the Bible in popularity during the Middle Ages.

St Benedict (480-547)

It is not so much that Benedict himself was a great preserver of Greek knowledge, but rather that he created the conditions whereby, throughout the Early Middle Ages, groups of dedicated men could focus their lives on religion, and – almost as a by-product – preserve some elements of the vast body of (secular) learning that existed in the West at the time of the Empire's collapse. Of noble birth in Umbria, Benedict forewent the earthly pleasures of youth in favour of shutting himself away in a cave above Subiaco, not far from Tivoli. Legend has it that for three years he lived as a hermit, intermittently being supplied with food by a local monk.

Some years later Benedict founded his famous monastery at Monte Cassino, and it is here that he developed his *Rule* – 73 short chapters that contain a mixture of the main tenets of a Christian lifestyle, and the detailed way in which a monastery should be administered. St Benedict's *Rule* became the basis on which hundreds of monasteries came to be run in Italy and throughout the rest of Europe, and it has continued to serve as a model approach right up to the present day.

Cassiodorus (c485-c585)

Born into a well-to-do family in southern Italy, Cassiodorus learned law while being an aide to his father, the Governor of Sicily. In living such an incredibly long life – he succeeded Boethius as 'magister officiorum' to Theodoric in 523, aged 38 – Cassiodorus was a key witness to the fragile relationship with Constantinople, which became no easier under Theodoric's heir Athalaric. The rest of his 'professional' life matched the rule of Justinian (who died in 565) and the Byzantine wars to recover Italy from the Goths. Through most of this period Cassiodorus lived in Constantinople, rubbing shoulders with the elite and improving his religious knowledge and literary skills.

Returning to Italy on Justinian's death, aged 80, his place in our story is secure through his having established in old age not only a monastery at Vivarium (on his family's land beside the Ionian Sea) but – *most crucially* – a library in which there was a 'scriptorium', wherein keen students copied out ancient Greek and Roman texts. Such establishments proliferated in Byzantium, but this first such venture in Italy was the direct result of the long sojourn of Cassiodorus in the east, and it served as a model for other monasteries that were struggling to establish themselves, in developing an almost complete monopoly on scholastic endeavour as Italy descended into ever greater chaos.

We owe an incalculable debt to the dedicated and – at that time largely incorruptible – monks, thousands of whom spent part of every day classifying and copying such ancient texts as came into their possession, many of which came to be unique sources of the vital information so eagerly pored over and absorbed hundreds of years later.

The early Popes

As can be visualised, the early Popes ('Pope' means 'father') had a fraught existence, struggling to exert their authority in such a troubled environment. Galasius I is recorded as showing real leadership, but only from 492 to 496, and there was then a gap of nearly 100 years before Gregory the Great (Pope between 590 and 604) revitalised the Church's missionary role. He is particularly credited with the Gregorian mission, wherein Augustine of Canterbury was dispatched to England to evangelise the pagan Anglo-Saxons. Pope Gregory's life-span paralleled that of St Gregory of Tours (c538-594), who dedicated his life to fighting heresies that kept arising. In the following centuries a series of Popes were ineffectual, being dominated by successive 'exarchs' (Eastern emperors).

Celtic and Anglo-Saxon Christianity

Before the Empire collapsed in the West, the armies and parallel administrators garrisoned in the far north and west of England and France were withdrawn in 407 to protect Rome. Hordes of invaders filled the vacuum, driving many of the native tribes into the regional extremities of Cornwall, Wales, Ireland, Scotland and Brittany. And since Christianity had previously become well-established, local priesthoods automatically became beacons of literacy in beleaguered communities that were often cut off from each other, not for weeks or months but in many cases for years or decades.

In Ireland – which had never been part of the Empire – St Patrick (a Briton) devoted his long life in the 5th century to bringing Christianity and the written word to this previously backward island. Somewhat later, in the 6th century, St David performed a similar role in Wales. Scotland derived much of its early Christianity from Ireland, with Palladius preceding St David in the 5th century, followed by St Columba in the 6th century, who established his famous monastery on Iona, where he ran a school for missionaries and is believed to have transcribed as many as 300 works.

In England in 595, Augustine's support for the Saxon ruler of Kent, newly married to the (Christian) daughter of a Frankish prince, was only a partial success. As the first Archbishop of Canterbury, Augustine sought to establish supremacy over the whole of Britain, stating: 'But as for all the bishops of Britain, we commit them to your care, that the unlearned may be taught, the weak strengthened by persuasion, and the perverse corrected by authority.' The bishops refused to accept his dominance.

The tortuous development of Christianity in Europe is exemplified by the strongly held opinions in Britain of, on the one hand, the version promulgated by prelates with strong links to Rome, who held sway from Canterbury to York and, on the other, the way in which the 'Ionian' faith had developed in Scotland (from Ireland) and permeated southwards into the Borders. A prime example of the differences between these two schools of thought was the way in which the date for Easter was calculated. Matters were brought to a head at the Synod of Whitby (664) wherein a common date was agreed, and the Northumbrian Church agreed to return to the Rome-orientated fold, in so doing submitting to the jurisdiction of York.

The Venerable Bede (c673-735)

Our knowledge of this Synod, and much else from that age, is largely due to the writings of St Bede, who lived virtually all his life at the twinned monasteries of Wearmouth and Jarrow in North East England. He remains a beacon of light for us, in providing a rare – but comprehensive – insight into early-8th-century Britain, and is known as 'the father of English history' due to his major work, *The Ecclesiastical History of the English People*. Completed towards the end of his life, the book traces events from Caesar's first invasion in 55BC right up to Bede's own era, with fascinating details of his own life. He wrote in Latin – with a knowledge of many classical Roman authors – but also had a grasp of Greek and Hebrew. His monastic library is estimated to have held 300-500 books, and he himself wrote learned texts on such diverse subjects as grammar, music, theology and astronomy. In all he wrote some 60 books (which included some poetry), most of which survive.

Brittany

Brittany saw the arrival of missionaries in the 6th century, from Wales. Known as the seven saints, they included St Tudwal and St Malo (who established the town of that name). There is evidence that other missionaries also reaching France, preaching their particular brand of English Christianity.

(Meanwhile, Christianity in the southern half of France had emanated from newly Christian Rome in the 4th century, and populous and economically successful cities in the fertile Rhone delta – such as Uzes and Nimes – enjoyed continuous bishoprics. On the other hand, the continuity of links south of the Pyrenees became very tenuous.)

The grip of the Dark Age

The reason that Chapter 12, on the onset of the Mediterranean Dark Age, and the first half of this chapter are both fairly brief is that there simply was not enough 'going on' in either era – as regards the flow and development of knowledge – to warrant a more lengthy discourse. Certainly there was plenty of militant activity in the European Dark

Age, but it was as generally disruptive as the activities of the 'Sea Peoples' had been some 1,500-2,000 years earlier throughout the Mediterranean. Conditions for systematic education and the exchange of ideas were almost entirely absent, except for the steadfast efforts of monastic scholars, almost as a by-product of their 'official' Christian mission.

Thus, in a west European peninsula increasingly isolated from Byzantium, the knowledge vacuum reached its nadir in c550, with no chance of recovering from this deep trough until more stable conditions started to emerge almost 200 years later. At this point, however, we should pause to acknowledge the astonishing artistic skills that were emerging. Using discoveries in England as a prime example, dating from the Sutton Hoo find from 1939 there has been a stream of exciting treasure trove revealed, year by year. At Sutton Hoo the ship burial, iconic helmet and beautiful jewellery, which date from the 6th and 7th centuries – all of which have design linkage to continental Europe, especially Scandinavia – serve as proof that, as with the Mediterranean Dark Age before, this era was not quite as 'black' as originally painted.

Emergence from the shadows

Now we move forward to examining the Early Middle Age period, which can be said to have started in c730, and – for our purposes – ran for some 330 years. Gradually, in what would become key geographical areas, strong and (slightly) more enlightened regimes began to assert themselves, so that almost imperceptibly at first – in the last quarter of the first millennium – the climate for learning, and crucially the exchange of goods, ideas, students and artists, began to emerge. Nevertheless it is illuminating to realise that in Charles Van Doren's book A *History of Knowledge*, he takes 100 pages to reach the Dark Age that started in c500, only 10 to cover the next 500 years, then nearly 100 pages again to take the reader from c1000 to c1500, by which time the Renaissance was in full swing.

With the key exception of Italy, where mini-kingdoms/ principalities/city states began to flourish *despite* continuing turmoil, this prerequisite of *stability* became established in one region or country after another, and we will examine – in approximate sequence – the key ruling personalities, and the fragile shoots of learning that they sponsored, and in certain cases in which they participated. Once again in this volume we are not so much concerned with the rulers themselves – whose rise and fall has been copiously documented by historians over the last half-millennium – but rather with the flickering signs of special knowledge, and the gradual appearance of brilliant writers, as well as remarkable architecture.

The Italian peninsula

In *The Oxford History of Medieval Europe* (edited by George Holmes), the first section, written by Thomas Brown, shows two maps of Italy. The first provides a picture in the 7th century, wherein there are more than 15 separate entities. The second map – far from any signs of unification – shows a position some 250 years later (at c900), with more than 20 states of one kind or another, covering a territory not much larger than the United Kingdom as it stands today. Even at the height of the Renaissance – after the Peace of Lodi in 1454 between Milan and Venice – while the southern half of the peninsula, together with Sicily and Sardinia, comprised the Kingdom of Naples, the northern half (stretching from Rome to the Alps, and from modern-day Slovenia to the Cote d'Azur) was even more fragmented than had been the case 550 years earlier!

Searching for 'signs of life', we can quote Thomas Brown:

'Eastern influences served as a catalyst in such areas as Rome, where the work of Greek craftsmen was visible in the art commissioned by Pope John VII (705-707). A particularly impressive example of oriental influence occurs in the frescos of Santa Maria "Outside the Walls" at Castelseprio north of Milan.'

Brown also cites the distinctive churches built during the reign of Liutbrand, King of the Lombards from 712 to 744. However, apart from these isolated examples, what started to fuel the later explosion of intellectual activity was the rise in prosperity. Quoting Brown again:

'As a land market developed and rents were increasingly paid in cash, increased demand and monetary circulation stimulated commerce and urban development. Milan had already grown to the full extent of its walls, and the vitality and collective awareness of townspeople can be glimpsed in episodes such as an uprising of Cremona merchants against their bishop in 924.'

Please note, though, that it took more than half the period we are reviewing for this display of popular dissent to manifest itself!

Another tangible portent was the appearance in c700 of the system of 'Doges' (Dukes) as elected rulers of the cluster of settlements around lagoons in the north-east of Italy known as Venice. The first historical figure was Orso Ipato – Ursus (726-737) – who was assassinated after only a decade in office. Although most of his successors in the 7th century suffered a similar fate, or were forced into exile, a system of government had edged its way onto the stage, which saw Venice eventually become an architectural jewel and the most powerful state in the central Mediterranean.

The Carolingian dynasty

In stark contrast to the seemingly perpetual fragmentation throughout Italy, the pattern in much of modern-day France took a totally different course. The Carolingian dynasty can be said to have started with Pepin the Elder, who came to prominence early in the 7th century, but it was his descendant Charles Martel (676-741) who – as a military genius – achieved everlasting fame through his turning back of the seemingly unstoppable Muslim army at the Battle of Tours in 732. The self-styled Prince of the Franks, Martel was one of the founding figures of the Middle Ages, and a progenitor of both feudalism and the concept of knighthood.

Martel's son Pepin the Short (714-768) consolidated his father's work. In being elected the first King of the Franks, he turned back the Lombard threat, defeated the Muslims at Narbonne in 759 (ending their presence in France), and assumed control of Aquitaine. But even Pepin's achievements are pallid compared with those of his son Charles the Great – 'Charlemagne' (c742-814). This towering figure can be said to have defined Western Europe and the Middle Ages. Known as Karl der Grosse in Germany, he became King of the Lombards in 774, and was crowned Holy Roman Emperor by Pope Leo III on Christmas Day 800 in the basilica of St Peter's, Rome. His only severe military setback came after an ill-advised incursion into northern Spain, when his retreating army was trounced by the Basques at the Battle of Roncevalles in 778, immortalised in the (heavily fictionalised) *Song of Roland*. Although (to the east) he never defeated the Saxons, he managed to promote their conversion to Christianity, which paved the way for the Ottonian dynasty. One other certainty is that Charlemagne's greatest legacy was to usher in a (mini) 'Carolingian' renaissance.

Alcuin of York

The stability achieved by Charlemagne, who wanted to promote learning in many disciplines, encouraged budding scholars to his court, with much of the inspiration derived from the resident polymath Alcuin of York, whose lifespan (c735-804) almost exactly matched that of his mighty patron. We know that Alcuin was born in Northumbria, but little else of his background. Being a child prodigy caused him to be sent to the school in York, founded in 627, which was subsequently named St Peter's. York had not long been raised to an archbishopric, with many resident devotees of Bede who had access to his works. As well as being a religious centre, the school was vibrantly involved in the arts, literature and science, with Alcuin being particularly fascinated by (the somewhat frowned-upon) classical poetry.

While on a mission to Rome in 781 to secure papal confirmation of York's elevated status, this now highly respected teacher was introduced to Charlemagne in the city of Parma. Charlemagne's fascination with intellectual matters helped persuade Alcuin to accept his invitation to join other prominent scholars at the palace court in Aachen. Bringing several assistants from York, Alcuin taught the king, his sons and family from 782 until 790. So influential did Alcuin become that his palace school became known (after one of his nicknames) as 'the school of Master Albinus'. In teaching a whole range of subjects to the royal family, Alcuin eventually persuaded Charlemagne that the ultimate sanction for paganism was pointless – 'You can force people to be baptised, but you cannot force them to believe.' Charlemagne abolished the death penalty for paganism in 797.

Despite returning to his beloved homeland in 790, Alcuin was persuaded back by Charlemagne in 792. Exhausted by the strenuous life at court, he leapt at the opportunity to become Abbot of St Martin at Tours in 796, and lived out the rest of his life there, dying (at an estimated age of 70) on 19 May 804. Buried at St Martin's church, a section of his epitaph reads: 'Dust, worms and ashes now... Alcuin my name, wisdom I always loved, Pray, reader, for my soul.'

As the most prominent scholar of his age, it is almost impossible to exaggerate Alcuin's influence: more than 300 of his letters survive, many written to Charlemagne; notwithstanding his piety, these letters and other writings show how important Alcuin was to the cause of humanism; he wrote works on grammar and rhetoric, many of the latter in the form of an imaginary dialogue between himself and Charlemagne; in 782 Italian influence was predominant at the Aachen court, but for the next 15 years its position was trumped by Alcuin, who introduced to the mainland priceless Latin texts (and culture) that had uniquely survived in isolated corners of the British Isles; lastly – as if all this were not enough – Alcuin was almost certainly the author of a mathematical textbook, which posed more than 50 problems, offering the correct solution in each case.

Theowulf

To illustrate how keen Charlemagne was to attract the very best scholars, Theowulf was a contemporary of Alcuin at court. He was a Christian Visigoth by birth, born in Spain in c750, who fled Muslim domination. He is remembered particularly for translating a handful of (for that time) rare Greek and Hebrew texts, and for becoming Bishop of Orleans, near where he built an oratory at Germigny-des-Pres, which still holds a wonderful mosaic of the Ark of the Covenant (dated to 806).

Alfred the Great (849-899)

Alfred's crucial importance in history is that his stubborn resistance – from his Wessex stronghold – was all that prevented England from becoming a Viking colony. As we shall see later, the Normans – also Vikings – developed in a 'French'-influenced manner in their adopted Normandy. If the Vikings had captured all of England, its future as a Nordic/Danish dominion would have been very different, and William would probably never have invaded his 'cousins' 200 years later, which led to the Norman/Anglo-Saxon cocktail that made the 'English' character, and guaranteed an orientation towards France.

As to Alfred, it is worth noting that, as the eventually self-appointed king of the Anglo-Saxons, he made huge efforts to reform the administrative and legal systems within his realm, and initiated the rebuilding and fortification of London. Perhaps following the example of Charlemagne, he sought to promote literacy and learning, and established a school at court, primarily for the benefit of his family and senior courtiers. Alfred's reign is also inextricably linked to the epic poem *Beowulf*, which was set in Scandinavia and written some time between the 8th and 10th centuries. Consisting of more than 3,000 lines, the heroic story somehow came to be translated into Old English, only one manuscript of which survives, known as the Nowell Codex.

Cluny Abbey

Although, after Charlemagne, progress in France was spasmodic, a shining example of piety, learning and architecture was initiated a century after the great man's death by William I, Count of Auvergne, when work commenced on the abbey complex at Cluny, 12 miles (20km) north-west of Macon, in 910. Established to follow the rule of St Benedict (see above), Cluny became a beacon for monasticism in Western Europe from later in the 10th century onwards. So admired did the Benedictine Order become that successive abbots of Cluny came to be treated as leading statesman in a European world that was edging its way towards increased stability.

Ottonian dynasty

This dynasty inherited (indirectly) from Charlemagne the role of Holy Roman Emperor, in the crucial century that further stabilised European government, from 919-1024. Otto the Great (son of Henry I) was justly the most famous member of this lineage, on whom we will concentrate. Born in 912, Otto I married Eagdyth of England in 929, and became king of the Eastern Franks upon his father's death in 936. He set about unifying six duchies, including Lorraine, Saxony and Bavaria, into the state of Germany. Despite inevitable setbacks, Otto became so successful that he secured control of great swathes of Italy, became crowned as Emperor in Rome in 962, and did not die until 973, after being the dominant figure in Europe for nearly half a century.

Otto was extremely astute in controlling his burgeoning 'Empire', generally placing himself on the side of the Church and its bishops so as to continually outsmart the ambitious nobility in each region.

However, his great legacy was to extend eastward the Carolingian (mini) renaissance that he so greatly admired. Notably, he facilitated the art form of illuminated manuscripts, and produced a *Pontifical Book* specifically to counter the laxity he saw to be prevalent in Rome.

One example of the extent of Otto's reach is the case of the envoy to his court from the Caliph of Andalusia in 955, who so dazzled the scholarly nun Hroswitha with his descriptions of Cordoba that it was she who described that wondrous place as 'The brilliant ornament of the world shone in the west, a noble city...' (Menocal). This was two years after Otto had sent John of Gorze at the head of a mission to Cordoba, but we shall cover his 'feedback', together with that of many others, in Chapter 21!

The Normans

'Norse Men' from a range of Scandinavian countries – including the Viking-held eastern side of England – were tough and resourceful raiders who started settling on either side of the Seine estuary (between modern-day Le Havre and Rouen) from 880 onwards. Headed by their leader Rollo, they were coarse, illiterate and pagan, but, as we have found elsewhere (most remarkably with the earliest Greeks), an unfathomable mix of origins, ethnicity, new environment, intermarriage and religious conversion, etc, somehow created an unbeatable combination in every crucial sphere. What is more, the transformation from Viking raider to Norman empire-builder only took half-a-dozen generations, a period of little more than 150 years.

English people are still fixated on how the country fell precipitously to William in 1066, but with respect to this pivotal moment in one nation's history – which was initiated by a short (admittedly very hazardous) sea crossing – the *simultaneous* achievements of the Normans 1,000 miles (1,600km) away in the Mediterranean were quite breathtaking, and equally momentous in their effect. We will examine the 'Norman whirlwind' at the start of Chapter 21, and confine ourselves here to a brief examination of their progress in France up to that pivotal decade.

In 911, the Carolingian ruler Charles the Simple – fed up with ceaseless Viking incursions into the north-western fringe of his realm – formally allowed Rollo (within the Treaty of St Clair-sur-Epte) to settle a small area of territory. Quickly bringing across their families, these new 'colonists' soon converted to Christianity. They started to interbreed, and largely adopted the local 'Frankish' language, though retaining features of their native tongue. Given the awe in which these warriors were held, there was little resistance as they expanded their territory westward, taking in the Cotentin peninsula, and brushing up against the defiant Celtic tribes of rugged modern-day Brittany.

Possibly the most remarkable transformation in this 150-180-year span was that – by the time the Normans launched themselves in a series of lightning and far-flung campaigns, and immediately showed an amazing flair for government – their version of Romanesque architecture was somehow ready to be bestowed on so many countries. As we will discover, this wonderful physical evidence is a constant reminder to travellers throughout Western Europe of the unique talents possessed by these so recently near-barbaric invaders.

Chapter 18

From Babylon and Baghdad to the Parthian Empire

In the 'time-line' included with this book, the fade-out at Chapter 3 links directly to this chapter, which in turn links to Chapter 19. This signifies that, in the 7,500 years of Middle Eastern and Western history that the book straddles, the huge geographical area that comprises modern-day Iraq, Kurdish Turkey, the west-facing slopes of the Zagros Mountains, south-eastern Iran and the whole of the Fertile Crescent sustained a dynamic activity *throughout*, of which we have a continuous record. From the decline of Sumerian power in Mesopotamia after 2500BC, it is true that – unlike in Egypt or Minoan Crete – no one dynasty held sway for more than a few hundred years at a time in any part of this vast 'Middle East', but there were only very brief *unrecorded* 'dark' periods. In marked contrast, throughout the Mediterranean (except in the Nile delta), even after 150 years of increasingly sophisticated research in our modern era, the picture of what was going on for more than 300 years between c1180BC and c850BC is still largely a blank canvas.

The Akkadian Empire (2334-2160BC)

As we saw in Chapter 3, it was the Sumerians – in the south of modern-day Iraq – who set the pace throughout the 4th century BC. Around 3000 – in what today is central Iraq – the closely related 'Akkads' came to the fore, but these two 'cousin' societies developed quite happily alongside each other for fully half a millennium. Indeed, with each handful of cities abutting – and the mighty twin rivers 'fertilising' the needs of both – their progress in language and lifestyle was deeply intertwined. However, some time after 2500BC the Akkads began to assert their authority over the region and the catalyst for a decisive shift was the rise to power of King Sargon in 2334. We know that Sargon rose from a humble birth, and that – over a 56-year reign – he created an empire that stretched from the Arabian Gulf in the south to eastern Turkey in the north, and almost to the Syrian coastline.

In 1975 at Ebla, east of the Orontes River near modern-day Tell Mardikh, the Italian archaeologist Paulo Matthiae discovered more than 1,800 complete clay tablets (and thousands of fragments) in the ruins of the ancient palace, all of which dated from c2500 to 2250BC, when the city was destroyed. This sensational find comprises the largest and oldest collection yet discovered in the Middle East. Written in Sumerian or 'Eblan' – since identified as a proto-Canaanite language – the wonderfully preserved tablets are a mine of information on Ebla as a centre of trade and learning in the Early Bronze Age. This chapter, and the next, will not stint on just how advanced were the successive Middle Eastern cultures; it is food for thought that the Ebla tablets alone exceed the combined Bronze Age discoveries in the Mediterranean, and precede (for example) the Linear B tablets found at Pylos by 1,000 years!

Written records show that Sargon built a new capital city, Agade (which has never been found), and that he and his successors defended their hard-won territories with great difficulty. According to *Babylon* by Joan Oates, a later poem known today as 'The Curse of Agade' blamed Sargon's grandson Naram-Sin for the destruction of Agade, the deity's revenge for the hitherto omnipotent ruler's sacking of Nippur. What can reliably be said is that the Akkadian regime was overrun by the Gutians, an (allegedly) barbarian people from the Zagros Mountains – according to Sumerian sources.

Revival of Ur: the 'third dynasty' (2112-2004BC)

Though Gutian successors appear listed as kings in the region, there was a brief Sumerian revival based on the city of Ur. While their kings continued links with the far-flung cities of the Akkadian Empire, there was a preoccupation with parochial affairs. We know this from the vast number of recovered tablets that date from this era, and which signify a mind-numbing obsession with 'accounting' for the movement of every animal. There are hundreds of thousands of 'entries', which extend to detailing all types/volumes/values of imported and exported goods. We also know that silver was becoming a traded 'currency' at this time, and we have been able to learn much about such diverse activities as contemporary judicial practice, and the rapidly developing use of brick within a precocious 'architectural' framework, particularly with regard to the design of increasingly sophisticated ziggurats.

Either side of 2000BC: overlapping regimes

It would be bewildering – in the space available – to go into details of all the competing city states in the last 100 years or so of the 3rd millennium and the first 200 years of the 2nd millennium BC, but the main participants in this turbulent period were Lagash, Larsa, Isin and – more significantly – the Martu (literally 'from the West') or Amorites, who gained control of Babylon c1900. It was also around 2000 that the origins of the Assyrian Empire were founded at Ashur (or Assur) on the Tigris, in the north of Iraq.

Technological achievements up to 2000BC

By around 2500 we know that dice existed (from Mosul) and a type of backgammon (the 'Royal game of Ur'). A most beautifully decorated lyre was also discovered at Ur, from this date. By 2000 the spinning of yarn had been perfected, in exactly the same manner as can be seen among Bedouin tribes today. We also have plaques that show drummers and boxers. Most notably – and well before the rise of Babylon – the Sumerians had developed the sexagesimal system, i.e. the use of the number 60. They realised that 60 was a highly composite number, having no fewer than 12 factors. Ever since, 60 has been used for measuring time, angles and geographic coordinates, and has never – over the ensuing four millennia – being usurped by any other system.

The Amorites in 'Old Babylonia': the First Dynasty (1894-1595BC)

Though mentioned several hundred years earlier, Babylon – on the Euphrates in central Iraq – rose to prominence from the moment of its adoption by the (previously nomadic) Amorites in 1894BC. Though the city was a name to conjure with for the next 2,000 years, we are concerned at this stage with the glorious period up 1595BC, when it was sacked by the Hittites. During this period Old Babylonian is the term used to describe the cuneiform language used, which has been preserved for us in so many documents. In the early phase of the dynasty, rulers of the city and surrounding region were competing against rivals from other cities we have already mentioned, with mixed success.

However, the prospects for Babylon were transformed by the accession of the great King Hammurabi, who reigned from 1792 to 1750BC. Records show that, in his early years, he struggled to assert himself beyond the surrounding territory, and was confined to building up his immediate power base. This period included great attention to matters of justice, based on his elaborate *Code* – most of which (in Akkadian) has fortunately come down to us. The best-preserved copy – a stele in diorite, standing 7.5 feet (2.25m) high – can be seen at the Louvre, in Paris. It describes 282 laws, including those that appear subsequently in the Old Testament, such as 'an eye for an eye, and a tooth for a tooth'.

Only as he approached the last decade of his reign (c1760BC) did Hammurabi start to extend his authority, struggling to secure Mari to the north, and making incursions into Assyrian territory. Though his grip remained tenuous, his crucial legacy was to make Babylon the supreme city in the region – with a population that may have reached 200,000 – and a religious centre that survived until after the birth of Christ. In this vast melting pot it seems that class divisions rested on economic grounds – those who controlled affairs, and those who did their bidding, including slaves – rather than on any religious hierarchy.

From all the records that have been preserved, it is clear that there was a fully fledged government, which administered every aspect of society and the economy, a few examples (apart from the law) being: tax collection; maintenance of the canals and irrigation systems; supervision of a wide range of crafts; religious practice; merchant activities; and the monitoring of far-flung trade. And it was at the height of Babylon's flowering that its remarkable achievements in astronomy, medicine and – especially – in several branches of mathematics were developed. A wonderful relic that typifies Babylon's advanced understanding is a clay tablet from 1800BC, in the form of a textbook of geometric problems. Squares and triangles are accurately delineated with a fine stylus, the lengths are declared, and the student is tasked with calculating the areas in each example. Perhaps even more impressive is a cuneiform tablet (recovered from Tell Harmal), dated to the same era, which shows a crisp right-angled triangle in an 'exam paper', which anticipates the theory first expounded by Pythagoras well over a millennium later!

The fall of 'Old Babylon': the Kassite dynasty (1570-1150BC)

Following Hammurabi's death, although his son Samsu-iluna (1749-1712BC) retained a firm grip in the north, it is clear that the 'old' cities to the south kept trying to reassert their historic independence. The gradual weakening of Babylonian hegemony continued in the 16th century BC, culminating in the unthinkable: the dynamic Hittite King Murshili I (from central Anatolia) overran much of Syria, and continued southward, almost unopposed, to sack Babylon itself in 1595BC.

Murshili almost immediately returned to his homeland, but the damage was done. Other predatory tribes vied to take control of Babylon's fabulous riches, with the Kassites (probably originating in the Zagros Mountains) eventually seizing control in c1570BC. It is perplexing that these people – who became totally absorbed in Babylonian traditions – have not been studied in greater depth by Mesopotamian experts, with a majority of the tablets recovered from this era still not interpreted. Yet, while there was continual 'turbulence' to the north, with Hittite, Hurrian and (emerging) Assyrian regimes vying for supremacy, the Kassites controlled Babylon for some 400 years.

The Amarna letters

As touched on when mentioning John Pendlebury in Chapter 6, one of the most remarkable caches of documents was discovered in 1887 by a local woman digging in the ruins of Pharaoh Akhenaten's capital on the Nile, Tell el-Amarna. Although most of the 350 tablets eventually recovered were dispersed around the globe, these are diplomatic letters of prime importance to our understanding of the mid-2nd millennium BC. The documents – written in Akkadian – have since been complemented by similar finds elsewhere in the Middle East, and they throw considerable light on the Kassite 14th-century-BC period.

The correspondence highlights the giving and receiving of 'royal' presents, and tells us much about the systematic patterns of trade throughout the region. One example is that large quantities of gold were supplied by Egypt so as to embellish Kassite buildings/monuments in Babylon itself, signifying the pre-eminence that the city maintained in Mesopotamia. It is also clear that – apart from the exchange of incredibly lavish gifts – diplomatically inspired marriages preoccupied the respective rulers of Egypt, Babylon, and Anatolia. Here again we come across the 'pyrrhic' Battle of Qadesh in 1274BC, which – despite the subsequent rhetoric of Rameses – was certainly a moral victory for the Hittites.

Technology and art in the Kassite era

A key piece of technology – developed in an 'arms race' with the Egyptians, Hittites and Assyrians, and embracing many skills – was the high-speed lightweight chariot for a highly skilled team of two or three, with spoked wheels and a suspension mechanism that helped prevent the occupants from being thrown out over rough terrain! Practical art and writing skills were poured into exquisitely crafted boundary stones, of which many precious examples have survived. In pure artistic terms, the incredibly complex core-moulded glass vessel – dated to c1450BC – found at Tell al Rimah shows a degree of sophistication not matched in Western Europe for another 1,000 years. Dated to the same period is a remarkably life-like clay figurine of the head of a lioness, found not far north of Babylon city.

The end of Kassite supremacy, and the aftermath

Experts believe it is coincidental that the Kassite dynasty withered away in c1150BC, just as the Dark Age swept through the Mediterranean. Its demise was the result of repeated incursions from Assyria to the north – hundreds of miles east of the havoc being wrought by the 'Sea Peoples' – for example by the rampaging Philistines who devastated the Palestinian coast and hinterland. (Ever more scientific research indicates that a key reason for this turmoil may have been a prolonged period of much drier climatic conditions – with the inevitable stresses that shortage of water and food would have brought to those regions with a hitherto fast-growing and prosperous population.)

An important aspect – which we touched on after the Hittite collapse, as it affected the Greek mainland – was the spread to the east of iron-making technology. Joan Oates postulates that the collapse of Hittite control over this demanding technology allowed the technique

264

to be spread among a much wider 'audience', even during the chaotic 12th century BC. Hence – in the Middle East as elsewhere – the use of iron for 'industrial' purposes (as opposed to decoration) became widespread by the 10th century BC, just as the Mediterranean Dark Age was drawing to a close.

'Babylonia for the Babylonians' (proposed title by J. A. Brinkman)

In similar fashion to the comments made about the Balkans early in Chapter 14, both native and western archaeologists have been unable hitherto to maintain continuous research programmes over the past century; in other words, given a long period of stability at some point in the future, there must be 'a lot more to come'.

There now followed a thoroughly unstable period of c400 years, during which Oates says that for the first time Babylon was actually under the control of native Babylonians. As best as can be analysed – again from correspondence that has survived, the wealth of inscribed stelae, and boundary stones – it appears that there were six dynasties. The famous name of Nebuchadnezzar first appeared in 1125BC, as the king who avenged the earlier Elamite sacking of Babylon, precious details of which – such as the blistering heat in which the campaign was fought – we know from a wonderful stela in the British Museum, known as the 'kudurru for Ritti-Marduk'.

This highlight stands out against an interminable period of repeated instability, during the last 200 years of which loomed the ever-growing threat from Assyria. All in all, more than 40 kings have been identified as rulers during this 400-year span, an average reign of barely 10 years. Still, again it must be repeated that we have a continuously documented record throughout this turbulent near-half-millennium, which ended in c725BC, a date at which no parallel Greek history had even started to be scripted, other than the single example of Homer's works that were probably just at the point of being committed to papyrus or parchment!

The Assyrian Empire (1120-612BC)

Founded at Ashur, on the northern Tigris – and without the fertility offered in southern Iraq – by the 8th century BC the nascent Assyrian power had been growing for at least a millennium, built on proactive trading with Hittite Anatolia and the aggressive acquisition of territory. It was constant Assyrian threats and invasion that motivated the Canaanites, and their illustrious successors the Phoenicians, to first explore the Mediterranean Sea, then to forsake the Syrian/ Lebanese coast once and for all to seek a different future as far away as was then thought possible, just inside the 'Pillars of Hercules'. In the same year (721BC) that a competent Chaldean ruler named Merodach-Baladan II became King of Babylon, Sargon II seized control of Assyria and revitalised the expansionist programme.

Sargon's armies marched through Palestine, and even forced mighty Egypt to sue for peace. With Merodach-Baladan faltering in his attempt to consolidate his power, Sargon turned his fire on Babylon in 710, and had colonised the whole territory by the time he was killed in battle in northern Assyria in 705. Once again a chaotic period followed – for the next 70 years – with control of Babylon oscillating between a tenuous independence and subservience to Assyria. Its last great king, Ashurbanipal – born in c685, reigned 668-627BC – left for us not only the wonderful monuments that have been so assiduously recovered and restored at Nineveh and Nimrud, but also his personal library at Nineveh – discovered by Austen Henry Layard in 1853 – which represents the most important collection of cuneiform tablets ever recovered, including a copy of the *Epic of Gilgamesh*.

At this time the achievements of the Assyrians reflected their understanding of what we today would call 'science and technology'. They were superb engineers and roadbuilders, they were masters of irrigation techniques, and – as a complete contrast – had a sophisticated grasp of astronomy. Oates relates Ashurbanipal's famous inscription from his boyhood, when he learned

'...the hidden treasures of all scribal knowledge. I solve complex mathematical reciprocals and products with no apparent solution; I read abstruse tablets whose Sumerian is obscure and whose Akkadian is hard to construe...'

(This extract shows vividly how deeply engrained were all aspects of advanced learning among the ruling class in each society c670BC throughout the vast region of the Middle East – again, as an example, more than 50 years before Thales [the first Greek philosopher/ scientist] was even born!)

Babylon Renaissance (625-540BC): Nebuchadnezzar

After Ashurbanipal's death in 627, there followed the most remarkable (and widely known) phase in the proud city's history. In a short span of about 85 years, three outstanding Chaldean kings ruled for all but seven years, starting with Nabopolassar (625-605), seizing control from a weakened Assyria. After an inauspicious start, Nabopolassar benefited from assaults on Assyria by the now-powerful Medes – successors to the Elamites in western Iran – and after many setbacks he was part of the alliance that finally determined Assyria's fate through the sacking of Nineveh in 612. The total collapse of the once-mighty Assyrians followed their defeat (in alliance with Egypt) by Nabopolassar's son Nebuchadnezzar at the Battle of Carchemish, on the Euphrates border between Syria and Turkey, in 605. Any celebration was cut short by Nabopolassar's death in the aftermath, causing his son to race back to Babylon to secure his succession. Thus began the 50-year span of Babylon's greatest age in its long history, under the guidance throughout of a single monarch, one of the most famous rulers in history.

Quite exceptionally – even by modern standards – Nebuchadnezzar ruled for more than 50 years until 562, although not without challenges to his authority in the early part of his reign. Abroad, he secured huge swathes of territory, and one way in which he resonates with us today is due to his repeated appearance in the Bible, as he strove to subjugate the Jews either side of 600BC – famously (or notoriously) taking thousands in captivity to Babylon. Perhaps even more famously – aided by the vivid account of Herodotus, written only about 125-150 years later – are the wonders that Nebuchadnezzar created in Babylon: his palace; the 'hanging gardens'; the hundreds of temples; the rebuilt and enlarged ziggurat; and (still in evidence today) the beautifully decorated Ishtar Gate, through which passed the Processional Way, en route to the temple of Marduk.

Nebuchadnezzar's death in 562 was followed by a period of chaos, only ended when Nabonidus (a non-family official) was installed on the throne in 555. (After the discovery of a stele in 1956 at Harran – near the Syrian border in Turkey – no commentary on Nabonidus can exclude mention of his remarkable mother. The stele states that she was born in c650, that her life was dedicated to the god Sin, and that she did not die until c546, aged well over 100! This means that she was in her 20s when this Chaldean [or neo-Babylonian] dynasty commenced, and almost saw it through to its end.) Not surprisingly, Nabonidus was a devout adherent to the god Sin, and primarily concerned himself with religious issues. He neglected civilian affairs, and became thoroughly unpopular by decamping to the Arabian desert for a large part of his reign. In 539 the Persians, led by the ambitious Cyrus the Great, captured Babylon, and murdered the devout Nabonidus.

The Persian (Achaemenid) Empire (540-330BC)

The latter part of this chapter, and the first part of the next, covers the 1,200-year period of 'Iranian' prominence, before the Muslim conquest overran the Sassanid Empire. As posed by Michael Axworthy in his book *Iran: Empire of the Mind* – who were these people? Even to this day, the close relationship between the Persian language and Hindi, German and English tells us that their origins lay in the Russian steppes, and – as Axworthy relates – they were one of the many Indo-European peoples who migrated in repeated waves to settle also in Europe, Central Asia and northern India.

For a decade Cyrus – about whose birth and youth many legends abound – had been flexing his muscles, and the conquest of Babylon was but a stepping stone towards establishing the mightiest (pre-Roman) empire the 'western' world had ever seen. Cyrus's everlasting legacy to the modern world is the 'Cyrus Cylinder', which he had inscribed with what we would now call a 'Bill of Rights'. Crucially, on its surface he decreed (in cuneiform script) that all conquered peoples enslaved in Babylon, including descendents of the Jews taken by Nebuchadnezzar, should be free to worship as they pleased and to return to their homelands. This political masterstroke won Cyrus the gratitude of the recipients of his largesse, and the admiration of peoples throughout the Middle East, thereby making his territorial ambitions much easier to achieve and sustain. (It is left for the reader to contemplate any of several ironies that could be deemed to surround both the recent agreement by Britain to have loaned the Cylinder to Iran, and the safe return of this priceless artefact to the British Museum as recently as April 2011.)

For more than 200 years – 550 to 330BC – the Persians were the predominant force in the Middle East. At the height of empire under

Darius I soon after 500, their suzerainty stretched from Egypt (south-west) and Thrace (north-west) to Central Asia (north-east) and India (south-east) – an area of more than 3 million square miles (8 million sq km). It was Darius who commissioned the construction of the religious centre of Persepolis, hundreds of miles south-east of the historic Persian – and previously Elamite – capital of Susa. He undertook other massive 'civil' projects, most notably the 1,550-mile (2,500km) Royal Road from Susa to Sardis in western Turkey, and he caused to be dug a forerunner to the Suez Canal.

The near-century from 521 to 424BC saw only three rulers, Darius I, Xerxes I and Artaxerxes I, during which this dynamic trio consolidated the methodology of managing their huge empire, many features of which were later adopted by Rome. These revolutionary steps included the promotion of Aramaic (which originated in northern Mesopotamia) as a common language with only 22 letters; the creation of a proper currency system, based on standard silver coinage; a standardised (though harsh) taxation policy; an efficient 'civil service'; a system of provinces with regional governors ('satraps'); and full enactment of Cyrus's dictate to emancipate all slaves, including Jews – a decision that was compatible with the Zoroastrian beliefs of the Persians. As Axworthy emphasises, with their connections to the Medes and realising the historic importance of Elam, these great rulers followed the wisdom of Cyrus in ensuring the empire 'flowed around and absorbed powerful rivals. Its first instinct was *not* to confront, batter into defeat, and force submission'.

As the empire grew, the relative importance of Babylon declined. It was not situated in the Persian homeland, and its masters threw vast resources into constructing impressive temples far and wide. Persian architecture was very sophisticated and exotic materials from every corner of the empire were used to adorn key public buildings. Great attention was paid to works of art – with skills drawn from far and wide – and the quality of sculpture that can still be seen set a benchmark for later achievements in the Greek world. A key cultural feature was devotion to truth. As tablets recovered from Persepolis in the 1930s show, this fundamental tenet was remorselessly instilled into the young, from all walks of life. 'Never get into debt!' Why not? 'Because being in debt may sorely test your ability to stick to the truth!'

(Reverting to a main theme of this book, it must be remembered that the Greeks survived desperately close-fought wars with their deadliest enemy the Persians, and – in any case – considered all who were not Greek to be barbarians! Nearly everything that came down to us – until 150 years ago – ignored or dismissed the ancient achievements throughout western Asia. It is only comparatively recently that the results of millions of man-hours of unbiased scholastic research has shown us (as in the above snapshot at 450BC, for example) the wealth of achievements attained in a world apart from Greece and Rome, but from which both absorbed many lessons.)

Macedonian conquest and the Seleucid dynasty (330-c100BC)

Referring back to the opening paragraph of this chapter, successive dynasties continued to dominate the vast area that we know as the 'Middle East' from the date of Alexander the Great's invasion (330BC) through to the point when the origins of the fundamental Muslim schism took place in Damascus (750AD) and on still for another 800 years, until the Ottoman Empire finally snuffed out the Baghdad candle of intellectual brilliance, less than 500 years ago. It might have been the case that some or all of these upheavals involved the destruction of the achievements and culture of predecessors. In fact, though much blood was frequently shed, it is in examining the degree of *continuity* that a crucial point of difference with what took place in Western Europe emerges.

In the latter case, we have seen how (BC) the great achievements of the Hallstadt, La Tene and Celtic cultures in central Europe and France, the Etruscans in northern Italy, and the Phoenicians in the western Mediterranean, were all largely wiped out by the Romans, and that then *their* heritage (which held within it a huge Greek legacy) substantially disintegrated at the onset of the Dark Age. Only 'Greater' Greece itself – the central Mediterranean 'pivot' where the Roman Empire later metamorphosed into Byzantium – managed to continue evolving without devastating trauma. However, in the Middle East – both in the thousands of years before Alexander, and during nearly 1,800 years after his death – each tyrannical regime largely preserved and *adapted* the complex cultural landscape that it inherited, for reasons that may never be fully explained.

We saw in Chapter 15 how Alexander and his immediate successors – while introducing the Greek way of life with remarkable speed – largely

270

adopted a benign attitude within the conquered peoples, and were open-minded in absorbing attributes that augmented (rather than competed with) their own accomplishments. Since Chapter 15 dealt with Alexander's legacy, we will now move on to the subsequent dynasties that dominated the Middle East – mostly described in the next chapter – and continue to trace the way in which civilisation and culture *developed*, without any one 'empire' obliterating the legacies of its predecessors.

The Parthian Empire (247BC-224AD)

Whereas the power-base of the Persians had been in the south of modern-day Iran, the Parthian (or Arsacid) dynasty had its foundations in the north-east of the country, as it is delineated today. In 247BC Arsaces I rebelled in the satrapy of Parthia against the declining Seleucids, who were then involved in trying to fend off the attentions of Ptolemy III in the far south-west of their sprawling empire. The balance of power shifted markedly when Mithridates I, who ruled from 171 to 138BC, seized control of Media (north-west Iran) and Mesopotamia. The momentum in favour of the Parthians continued, with the Seleucid hegemony eliminated by 100BC. A century later – at its height – the new empire encompassed the whole of modern-day Iraq. Inevitably, the Parthians came up against the might of Rome, and though they won a famous victory (against Crassus) in 53BC at Carrhae, just inside Turkey, close to the Syrian border, the Romans reacted vigorously.

Thereafter, the Parthians became land-locked in the west, with Rome controlling the coastal strips of modern-day Syria, Lebanon, Israel and Egypt. Since the silk route ran through the Parthian Empire, successive kings presided over vibrant trade and commerce, as between China and Rome at the eastern and western extremities, with the crafty involvement of generations of Greek middle-men continuing to be respected. As alluded to earlier, the Parthians adopted much of the cultural and artistic heritage of their predecessors and, until late in their control of this huge region, Seleucid (Greek) influence was tolerated, almost certainly so as not to 'rock the boat' economically. Also, as the empire grew westwards in the 1st century BC, while the capital, Ctesiphon, was established on the Tigris, nearby Seleucia continued to be the administrative hub (both being adjacent to the much later city of Baghdad).

While the Arsacids styled themselves 'Kings of Kings' after the fashion of their Persian predecessors, they also professed themselves 'Philhellenes' – friends of the Greeks. Greek drachma coinage remained the standard currency throughout most of their near-half-millennium of supremacy, and even later, when Parthian coinage became prominent, Greek legends were always incorporated, as was the word 'philhellene'. In the arts, Greek plays were very much in favour – a graphic (though gruesome) example being when Orodes I, and his Armenian guest Artavasdes II, were watching Euripides's play *The Bacchae* in 53BC, the head of Crassus was brought to him and the producer of the play promptly decided to use the 'real thing' as a substitute for the stage-prop head of Pentheus (in mythology, the King of Thebes)!

However, while the Parthians had periods when they fended off the Roman might, intermittent conflict over the decades on their western and north-western frontiers only served to weaken their capabilities, and the start of the 3rd century AD saw the rise of – arguably – the greatest of all the 'Persian' empires, whose subsequent expansion dwarfed the achievements of their immediate predecessors.

Chapter 19

From the Sassanid Empire to the Muslim enlightenment – Greek into Arabic

The Sassanid Empire (224-641AD): contemporaries and successors

This remarkable 400-year period of Persian revival started shortly before Diocletian's decision to split the Roman Empire into two halves, a move that singularly failed to prevent the inexorable decline and collapse in the West 200 years later. The Sassanids then ran up against the first 200 years of the Eastern (Byzantine) Empire, including the era in which Justinian strove mightily to recreate the earlier unified entity.

At their apogee (c600AD) the Sassanids held together vast swathes of territory, but it is the cultural legacy to their Muslim conquerors that is crucial for our story. We have plotted in the previous chapter how their Achaemenid and Arsacid predecessors – interspersed by the Greek Seleucids – largely profited from each civilisation successively. In this chapter we will see how the Sassanids continued to build on their cultural inheritance, and how crucial the strands of these Middle Eastern developments proved to be for their Muslim conquerors. For, as the famous Iranian scholar Abdolhossein Zarinkoob (1923-99) has said, much of what later became known as Islamic culture, architecture and writing was developed from the Sassanid Persians.

The Sassanid Empire falls into five distinct phases.

Origins and early history (205-310AD)

Exactly who Sassan was is the subject of conflicting accounts, which may never be resolved. He was almost certainly a 'warrior prince', and possibly a forebear of Ardashir I, who had been building his power base in the Parsis province of south-west Iran (modern-day Fars) for some 20 years. Always one of the most influential regions of Iran, Parsis or Fars gives its name to the Persian language – Parsi or Farsi – and its capital Shiraz gave to the world one of the most highly regarded wines (alternatively known as Syrah), which had already been famous throughout the Middle East for well over a millennium.

Ardashir (died 241) overthrew the last Parthian king Artabanus IV in 224, and – to stamp his authority over the whole region – had himself crowned 'King of Kings' at the Parthian capital of Ctesiphon on the Tigris. But, just as the Parthians had laid bare their eastern flank through waging interminable wars with Rome, Ardashir and his successors proceeded to throw unaffordable resources in the same direction, and progressively engender the same fundamental weakness. Aided by his son Shapur I (241-272), a number of pivotal battles were fought, with the latter eventually gaining a stunning victory over the Emperor Valerian, who was captured at the Battle of Edessa in 259, together with much of his army – some of whose skills (as prisoners) were deployed in the aftermath to build roads, bridges and dams, still in evidence today. Parry points to a combined dam and bridge near Susa in Iran:

'...the 516m-long (1,700ft) structure, much of which survives until today as a lasting reminder of Rome's shame... While Roman effort and perhaps technology, however unwillingly, went into the Shushstar Bridge, it does not have the characteristics of a typical Roman bridge. The pointed arches are quintessentially eastern, as is the combined purpose of the structure to act both as a bridge and a dam, which accounts both for its twisting alignment to cross the river following the line of the rock outcrop and for pier widths exceeding the arch openings. Roman touches include construction of the 41 piers; each had a rubble core faced with masonry and arched openings in the spandrels to increase flood flow capacity.'

Under Shapur, a more vibrant economy developed, served by expanding agriculture. This in turn was facilitated by an innovative method of irrigation, i.e. underground canals ('qanat') that carried

274

water from mountainous areas down to groups of villages for distribution in the surrounding fields. It has been established that the qanat was an Iranian invention some 2,700 years ago. Since that time the technology, which requires experienced engineers to not only establish a satisfactory source, but also to plot a workable route, and construct a long-lasting tunnel – with intermittent maintenance shafts – has been imitated around the whole of the Middle East region, and still constitutes a vibrant civil engineering activity in some countries. The system avoids large-scale evaporation, can be tapped into so as to cool adjacent houses – and can even assist in maintaining ice-pits (invented in Iran c400BC) through the intense summer heat. Many systems are still in perfect working order, two notable examples in Iran being the ancient qanat – 28 miles (45km) long – which still supplies water to 40,000 inhabitants of Gonabad, and the one that surfaces in the famous Fin garden, from a source believed to be several thousand years old, known as the 'Spring of Solomon'.

The influx of Roman subjects, including native Greeks and Syrians, prompted renewed interest in Greek learning, although a questionable aspect was the emergence of the prophet Mani (216-277). Born a Christian, his 'puritanical' outpourings – perhaps based on earlier 'Gnostic' ideas (linked to Platonic philosophy) – which led to the splinter movement Manichaeism, has contributed to all manner of subsequent Christian schisms. At the root of his depressing ideas was the concept of 'original sin' (i.e. from birth) and the declaration that pleasure was an abomination, especially in the area of sexual relations, with only death bringing spiritual relief. After Shapur I died in 272, there were six successors in the 37-year period up to 309, and consequently weak regimes could not prevent repeated Roman incursions. But this dismal period was followed by a remarkable era.

First Golden (military) Era (309-379)

This 70-year period benefited from having a single ruler, from the moment that the boy-king Shapur II (great-grandson of Shapur I) overcame a year of uncertainty over the succession, although in his infancy his mother and key nobles operated a 'regency'. One key achievement throughout his long reign was to oversee completion of codification of the Mazdaean religion, which had emerged from its longstanding Zoroastrian origins, a transformative process initiated by his illustrious predecessor in the middle of the previous century.

275

In terms of his relationship with the (Eastern) Roman Empire, Shapur II reigned first through the period when Constantine pronounced that Christianity was to be adopted 'everywhere', then had to face (in 363) his militant pagan successor Julian. A huge Roman army penetrated Mesopotamia, reaching as far down the Euphrates as Ctesiphon. A comparison with Napoleon penetrating deep into Russia springs to mind, except that in this case it was the heat and disease that sapped the will of this seemingly irresistible force. Julian was killed in mysterious circumstances, and the Romans were forced to sue for peace. Sassanid borders were restored to those achieved by Shapur I, together with suzerainty over the endless 'pig in the middle' country – the always contested (and now nominally Christian) territory of Armenia.

Intermediate Era (379-498)

In total contrast to the stability that mostly applied under Shapur II, the next 120-year span saw ten individual rulers of differing abilities – 11 if one includes the first eight-year stint of Kavadh I, from 488 to 496. Not surprisingly, an inconsistent approach appertained towards religious tolerance, since even as the empire's borders waxed and waned a substantial proportion of the population was Christian, Jew, pagan Greek, and Arab. The situation with 'Rome' (i.e. now the Eastern Empire) also ebbed and flowed. Worse still, early in the 5th century the porous eastern borders were punctured repeatedly by the semi-nomadic Hephthalites (White Huns).

Towards the end of this era, Manichaeism reared its head again, when a sect emerged known as Mazdakism, after its leader Mazdak, which preached what we would now call 'communist' theories, ranging from free food for all to free love for all! The newly appointed Kavadh fell for this insidious (ungovernable) movement, which temporarily cost him his throne in favour of his brother. Apparently imprisoned, legend has it that Kavadh eventually escaped only through the feminine wiles of his daughter being brought to bear on his gaoler, and was soon reinstated as monarch, with the aid of an army sponsored by erstwhile enemies – none other than the Hephthalites.

Second Golden (cultural and military) Era (498-622)

The link between stability and length of kingship was never more emphasised than when examining this buoyant 125-year period –

culturally as well as militarily – during which only four kings ruled throughout the Sassanid Empire's most successful phase. Kavadh's second reign lasted from 498 until his death in 531, and he spent most of this time embroiled in battles with the Eastern Roman Empire, coming up against the famous general Belisarius. Even so – and despite being in hock to the menace on his eastern border from the Hephthalites, who had restored him to the throne – he initiated a programme of reforms.

Kavadh modernised the system of government and tax collection, which process – according to Axworthy – created a new class of rural gentry, the 'dehqans', and it is they who came to provide the 'game-changing' cavalry to their rulers, *and* eventually ensured that Sassanid traditions and culture 'were preserved and transmitted onward in time after the Islamic conquest'. Kavadh also found the will to tackle the influence of Mazdak, who later in his reign he perceived to be malign. With the aid of his son and heir, Kavadh plotted to round up and kill the key followers of this 'communist', then had him ruthlessly assassinated.

In the year of Kavadh's death, the Persians finally achieved a victory over Belisarius, and one of the first acts of his son Khosraw I (reigned 531-579) was to conclude an 'eternal peace' with the new emperor Justinian. Khosraw broadened and deepened the reforms that his father had initiated. He especially made the tax system 'transparent', based on a comprehensive survey of land ownership, and he deepened the concept of dehqans, since in funding them they became more committed to his leadership, and less so to the local lords who had previously held sway in this vast territory.

But – even more so than with his father – Khosraw, in broadening the social and political structures, set in motion a more tolerant age. The most famous of all Sassanid kings, he earned the title 'Anurshivan' ('He with the immortal soul'). His reign largely coincided with that of Justinian (reigned 527-565), and after the latter had closed the Plato Academy in Athens in 529, Khosraw welcomed a group of (unwanted) scholars, who brought with them precious works of philosophy, literature and science. Allegedly the guests were appalled at (in particular) the lifestyle of the Persians, and felt honour-bound to return to a perilous future in Greece. Axworthy quotes Gibbon as commenting:

'From this journey, however, they derived a benefit which reflects the purest lustre on the character of Khosraw. He required that the

277

seven sages who had visited the court of Persia should be exempted from the penal laws which Justinian enacted against his pagan subjects; and this privilege, expressly stipulated in a treaty of peace, was guarded by the vigilance of a powerful mediator.'

Khosraw sponsored the translation of texts in several languages into Persian (Farsi), saw that a complete history of Persia was written, and – though reaffirming Zoroastrianism as the official religion – was tolerant of all others, with one of his sons becoming a Christian. He was revered outside his borders and famed for building a fabulous palace at Ctesiphon, and keenly promoted the study of astronomy. Not forgetting his predecessors' territorial ambitions, he succeeded – on balance – in holding his own against the Romans (Byzantines), finally hammered the Hephthalites to the east, moved into India, Afghanistan, central Asia, Turkey and Syria, and, most important perhaps strategically, started the process whereby his successors secured the whole of the eastern and southern Arabia coastline, thereby controlling access to the Red Sea.

The 11-year reign of Khosraw's son Hormudz IV (579-590) was a comparatively dismal period with endless wars; a disaffected general, Barham, eventually overthrew and murdered the king. Barham's attempt to rule was thwarted with difficulty by Hormudz's son Khosraw II, and the over-ambitious general had to flee to Turkey, where he was in turn murdered.

Because of this insurgency, Khosraw II (590-628) did not fully establish himself until c600. In a reign of contrasts, on the one hand he proved (like his father) not to be a patch on his illustrious grandfather in terms of the way he handled his people, and he lived an outrageously grandiose lifestyle, even for a mighty king/emperor. On the other hand, he achieved almost unchallenged military successes that his forebears could only have dreamed about.

By 610 – and during the following decade – Khosraw II (named 'Parvaz', 'the victorious') all but restored the boundaries of the empire that had been reached by Darius in the first Persian (Achaemenid) Empire 1,100 years earlier. With what we will now refer to as the Byzantine Empire in one of its periodic crises, the Sassanids achieved control – in a clockwise direction – not only of the eastern and southern coastlines of the Arabian peninsula, but also the whole of northern Egypt, stretching into Libya, the entire Middle East to the Mediterranean shore, the eastern half of Turkey, Armenia and the whole of the Caucasus, the whole of central Asia and Afghanistan, and most of what is now Pakistan. As to famous cities that were trade and cultural centres with fabulous wealth, Antioch fell in 611, Damascus in 613, Jerusalem (sending shock-waves throughout the Christian world) in 614, and Alexandria in 619.

Decline and fall (622-651)

However – with parallels to Hitler's Europe in 1942-43 – this dramatic Sassanid expansion had exhausted the Persian armies, as well as material resources and much of the fabulous treasury. Having suffered a devastating setback in 613, the Byzantine Emperor Heraclius now turned the tables. Between 622 and 628 he recovered all his previously lost territory, and – advancing down the Tigris – almost reached the gates of Ctesiphon, from where in 629 (most famously) he managed to seize the True Cross taken from Jerusalem 15 years earlier, and restore it to its rightful place in a magnificent ceremony. With Khosraw dead, a chaotic state of affairs ensued among his successors. Having suffered terrible setbacks from the north-west, the shattered armies were in no position to fend off the well-organised Arabs, who had just become newly united under Islam. Despite the occasional counterattack, the Arabs swept through Iraq and captured Ctesiphon in 637, forcing the fleeing Sassanids to leave behind their remaining treasury. Because the Persians resisted strongly in their Iranian homeland, the empire disintegrated on a dismal note; many wonderful buildings, including priceless books and works of art, were utterly destroyed by fire in the final Arab conquest.

Islam from the birth of Muhammad (570) to the end of the Umayyad dynasty (750)

It has never been more important than now to understand the world in which Muhammad grew up, and the core beliefs that he espoused in the Quran (Koran) – translated as 'Recitation'. It is perhaps the most supreme (and deeply worrying) irony of our age that, at a time when the 'West' at large is most suspicious of the motives of many Muslims ('those who submit to God'), today's scholars and historians have secured a better insight into the prophet's *actual* thinking and pronouncements than at any time hitherto. It seems to the writer that, just as repeated schisms in Christianity require that we should never forget the core principles of Christ's original teachings, so we should never lose sight of what Muhammad himself set out to achieve.

A significant proportion of what follows is owed to Karen Armstrong's excellent book *Islam* (the word meaning 'surrender' – to the will of God). Since she served as a Roman Catholic nun for seven years, and is well known for her measured writings on Christianity, Karen Armstrong has to be respected for her well-researched and thoughtful histories of the prophet Muhammad, and on Islam throughout the ages (as well as on Buddhism). Our script will also include the original/literal translations of Arabic terminology, so that we can assert their original meaning.

Arabia at the time of the prophet's birth

The enormous peninsula was peppered with small settlements, the two sizeable cities being the agricultural centre of Yathrib (later Medina) and the trading/financial centre of Mecca. The population was partly sedentary and partly nomadic, with the latter having little compunction in raiding oasis communities or travelling caravans for their requirements. In a harsh desert environment, tribal loyalty was supreme, evidenced by hundreds of statues of (pagan) patron deities at the Kaaba shrine in Mecca, the site of an annual pilgrimage. Tribal feuding was ceaseless, with a seemingly perpetual cycle of blood-shedding vendettas; this aspect, more than any other, held back the Arabs from the (social) progress seemingly being made by their ethnic 'cousins' in the wider Middle East.

Arabs knew about Judaism and Christianity, as many such communities were intermingled with their own – to whom they were indeed related by blood – and they were perhaps envious of their monotheistic beliefs, which made a deep impression, partly because they were written down. Indeed, a minority among the mainly pagan population were 'hanifs', a largely monotheistic group who believed themselves to be direct descendents of Abraham (Ibrahim) and who had a somewhat vague notion of Al-Lah (the one 'God'). Muslim tradition has it that Muhammad (570-632) was a direct descendent of Abraham's son, Ishmael.

Muhammad's early life and revelations

Muhammad ibn Abdallah's father died before he was born, as did his grandfather when he was only aged six. With his mother unable to support him, tradition has it that he became an adopted member of the Quraysh tribe, which had grown wealthy from its part in Mecca's trade with the wider world. He himself became a successful businessman, though troubled by the way in which his tribe in particular had achieved success at the expense of weaker brethren – with the old tradition of the strong supporting the weak becoming lost. When he was 25, he married the 40-year-old Khadija, and – unusually – she remained his sole wife until her death in 620, aged 65, after which he took several more wives.

Being a deep thinker, Muhammad used to retreat during Ramadan, the ninth month in the Arabic calendar, with a fasting practice that long predated Islam. His chosen place for meditation was a cave on Mount Hira, near Mecca, and it is there in 610 that the angel Gabriel appeared to him in a vision. Essentially, Gabriel revealed to Muhammad pronouncements that he must make, which left him sorely distressed. For two or three years he only confided in his wife and her Christian cousin that he held the beginnings of an Arabic scripture that he was preparing to pour out.

Eventually, in c613, convinced he was possessed of the word of God, Muhammad began to pass on this wisdom to his four closest companions, to all but one of whom he was but distantly related: Abu Bakr, Umar ibn al-Khattab, Uthman ibn Affan (a descendant of Umayya, founder of a powerful clan), and his much younger close cousin Ali ibn Abi Talib, then aged about 10.

Muhammad's teachings

Slowly Muhammad started to attract converts, many of whom were poor and female – and disillusioned by the inequalities of life in Mecca. To quote Armstrong:

> 'Muhammad's message was simple: He taught the Arabs no new doctrines about God: most of the Quraysh were already convinced that Allah had created the world and would judge humanity in the Last Days, as Jews and Christians believed. Muhammad did not think he was founding a new religion, but that he was merely bringing the old faith in the One God to the Arabs, who had never had a prophet before... If the Quraysh did not mend their ways, their society would collapse...'

281

Muhammad was illiterate, as were most of his growing band of believers. As the Quran was progressively revealed to him – almost until his death – so in turn did Muhammad rely on learned scholars to write down, then continuously recite the ever-growing number of chapters to him and his followers, verse by verse. As Armstrong again describes:

'The revelations were painful to Muhammad, who used to say: "Never once did I receive a revelation, without thinking that my soul had been torn away from me."'

It is clear that it was the remarkable mixture of the message itself, and the beautiful prose, that began to appeal – with electrifying effect – to an ever-widening audience. A classic case was that of one of the four 'companions', Umar ibn al-Khattab, which has a resonance with St Paul's conversion on the road to Damascus. Umar, a pagan who was determined to crush the new sect, was fortuitously also well-versed in Arabic poetry, and the first time he heard extracts from the Quran he was overcome. According to Armstrong, he said, 'When I heard the Quran my heart was softened and I wept, and Islam entered my soul.'

Muhammad preached the virtues of justice and compassion between human beings, core beliefs that were extremely close to those propounded by Christ 600 years earlier. Each group of early followers was committed to creating a small community ('ummah'), which practised these virtues. In addition, as a repeated acknowledgement to the commitment of 'surrender to God', all Muslims were required to prostrate themselves three times a day in ritual prayer ('salat'). Crucially also, the Quran repeatedly points out (Armstrong again) that:

'Muhammad had not come to *cancel* the older religions, to contradict their prophets or to start a new faith. His message is the same as that of Abraham, Moses, David, Solomon, or Jesus ... he commands Muslims to respect the beliefs of Jews and Christians, whom the Quran calls "ahl al-kitab" ... "People of the Book".'

Mecca and the surrounding area was – by ancient tradition – inviolate against the internecine tribal bloodshed that so marred Arabic life elsewhere in that vast region. This degree of protection was linked to the annual pilgrimage ('hajj') from far and wide to the Kabah, the long-standing cube-shaped shrine that stands in the centre of the city. Arabs from the far north, who had been influenced by Byzantium to convert to Christianity, joined in the ritual, which saw all involved performing their prayers, facing towards Jerusalem, a practice to which Muhammad made his followers adhere in those early days.

A summary of Muhammad's struggle for survival

In the space available it is simply not possible to detail the tortuous path trodden by Muhammad in order for his message to survive, which was the prerequisite for his growing band of adherents to eventually prosper. There follows therefore a summary, which can easily be expanded upon by reading any number of texts, including that of Karen Armstrong.

By 616 Muhammad's relationship with the pagan hierarchy that controlled Mecca had almost reached breaking point. They saw their rich and comfortable lifestyle being endangered by a man they accused of being a charlatan, and – in further echoes of the life of Jesus – followers of the prophet were increasingly persecuted. Muhammad's own position became more perilous when, in 619, his uncle Abbas, who had protected him from early childhood, died, leaving him vulnerable to assault or even death, with any assailant knowing there was no 'godfather' to answer to. By good fortune (or providence), leaders in the settlement of Yathrib (Medina – the 'city') were fed up with their own endless infighting, and during the 'hajj' of 620 they converted to Islam and invited Muhammad to 'emigrate' north across the desert, with their promise of a stable future for him and his followers.

With his first wife dying in the same year, Muhammad took several others during the remainder of his life, his favourite being Aisha, the daughter of another of the 'companions', Abu Bakr. He also married one of his daughters to a third 'companion', Uthman, and another to the fourth, his young cousin Ali. It is important to note that Muhammad expressed his real enjoyment of female company, and that he favoured their emancipation. As Armstrong recounts:

'The Quran gave women rights of inheritance and divorce centuries before Western women were accorded such status ...

there is nothing in the Quran that requires the veiling of all women or their seclusion in a separate part of the house. These customs were adopted some three or four generations after the prophet's death.'

In 622 the still small Muslim community in Mecca (perhaps only 70 families) made the migration ('hijrah') to Medina. Officials in Mecca had Muhammad closely watched, and both he and Abu Bakr only escaped assassination through the heroics of Ali, his 22-year-old cousin and new son-in-law, an act that would later help to precipitate the fundamental schism within Islam, which has never been reconciled (see below). The first effect of the 'hijrah' was that Muhammad – after winning over the disparate local factions through the Constitution of Medina – was able to openly promulgate his message to the wider population, thus marking the start of the Muslim era proper. The second effect was the vicious reaction of the 'old order' in Mecca, who considered Muhammad's action treacherous, and vowed to secure revenge.

There now followed a period of great uncertainty as to which side would win the ensuing struggle. The year 624 saw the (still small) Muslim army secure a dramatic victory, only to suffer a crushing defeat in 625. This resulted in the expulsion of Jewish tribes from Medina, for having sided with Mecca. It was Muhammad's disillusion with the Jews at this time that caused him to have his followers perform their prayers facing Mecca instead of Jerusalem.

Again, the Muslims gained the upper hand in 627 with a stunning victory at the 'Battle of the Trench' – and this time the militia of another Jewish clan that had supported Mecca were all put to death. Despite this drastic action, the Quran portrays no general hostility to the Jews, but on the contrary reveres their prophets.

To quote Armstrong again:

'…later Jews, like Christians, enjoyed full religious liberty in the Islamic empires. Anti-semitism is a (centuries old) Christian vice. Hatred of the Jews became marked in the Muslim world only after the creation of the state of Israel in 1948 and the subsequent loss of Arab Palestine.'

(A remarkable 800-page book that gives a graphic insight to the relationship of Arabs and Jews is *One Palestine, Complete* by Tom

Segev, which primarily covers the first half of the 20th century. This even-handed history starts in Jerusalem, with the intermittent – and moving – relationship between a notable Christian Arab writer, Sakakini, and a Jewish businessman, Levine. It then plots in detail the tragic circumstances that have led all the way to the continuing Israeli/Arab impasse.)

It is quite crucial to note the above pair of paragraphs, when considering the next three chapters.

A major turning point followed in 628, when Muhammad put out peace feelers to Mecca, and marched towards the Holy City with a large band of unarmed supporters. This was obviously a huge risk, and the intrepid group camped outside Mecca, at Hudaybiyyah, to await the response of the pagan traditionalists. Eventually a tentative peace treaty was signed, the reward for Mohammad being an irreversible tide of conversion to Islam by thousands of amazed bystanders in the region, who were bowled over (from a religious and secular standpoint) by the prophet's faith, courage and dynamism.

Mohammad's supreme achievement, and death

Not surprisingly there was unease on all sides, and Meccan violation of this Treaty of Hudaybiyyah resulted in Mohammad marching on the city with a major force in 630. The old guard in Mecca realised that the game was up, and the Muslims took control without further bloodshed. Muhammad destroyed all the idols around the Kabah, and dedicated the ancient shrine to Allah. However, he made it clear that there would be no forced conversion to Islam. Now nearly everyone became convinced of the merits of this remarkable man, and soon the vast majority throughout Arabia had taken up the Muslim faith. Muhammad's astonishing achievement was to put an end to centuries of deadly infighting among the hundreds of Arabian tribes. In so doing he created a united force that would soon prove unstoppable throughout the Middle East, and beyond.

Tragically – again echoing the divisions in Christianity that soon broke the bonds of the idealistic early Church – we can see that, in the respect of unity, the point at which Mohammad died in 632 was most unfortunately the supreme moment. A few months after his final pilgrimage to Mecca, at the end of which he delivered what is known as his Farewell Speech – and from which *crucially different interpretations* arose as to his chosen successor – Muhammad fell ill. He died at his home in Medina, with his wife Aisha, on 8 June 632 at the age of 63, his final words being recorded as, 'Rather, God on High and paradise.'

The Rashidun: the four 'rightly guided' caliphs (632-661)

After the peaceful 'conquest' of Mecca, Muhammad had dealt effectively with recalcitrant tribes – mainly in northern Arabia – as a result of which the absence of fighting between Arabs became more pronounced, and thousands more converted to Islam. After his death, Muslims therefore were left with the twin benefits of a largely united population *and* a real sense of purpose, which was guided by the accumulated wisdom of the Quran. The questions were: with their unique leader no longer at the helm, who would/could now possibly take his place, and what was the direction in which the (very newly enlarged) Arab 'ummah', or federation, should proceed?

We have already seen that the prophet had shared his life with his four closest companions. In a society where blood ties were considered sacred, three of these were only distantly related, but mature 'elder statesman'. The fourth, Ali, was aged just over 30, but Muhammad's quite close cousin, son-in-law, *and* the young man whose selfless impersonation of his uncle had enabled the latter and Abu Bakr to escape assassination when they had been compelled to flee from Mecca. As we shall see, in the decisions that were now taken lay the seeds of eventual and interminable schism.

Fatefully, after some deliberation, it was Abu Bakr – only 10 tumultuous years after he had been saved by Ali's heroism – who was elected as the first caliph ('khalifah', or 'successor') from 632 to 634. With Muhammad's charismatic hold over the different tribes gone, several tried to break away, and Abu Bakr successfully oversaw a crucial period of ummah reintegration or consolidation. A particular grievance had been the Muslim requirement to cease raids ('ghazu') on neighbouring territory, thus choking off a main source of tribal 'income'. And it was in seeking a new purpose so as to keep the ummah united and well-victualled – rather than as a result of Islamic fervour – that Abu Bakr (and his immediate successor) conceived the notion of carrying the ghazu to *non-Muslim* lands. Little did he know what he had started!

On the death of Abu Bakr, the role of caliph passed to another of the prophet's companions, Umar ibn al-Khattab, between 634 and

644. In this 10-year period the conquests of the ummah were truly astonishing. Much aided by the fact that the Byzantines and Sassanids had fought each other to a standstill, the ever-more-professional Muslim army defeated the Persians in 637 at the Battle of Qadisiyyah, seized Ctesiphon, and set in train capture of the whole of the eastern Sassanid Empire. In the west, while making little progress in Anatolia, they defeated the Byzantines at the Battle of Yarmuk in 636, conquered Jerusalem in 638, and by 641 held control of Syria and Egypt.

It is of great significance – as we will observe later from a cultural point of view – that a number of factors combined to avoid huge mutiny, bloodshed and upheaval in these conquered territories. In the west, local populations quickly preferred the *religious tolerance* of the Muslims, as opposed to the dogmatic strictures of the Greek Orthodox Church. Indeed, since Muslims believed that they were linked by blood to the House of Abraham, they quickly realised themselves that most of the indigenous peoples were 'People of the Book'. To add to this, Muhammad had laid down a strict code for the protection of weaker brethren ('mawali'), whether or not they shared original ethnic ties. Finally, being protected subjects ('dhimmis'), Christians and Jews – as well as (mainly Persian) Zoroastrians – were protected from any form of attack or persecution, in return for paying a 'levy'.

This brief period of law and order – after such heady triumphs – was severely threatened after Umar was murdered in the Medina mosque by a Persian prisoner-of-war. It may have been logical to elect the last surviving older companion of the prophet as the third caliph, but Uthman ibn Affan (644-656) was no patch on the first two caliphs, in terms of wise governance. On the one hand he oversaw continued military success in North Africa, the Caucasus, Afghanistan, Iran and India, together with the capture of Cyprus. But by 650 he had unsettled his commanders by sticking to Umar's policy of not allowing them to acquire private land in the conquered territories, and – as an even greater portent of incipient trouble – had infuriated Muslims in Medina by awarding most of the key levers of power to members of his large Umayyad family.

Ironically, this discontent was unrelated to the outstanding ability of some members of the Umayyad clan, the prime example being Muawiyyah, a devout Muslim and a very able administrator who was appointed Governor of Syria. Dissent in Medina reached boiling point in 656, with unrest culminating in a full-blown mutiny by members of the army who looked up to the prophet's cousin, Ali ibn Abi Talib, by now more than 55 years of age. It was known that Ali had had his disagreements with at least two of the first three caliphs, and in his name the mutineers raided Uthman's home and murdered him.

And so, after being overlooked for nearly 25 years since Muhammad's death, Ali finally became the fourth caliph (656-661). However, given no time to enjoy his appointment, he soon became locked in what amounted to civil warfare – the first 'fitnah' ('temptation'). Immediately, the prophet's widow Aisha rebelled with her clan, accusing Ali of failing to punish Uthman's killers. Her group of followers established themselves at Basrah, but were heavily defeated by Ali's forces at the Battle of the Camel. Much more dangerous to Ali was his rejection by Muawiyyah, whose power-base was Damascus, but who was supported by many wealthy Meccans. Attempts at conciliation between the two factions failed, and Muawiyyah flexed his muscles by pronouncing himself caliph, in Jerusalem. Though Ali and his followers resisted this Umayyad-based drive for supremacy, Muawiyyah had overcome most resistance in Arabia by 661, with Ali, the last of the four Rashidun, being murdered by a member of the Kharajis rebels – 'seceders' from the ummah, who believed the principles of the Quran had been abrogated.

With Damascus as his capital, Muawiyyah made serious efforts to reunite the ummah, but the seeds of everlasting dissent had been sown. Many Muslims in Arabia and Iraq could not be reconciled to Muawiyyah's caliphate. Believing Ali to have always been the rightful heir to Muhammad, they appealed to like-minded Muslims to join them in the struggle ('jihad'), and claimed that they belonged to the Shia I Ali ('the party of Ali').

The term Sunni is derived from the term 'Sunnah' – implying the tradition of Muhammad – and is today followed by a clear majority of Muslims worldwide, their original core difference from Shia Islam being the Sunni reverence for *all four* caliphs of the Rashidun, *in equal measure*.

The Umayyad dynasty (661-750)

After the ghastly events of the first fitnah – so alien to the ideal of the ummah – Muawiyyah (caliph from 661 to 680) set about restoring unity throughout the empire. He stuck to Umar's policy of not allowing Muslims to build private estates in the conquered lands, and because his fellow Arabs had (in the early years) no way of knowing how to govern such a complex *existing* 'society', had the wisdom to allow officials from the dhimmis community to operate the 'civil service'; after all, Damascus and Jerusalem were already two of the longest-inhabited cities in the world, just as they both remain today, just 1,350 years after the start of this dynasty!

(Recent carbon dating shows that Damascus was inhabited before 6000BC. Josephus, the 1st-century-AD Jewish historian, wrote that Abraham and his followers (emigrating from northern Iraq) settled in Damascus before moving on to 'the land of Canaan'. This modest settlement was greatly expanded once the Aramaeans – Semitic nomads from Mesopotamia – moved into the Barada valley in the 11th century BC. They constructed channels and tunnels to give the rapidly growing city a secure water supply, a system later improved by both the Romans and Umayyads, and still partially in use today. The Romans developed the city both strategically and culturally and, even though bitterly fought over in later centuries, the status of Damascus as a major centre was assured long before Muawiyyah decided to base his caliphate there. This city, to which St Paul was travelling when he had his 'Damascene' conversion, has bequeathed us several other legacies, including Damascus steel, Damask textile fabrics, glass-blowing technology; and the Damask rose.)

Muawiyyah did his utmost to balance several competing factors: Islamic ideals with secular government; the rural poor with the wealthy city-dwellers; and the legacies of the Sassanid East with the still partially Hellenistic (Byzantine-facing) West. He did not see himself as an absolute ruler, but as a 'first among equals' who did not enjoy a lavish lifestyle. Arguably, his mistake was to nominate his son Yazid I as his successor (680-683).

There now followed a chaotic five-year period (680-685) of three rulers, with Yazid, *his* son, and Muawiyyah's cousin Marwan I becoming caliph in rapid succession. In the second fitnah that ensued, the seeds of the permanent Sunni-Shia split were further nurtured through the killing by Yazid of Ali's second son Husain – and his children – at Kerbala, south of modern-day Baghdad. Further rebellion against the Umayyads took hold in Medina and Mecca, and was only put down after a bitter struggle. Only when Marwan's son Abd al-Malik became caliph (685-705) did the Umayyads reassert their hold over the ummah. Abd al-Malik is considered to have governed well, but he moved close to being an absolute monarch, started to allow Muslims to acquire private property in the conquered lands, relied ever more heavily (see below) on the cultural contribution of non-Muslims, and was perceived – particularly in Arabia and southern Iraq – as moving away from Quranic ascetic principles.

During the first half of the 7th century a series of devout adherents to the Quran sprang up, the most famous of whom was Hasan al-Basri (died 728). He based himself at Basrah, preached unswerving obedience to the Quran, and fearlessly asserted that the caliphate should be bound in the same way as the ordinary citizen. He was brought before Abd al-Malik, but so strong was his following that the caliph felt unable to punish him. Hasan al-Basri nevertheless accepted Umayyad rule, thus initiating the centuries-long 'creative tension' between the political and religious wings of Islam.

Although Abd al-Malik nominated his son to succeed him without opposition – and the empire continued to expand as far west as Spain – governance from Damascus became ever more difficult. Yet again there was Shia discontent, with the conviction growing in Arabia that Ali should have been the (rightful) first caliph. The attempt by the Umayyads to maintain control was not helped by there being no fewer than nine caliphs between 705 and 750. Shia ideology led to the conviction that as close a relative as possible to the prophet should become their leader, and they chose a descendant of Muhammad's protective uncle, Abbas, as their leader.

Thus began the Abbasid revolt, which gathered momentum with amazing speed, and resulted in defeat of the last Umayyad caliph Marwan II (744-750), who governed from Damascus, in 750.

The Abbasids ruthlessly slaughtered the entire Umayyad family, or so they thought – as we shall see in the next chapter!

'A new Byzantium'

This term was used by Colin Wells in his fascinating book *Sailing from Byzantium*, to head the chapters that describe how much Abd al-Malik and his successors borrowed from an unbroken Roman/Hellenic/ Byzantine architectural and cultural lineage, as the new caliph set out to display the supremacy of Islam under Umayyad leadership. The act for which he is most famous was to build in Jerusalem (to which city

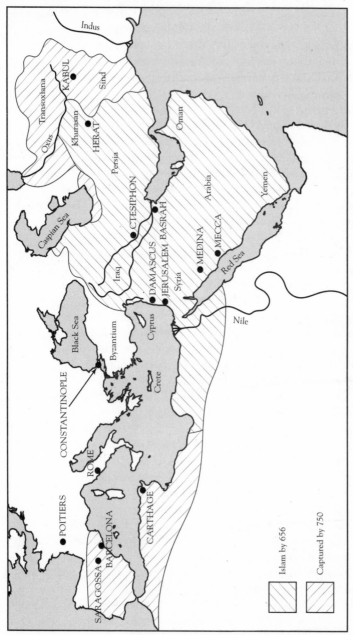

Map viii – Extent of the Umayyad Empire at 750AD

the prophet had had his followers in Medina initially pray) the Dome of the Rock. At that time also, though Jerusalem and Damascus were under Umayyad control, both Mecca and Medina were in the hands of Abd al-Malik's opponents. As the oldest public building in Islam, this remarkable shrine still dominates the skyline of the ancient city. In proclaiming the arrival of a new power, Wells states, the Dome of the Rock 'perfectly symbolises Byzantium's influence on the emerging civilization of Islam'. He goes on to describe how, even as the fabulous edifice was being constructed on Byzantine lines, the Umayyads were ousting the Christian empire from the eastern Mediterranean and North Africa. Crucially, he notes that Quranic inscriptions in the Dome of the Rock – while acknowledging Christians (and Jews) as 'Peoples of the Book' – firmly propounds that in 'introducing the idea of the Trinity, Christians have corrupted the original monotheistic message of God's unity'.

If now Islam was becoming a civilisation as well as a faith, Persian and Byzantine influence was inescapable. While on the one hand, up to 600AD those influences had largely bypassed Arabia because of its inaccessibility and partly nomadic structure, so strong were those (competing) influences in the lands the Arabs conquered that the Umayyads could not administer daily life – over such huge swathes of territory – without relying on the methods and structures of the indigenous population. So it followed that the *cultural* heritage of these earlier invaders seeped into the minds of the new rulers.

To add to the above, it cannot be emphasised enough that the Muslim conquerors specifically did not attempt to convert their captive peoples to the new faith. As the new empire spread, a crucial tool of government was to encourage normal life to continue, so as to ensure stability – much aided (in the Near East) by subject peoples previously having been persecuted by the Orthodox Greek Church. Nowhere was this 'administrative' practice more apparent than in Alexandria in 641, after which Byzantine propaganda would have the world believe that the Muslims deployed a 'scorched earth' policy – most damagingly in the fantasy of the destruction of the greatest library in antiquity.

Much damage had been done centuries earlier, and precious manuscripts lost, at least once through Christian invasion, and it is highly questionable as to whether the Muslims caused any severe loss of priceless texts. An example of such earlier chaos has recently been brought to a wider public through the recent release of a film, *Agora*, covering the life of Hypatia, a female Greek scholar in mathematics, who was killed by a Christian mob in 415. As we shall see later, the 'proof of the pudding was in the eating', namely: how could an entire corpus of Greek works have existed in Arabic texts – in Baghdad – by 1,000AD, if earlier Islamic conquerors of the Middle East had eradicated (wittingly or unwittingly) so much of the accumulated knowledge that had fallen into their hands, as they overran not only Alexandria but such other famous seats of learning as Damascus (which the Arabs particularly respected), Jerusalem and Antioch?

In an intriguing passage from his book, Wells describes how the Arabs' first teachers in pomp and circumstance were the Byzantines. Quoting the great 14th-century Muslim historian Ibn Khaldun (see the end of Chapter 24), Wells continues: 'In his [Muawiyyah's] defence, he explained "that Damascus was full of Greeks, and that none would believe in his power if he did not behave and look like an emperor".' Quoting again on the need to 'keep the wheels turning': 'The Muslims were illiterate Arabs who did not know how to write and keep books. For bookkeeping they employed Jews, Christians, or certain non-Arab clients versed in it.'

Wells also refers to the new Muslim masters – in adopting a sedentary lifestyle, as opposed to their centuries-old Bedouin ways – relying heavily on their subject 'tutors', in all manner of necessary skills. They were also much influenced by Byzantine and Persian artists and musicians; although well-versed in oral poetry, Ibn Khaldun also wrote that 'before the conquests, the Arabs had not known singing'.

The Abbasid switch to Baghdad, and cultural renaissance

After the appalling bloodshed of 750, the Abbasids soon decided that – rather than base themselves in Damascus, Mecca or Medina – they would build a new capital from scratch. They chose Iraq, and after basing themselves briefly at Kufah, caliph Abu Jafar al-Mansur (754-775) founded Baghdad on the Tigris in 762 – a location just 19 miles (30km) from the Sassanid city of Ctesiphon. From that moment the Byzantium-centric milieu, which had been favoured by their Umayyad predecessors, was replaced by the cultural influence of the Persians. Even the Arabic name bestowed on the new city by al-Mansur – Madinat as-Salam, 'City of Peace' – soon gave way to the Persian name used ever since.

So well sited from a trading point of view, Baghdad grew rapidly, and by the time of caliph Harun al-Rashid (786-809) had a population of several hundred thousand. Quoting Karen Armstrong again:

'Harun al-Rashid was a patron of the arts and scholarship, and inspired a great cultural renaissance. Literary criticism, philosophy, poetry, medicine, mathematics and astronomy flourished... Dhimmis participated in the florescence by translating the philosophical and medical texts of classical Hellenism from Greek and Syriac into Arabic. Building on the learning of the past, which had thus become available to them, Muslim scholars made more scientific discoveries during this time than in the whole of previously recorded history.'

Colin Wells records that Harun al-Rashid's son, caliph al-Mamun (813-833), is purported to have had a dream that energised his interest in ancient Greek, wherein a handsome man identified himself as Aristotle. In his dream, the story goes, al-Mamun asked the famous philosopher to answer a question: 'What is good?' 'Whatever is good according to reason,' Aristotle replied. 'What else?' asked the caliph. 'Whatever is good according to religious law,' came the answer. 'And what else'? 'Nothing else,' said Aristotle.

Although the formality of the institution has recently been cast into doubt, caliph father and son created the 'House of Wisdom', a centre for a library and translation. While the Persians had long been working on Greek texts, there is no question that from c800AD onwards the Arabs in their new capital city were seized by a desire to understand as much of Greek learning as possible – and to use the results to further their own civilisation and culture.

The most famous translator of this age in Baghdad was the local-born Hunayn ibn Ishaq, who lived from 808/809 to 873. The son of a pharmacist, Hunayn was born a Christian, well educated and widely travelled. Known later in Western Europe by his Latin name Johannitius, Hunayn's reputation was staggering in his own lifetime, which straddled the rule of nine caliphs. If anything, his reputation in modern times is even more legendary, and it is well worth quoting Wells verbatim:

'Hunayn is credited with literally hundreds of translations, from disciplines that included medicine, philosophy, astronomy,

294

mathematics, magic, and dream interpretation, and even a highly praised version of the Old Testament. He also wrote around a hundred works of his own, many summarising his translations. Modern philologists have found Hunayn's techniques almost unbelievably advanced – essentially the same as those used today, though reinvented in the West nearly eight hundred years later by Lorenzo Valla and his successors. *Textual critics have used many of Hunayn's translations to help restore the original Greek text in cases where no Greek manuscript survives.*' (Author's emphasis)

Galen of Pergamun (born 129, died probably in 216) was arguably the most accomplished medical researcher of his day. His written output was so prolific that it constitutes a substantial proportion of all extant Greek manuscripts. It is not surprising, therefore, that Hunayn's record of Galen's works contains no fewer than 129 separate translations. These he mainly translated into Syriac, because that language was known to the majority of his students, who could then easily change the finalised copies into Arabic. In addition, Hunayn's translations were accompanied by a wealth of informative notes and observations. Wells gives an example regarding one text, Galen's *On Dissection*, over a span of many years:

'I translated it [into Syriac] when I was a young man ... from a very defective Greek manuscript. Later on, when I was about forty years old, my pupil Hubaish asked me to correct it after having collected a certain number of [Greek] manuscripts. Therefore I collated these so as to produce one correct manuscript, and compared this manuscript with the Syriac text and corrected it. I am in the habit of proceeding thus in all my translation work. Some years later I translated it into Arabic for Abu Jafar Muhammad ibn Musa.'

Hunayn's translations also covered a majority of the crucial works of Plato and Aristotle, but he shunned the plays and other works of Greek literature. He and other translators simply could not comprehend the flowery language/satirical jokes/double entendres. In any case, to the serious-minded Syriac Christians and Islamic Arabs, such works would have seemed at once irrelevant and profane.

So successful and revered did Hunayn become that – perhaps also because he was paid enormous sums for his work – he fell foul of one caliph, who had him imprisoned. Much worse, he had the precious library that he had built up confiscated. Although eventually rehabilitated, it is not known whether he ever recovered his treasured life's work.

A key facilitator for Hunayn's startling output was the Arab development of volume paper production in the 9th century, based on skills acquired from China. Specifically, they constructed machines that could produce uniform sheets, which were thick enough to take condensed writing, and withstand being folded, passed from hand to hand, and transported long distances. It was at this time, and partly for this reason, that the parallel translation movement in Constantinople gained such momentum (see Chapter 23).

However straight-laced Hunayn may have been as regards the Greek playwrights, the era in which he lived saw the mass-popularity of the game of chess become a reality. Originally developed in the Sanskrit (Indo-Iranian) language, the game was first adopted by the Persians in the 7th century, before coming into the hands of the Abbasid dynasty as it spread east to Baghdad and beyond. As with so much else, chess spread along North Africa into Spain, to become yet another filament of medieval European society that was soon taken for granted.

Let alone today, how many educated Europeans 500 years ago would have known that the term 'checkmate' was derived from a Persian phrase 'Shah Mat', the literal meaning of which is 'The king is helpless'?

By the year 1000, as Wells relates, Arab/Syriac translators had translated every Greek text that they had earlier laid their hands on that they considered to be 'useful'. He continues:

'It seems quite apparent that the translation movement ended precisely because Arabic scientists and philosophers were breaking new ground: they had moved on, and the Greeks had nothing left to teach them. All the relevant works had been translated long since, and the Greek material that had sparked the Arabic Enlightenment was no longer on the cutting edge.'

A new movement sprang up, known in Arabic as 'falsafa', a translation of the Greek term 'philosophia'. A succession of philosophers

296

('faylasuf') took centre stage, the first being the aristocratic Arab al-Kindi, a contemporary of Hunayn, and likewise a devotee of Aristotle, both men dying in the same year (873). He was followed by a Persian, Abu Bakr al-Razi, better known to us as Rhazes (865-925), who was a Platonist, and who also followed the medical teachings of Hippocrates. Illustrating the widespread educational possibilities in the Middle East melting pot a thousand years ago, Rhazes's most notable near-contemporary was the Turkish-born faylasuf Muhammad al-Farabi (872-950), whose Latin name was Alpharabius.

However, even these illustrious polymaths were surpassed a century later, in terms of lasting influence, by Abu Ali ibn Sina (980-1037), known in the West as Avicenna. He was born near Bukhara in modern-day Uzbekistan, which the Samanid successors to the Abassid dynasty made their capital. We know more about this multi-talented Persian than about his predecessors, mainly because he left an autobiography chronicling his hazardous life; he was only 20 when his Samanid patron, their ruler Nuh ibn Mansur, was overthrown by the Ghaznavids. Avicenna then had a peripatetic existence for many years, before settling in Hamadan (western Iran). Here, in managing to dodge the fallout from political instability, he wrote on a wide variety of subjects – including medical matters – his most famous work being a huge 15-volume summary of Greek learning in all its aspects, known in Latin as *La Sufficientia*.

Decline in the East

A century after Avicenna, the end of the falsafa movement was hastened by the writings of Abu Hamid al-Ghazali (1058-1111), who – being deeply committed to mysticism – repeatedly questioned the faylasuf interest in the Greek philosophers, and their whole attachment to 'reason'. It was at the other end of the Mediterranean – building on the spectacular territorial achievements of adventurous Muslims in the 8th century (one of whom in particular felt he had no choice but to flee from the east) – that the most famous faylasuf of all lived and worked in the 12th century, whose wisdom and attraction to a wide number of European scholars changed everything in Western Europe (see Chapter 22).

In Baghdad a decline in every branch of scholarship was hastened through a growing rift between rational scholars and Islamist zealots.

The seeds of what became Wahabbism (practised most strictly today in Saudi Arabia) were sown. As this once mighty empire that led the known world in science and technology became more introverted, military pressure from the Turks – then destruction through Mongol invasion – brought intellectual adventure to a shuddering halt. So, long before the final absorption of most of the Middle East by the Ottoman Empire in c1550, as Colin Wells describes:

'The Arabs had occupied Jerusalem and made it their own, but straitened circumstances led them, metaphorically, to abandon Athens. This was the same choice that the Byzantines … would ultimately make …. in the age of Hesychasm.' (See Chapter 23)

Chapter 20

Moorish Spain, from the Umayyad to the Nasrid dynasties

We start with a summary of two most instructive books, which broke new ground when they first appeared.

The late Richard Fletcher – Professor of History at York University – had his book *Moorish Spain* first published in 1992. The back cover of the paperback edition states:

'The Islamic presence in Spain would last for nearly a thousand years, stamping an indelible mark on the language, art and culture of the country and profoundly affecting the course of European history. Critically, the scientific and philosophical learning of the Greeks and Persians had been lost to the West but was reintroduced to European intellectual life via the Islamic influence in Spain. The work of Newton would have been inconceivable without Islamic mathematics, and navigational instruments such as the astrolabe made possible the great voyages of discovery.'

Cuban-born Maria Rosa Menocal – currently director of the Yale Whitney Humanities Centre – produced her masterpiece in 2002. Included in the 'Acclaim' section is a short eulogy by the late (and lamented) Christopher Hitchens:

'Little Brown has chosen the perfect moment to publish *The Ornament of the World* [just eight months after the appalling acts of '9/11']. It is a history of medieval "al-Andalus" or Andalusia: a culture where there was extensive cooperation and even symbiosis among Muslims, Jews and Christians, and where civilisation touched a point hardly surpassed since 5th-century Athens... It is no exaggeration to say that what we presumptuously call "Western" culture is owed in large measure to the Andalusian enlightenment... This book partly restores us to a world we have lost, a world for which our current monotheistic leaderships do not even feel nostalgia.'

The Visigoths in Spain

The Visigoths – whose ancestors had sacked Rome in 410, and had then settled in southern France as 'foederati' (tribal people bound by treaty) – soon threw off any obligations to the dying Empire. Instead, they moved into Spain – ousting the remaining Vandals – in the century after Rome had shown it could no longer defend the peninsula that had provided so much of its wealth, ever since the third Punic War some 600 years earlier. Although the history of 6th-century Spain is hazy, we do know that at c589 the Visigoth king Reccared I converted his people from their Arian branch of Christianity to the more widely accepted Nicene faith. The motivation for this move derived from the erosion of ethnic distinctions between the Visigoths, Romano-Hispanics, and other minorities.

In the 7th century, successive Visigoth kings promulgated a series of laws, first pulled together by Bishop Braulio of Zaragoza. This *Visigoth Code* for all subject peoples (in Latin the *Liber Judiciorum*) appeared in its final form in 654. It covered most aspects of life, was later respected by the Moors, and remained a key pillar of Catholic jurisdiction within the country for hundreds of years. However, after King Roderic invited Berber soldiers (from across the Strait of Gibraltar) to help subjugate dissident tribes in 710, the latter reported back that southern Spain held riches beyond their wildest dreams. Unable to resist the temptation, in 711 a full-scale Arab/Berber invasion of Spain took place that defeated the Visigoths at Guadalete (probably killing Roderic) and proceeded to sweep all before it.

Muslim North Africa

During the time of the Rashidun (632-661) the Muslims first overran most of the North African littoral in 647, although Egypt (and

Alexandria) had been captured in 641. However, the upheavals within the Rashidun enabled the Byzantines to recover much of the territory they had lost. At the start of what became the Umayyad dynasty (661), Muawiyyah had much work to do closer to home, but a second invasion took place from 685 to 689, with the overstretched Muslim armies only being held by Berber defenders at the gates of Tangier. (Shades of the ebb and flow of the desert campaigns during the second World War – and of the uprising in Libya of 2011 – spring to mind when attempting to evaluate the logistical feat of trying to gain, then hold, this vast stretch of inhospitable terrain!)

Once again, turmoil following the death of Muawiyyah in 680 meant that an inconclusive situation existed until – in the reign of Abd al-Malik – a third invasion was mounted, wherein by 698 most of the region had again been conquered. Despite being able to field ever-larger armies, as the Muslim writ over the whole Middle East became consolidated, the Arabs faced repeated rebellion in this region from the fierce but (usually) disunited Berber tribes – with the immensely long coastline being vulnerable to intermittent attack from the Byzantine navy. Algiers was not taken until 700, and only in 709 could the Umayyads be said to be in total control of the entire coastal strip, from Gaza in the east to Agadir in present-day Morocco – a distance of no less than 2,500 miles (4,000km)!

The enabling of a settled regime to prosper was aided by a combination of military employment for a large proportion of the able-bodied subject tribesmen, and a programme of conversion of the willing to Islam. Seemingly without a pause for breath, the foray into Spain in 710 was swiftly followed by the full-blown invasion of 711, referred to above. The invitation in 710 seems surprising, when only a dozen years earlier the Visigoths had helped the Berbers and Byzantines thwart Muslim ambitions south of the Strait. This volte face must say a lot about the known disputes among the Visigoths themselves, allowing the Muslim general Tariq ibn Ziyad (a converted Berber slave), under the overall command of the Yemeni Musa bin Nusair, to seize a golden opportunity for further (Umayyad) glory in the name of Islam. We should note, at this stage, that the term 'Berber' never denoted any ethnic significance. Rather, it is derived from the Roman word 'barbari', which categorised most foreigners as 'barbarians' or 'outsiders' – and for some reason the description stuck to these disparate and warlike peoples.

Muslim advance in Spain, and France (711-756)

Though there are scant historic records of this period, it seems that only a very small Visigoth presence had held control over the diverse and fractious peoples of Hispania. In the aftermath of the victory at Guadalete, the Muslims made sweeping advances through most of Spain in the next few years. Only in the mountainous north-west and in the Basque region of the Pyrenees did the local tribes hang on to their independence. In about 714 the elderly Muslim commander Musa bin Nusair (born c640) must have felt confident of his territorial grip, because he made the immense journey back to Damascus with a huge contingent of surviving Visigoth leaders and Hispanic slaves – the first of many occasions when European captives would be paraded in the Islamic heartlands. As a typical act of assimilation, Musa's son married the daughter of Roderic, just before the old warrior died in 716 while on the annual pilgrimage ('hajj') to Medina or Mecca.

Back in Spain, the Muslims made their first capital Seville – though this was shortly moved to Cordoba – and with most of the conquered territory (temporarily) stable, they could not resist the lure of Aquitaine in south-west France. Making serious inroads from 718, they suffered a severe setback through a crushing defeat at Toulouse in 721. Undeterred, a new assault took place in 732, wherein the Muslim army defeated the Duke of Aquitaine on the Garonne, and charged northwards with the aim of seizing Paris. At a pivotal moment in European history, their advance was finally checked by Charles Martel's Merovingian army at the Battle of Tours (actually between Tours and Poitiers) on 10 October 732. Although the Muslims sniped away at France over the following 200 years, making serious inroads along the southern provinces for decades at a time, there was never again a serious threat of its total subjugation.

However, still today it is tantalising to see the number of Saracen towers scattered along the South of France – all the way to Italy. One of the most evocative, and accessible – and from which there is a commanding view of the Rhone valley – stands high up in 'Les Dentelles de Montmirail', above the vineyards behind the village of Gigondas.

The next 20 years saw renewed instability within Hispania, from the intermittent tribal uprisings, from the direct or indirect effects of turmoil in North Africa, which provided the only overland link between al-Andalus and the Islamic 'motherland', and from the chopping and changing of rulers that prevented any chance of governing continuity. However, all this was about to change in a remarkable manner. Who knows how influential Muslim Spain might have been for the rest of Europe, centuries later, had it not been for the man who made a seemingly miraculous transformation almost overnight – being metamorphosed from haunted 'desperado' at one end of the Mediterranean to charismatic leader of a gradually less fractious set of peoples at the other?

Abd al-Rahman I (born 731, ruled 756-788)

After the capture of Damascus in 750, the Abbasids were not quite sure if they had managed to kill the entire Umayyad family, and caliph Abu al-Abbas instructed his militia to hunt down and assassinate any remaining members. Having managed to survive the initial slaughter, 19-year-old Abd al-Rahman (grandson of caliph Hisham, 724-743) fled east with a tiny band of followers, and – so the story goes – only narrowly avoided his determined pursuers on several occasions. The most famous moment was when they had to fling themselves into the Euphrates to escape, with his brother Yahia making the fatal mistake of turning back. Following a circuitous route, the diminished group managed to cross Palestine and the Sinai desert into Egypt. Even then they were not safe in what had once been Umayyad-controlled territory, since local governors were told by the Abbasid victors that they would harbour any of the vanquished at their peril.

It is reckoned that – after a tortuous period of wandering and hiding – Abd al-Rahman eventually reached north-west Africa (the Maghreb, his mother's homeland) in 755. Since his grandfather had reigned from Damascus when al-Andalus had been first conquered, Abd al-Rahman had reason to believe that he would be welcomed across the water with open arms. After at least 20 years of instability, however, the likelihood of a hospitable welcome was further confused by infighting between Arab and Berber settlers. Abd al-Rahman took his chance in crossing the Strait, almost being captured by Berbers as he set sail from Ceuta. Landing in late 755 near Malaga, the last surviving Umayyad heir (still aged only 24) had a grim struggle to assert his authority; one window of opportunity was that many of those opposed to him were – at that precise moment – having to deal with an uprising at Zaragoza.

303

Abd al-Rahman soon faced a confrontation at the Guadalquivir River near Cordoba, with the difficulty in handling his supposed Yemeni allies proving almost as difficult as fighting his enemies. Eventually he proved victorious and, after further minor skirmishes, felt confident enough to pronounce himself emir (a lesser title than caliph), and sent out a 'call to arms' for all Umayyad loyalists to join him from wherever they had been scattered. Thousands flocked to Spain, including his son, whom he had reluctantly had to abandon beside the Euphrates some 10 years before as a four-year-old. Any thoughts that he could now settle down to improving the government of al-Andalus were soon put aside as Abd al-Rahman faced his biggest test.

In 763, the Abbasid caliph al-Mansur – now based at his new capital of Baghdad – was incensed at the news from the far west, and sent his African army to deal with the Umayyad upstart. Led by general al-Ala ibn-Mugith, this much superior force probably landed in Portugal, and laid siege to Abd al-Rahman at Carmona. After a desperate two months, Abd al-Rahman's men broke out at night and caught the attackers completely by surprise, achieving a complete victory of unremitting bloodshed.

Even though this resounding success put paid to any further assault from the Abbasids in the east, civil war flared up repeatedly, the worst instance being in 778 when Charlemagne's help was enlisted by the (then disaffected) Muslim governors of Zaragoza and Barcelona. This unlikely alliance soon fell apart, with the retiring Franks being harried all the way back to France by Basque and Gascon rebels, inspiring the epic *Chanson de Roland*. In the end Zaragoza's defensive walls were only breached in 783, and Abd al-Rahman could then be said to have brought all but the north-western quarter of the peninsula under a reasonable degree of control. In the last five years of his life Abd al-Rahman set in train several major initiatives to try and secure his legacy: civil engineering projects, including roads, aqueducts and irrigation; the recruitment of a vast *standing* army, mainly comprised of Berbers and slaves; the creation of a 'civil service'; the start (in 786) on what would become the Great Mosque of Cordoba; and the creation of a regime whereby – as in the days of Muhammad – Jews and Christians were allowed religious freedom, in return for paying a tax, which was perhaps the leading factor in encouraging a steady stream of conversions to Islam over the next two centuries.

Having led a life of extreme rigour over a period of some three decades, it is not perhaps surprising that Abd al-Rahman (allegedly) became mentally unstable – even paranoid – in the last years of his life, though he did his utmost to leave an orderly succession to his son Hisham I. The best tribute to this previously indomitable man came from his Abbasid enemy al-Mansur. First, after the defeat of al-Ala, he called Abd al-Rahman the 'Hawk of Quraysh' – the prophet being of the Quraysh tribe. Second, when posing the question to his courtiers as to who deserved the exalted title 'Falcon of the Quraysh', or 'Saqr Quraysh', he astonished them by bestowing this honour, not on himself, but on his sworn rival.

Umayyad rule in al-Andalus
(emirate to 929, and caliphate to 1031)

From the groundwork so painfully laid by Abd al-Rahman I, Umayyad dominance of al-Andalus reached its zenith during the near-century of rule by three of his direct descendents, in succession Abd al-Rahman III (912-961), Al-Hakam II (961-976) and Hisham II (976-1008).

After that, the eight caliphates up to the end of the dynasty were increasingly dysfunctional and chaotic. In the 125 years after Abd al-Rahman I's death that preceded the near-60-year rule of Abd al-Rahman III (half as emir, half as caliph), the economy of the country began to improve, as compared with the harsh conditions that still existed in the second half of the 8th century. But after this, as Menocal writes:

'...within the stability of the long reigns and orderly successions ... other kinds of revolutions occurred. There was a vast economic revival: the population increased, not just in the invigorated and ever more cosmopolitan cities, but even in the once decimated countryside, where the introduction of new crops and new techniques, including irrigation, made agriculture a prosperous concern; and the pan-Mediterranean trade and travel routes that had helped maintain Roman prosperity, and which were vital for cultural contacts and continuities, were reconfigured and expanded.'

A point to note in the 10th century is the ethnic mix of al-Andalus: Arabs, whose forbears had lived as far afield as Syria, Persia, Arabia or North Africa; long-settled Romano-Hispanics; Visigoth descendents;

Jews; Frankish Christians; Berbers; and many other minority groups. Of course, the Arabs controlled affairs and, as the conversion rate to Islam grew, so did the dominance of the Arabic language. Until 909 the al-Andalusian Umayyads showed a degree of respect to the Abbasids in Baghdad, and it was this tolerable relationship that had allowed the crucial cultural flow across North Africa to take place, mainly from east to west. It was in this century that Alvarus of Cordoba famously documented the inability of young Christian men to write anything of note in Latin, but (Menocal says) they were doing their utmost to write 'odes in classical Arabic to rival those of the Muslims'.

In 909 a Shiite movement in North Africa, in breaking away from Abbasid (Shiite) Baghdad, began to assert itself, and it was this potential threat that finally made the Umayyad (Sunni) Abd al-Rahman III declare himself caliph.

In effect, he finally felt compelled to give up any pretence of deference to the erstwhile Muslim capital of Baghdad, pronouncing the fully fledged independence of his burgeoning state. At this pivotal stage, never was established Muslim policy to prove more fruitful than as regards the 'Peoples of the Book' – the 'dhimmi'. The brilliance of this 'Ornament of the World' – so described by the famous German nun Hwroswitha – that was to shine ever brighter over the coming centuries, owed an immense amount to the policy towards the dhimmi, which *uniquely in Europe* developed to the point of a symbiotic relationship.

By the beginning of the new millennium it is calculated that the library of the caliph in Cordoba – one of 70 in the city – held (Menocal again)

'…some four hundred thousand volumes, and this at a time when the largest library in Christian Europe probably held no more than four hundred manuscripts.

The Andalusians, thanks to their regular intercourse with Baghdad, which had made translation of the Greeks a prized project, also housed the libraries of crucial traditions long lost to those in the rest of the Latin west, and unknown to them still in the tenth century.'

Before leaving the 10th century, we should try to imagine the impression given to European diplomats through their contacts with al-Andalus. If – in their own country – they were disbelieving of the stories woven by Muslim envoys, the astonishment of European court visitors to Cordoba must have been stupefying, as Fletcher describes.

First, the richness of the caliph's palace, in terms of architecture, decoration, clothing – and all around an air of military might, scholarship in a bewildering array of scientific subjects, and patronage of the arts – must have combined to produce overwhelming sensations in the eyes of the visitor.

Second, there was a staggering variety of industrial skills within the city and the surrounding region, from all kinds of armaments to 'metalwork, ceramics, glass, woodwork and leatherwork, silk and woollen textiles, paper-making, book production, ivory-carving, to name but a few'.

Third, the visitor would learn of the far-flung mining industries – not just of silver, for which Spain had long been famous, but of 'rare minerals like mercury from the cinnabar mines at Almaden, between Cordoba and Toledo, which was exported all over the Islamic world'.

Fourth, in stepping out to the countryside, the impression given by thousands of waterwheels irrigating a vast acreage that turned a near-desert into a 'Garden of Eden', must have raised the spirits of any weary traveller.

And last the produce: 'rice, hard wheat, sorghum, sugar-cane, cotton, oranges, lemons, limes, bananas, pomegranates, watermelons, spinach, artichoke and aubergine', not to mention a profusion of figs, some being exported to Baghdad.

The 'Taifa' kingdoms, the Almoravid dynasty and the Almohad caliphate (1009-1248)

It is impossible, in this book, to do justice to the incredibly complex military and political upheavals that took place over the nearly two and a half centuries that followed the relative calm of the Umayyad 10th century. The twists and turns of events are made even more difficult to grasp – and retain! – because the time-spans of these eras were not clear-cut, with each tending to overlap its predecessor by several years or longer. All we can do is summarise these three phases, throughout which one would have thought it impossible for the key seats of learning to flourish, let alone for them to play host to hundreds of scholars from the rest of Europe, with the unquenchable thirst of the visiting 'students' for the 'new' knowledge.

And yet somehow it happened. What is more, it happened against the most unpromising background, with most of this precious knowledge being 'transferred' between 1150 and 1250, a century during which the Catholic north was remorselessly prising away from the Muslims all but the south-eastern corner of Spain. What is more, this flow of scholarship continued against the backdrop of the Crusades, wherein most of Christian Europe pledged itself to rid the Holy Land of the 'infidel' Muslim.

Technically there were nine crusades to the Middle East. The first five were the most 'robust', and took place – at intervals – between 1095 and 1221. On a scale of ignominy, the fourth crusade arguably ranks as the worst, in that it never got further than Byzantium, where all hell broke loose in 1204 between the two wings of Christianity (see Chapter 23). The last four crusades were much less substantial, taking place between 1228 and 1272.

The Taifa (petty emirate) kingdoms (1009-1091)

Throughout three-quarters of the 10th century, father-and-son rule had held control of all but the north-west of Spain. Apart from their forceful characters, they had delegated authority to their most trusted lieutenants in the regions that covered this (nearly square) country measuring more than 600 miles (1,000km) from the Pyrenees to Gibraltar, and c450 miles (700km) from Valencia to Lisbon. However, the seeds of disintegration were sown in 976 when 10-year-old Hisham II was effectively reduced to puppet status through the corrupt guardianship of his father's closest advisor, Al-Mansur ibn Ami Aamir. Any sense of unity became progressively lost through factional disputes and distrust between competing officials.

From 1009, when the small region of Alpuente (near Valencia) and Badajoz (the much larger area in the west towards Lisbon) broke away, the divisions gathered pace, until there were more than 30 Taifa states at 1031, the Cordoba caliphate being the last to become reduced to this status. It is the case, however, that through the next half-century Taifa military rivalry was thankfully outdone by the intense desire to compete culturally, with emirs vying with each other to attract the most famous poets and artists, and the very best craftsmen. Nevertheless, it was their divisions that allowed Alfonso VI, King of Leon and Castile, to capture Toledo in 1085, although not all the surrounding territory simultaneously.

308

Almoravid rule (1090-1147)

This Berber dynasty flourished in present-day Morocco in the middle of the 11th century, with its leaders being the founders of Marrakesh. At its height in Africa, the empire stretched from western Algeria down to modern Senegal. As we know, there had been a very strong Iberian/Berber linkage for centuries, and in 1086 a group of Taifa emirs implored the Berber leader, Yusuf ibn Tashfin, to help them fight off Alfonso VI, so as to prevent him making further inroads. This was accomplished at the Battle of az-Zallaqah, within the Taifa of Badajoz. Yusuf then had to deal with urgent problems in Africa, but returned in 1090 with the express purpose of removing the multitude of Muslim emirs – knowing that he had popular support against the perceived or actual sufferings of the ordinary citizen. By 1094 Yusuf had deposed the emirs from every Taifa except Zaragoza, and had recovered Valencia from the Christians. He reunited Muslim power and checked any southward Christian expansion, dying as a heroic figure in 1106 at the reputed age of 100.

Yusuf's death marked the high point of Almoravid rule, as – once again – pallid successors and internal strife encouraged incursions, this time by the Christians. Although Yusuf's son Ali ibn Yusuf nominally ruled until 1143, he seemed to prefer piety to strong government, and his armies were defeated in turn by Alfonso VII of Leon, and Alfonso I of Portugal. Ali's sons were finally undermined when Marrakesh fell to the Almohads in 1147, with this loss of their original power base ushering in yet another era.

Fletcher graphically shows how – over 200 years from 1050 to 1250 – the Christian kings gained all but the south-eastern corner of Spain. By 1150, a snaking line from the Mediterranean to the Atlantic shows that they controlled the cities of Tortola, Toledo and Lisbon – and most of the natural boundary made by the River Tagus, which stretches for more than three-quarters of this distance, before meeting the sea at Lisbon.

Almohad rule (1147-1212)

The Almohad dynasty arose in Morocco under the leadership of another fervent Muslim Berber grouping. Founded by the zealous Ibn Tumart, who died in 1130, his brilliant Algerian lieutenant Abd al-Mu'min took up his cause, and ousted the Almoravids from the whole of North Africa, seizing the capital Marrakesh in 1147, the same year as he took control in al-Andalus. Abd al-Mu'min died in 1163, but so confident was the new regime that in 1170 the capital was moved to Seville – immediately followed by the foundation of the Great Mosque.

Almohad leaders, who styled themselves caliphs, varied in their attitude to Jews and Christians, an inconsistency that was influenced by their fairly frequent succession, three rulers spanning the 50 years from 1163 to 1213. At times the 'unbelievers' had to take refuge in the Christian north; they lived a precarious existence, as did the growing band of (mainly Muslim) philosophers.

After near-constant border wars with Christian kings, the third of these able rulers, Muhammad III (al Nasir), was heavily defeated in 1212 by an alliance of Castile, Aragon, Navarre and Portugal, at the Battle of Las Navas de Tolosa. With this crushing defeat, Almohad control of southern Spain crumbled. Badajoz (1230), Valencia (1238), Murcia (1243), and Faro (1249) fell, together with a host of lesser cities. Much more traumatic, and symbolically devastating, was the loss of Cordoba in 1236, and Seville in 1248. Thus, referring to Fletcher again, by 1250 the Muslim writ only ran south of the Guadalquivir River, including the cities of Ronda, Malaga, Almeria and, most crucially, Granada.

The Nasrid dynasty (1238-1492)

Following the series of Almohad setbacks, resentment in Granada boiled over in a civil revolt, with the Nasrid (Banu Nazari) dynasty emerging dominant. Starting with Muhammad I ibn Nasr, who ruled until 1272, some 20 sultans ruled the shrunken state successively, most of the time owing some form of allegiance to the increasingly dominant Christian kings. Amazingly, an uneasy sort of peace – albeit with endless border incidents – managed to exist for no fewer than 280 years, following the pivotal Battle of Las Navas de Tolosa in 1212. This remarkably long period is termed 'La Conviviencia' ('Coexistence'), during which, following a similar pattern to that of Almoravid and Almohad rule, Muslim, Jew and Christian continued to live and work side-by-side in a largely benign and hugely productive manner.

It is impossible here to provide details of the palace complex (the Alhambra) in Granada, but it remains one of the 'wonders of the world'. Largely built by the Nasrids in the 14th century, and now a

UNESCO World Heritage Site, the use of water throughout and the amazing geometric designs are testament to two of the most cherished Arab treasures, both of which were legacies of Umayyad Damascus no fewer than 800 years earlier. (Following harsh lessons that peoples of the Middle East had learned over several millennia, the comprehensive way in which Andalusia was irrigated by the Moors made it incredibly fertile. Their elaborate water management systems fell into decay from 1500 onwards, and it is no exaggeration to say that agricultural productivity in the region only returned to the levels that were achieved between 900 and 1500 when modern Spain became a beneficiary of European Union munificence some 35 years ago.)

Perhaps 'La Conviviencia' could have continued into the 16th century, but any hope of this was shattered in the aftermath of the Ottoman capture of Constantinople in 1453. Throughout the Christian world, a mood to launch a counterattack developed, with the notion of 'Reconquista' gathering momentum in Spain, further fuelled by the accessions in 1474 of Ferdinand to the throne of Aragon, and Isabella to that of Castile, the two heirs having married in 1469.

As Fletcher recounts, fortune favoured the gilded Catholic couple when the Castilians captured Boabdil (the rebellious son of Granada's ruler) in 1483, and set him up as a puppet ruler, Muhammad XII.

'This diplomatic ace secured, Fernando prosecuted the war steadily by means of devastation and siege. Ronda fell to him in 1485; Loja in 1486; Malaga in 1487; Baza in 1489; Almeria in 1490. Granada itself was besieged for eight months in 1491. Terms of capitulation were arranged in December. Castilian troops took over the Alhambra on 1 January 1492. On the following morning the Catholic Monarchs received the keys of the city from Boabdil: curiously enough, they had chosen to dress themselves in Moorish costume for the ceremony. Among those who witnessed it was Christopher Columbus, who was in attendance upon the court in his quest for royal sponsorship of his projected voyage of discovery into the Atlantic.'

Menocal also writes:

'There was no bloodshed in the city and no damage done to the precious palaces. The well-known expression "the Moor's last sigh" refers to Boabdil's own grief on leaving Granada, city of the Nasrids for nearly three centuries.'

And so, nearly 800 years after the Muslims first crossed the Strait of Gibraltar, their involvement in Spain was almost at an end. Almost, but not quite, since while all Jews were immediately exiled, the defeated Moors were (by treaty) allowed to move into the nearby Alpujarras hills – hence the unique architecture of the white-painted houses we can still see today.

But this apparent leniency did not last for long, as within only a few years all Moors had been compelled to convert to Christianity, or leave the country. However, nothing that the Christian conquerors could do – including subsequent book-burning rituals – could destroy the remarkable legacy that had already been bequeathed to the rest of Europe, as we shall examine in Chapter 22, starting with the preservation of two priceless Greek inventions, and leading on to the most notable scholars of the centuries-long Muslim era.

Chapter 21

Europe in the High Middle Ages, 1066-c1400

The crucial role of the Normans

Chapter 17 finished just at the point where William was about to invade Britain, but – however symbolic to English history – that date signifies the decade during which Norman influence came to be stamped on many areas of Europe, in particular southern Italy, including Sicily. The marauding instinct of the Vikings ran deep through Norman veins, but after 150 years of Frankish influence they became good administrators and – most of all – supreme *builders* throughout their conquered lands.

It may be that William had a good excuse (picked over by a thousand historians) for invading England in 1066, but judged by Norman exploits elsewhere it was inevitable that this invasion would happen sooner or later. Apart from the actual defeat of Harold, William moved swiftly to subdue the rest of England, putting his loyal nobles in control, building magnificent stone castles at every strategic point, promoting the French language above the native tongue, causing the unique Domesday Book to be compiled (in Latin) in 1086, and – from the first decade of 'occupation' – initiating a church-building programme so ambitious and masterful that, nearly a millennium later, these wonderful places of worship are one of the defining aspects of English culture.

Amazing as this list of achievements is, we now turn to the Norman presence in Italy and the surrounding islands, because – nearly 70 years before William's momentous exploits close to his homeland – his intrepid kinsmen were making an impact hundreds of miles away. History records that in 999 a group of Norman knights returning from a pilgrimage to the Holy Sepulchre in Jerusalem put into Salerno. Witnessing feeble defence against a Saracen attack, the visitors rallied their fellow-Christian hosts, and caused the normally resolute Muslim raiding party to flee. Summarising a story of piecemeal successes, in the next 150 years the Normans ultimately secured the whole of Italy south of the Papal States. In Sicily they captured Messina in 1061, and Palermo in 1071. Eventually they captured the whole island – no mean achievement – which became the Kingdom of Sicily under Roger II, who was crowned in Palermo on Christmas Day 1130. It survived as a separate entity right through to the unification of Italy in 1861.

By c1150 the Normans had also left their mark on Corsica, Sardinia, Malta and the North African coast. But it is in Sicily itself that their most enduring legacy lies, the greatest symbol of which is arguably the quite stunning Cathedral of Monreale, which lies to the south of Palermo. This jewel of Norman aesthetic architecture, commissioned in 1174 by King William II, is one of the finest examples of their work anywhere. Although little of the adjacent palace or monastery still stands in its original form, the Norman cloister – built around 1200 – is also outstanding both for its size and beauty. Sicily, previously governed by successive caliphs from Cordoba, had been wrested from Arab control, and one can clearly see the influence of Muslim craftsmen when intriguing comparison is made with churches that can still be seen today in Syria.

The above point indicates the respect that the Normans had for Muslim achievements, and their own tendency to 'go native'. Maria Rosa Menocal, in *Ornament of the World*, tells the story of the capture of the small town of Barbastro in the southern foothills of the Pyrenees by a mix of Normans and Aquitainians in 1064. She recounts how here, in a perhaps apocryphal tale, the conquerors adopted the culture of the conquered, as happened often elsewhere in the Mediterranean. A Jewish friend of an ousted Muslim was asked to try and rescue his daughter from her captors. The Jew reported back that the Christian (Norman), who had taken up residence in the Muslim's house, was found seated on the floor in Arabic garb, having apparently taken the Muslim girl as his wife, in rapt attention as other Muslim girls sang traditional folk songs! Why such a contrast with the ruthless 'Frankification' of England? Because there was so much of the Muslim world to learn from and respect, which was simply *not the case* with comparatively backward England.

One Islamic writer, Said al-Andalusi, described in 1068 a list of eight nations that had contributed most to knowledge, but, in underestimating the absorptive powers of the Normans, wrote that 'northern Europeans have not cultivated the sciences ... they lack keenness of understanding and clarity of intelligence.'

Menocal records that – almost 200 years later – the Arabised half-Norman/half-German King Frederick II of Sicily (1194-1250) was so steeped in learning that he was known as 'Stupor Mundi', or 'Wonder of the World'. This remarkable man spoke Arabic among many languages, built the spectacular Caste del Monte in Apulia, and was involved in the Crusades. But this did not stop him having such a thirst for knowledge, including science and the arts, that at court he employed Jewish translators of priceless Arabic texts.

Notable individuals of the 12th-14th centuries

Since European history in this period – from a military and kingship point of view – has been exhaustively examined, we will concentrate on a handful of the most notable individuals, each of whom made a unique contribution to the advance of scholarship in a wide variety of fields. A particular feature in almost every country was the foundation of universities, although, in many cases, the date of transition from a church or monastic school is difficult to pinpoint, and does not take into account the Madrasahs in Islamic Spain or Sicily. As far as can be ascertained, assumed dates for the founding of 'western' universities are as follows:

In Italy: Bologna (1088), Modena (1175), Padua (1222)
In France: Paris (recognised in 1150), Montpellier (1220), Toulouse (1229), Orleans (1235)
In England: Oxford (teaching from 1096, recognised in 1167), Cambridge (1209)
In Catholic (northern) Spain: Palencia (1208), Salamanca (1218)
In Portugal: Coimbra (1288)
In 'greater' Germany: Charles University in Prague (1347)

Following the handful of remarkable men profiled towards the end of Chapter 17, it is highly significant that, among *this* schedule of outstanding scholars and writers, the earliest date at which any individual began to make an impact was soon after 1100, with first Peter Abelard, then his arch-rival Bernard of Clairvaux. There is then a lapse of perhaps a century before Wolfram von Eschenbach wrote *Parzival*, in around 1200. All this goes to show just how slow Western Europe was to gain intellectual momentum, at a time when – as we shall see in the next chapter – the huge accumulation of classical knowledge, powerfully augmented through centuries of learning in the Middle East, was just waiting to be 'exported' from the vibrant Muslim cities of al-Andalus.

Peter Abelard (1079-1142) – forever linked to Heloise (c1098-1164)

Born near Nantes in southern Brittany, Abelard was a child prodigy who – forsaking his comfortable family life – started travelling in his teens in search of knowledge. Still not much more than a boy when he reached Paris, Abelard quickly overcame in debate his teachers in philosophy, then in theology. He became a charismatic teacher himself, and by 1115 (aged 35) had secured the chair of the famous Cathedral School of Notre Dame. So famous did he become, with his exceptionally keen thinking and bold theology, that hundreds of students at a time clamoured to attend his lectures.

Fatefully, at this time Abelard lodged with Canon Fulbert, whose ward was his 17-year-old niece Heloise – herself a brilliant student, and well-versed (unusually) in Greek and Hebrew. Quite at odds with his highly disciplined lifestyle hitherto, Abelard indulged in an affair with Heloise, and they were secretly married, resulting in a son (named Astrolabe, see Chapter 22). It can be no surprise to know that jealousy, intrigue and misunderstanding then had a catastrophic effect on both their lives. Heloise was packed off to become a nun most reluctantly, while an outraged Fulbert had Abelard waylaid by hired gangsters and castrated.

But despite the misery of their subsequent lives – and most fortunately for us today – far from forgetting each other Abelard and Heloise later managed to have published a collection of their love letters, described by Van Doren as 'one of the most beautiful and revealing medieval books'. Also, in an age where religious and philosophical argument raged constantly, Abelard produced his most famous work, *Sic et Non* (*Yes and No*). Here he sets out a series of contradictions, in each case commentating on how a resolution could be reached. He also wrote *Scito te ipsum* (*Know Thyself*), where he stated that sin was not so much in the deed as in the intention.

Abelard lived a miserable last 25 years, moving from one refuge to the next, only interspersed by clusters of students who caught up with him from time to time. On learning of his death, Heloise took care of his remains, and 22 years later she ensured that she was buried beside him, though controversy still rages as to where they now lie. Abelard was the greatest thinker of his day, in the mould of Aristotle and Boethius, all three convinced that reason and logic must be allowed to shape religious attitudes. In this he could not have been further from his adversarial contemporary.

Bernard of Clairvaux (1090-1153)

Bernard was the complete antithesis of Abelard. Born into a wealthy family in Burgundy, he joined a Cistercian (Trappist) monastery as a young man, and founded a new abbey at the age of 25 in an isolated valley south-east of Bar sur L'Aube. He called this Claire Vallee, hence 'Clairvaux'. Although Bernard had what would later become 'Protestant' tendencies, he rejected the philosophy of 'humanism' and any notion of theology being understood through 'reason'. So prominent did he become that when Pope Honorius II died in 1130, at the council convened by Louis VI (of France) it was to Bernard that the bishops turned to choose the next Pope.

Bernard, whose way with words earned him the soubriquet of 'doctor mellifluous', became the confidant of no fewer than five Popes, wrote copiously (though none of his works had the startling effect of Abelard's manuscripts), and became the scourge of this hard-pressed rival for hearts and minds, who had earlier been brought so low. Bernard wrote of Abelard, in the course of their unequal tussle: 'This man presumes to be able to comprehend by human reason the entirety of God.' As Van Doren puts it:

'Thus it was Bernard who got the Pope to silence Abelard, to reduce him to a meagre life in the monastery at Cluny, and who probably broke his heart. Bernard was one of the greatest Augustinians, and the supporters of Aristotle still had a long and weary road to travel.'

Devout as he was, even Bernard had his comeuppance. With papal support he proselytised the merits of the Second Crusade with great intensity, but its failure saddled him with an overwhelming responsibility. In his apologia, Bernard blamed the fiasco on the sinfulness of the crusaders themselves, a dubious line of argument only made worse when his call for a third crusade fell on deaf ears.

Wolfram von Eschenbach (c1170-c1220)

There were, of course, notable thinkers and writers in the second half of the 12th and early part of the 13th centuries, but from this era only Wolfram left an indelible mark, entirely through his works, since there is no record of his life. One subject that gave rise to a specific genre was the mysterious Holy Grail, said to be the drinking vessel used by Christ at the Last Supper. The legend may have had Celtic origins, and it certainly became a part of Arthurian folklore. First appearing in literature at the end of the 12th century, the story emerged in an incomplete poem by Chretien de Troyes, entitled *Perceval, le Conte du Graal*. Wolfram's epic poem *Parzival* was based on this work, and became immensely popular in the following centuries, as testified by there being no fewer than 84 surviving manuscripts.

Several translations of *Parzival* have been published in modern times, the most famous interpretation having been undertaken by Richard Wagner in his opera *Parsival*.

Daniel of Beccles (dates uncertain)

It is probable that this earthy individual lived and wrote early in the 13th century, since a Daniel of Beccles was thought to have occupied a position in Henry II's English court for as long as 30 years. He features here, not so much for any brilliance in his prose, but as an indication that familiarity with writing was beginning to be a factor outside the domain of the Church.

Daniel's *Book of the Civilised Man* comprises 3,000 lines of Latin verse. It is the first known English 'courtesy book', on which subject hundreds of tomes were written in the following centuries. That the writer felt the need for such a guide to 'etiquette' (for which French term we still struggle to find a precise English equivalent) shows how far behind the rough-and-ready natives were in terms of correct behaviour at the comparatively sophisticated Francophile court – 150 years after William's lightning conquest of the island.

Essentially, three themes are covered: social hierarchy, self-control and sexual morality. Today's comedians still delight in quoting certain lines such as 'don't mount your horse in the hall', which should not undermine the serious message of 800 years ago. The book ends with the statement, 'Old King Henry first gave to the uncourtly the teaching written in this book.'

Roger Bacon (c1220-1292)

Bacon features in our story specifically because he was the earliest European (non-Muslim) scientist of his day. Modern research has shown that he was not alone in his field, and that the degree to which he was persecuted resulted more from his provocative and outspoken behaviour than from religious hostility to his experiments. Little is known of his early years, except that he was born in Somerset into a well-off family, and studied at Oxford. Some time around 1240 he started teaching in Paris, then the centre of European intellectual life. Bacon was an avid student of Aristotle and Plato, with a particular fascination for their scientific theories. He also caused hostility by expressing his outrage that Parisian students revered Albertus Magnus as an equal of these classical giants, as well as the equal of Avicenna and Averroes.

In his *Opus Majus*, Bacon wrote on a huge range of subjects, propounding his view that there was no substitute for detailed experimentation and analysis. He covered the field of mathematics as well as alchemy, including the manufacture of gunpowder. Most notably, he showed his fascination for optics, forecasting the later inventions of the telescope and the microscope. He dealt in extraordinary detail on this field, drawing heavily on the research of earlier Muslim scholars in such areas as the anatomy of the eye, light, distance, vision, refraction, lenses and mirrors – while also acknowledging his debt to an earlier Englishman fascinated by the same subject, Robert Grosseteste, scholastic philosopher and Bishop of Lincoln.

In about 1256 Bacon became a friar in the Franciscan Order, whose code was supposed to have restricted his ability to publish written works. He provoked further controversy by urging a return to original religious texts, and less reliance on the interpretations of his day. So unpopular did he become in Paris that he was placed in solitary confinement by his superiors in 1267, probably being restricted for a full decade.

319

Thomas Aquinas (1225-1274)

Thomas became the dominant figure of the second half of the 13th century within the huge sweep of Christian Europe that still remained an intellectual desert compared with Byzantium, Baghdad, the cities of al-Andalus and Norman Sicily. Thomas had a privileged start in life. He was born in Aquino, probably in the wonderful Norman castle mentioned earlier in this chapter; he was indeed related to the Hohenstaufen dynasty of Frederick II ('Stupor Mundi'), who ruled the Kingdom of Sicily for the first 25 years of Thomas's life; and his education started, at the age of 5, at Monte Cassino, before he was moved to the budding university at Naples.

It was at Naples that Thomas was introduced to the work of Aristotle, and to Averroes and Maimonides (see Chapter 22), all of whom would have a deep influence in his formative years. At this time Thomas became well-versed in mathematics, geometry, astronomy and music – but most of all, by his late teens, in the branch of the Church that had been approved by Pope Honorius III in 1216, the Order of Preachers, more commonly known as the Dominican Order. Aged 19, he left for Rome to pursue this calling – instead of becoming a Benedictine monk – but was famously kidnapped by his brothers en route, and was imprisoned for two years in the Norman-built castle Monte San Giovanni Campano. Eventually escaping (in which his mother was complicit), Thomas finally reached Paris University via Naples and Rome, where he enrolled under Albertus Magnus, taking a full seven years to obtain his degree in theology, and finally obtaining his licence to teach at the age of 30. Then, after this slow start, Thomas became embroiled in the heat of endless (deeply complex) debates concerning philosophy and theology. He published innumerable works, and here we can only try to summarise the key issues.

First, there was the 'doctrine of universals', with a divide between Realists and Nominalists, with Aristotle being placed as a 'Modified Realist'. As Van Doren writes, with his brilliant mind Thomas wrestled with such puzzles as: 'Had God really not meant for man to think? Had he meant for man to pass through the Earthly City with blinkers, and with his eyes on another existence in the future?'

Second, there was the question of nature itself – the natural world. In effect, Thomas strove to reconcile the 'City of Man' with the 'City of God', showing himself to be the greatest force for peace in his lifetime between these seemingly irreconcilable issues. In this he so antagonised the Church hierarchy that at the end of his life he was summoned to a council in Lyons, and bitterly criticised. Unlike Abelard more than 150 years earlier, however, his reputation as a true Catholic Christian acted as a shield, and he escaped draconian censure.

Known also within the Catholic faith as the 'Angelic' or 'Universal' Doctor, Thomas was a master theologian, whose works pronounced on such aspects as Revelation, Creation and Ethics. As he moved around Catholic Europe his brilliant mind was being constantly challenged by highly placed priests of a more conventional persuasion. In his lifetime, and – even though he was declared a saint 50 years after his death – for centuries afterward, his reputation ebbed and flowed. Only finally in 1879 did Pope Leo XIII issue an encyclical that stated that Thomas's theology was a *definitive* exposition of Catholic doctrine.

Of course, unlike the unsurpassed thinkers of Classical Greece, whose lives were lived in awe of the pantheon of pagan gods, Thomas's mind was cloaked in Christianity. That said, as the Middle Ages drew closer to a full-blown Renaissance, many of the issues that so exercised his every waking hour (as with Abelard before him) – and which had lain so dormant – were exactly the same as those that had been so exhaustively fought over in Athens no fewer than 1,500 to 1,800 years previously!

'The Pyrrhic victory of Faith over Reason' is a description given by Van Doren to the period that immediately followed the lifetime of Thomas Aquinas, wherein conventional (and militant) Church doctrine suppressed would-be humanist philosophy. In the end we know that Reason triumphed, but the practical effect was that the 13th century ended with a whimper in terms of any follow-up to Thomas's questioning views.

It took one man in particular to blow life into the torch embers of medieval literature, very soon after the turn of the 14th century.

Dante Alighieri (c1265-1321)
Born in Florence, not very much is known about Dante's early life and education. What we do know is that he grew up within the ceaseless turmoil among the numerous petty states of northern Italy – between the Guelphs (supporters of the Papacy) and the Ghibellines (supporters of the Holy Roman Emperor). Even more depressing – after the Guelphs had defeated the Ghibellines – was the split (when Dante was about 30, in c1295) into the White Guelph, which Dante

supported, and the Black Guelph factions. Initially the White Guelphs dominated, but in 1301 – while Dante was on a political delegation to Pope Boniface VIII in Rome – Charles de Valois (brother of Philip the Fair, King of France) led a savage assault on Florence by the Black Guelphs. Dante stayed in Rome, courtesy of the Pope, and became permanently exiled from Florence, never returning in the remaining 20 years of his life, and eventually dying in Ravenna.

Going back to Dante's youth, it is known that he studied Tuscan poetry, much influenced by the 'Sicilian School'. He was also interested in the troubadours of the Occitan (southern France and Catalonia) as well as classical Latin poetry, Virgil in particular. Critical to his greatest work was his unrequited love for a young lady he only met in the streets of Florence when very young – Beatrice Portinari. It was in 1300, a year of special Christian celebration, that Dante conceived the notion of his *Commedia* (*Comedy*) – all works that were not written in Latin *and* were not about religion were deemed to be 'comedies'. Furthermore, Dante's stupendous work did not attract the term *Divina* (*Divine*) until Boccaccio (see Chapter 23) so named it later in the 14th century.

One remarkable feature of the *Divine Comedy* is that it was written in a mixture of the Tuscan dialect, other regional influences, and only certain elements of Latin – deliberately so as to be available to a much wider audience than would be the norm at the end of the 14th century. In pursuing this path, Dante secured his place as the 'father' of the Italian language. The other aspect that made the *Divine Comedy* arguably the greatest work of Italian literature was the breathtaking sweep of his mystical journey: first most vividly through *Hell* (*Inferno*); then through *Purgatory* (*Purgatorio*), guided by Virgil and other poets in a lyrical and human manner; then finally *Paradise* (*Paradiso*), led by Beatrice, admitting that he is barely able to express himself when face to face with God – '…at this high moment, ability failed my capacity to describe.'

Having been sentenced to death in absentia, when many years later Dante had the chance to return to Florence, his uncompromising stance at his treatment ensured that he never returned. Moving to Ravenna in 1318, he travelled to Venice in 1321 on a diplomatic mission, and possibly contracted malaria from the notorious marshland. He died in September of that year and was buried in Ravenna at the church now called San Francesco.

At the start of this chapter, we highlighted the difficulty in adhering to the lives of those key 'Europeans' whose development was mainly 'native'. Although greatly influenced by earlier Muslim scientists in the field of optics, Roger Bacon belongs in this chapter because, in so many other areas of his life's work, the major influences were English or French. The scene in Italy in the 14th century was much more complicated, because of the growing influence from Constantinople. Two Italians feature in Chapter 23, because their adopted Byzantine 'heritage' is considered to outweigh the contribution of their country of birth – Barlaam (1290-1348), who lived for a full decade in Constantinople, and Boccaccio (1313-1375), who was in effect a key disciple of Barlaam.

Petrarch (Francesco Petrarca, 1304-1374)

An almost exact contemporary of Boccaccio, Petrarch was born in Arezzo, though he later encouraged the idea that he was a Florentine – a city of growing sophistication. His father was involved with the papacy that took refuge in Avignon from 1309 to 1377, where the family lived for many years, as well as at nearby Carpentras. Petrarch studied in various cities, but before he was 20 he had a position at the papal court. Being a dedicated student of Latin, he soon took educated Europe by storm with his first major work, *Africa*, the epic story of the great Roman general Publius Cornelius Scipio (Africanus). So famous did this make the emerging polymath that he became 'crowned' the first poet laureate since antiquity in Rome's Capitol on 8 April 1341.

This man of many parts (unusually) travelled for pleasure, in the course of which he climbed Mont Ventoux in April 1336, the sole mountain in the Vaucluse, at more than 6,250 feet (1,900m) towering above the Rhone valley and the surrounding hills, in one of the most beautiful regions of France. Only the incredible views from the summit, and the mountain's constant presence when one is anywhere within its phenomenal range of vision, can convey the hold it has over the visitor. Petrarch took with him St Augustine's *Confessions*, and was deeply moved when the page fell open at the following words:

> 'And men go about to wonder at the heights of the mountains, and the mighty waves of the sea, and the wide sweep of rivers, and the circuit of the ocean, and the revolution of the stars, but themselves they consider not.'

With echoes of Dante, Petrarch records that his life was marked above all by his meeting in 1327 (aged 22) of a lady called Laura, in a church in Avignon. There are those who have written that he was merely copying Dante, but – whatever the truth – some of Petrarch's most beautiful poetry is derived from the inspiration that Laura (who apparently died in 1348) gave him. Initially he was bound up with praising her beauty, only later seeking to praise her spirit above her physical attributes. Laura was but one manifestation of Petrarch's amazing literary output, sometimes in Latin and otherwise in the developing Italian language, which ranged from theology in *Secretum* (*My Secret Book*) to a self-help book that remained popular for centuries, *De Remediis Utriusque Fortunae* (*Remedies for Fortune Fair and Foul*) and a travel guide, *Itinerarium* (*Petrarch's Guide to the Holy Land*).

But our greatest legacy from this 'Father of Humanism' is derived from his collaboration with Boccaccio in the last 25 years of his life. They had long admired each other, and in Chapter 23 we refer briefly to the latter's mostly unsuccessful attempts to teach Petrarch Greek so that he could access the Classical works that were then being transferred from Constantinople. That setback aside, these giants of learning – who together ushered in many elements that constituted the Renaissance – joined forces to scour southern Europe in a relentless search for lost manuscripts of Classical Rome. In particular they discovered a cache of lost works of Cicero in 1345, which fired Petrarch into writing 'letters' for the remainder of his life to Virgil and Seneca, as well as to Cicero.

Petrarch never married but sired two children, and spent his last years with his daughter Francesca and her family in the small town of Arqua, near Padua. The house where this revered man died (the day before his 70th birthday) still stands. He left Boccaccio, who was to die a year later, 50 florins, but his library of manuscripts – originally earmarked for Venice – was seized by its enemy Padua. It seems that Petrarch's works became widely scattered, but a core found their way into the hands of Cardinal Bessarion (see Chapter 23), whose wider collection (of mainly Greek texts) formed the nucleus of the Biblioteca Marciana in Venice.

It is clear to see that – however fractured Italy was physically – the combination of its men of genius in the 14th century, with the huge impetus they alone derived from being the prime refuge for brilliant scholars escaping from collapsing Byzantium, enabled its vibrant competing cities to be at the forefront of the drive to the cusp of the Renaissance. Germany and – to a lesser extent – Paris lagged behind, as did England, but in these regions furthest away geographically from Italy a number of notable writers emerged in just the same era as their illustrious Byzantine counterparts.

Four other notable writers

'Sir John Mandeville'

Probably a pseudonym (details of his life are unknown), this is an excellent demonstration of the growing thirst for knowledge. His book of extraordinary travels – written in Anglo-Norman French – was immensely popular throughout much of Europe, causing it to be translated into many languages. It is a fantastical travelogue, which held late-medieval readers spellbound by a 'hero' who travelled everywhere in Europe as well as the entire Mediterranean and the Middle East, and who saw everything, met everyone, and held every kind of exalted position! Painstaking research has shown that the volume (written between 1357 and 1371) was at least in part compiled by a Liege physician named Jehan a la Barbe – certainly the book contains a remarkable insight into his chosen profession, as well as philosophy, astrology and naturalism.

Anonymous: *Sir Gawain and the Green Knight*

This epic poem covers one of the long-known stories within the Arthurian legend. Experts have placed the written English as reflecting a Midlands dialect, but that is all that is known about the author to date. The poem survives in a single manuscript, which includes three religious pieces. The language is rich, and the plot complicated, but what attracts literary critics is the heavy use of medieval symbolism, which effectively draws on all the ethnic origins that had come together by that era to make up the Welsh and English national composition.

William Langland's *Piers Ploughman*, c1360-1387

This example of 'Middle English' writing is considered to hold its place alongside *The Canterbury Tales* (see below) as one of the finest examples of early English literature. The poem covers the story-teller's search for a pure Christian life. It starts in the Malvern Hills, where a man named Will has a vision while asleep, and goes on to examine the lives of three characters – Do-well, Do-better, and Do-best – through a series of dreams.

Julian of Norwich (1342-1416)

Uniquely (for the age) this writer was *female*, a semi-hermit lady attached to a church in Norwich. Aged 30 she nearly died, and during her severe illness had a series of powerful visions of Jesus Christ. Recovering in May 1373, she immediately set down her 'Short Text' of these visions, but another 20 years passed before her 'Long Text' explained in detail their full significance to her – this being written in English and published as 'Sixteen Revelations of Divine Love' in 1393. Written during the Black Death (see below), one reason for Julian's fame was her unquenchable optimism, and the belief that God wanted to save everyone. This was in marked contrast to the popular (and deeply depressing) notion that the Plague was simply God's retribution for all Man's wickedness.

Geoffrey Chaucer (c1343-1400)

A detailed examination of Chaucer's life would capture perfectly not only his amazing experiences and his versatility, but also – harking back to the beginning of this book and the central theory of Fernand Braudel about what took place thousands of years earlier – the dramatic effect that the flow of commercial trade, diplomatic exchange, and knowledge were all having throughout late-13th-century Europe.

Though not very much is known of Chaucer's early life, we do know that his family were quite well-to-do London vintners, with good connections. We first learn of him as a 14-year-old page to Elizabeth de Burgh, Countess of Ulster, and thereafter his life and career are detailed in hundreds of extant documents. Chaucer compares favourably with Petrarch, in that – before even considering his poetry – he stands high among his contemporaries as courtier, bureaucrat, diplomat, traveller, philosopher, and – most notably – translator. In his *Troilus and Chrysede*, his main sources were Boccaccio (Chapter 23) and Boethius (Chapter 17), but he also translated the latter's seminal work *Consolation of Philosophy*. Chaucer was also fascinated by science, and wrote *Treatise on the Astrolabe* (see Chapter 22), describing that instrument in great detail. Also, only discovered in 1952, is *Equatorie of the Planetis*, which may eventually be proved as Chaucer's, since it seems to continue the ideas of the Astrolabe and is written in very similar language and handwriting.

Turning to the area for which he is most famous, Chaucer was extremely prolific, finding time – from c1375 onwards – to write copiously of his life and times. Credibly described as the father of English literature, he firmly focussed his (mainly lay) successors on the virtues of the English language, as then developed, as opposed to Latin or French. Chaucer's most famous work, *The Canterbury Tales*, was probably started in the 1380s, while he worked as Comptroller of Customs for the Port of London, during which phase he went to live in Kent, becoming Member of Parliament for the county in 1386. What made *The Canterbury Tales* mark a watershed in English literature was the realism in the script, the sheer variety of the stories, and the vibrant personalities of the pilgrims on their way to Canterbury, most of whom were taken from real contemporary life. We do not have the space here to detail the widely differing experiences that Chaucer crammed into (at most) 40 years of active adulthood, but doubtless it was this richness that gave such colour to his chosen subjects.

The Black Death

It is extraordinary to realise that the blossoming of literature in mid-14th-century Europe occurred at *exactly* the moment of a terrible crisis, caused not through yet more military confrontation but by the worst collapse in human health in recorded history. The Plague of Justinian, which devastated the Eastern Roman Empire in 541-542AD, had not been repeated anywhere in the West during the next 800 years. However, the Medieval Warm Period, which ended around 1250, immediately gave way to the Little Ice Age. Agricultural output in most of Western Europe collapsed, giving rise to sharply escalating food prices – disastrously compounded by both Edward III of England and Philip VI of France promoting a policy of higher rents on tenants, so as to protect the living standards of the ruling classes.

Widespread starvation ensued, bringing severe health problems – and increased death rates – among the wider population, who were already ravaged by a series of bitter winters. Then, almost from nowhere, the bubonic plague struck. Only as recently as 2010 have medical geneticists finally proved that the plague originated in China, to be carried along the silk route by rodent-borne fleas. The (almost always fatal) disease erupted in the Crimea in 1346 and, probably brought to Italy by fleeing Genoese traders, proceeded to devastate a panic-stricken Europe during the next five years before dramatically subsiding in 1351.

Modern assessment is that almost half the population of Europe was wiped out during this five-year period, though widely varying from as much as 80% in some major cities to 'only' 20% in others – with chronicles from this dreadful era consistently referring to the endless heaps of unburied dead. It is calculated that the overall population did not recover for at least 150 years, until after 1600.

But – as the worst stories of ghost towns, untended livestock, and overgrown fields emerged – a most remarkable series of interlocking factors came into play. Landlords (who had been affected least) had to pay sharply higher wages to the decimated peasantry to enable agricultural production to recover; sky-high grain prices then started to fall, lowering the cost of living; those able-bodied peasants who had survived were suddenly quite well off, precipitating the rise of a (previously non-existent) middle class; the iron grip of the Catholic Church, which had shown itself to be powerless to ameliorate the worst effects of the Plague, became severely weakened; as Boccaccio wrote in *The Decameron* (1353), with life so uncertain, people should 'live for the moment'; and, *most vital of all*, nowhere had suffered more than in the key northern Italian cities (among which Florence's population had declined from c120,000 to c50,000). It was these factors – together with those of the next two chapters – that combined, as the 14th century drew to a close, to initiate an explosion of scientific and artistic invention.

Juan Ruiz (c1283-1350)

It is perhaps appropriate to end this chapter with a brief description of an individual whose life was so closely bound up with the subject matter of the one that follows. Juan Ruiz was born close to Jaen, a town in Muslim al-Andalus, though little is known of his life other than he seems to have studied in Toledo, and become a priest. It would appear that he was imprisoned for the last 13 years of his life, but we do not know for what crimes. There is even speculation that – because his name was so common at that time – it might have been assumed, so as to represent a group of writers.

What we do know is that the massive poem of 1,728 stanzas – *Libro de Buen Amor* (*The Book of Good Love*) – with its content of religion, story-telling, unrequited love and autobiographical details, has caused the writer(s) of this fabulous work to be referred to as the 'Spanish Chaucer'. The whole book is written in exuberant style, and captures exquisitely the exchange of knowledge and literature that was giving such cross-border impetus at this time: colloquial Arabic; Asturian (northern Spanish) elements through the writings of the powerful 12th-century figure of Pedro Alfonso; classical Latin writers such as Cato and Ovid; and French literature through Tristan and Isolde.

Although three manuscripts of *Libro de Buen Amor* survive, it seems that its author was largely forgotten until an edited version was published at the end of the 18th century, but over the past 200 years Juan Ruiz has slowly become recognised as providing one of the crucial links between the various burgeoning High Middle Age cultures, which were soon to give way to the Renaissance.

Chapter 22

What al-Andalus taught Europe – Arabic into Latin

The Astrolabe

While we will shortly examine the Moorish teachers, and their enthusiastic foreign students, it is this 'machine' that so epitomises the way in which an item of Greek origin was taken up and developed in the Middle East, and, through then becoming ubiquitous in al-Andalus, held writers and budding scientists spellbound throughout the rest of Europe. Why otherwise would Abelard and Heloise have so named their only child? And why otherwise would Chaucer have written a treatise devoted solely to this subject? It was this device – in its many forms – that presaged clock-making, and which enabled maritime exploration to take off.

Initial development took place in Greece c150BC, whereby – in disc form – the early astrolabe acted as an analogue calculator for the purpose of astronomical positioning. It is widely believed to have been the invention of Hipparchus – the greatest astronomer of his day – whose research was rooted in Babylonian mathematical achievements many centuries previously. Theon of Alexandria wrote on the subject in the late 4th century AD, as did the Christian philosopher John Philiponus around 550. There were writings in Syriac on the subject in the 7th century, which indicates that the astrolabe was known in the Christian east before it was adopted by the Islamic world.

From the 10th century onwards Muslim scholars made almost continuous improvements to extend the machine's versatility, including its use as a navigational aid to reaching Mecca. The earliest surviving astrolabe is dated 315 in the Islamic calendar – 927/928AD. In the same era the famous Persian astronomer, al-Sufi, described it as having more than 1,000 uses in other fields such as astrology, horoscopes, surveying and time-keeping. It was around this period that Islamic scientists perfected a spherical astrolabe, which was combined with an armillary sphere, a long-established means of depicting the celestial world.

The mariner's (or sea) astrolabe was first documented in 1295 by Ramon Llull, a Majorcan philosopher/scholar. These were made of brass, which has enabled a growing number to be discovered in recent times by marine archaeologists investigating shipwrecks – 35 examples up to 1980, and more than double that number recovered by 2010. Though this device could not predict longitude, its reasonable accuracy as regards latitude was the key factor in enabling both Columbus to reach America, and Marco Polo to circumnavigate Africa.

The astrolabe was very influential in early astronomical clock-making, witness the very advanced mechanism manufactured by Richard of Wallingford in c1330. The Prague astronomical clock, dating from 1410, was also designed along an astrolabe-type display.

The Almagest (al-Majitsi)

This was another – originally Greek – phenomenon that enthralled Western European scholars in the High Middle Ages, partly because it provided the only insight into the mathematical genius of Hipparchus, all of whose original manuscripts were lost. This astronomical treatise proposed that the sun and planets revolve around the earth, which remained the accepted wisdom throughout the Islamic ascendancy, and into the early Renaissance. It is now almost proven that this masterpiece – of 13 sections, covering 152 pages – was published by Ptolemy of Alexandria in or just after 150AD.

As an indication of the passage through time and cultures undergone by *The Almagest*, we will briefly reflect on the sequence of titles given to this brilliantly constructed set of theories. The modern spelling of the originally written Greek is *Mathematike Syntaxis* (*Mathematical Treatise*); in turn this was *originally* translated into Latin as *Syntaxis mathematica*; in Arabic it became known as *al-kitabu-l-mijitsi*, for which the Latin (in c1350AD, some 1,200 years after its origin) was *Almagest*, or in English *Great Compilation*.

331

Turning to the great men of letters in al-Andalus, we already know from Chapter 20 that 'seepage' of knowledge – from southern Spain to the rest of Europe, and occasionally vice versa – had been taking place since the middle of the 10th century. A wonderful example of this exchange (from Richard Fletcher) involved a copy of the works of the 1st-century botanist Dioscorides that was brought to Cordoba in 949 by Byzantine emissaries. At this early date, no court scholar could be found who could translate the priceless Greek texts of the legendary scientist. Only the combined efforts of a monk drafted from Constantinople and a Greek-speaking Arab from Sicily could expound the texts to an intellectual group, led by the caliph's personal physician.

Outstanding Muslim scholars and visitors

The pace of travel accelerated at the onset of the 2nd millennium, mostly into Muslim-held territory, but in this chapter we can only handle the most outstanding Muslim scholars, and a handful of the intrepid visitors, always bearing in mind that the two-way exchanges reached a vital crescendo (for the future of European culture) between 1150 and 1250. We will start with one of the rare instances of a visitor from al-Andalus northwards.

Petrus Alphonsi (first half of the 12th century)

Originally Moses Sephardi ('Moses the Spaniard'), we do not know when Petrus was born, but we do know it was somewhere in al-Andalus and that he was baptised on 29 June 1106 at Huesca, in north-eastern Spain. While not considered to rank with the greatest intellectuals of his day, his place in history is secured in three particular ways. First, as a very young man he somehow made his way to England, where he lived for several years. It would appear that he served as one of the court physicians to Henry I, and also that he lived in the west for some time, because he discussed astronomy with Walcher of Malvern, who himself came from Lorraine. Second, Petrus wrote a stinging polemic against the Jews, *Dialogi contra Iudaeos*, in particular as to their role in Christ's death. Last, in complete contrast, he wrote – in Latin – *Disclipina Clericalis* (*A Training School for the Clergy*). This seemingly draconian title belies the content of 33 tales or fables, some based on the 'Arabian Nights'. So popular did this book become that it was later translated into most European languages, and was frequently used by later writers as a model, as well as by Christian preachers.

Averroes (1126-10 December 1198)

Long recognised as the towering figure and pre-eminent philosopher of the second half of the 12th century, whose influence was all-pervasive until at least 400 years after his death, Averroes – shortened Muslim name Ibn Rushd – deserves here not so much a biography as a brief commentary on each of the subjects in which he was so learned. Born in Cordoba to a wealthy and influential family, the young Ibn Rushd received an unparalleled education from the illustrious experts in al-Andalus, on medicine and every other subject set out below. In 1160 he was appointed a judge, but within a few years fell out of favour with the (new) Almohad dynasty, and was effectively exiled to Morocco, dying in Marrakesh – though his body was brought back to Cordoba.

In **philosophy and logic**, above all else Averroes's lasting fame is secured by his translation and interpretation of many of Aristotle's works, with many writers – up to the present time – regarding him as the father of secular or rational thinking in Western Europe. We have to go back to Boethius in c500AD to find any translation of Aristotle's works, from Greek to Latin (Chapter 17). Six hundred years later, while the entirety of extant Greek works resided in Byzantium, only in the eastern Muslim world had Aristotle been translated into Arabic, and criticised by sceptics such as Hamid-al-Ghazali (named Algagel in Latin – Chapter 19), who, as an advocate of mysticism, had denounced the rationalism of Avicenna in his work *The Incoherence of the Philosophers*. Averroes's vigorous riposte was set out in his famous tome *The Incoherence of the Incoherence*.

He commented on most of Aristotle's works – though he did not have access to a text of *Politics* – and he also expressed his views on Plato's *The Republic*. According to Averroes, there is no conflict between *religion* and *philosophy*. They are just different ways of arriving at the same (universal) truth. From the 13th century, though some were lost, many of his works were translated from Arabic into Hebrew, and later from Hebrew into Latin, while Michael Scot (see below) made direct translations from Arabic to Latin. To show how well Averroes's reputation survived, the most complete set of translations of his works appeared in Venice in c1570, nearly 400 years after his death.

In **astronomy** one of Averroes's early claims to fame arose through his detection of a previously unobserved star, when studying the heavens from Marrakesh at the age of 25. He also challenged Ptolemy's astronomical model, set out in *The Almagest*, at a time when most other commentators accepted Ptolemy's theories as gospel. Averroes also challenged the calculations made by the 6th-century Greek Alexandrian John Philiponus, on the arcane subject of celestial mechanics.

Regarding **legal matters** Averroes, being a judge, wrote copiously on many aspects of 'Shariah' (Law) and 'Fiqh' (Jurisprudence). He commented extensively on the equality of women, and on the concept of 'Riba' (Usury). While noting that it was not part of The Prophet's Shariah, he sided with the ban on alcohol imposed subsequently by the Rashidun Caliphate, agreeing that alcohol abuse had only become a problem among young men after Muhammad's lifetime.

As a physician, Averroes wrote 20 treatises on the huge subject of **medicine**, one of which was a vast encyclopaedia known in Latin as *Colliget* (in English *General Rules of Medicine*). As the title indicates, he covered every conceivable subject including hygiene, therapeutics, urology, sexual dysfunction, and the possibility of what came to be known as Parkinson's disease. Most notably, he had an acute understanding of ophthalmology and optics.

Physics, politics and psychology were all areas where Averroes contributed significantly. In all, we know that he wrote at least 67 works, and it is a sign of his pivotal role in emerging Western European thinking that the pre-eminent 13th-century Christian theologian Thomas Aquinas explicitly referred to Averroes in his own writings no fewer than 503 times.

Maimonides (1135-12 December 1204)

Born Moses ben-Maimon, also in Cordoba, this almost exact contemporary of Averroes was the other great al-Andalusian thinker and physician of the 12th century. Like Averroes he was frequently quoted by Thomas Aquinas, but – perhaps even more than Averroes – he is still revered today as one of the masters of Jewish theology and ethics, as well as a proponent of Aristotle. Being born nearly a decade after Averroes, he enjoyed a similar education into his teenage years. However, being Jewish, Maimonides's family was eventually expelled from al-Andalus under the new (less tolerant) Almohad regime (from 1148), and first resettled in Fez, Morocco, where the family house still stands. Maimonides never returned to Spain, living most of his adult life in Egypt. He spent time in modern-day Israel, and it is still hotly disputed as to whether he died in Tiberias or in Egypt. Although he led a peripatetic existence, Maimonides wrote copiously, among his most outstanding works being *Mishneh Torah*, in which he set down a comprehensive exposition of Jewish law, covering the widest possible range of subjects: his 13 principles of faith, still held to be obligatory by orthodox Judaism; and *Tzedakah* (*Charity*), in which he listed his famous 'Eight Levels of Giving'. *Mishneh Torah* contains many 'jewels', for instance Maimonides's frequently quoted maxim that 'it is better and more satisfactory to acquit a thousand guilty persons than to put a single innocent one to death'. In his acute perceptiveness, he observes that any deviation from this principle would lead to a 'slippery slope' for the judiciary (an occurrence with which we are all too tragically familiar, around the world, today!).

In his philosophical work *Guide for the Perplexed* (*Delalatul Ha'yreen*), which so influenced scholars that followed him, Maimonides showed that he had learned from both Muslim and ancient Greek philosophers in his earnest search for a reconciliation between Aristotle's teachings and those of the *Torah*. In an age when prophesy was still a considerable 'industry', and men were obsessed with the nature of evil, he strove to provide valid philosophical views on both preoccupations. He also drew a distinction between beliefs that were 'true' to God, and those that were vital for social order. Maimonides promulgated the notion of humility, and wrote extensively on the vexed questions of resurrection, immortality and the afterlife.

In his Aristotelian work *Treatise on Logic* (*Makalahfi-sina'at al-mantik*) he included the study of Avicenna's teachings when still in his 20s. As regards medical works, there is a document – *The Oath of Maimonides* – that he wrote as an alternative to *The Oath of Hippocrates*. There are known to be ten medical papers written by him – which have been translated into modern English – on subjects as varied as asthma, haemorrhoids and cohabitation!

There is one further giant of Muslim literacy, to whom – because of his influence on 'Western' writers and academics over the past 150 years – we will return in the concluding chapter. Now we will turn (in date sequence) to a sample number of travellers from the rest of Europe who were either sent by their masters to southern Spain, or who made the intrepid journey on their own account. The period of travel covers three centuries from c950, the last of which was the most fertile, in terms of the intensity of learning.

John of Gorze (c900-3 March 974)

Saint John – as he later became – was a well-born monk turned diplomat from Lorraine. In 953 he was sent by Emperor Otto II to be ambassador to the Caliph of Cordoba. John's official brief was to negotiate a cessation to the constant menace from the fortified Saracen port of Fraxinet (close to modern-day St Tropez). With the intercession of local Mozarabs (Christians within a Muslim community), John – who had a reputation for a photographic memory – became fascinated with Islamic learning, and eventually returned home with all the manuscripts he had been able to obtain.

Crucially, John – who had revitalised the decaying monastery at Gorze in 933 – saw to it in the remaining 20 years of his life that the duchy of Lorraine became a centre for the dissemination and circulation of Islamic learning and science.

Gerbert of Aurillac (c946-12 May 1008)

Born in south-central France, Gerbert entered the monastery at nearby Aurillac in 963. Singled out for his interest in mathematics, he accompanied the visiting ruler of Barcelona, Borrell II, back to Catalonia in 967, at a time when the province was under threat from Cordoba and in the era when the military threat from Muslim Spain was at its zenith. Even so, learning of the negotiations for peace from Borrell's courtiers, it occurred to Gerbert that the leaders in Cordoba were far more interested in the sciences and literature than they were in warfare.

From that moment the brilliant young Gerbert was intent on using every spare minute of his time to learn from Arab scholars, most notably the system of *Arabic numbers* – even though it is debatable as to whether he ever visited Cordoba. His passionate studies were interrupted when Borrell required him to travel to Rome with him in 969. Thereafter, Gerbert led a turbulent existence within the Church hierarchy, being promoted, becoming involved in French politics, and ultimately becoming the first French Pope, as Sylvester II, in 999.

It was when posted to Rheims that his scientific reputation became established. He wrote on arithmetic, geometry, astronomy and music. He made a revolutionary hydraulically powered organ for the cathedral, and acted as a promoter of Arabic learning in general. Gerbert had also brought back from Spain knowledge of the astrolabe and armillary sphere, both lost to Western Europe for half a millennium, as noted earlier – and he built models of these, wrote papers, and gave lectures to his students on their remarkable capabilities.

Beyond all else, however, Gerbert's place in history, as being far ahead of his time, was secured by his introduction of the abacus and Hindu-Arabic digits to his peers. However simple the abacus seems to us today, as Fletcher recounts, 'in the desperately backward world of 10th-century Europe it was revolutionary and liberating. The abacus made it possible to make rapid and exact calculations of hitherto unmatched complexity.'

Eighteen years after Fletcher's seminal work, the reader might like to refer to Nancy Marie Brown's 2010 publication *The Abacus and the Cross*. Interviewed for *Religious Dispatches* in January 2011, in an article headed 'Everything you think you know about the Dark Ages is wrong', Brown expresses her astonishment at discovering (after many years' study of the Middle Ages) that Gerbert (a Pope!) was the leading scientist of his day in Medieval Europe, and, what is more, that he learned 'everything he knew' from Muslim Spain!

Adelard of Bath (c1080-c1152)

Though little is known of Adelard's early life, it is certain that he became one of the most widely travelled scholars of his day – to France, southern Italy, and (he claimed) to the east for seven years. Indeed, so well did he master aspects of Arabic learning that it was considered he must have spent time in al-Andalus, until this assumption was recently disproved. Even so, Adelard's substantial literary output can be seen to result from his unique insight into the emerging convergence of French (partly through Gerbert), ancient Greek (via Norman Sicily) and Arabic knowledge.

Adelard promulgated Gerbert's work on the astrolabe, and on Hindu-Arabic numbering and the abacus. He wrote a work (*Eodem et Diverso – On the Same and the Different*) based on *The Consolation of Philosophy* by Boethius. In his *Questiones Naturales* (*Natural Questions*) he posed 67 questions about meteorology and natural science. And in translating Euclid's masterpiece on geometry, *Elements*, from Arabic to Latin, he cemented his reputation, since – following its printing in Venice in 1482 – Adelard's version was the prime mathematical textbook used throughout Western Europe for the next century.

Peter the Venerable (c1092-25 December 1156)

It was Peter who, from his powerful base at Cluny, was the antagonist of Bernard of Clairvaux, and gave sanctuary to Abelard (see Chapter 21), handing his remains to Heloise and – for her sake – pardoning the deceased genius of all his sins. Handed over to a monastic life from birth, Peter's greatest claim to fame was his insistence that the Church reappraise its relationship with Islam. In this he was greatly assisted by Herman of Carinthia and Robert of Ketton (see below).

Peter set in train a formal programme of translation of available Arabic texts into Latin, and in 1142 visited Spain to meet the team of translators, confirmed by J. Kritzeck as 'a momentous event in the intellectual history of Europe' (*Peter the Venerable and Islam* [1964]).

It is also worth noting that, at his weekly general audience in St Peter's Square on 14 October 2009, Pope Benedict XVI used Peter as an example of compassion, citing his governance of Cluny, diplomacy, and study of Islam.

Herman of Carinthia (c1100-c1160)

Herman was born in Istria (then part of Carinthia), which is the small peninsula protruding into the Adriatic and shaped like India – today partitioned between Slovenia and Croatia. Detailing his birthplace gives an indication of how far and wide serious learning was beginning to spread, which prompted this young monk to further his education in France, at the cathedral school at Chartres. Some time later he and his fellow student Robert of Ketton travelled for four years to the east, spending time at both Constantinople and at Damascus. The pair learned Arabic, and devoted the rest of their lives to translation and the understanding of Islam.

In 1142 both these men were in Peter the Venerable's team that visited Spain. It seems that, while Herman and Robert collaborated on each of the five main works tackled, the former was mainly responsible for two – *De generatione Muhamet et nutritura eius* and *Doctrina Muhamet*.

Herman was also deeply involved in translating works of Euclid and Ptolemy from Greek to Latin; translating Arabic texts on both astronomy and astrology; elaborating on previous mathematical works, including the astrolabe; and making his own philosophical contribution – *De Essentiis* (*On Essences*) – based on five Aristotelian categories.

Robert of Ketton (c1110-c1160)

Born in Rutland in England, not much is known of Robert's early life until we find him at Chartres, as a fellow student with Herman. When in Spain in 1142 Robert will have assisted Herman in his main translations, but is himself best remembered as being the prime translator into Latin of the Quran (Koran) – *Lex Muhamet pseudoprophete*. Completed in 1143, this became the standard work on the Koran throughout Europe, the more so when – though later known to include inaccuracies and exaggerations – it was printed in 1543, in Basel, and thereafter widely circulated.

Gerard of Cremona (c1114-1187)

Very early in his education, Gerard knew enough to realise the limitations of his Italian teachers. For most of the 12th century Toledo was accessible to Christians, and it is believed that Gerard arrived there in c1140, in the words of his pupils' obituary (as recounted by Fletcher): 'There, seeing the abundance of books in Arabic in every subject, and regretting the poverty of the Latins in these things, he learned the Arabic language in order to be able to translate.' Toledo had been captured by Alfonso VI of Castile in 1085, but was still a vibrant city of learning, with dozens of libraries holding tens of thousands of manuscripts.

Perhaps the greatest resident scholar was Gerard's contemporary, Rabbi Abraham ibn Ezra, and so completely absorbed did Gerard become in what he saw as his life's work that he never left Toledo – dying there after nearly half a century of constant endeavour. Gerard did not realise that a translation of *The Almagest* from Greek to Latin had been produced in Sicily in 1160 by Henricus Aristipus, and in 1175 he produced his famous translation from Arabic (again into Latin), which remained the most popular work on astronomy in Western Europe for nearly 400 years.

Gerard edited in Latin *The Tables of Toledo*, most of which was based on the work of the 11th-century Cordoban scholar Al-Zarqali (Arzachel). He also interpreted the work of the legendary 10th-century Islamic polymath Al-Farabi (styled as the 'second teacher' after Aristotle), whose book on science, *Kitab al-Ihsa al Ulum*, became *De Scientiis* in the hands of Gerard. In all Gerard translated 87 Arabic works, covering such subjects as arithmetic, geometry and astrology – and such original authors as Euclid, Aristotle, Ptolemy and

Archimedes – together with the father of algebra, Musa al-Khwarizmi (in Latin Algoritmi), from whom our legacy is the word 'algorithm'.

Daniel of Morley (c1140-c1210)

We include a brief survey of Daniel not because he could rival some of the travellers to Islamic Spain we have already discussed, but because he was an English pioneer in the thirst for Greek learning. Born in Norfolk and educated at Oxford, he then moved to Paris, but was appalled by the limited curriculum. As a budding philosopher he decided to follow Gerard and other scholars to Toledo, and is also notable as being one of the few who recorded his travels and thoughts. Eventually returning to Oxford, he submitted his manuscripts and other papers to his patron John of Oxford, Bishop of Norwich, who was enlightened enough to want to establish Oxford as a centre for the study of Greek philosophy.

Michael Scot (1175-c1235)

Born in Scotland, Michael went from early education at Durham to Oxford, then to Paris, specialising in philosophy, mathematics and astrology. After a spell in Bologna he divided most of his remaining life between Sicily and Toledo. Having learned Arabic, Michael's place in our story is assured by his being retained by Frederick II (see Chapter 21) at Palermo, as his most senior Arabic translator, within a court populated by brilliant scholars.

In particular, Frederick was obsessed with Aristotle, and Michael studied the 'Father of Philosophy' intensively through the works of Avicenna and Averroes. Michael also translated Aristotle's *Historia Animalium* (*History of Animals*), from which Frederick may have derived inspiration for his own work on falconry *De Arte Venandi cum Avibus*, which many experts believe to have been the greatest book on this subject ever written.

Plato of Tivoli (12th century)

The exact dates of Plato's life are unknown, but while born in Italy he lived his adult life in Barcelona, as a mathematician, astronomer and translator. One of Plato's lasting works was his translation of Ptolemy's *Tetrabiblios* (*Four Books*), the most popular book on astrology in antiquity, which had long been influential in Islam and, after this translation, held High Medieval Europe almost literally spellbound.

Plato also translated the Arabic astrologer Albohali's *Book of Birth* into Latin.

Ramon Llull (c1232-29 June 1315)

This most unusual man was born into a wealthy family in Majorca. Extremely well educated, he became tutor to James II of Aragon, married and had two children. Having led a fairly carefree young life, everything changed after his conversion to a religious life in c1265. At a time when the notion of 'La Conviviencia' had faded – and religious persecution was prevalent – the characteristic that singled out Ramon Llull from his peers was his obsession with not only learning and translating Arabic, but also with emphasising the areas of commonality between Jews, Muslims and Christians. It is true that he fervently believed that the answer to all religious divisions was that Jew and Muslim should convert to Christianity, but – most notably – he badgered the Council of Vienne in 1311 to foster linguistic education at major universities. As a result of his tireless efforts, it was decreed that chairs of Hebrew, Arabic and Chaldean should be created at Bologna, Paris, Oxford and Salamanca – as well as at the Papal Court. Travelling to North Africa in 1314, on yet another of his missions to convert Muslims to Christianity, he was stoned by a mob, but rescued by Genoese merchants who returned this 82-year-old man to Majorca, where he died the following year.

From 1250 the Nasrid dynasty was confined to ruling only the al-Andalusian stretch of the Iberian peninsula, in a westward arc that started on the Mediterranean coast approximately halfway between the modern-day cities of Almeria and Cartagena. The wonders of Granada lay at the apex of the arc, protected to the north by the Sierra Nevada mountain range. The Moorish-held enclave then followed the south-eastern flank of the Guadalquivir River, from its source through its 400-mile (650km) journey to the Atlantic – crucially excluding the once-fabulous cities of Cordoba and Seville, lost in 1236 and 1248 respectively. Throughout the succeeding 250 years, until the final surrender to Ferdinand and Isabella in 1492, access to this still-vibrant beacon of culture was largely prevented by growing Catholic militancy overland, and was hazardous in the extreme by sea, due to the twin threats of an emerging Spanish navy and ever-present ruthless piracy.

Chapter 23

Byzantium: 'The flame is kept alive' – Greek into Latin

In Chapter 21 we dwelt on the European story of emergence from the Dark Age into the Middle Ages – the traditionally regarded 'springboard' for the Renaissance. Then, in Chapter 22, we highlighted one of the other two crucial building-blocks for that so-called 'miracle'. Now we come to the third key contributor. As can hardly be emphasised enough, both the Byzantine (Orthodox Christian) and Arabic/Moorish (Islamic) contributions to the wonderful base of knowledge that the 'West' has inherited have only really emerged from the shadows of a jealously guarded European (Catholic and Protestant Christian) convention over the last 50 years.

A continuing search for unbiased truth by academics generally – archaeologists and historians specifically – has been promoted by our increasingly secular society, wherein long-held prejudices have largely disappeared; the absence of another World War, which has led to open-ended investigation and dialogue; and a realisation that the residual store of knowledge extant in Western Europe c1000AD could not in any way account for the remarkable transformation that swept through this most fortunate peninsula during the ensuing centuries.

Founding of Byzantium: early history

In 685BC Greeks from Megara had founded the colony of Chalcedon, on the western extremity of Asia Minor, close to the Black Sea, via the entrance to the Bosphorus. Not to be outdone, other Megaran citizens (in legend led by one Byzas) founded Byzantion on the much superior site directly opposite Chalcedon some 15 years later, in 688 or 687. Even a cursory glance at a modern map shows that, whereas both towns had access westward into the Aegean – through the Sea of Marmara, and the Dardanelles – this site was better placed because, protected on the southern side, as the headland jutted into the sea, it was also protected on the north-eastern side by the gulf known as the Golden Horn, which provided a superbly sheltered harbour; the peculiar wedge-shaped site only required (initially) a defensive wall facing west; and, whereas Chalcedon was an outpost at the western extremity of the huge Asia Minor continent, potentially under threat from the populous east, Byzantion was at the eastern extremity of the rapidly expanding Greek-influenced 'European' mainland.

For nearly a full millennium Byzantion had no special claim to fame, until two events in rapid succession transformed its prospects within the space of a generation.

Byzantion becomes Constantinople

As we have already seen, when Diocletian came to power in 284AD – after 50 years of chaos, during which there had been no fewer than 22 emperors – his solution to an ungovernable situation was to split the empire into two halves, with a separate emperor to govern the East and the West. Diocletian's ruthless grip ended with his death in 305, and after a burst of civil war Constantine muscled his way to the top. He was determined to reunite the Empire, but deemed a corrupt Rome to be an unsatisfactory capital city, even after its 1,000 years of supremacy, especially as – being a native of modern-day Serbia – he considered it lay too far to the west.

To him, Byzantion presented itself as the ideal location for a spectacular new headquarters, and he commissioned the construction of a completely new city, which took six years to complete. Consecration as Constantinopolis took place on 11 May 330.

Splendours of the new city

Being built in great haste, temples elsewhere in the empire were effectively dismantled and relocated. Great works of art were also transplanted 'overnight'. Constantine ensured the vibrancy of the city by distributing plots of land for housing, then perpetuated a grave mistake by Rome, in deciding to grant the burgeoning population free food. More land was brought within the official city boundary by the construction of the first great wall; this 'wall of Constantine' was started in the same year as the new city (324), and the Emperor did not live to see its completion. When completed, with intermittent towers, it covered a length of 1.75 miles (2.8km) and its path is known to have run in a west-facing north-south curve, starting from the 'Golden Horn', close to the current Ataturk Bridge.

The walls – practical and symbolic
The death of Constantine in 337 did not impede the development, and growing confidence, of the city. Within 50 years, however, the crushing defeat by the Visigoths at the Battle of Hadrianopolis in nearby western Turkey (378) sent shockwaves through the Empire. Ironically, though this traumatic event presaged eventual collapse in the West, it served as a salutary lesson to the early 'Byzantines'. Soon after Theodosius II was born in 401 (reigned 408-450) the erection of a far more robust outer wall was commissioned. In order to allow expansion of the fast-developing city, it was built 1 mile (1.5km) further west, ran for 4 miles (6.5km) from coast to coast, was 60 feet (18m) tall, and was of triple construction with massive towers built at strategic intervals.

This wonder of the early medieval world survived repeated earthquakes (though having to be quickly repaired each time) and successive sieges by Persians, Arabs, Bulgars and the Rus, not to mention civil wars. The only breach prior to the final onslaught by the Ottomans in 1453 was the capture of the city by crusaders in 1204. This one devastating incursion aside, the integrity of the city, surviving for a full millennium, is *pivotal* to the Byzantine legacy to Western Europe, as will be seen during the course of this chapter.

Lasting monuments
Territorially, the titanic efforts of Justinian in the middle of the 6th century to reunite the empire fleetingly recaptured the glory days of Constantine 300 years earlier. And enough of Justinian's monuments survive to enable us to have an insight into the richness of his reign. In Ravenna – revived as the capital in the west – the 'Justinian' panel in the church of San Vitale, with its attached panel depicting his empress Theodora, can truly be described as sumptuous.

But the reconstructed basilica that he commissioned to be built in Constantinople in 532 – the Hagia Sophia, largest cathedral in the world for nearly a full millennium, until Seville cathedral was finished in 1520 – can only be described as breathtaking. Its central dome rivals that of the Pantheon in size, majesty and decoration – and towers over the centre of modern Istanbul, one of the busiest cities in the world, with a population now close to 13 million.

In complete contrast, Justinian's Monastery of St Catherine, with its rustic basilica, was built at the foot of Mount Sinai, at the mouth of an inaccessible gorge. Virtually unscathed by time or marauder, the monastery still houses one of the world's greatest collections of ancient manuscripts, encompassing priceless works in at least six languages.

'The parting of the ways'

We have already seen in Chapter 17 the fate that befell Boethius in Rome as a result of his attempts to heal the incipient religious schism between Rome and Constantinople, and the legacy from the latter that Cassiodorus perpetuated in Italy beyond his death in 585. In truth, the façade of a unified church was being steadily eroded by language as much as any other factor, with a distinct east-west split between Greek and Latin speakers, and, more importantly, between writers – 'the parting of the ways', as Colin Wells describes it in *Sailing from Byzantium*.

Then, with continuing chaos in Italy for 200 years after Justinian's attempt to unify the empire, a despairing Pope Leo III sought protection from the increasingly powerful Franks. A terrible affront to Byzantines (who deemed themselves to head the empire, from Constantinople) took place on Christmas Day 800, when Charlemagne was crowned 'emperor' in Rome. It is the case that, thereafter, interminable wrangling over the 'true' emperor masked an increasing tide of contempt between east and west – centred not only on religious differences, but also on the issues of economic jealousy and what can be described as 'lifestyle'.

Wells describes how diplomatic envoys from the west to Byzantium in the 10th century reported visiting an alien world, where the food, sights, smells – and behaviour – were completely foreign to 'western' taste, and in many instances repellent. A more disastrous (and repetitive) clash of ideals was brought about with successive Crusades, wherein the route to the Middle East went via Byzantium. As it became clear to the Byzantines that the crusaders had no intention of returning conquered territory to their authority – rather, they established crusader kingdoms linked to the west – relationships between the 'facilitating' locals and the unruly 'league of nations' became stretched to breaking point, with dire implications for what was originally meant to be a *Christian alliance*.

The Fourth (French/Norman) Crusade

In 1202 yet another crusade was launched, deeply indebted to the hugely ambitious – and thoroughly unscrupulous – republic of Venice. Long before the heavily laden fleet neared Constantinople in the summer of 1203 – en route (ambitiously) to recapture Egypt – the seeds of confrontation were sown. On the one hand, Byzantium was enduring a phase of political instability, and on the other the crusaders were completely mesmerised by the vast sight that awaited them – the largest, most populous and wealthiest city by far in the known world.

The temptation to (somehow) create an opportunity to clear their debt to Venice became overwhelming to the seaborne army, who were supposed to be preparing for a holy war against the infidel Muslims 1,000 miles to the east. Aided by all-knowing Venetian pilots, the visitors abused their hosts' invitation to reside on the northern side of the Golden Horn, by seizing the tower from which the great chain across the harbour entrance was (normally) raised to prevent a naval incursion.

The rest is horribly predictable. Using this weak spot to gain access to the main city, a body of crusaders effectively became an occupying force, with the declared intent of not moving on until a massive bribe was paid. Matters dragged on until the spring of 1204, when the 'invaders' launched a 'Trojan horse' attack that quickly overwhelmed the demoralised Byzantines. There followed – even by the base standards reached worldwide over the following 800 years – one of the worst acts of sustained brutality and vandalism ever perpetrated by one set of Christians on another.

The crusaders' orgy of violence resulted in the murder and rape of countless thousands. To compound this human tragedy, the wondrous artefacts that had been gathered together in the city for a full millennium were wrenched from the walls and floors of churches, and public and private buildings alike. Many of the most famous works of art were taken to Venice intact, still to be displayed today. However, countless smaller or less durable treasures were either removed or mindlessly smashed by the less sophisticated crusaders, never to be seen again.

A supreme irony is that the now thoroughly degenerate 'army of Christ' never continued its original journey to 'rescue' Egypt. Instead, it stayed in Constantinople, on the feeble pretext of securing the city as a Christian bastion for Rome. The Byzantines in the wider empire eventually pulled themselves together as a united force, and threw out the invaders in 1261. Thus the chasm between east and west became unbridgeable, with Byzantine resentment never being mollified over its final 200 years of sparkling existence.

The intellectual gulf

In Italy – perhaps as a legacy of the inability of the Romans to fully comprehend Greek philosophy, and the subsequent death of the Greek language – Catholic (papal) interpretation and dogma became the supreme authority, leaving almost no room for secular thinking. The position in the Eastern (Byzantine) Empire was quite different. As early as the 4th century St Basil of Caesaria had set down a division between Greek literature (the Outside Wisdom) and Christian teaching (the Inside Wisdom). In the Greek-speaking East, a tradition was being established that clearly continued to respect the pagan-orientated 'classics', which – unlike in the West – were never to become lost. Basil went further, in an essay 'To young men, on how they might derive profit from pagan literature', which became a widely read tract in Byzantium.

As we will see, during the millennium from the 5th to the 15th centuries, while schisms occurred in the east, this vein of secular thinking and academic study survived alongside Orthodox Christianity, whereas under the disciplines applied by Roman Catholicism no such non-religious 'school' prospered in the west. This is not to say that Byzantium avoided a Dark Age, although it proved to be of shorter duration than in the west. And although all institutes of higher learning followed the fate (100 years later) of Justinian's closure of Plato's academy, the ancient authors continued to be read. Most notably of all, Homer's works – the foundation stone of all western literature – survived. It is when the first Byzantine Renaissance took place towards the end of the 10th century that we have records of over-awed visits from Italy taking place. But it is when the final flourish commenced in 1261 that the momentous schism emerged, with its ultimately 'life-changing' consequences for our ancestors in Western Europe.

'Hesychasm' and humanism

It seems that relentless pressures on Byzantium's borders only made this Last Renaissance (or Paleologan Renaissance – after the dynasty that ruled from 1261 to 1453) more vivid than anything previously seen, coincidental with a religious resurgence. As Colin Wells states, the most prominent Byzantine contributor to this burst of intellectual endeavour was the statesman Theodore Metochites (1270-1332), whose wealth enabled the fabulous mosaics in the beautiful Chora church to be created between 1315 and 1321. More than that, Metochites (claimed by some to be the first fully fledged 'humanist') promoted the preservation and understanding of Classical Greek texts. He created the best library in the city at the Chora church monastery, and (prophetically) begged the monks to 'preserve these exquisite objects and treasures undiminished, as they will be much desired by men for all time to come.'

By the 14th century the Greek term 'Hesychia' ('quiet' or 'peace') referred to a particular monastic practice that had existed for a thousand years, where for the 'Inside Wisdom' solitary meditation (by monks) was considered a purer form of devotion to God than liturgical practice (public worship). Meanwhile, followers of the 'Outside Wisdom' (humanists) had never died out. In the frenetic upsurge of learning, these two vigorous schools clashed very publicly in what is known as the 'Hesychast controversy'.

A key 'accelerant' to the controversy was the realisation that, sooner or later, the intermittently besieged Byzantine state would succumb to the Turkish menace. There may have been a majority of intelligentsia who were ambivalent, but on one flank were the humanists who were devoted to preserving the history and literature that had become so admired in the recovering west. On the other flank, put bluntly, were the devout monks who proselytised their beliefs ever more stridently.

As the dispute became ever more bitter, the one camp clearly believed that preserving the classical heritage, and – if necessary – forsaking an Orthodox form of Christianity for a Catholic version (so as to try and present a united front against the infidel), was a price worth paying. The other camp was equally convinced that adherence to the Orthodox tradition was the only true path, and that the probability of being overrun by the Muslim world was a lesser evil than giving way to despised Catholics.

Therefore we can see that this disastrous schism, which led to periodic civil war, only hastened the eventual collapse of Byzantium, with the fall of the long-beleaguered Constantinople enclave in 1453. But this is the same schism that proved so vital to our heritage, for as the Ottoman pressure grew, so did the rapprochement between intellectuals from the dying Eastern empire and their Western counterparts.

Key Byzantines in the west, and those they influenced

From early in the 14th to late in the 15th century, a migration of scholars from Constantinople (not all of whom were born 'Byzantines') to the west took place, who taught, wrote and debated on all aspects of Greek Classicism, mainly in Italy.

Barlaam (c1290-1348)

Born Bernado Massari in Calabria (southern Italy), Barlaam was an Orthodox monk in an area of Italy that had always been influenced by Byzantium. Brought up in the Hesychast tradition, he was a brilliant scholar in a wide range of subjects, and – crucially through his fascination with Aristotle – fluent in Greek. Moving to Constantinople in c1330, his reputation soon brought him to prominence and, although supposed to be promoting a reconciliation between Orthodoxy and Catholicism, he became embroiled in a bitter clash with Hesychast militancy.

With this long-running dispute unresolved, Barlaam was nevertheless sent in 1339 to the Pope at Avignon (exiled from Rome between 1309 and 1377) to try and pursue the – hopeless – chimera of Church unification. Back in the east by 1341 and again in conflict, Barlaam soon realised that that he had outstayed his welcome and returned to Italy. Landing at Naples, he was (as previously) welcomed at the court of King Robert (the Wise), and assisted in arranging the growing number of Greek manuscripts in the royal library. In 1342 he made his second visit to Avignon and, with his protégé Boccaccio (see below), promoted the rediscovery of great Latin literature, the best of which had relied so much on inspiration from Classical Greek texts, of which the most compelling is Virgil's *Aeneid*, largely based on Homer's *Odyssey*.

In the course of trying to impart his Greek knowledge to the Curia (papal court), Barlaam met Petrarch (Francesco Petrarca), the famous Italian poet and scholar, who is often referred to as the 'Father of (Italian) Humanism'. Petrarch was the first Italian to revive Roman belief in the 'humanities' – essentially a credo that careful study of literature could enhance one's grasp of humanity. Barlaam, Boccaccio and Petrarch found their attempts to study Greek together a frustrating experience, as they lacked adequate (Byzantine) books on grammar and vocabulary, as well as bilingual texts. All in all, the last few years of Barlaam's life were unhappy, with a spell as a bishop in Calabria, a final brief visit to Constantinople, and a return to Avignon in 1347 all leaving him sad, disillusioned and unfulfilled.

Giovanni Boccaccio (1313-1375)

Born in Florence to a father with influence, Boccaccio had no real affinity with his early career in banking, nor with his later tilt at the law. Moving to Naples while still an adolescent, he was absorbed into the court of Robert the Wise, which is where he met Barlaam in 1339. In his future collaboration with Barlaam – whom he revered for his knowledge of Greek – Boccaccio too realised that popularising ancient Latin texts was an incomplete exercise unless the works of Greek authors – on whom these great Roman writers (fluent in Greek) had relied – could themselves be properly understood.

Though his most famous works were the *Decameron* and *On Famous Women*, his friendship and exchanges with Petrarch – who also shared his enthusiasm for the concept of archaeology (!) – encouraged him to write *The Genealogy of the Gods*. It was in this work, which remained a key reference book on classical mythology for several centuries, that Boccaccio paid tribute to Barlaam: '…he stood higher than others in learning. Shall I not do well to trust him, particularly in all that pertains to Greek.'

Demetrius Cydones (1324-1398)

Born Demetrios Kydones in Thessalonica, Byzantium's second city, Cydones was a theologian and statesman, deeply involved in belated attempts to reconcile Orthodoxy and Catholicism, in the forlorn hope that such a move could ward off the ever-growing Muslim threat to Constantinople. One part of his legacy was his famous tirade against recalcitrant Greeks in his philosophical essay *De contemnende morte* (*On Despising Death*), his 'apologia' for his conversion to

Catholicism. As lost on ambivalent Christians now as it was 650 years ago, his words may still send a shiver down the spines of ecumenical believers:

> 'Then, as a battle fought in the dark, we will be striking at our own friends, and they at us. How the non-believers will enjoy our antics, because we Christians are engaged in endless bickering among ourselves, since none of us wants to concede anything to anyone else...'

As a young man, Cydones – a committed anti-Hesychast – knew and greatly admired Barlaam. This did not stop him becoming an assistant, and eventually 'premier' to the pro-Hesychast emperor in 1347, at the tender age of 23, though he spent most of his long life dodging violent criticism from the dominant Hesychast faction at court. He was luckier than several of his persuasion, who ended up having to flee to Italy. On his first retirement from public office in 1354, Cydones himself travelled to Italy, where he studied the writings of leading *philosophical* theologians. He translated major works into Greek, most famously those of Thomas Aquinas, and converted to Catholicism in 1365.

Cydones served different emperors twice more, accompanying John V Paleologos to Rome in 1369. On this despairing sojourn, the emperor professed his conversion to the Catholic faith, in an attempt to raise a coalition against the ever-more-oppressive Muslim encirclement of a shrunken Byzantium.

By 1380 the Turks had conquered Serbia and Bulgaria, reducing the once mighty empire to just a patchwork of outposts, together with Constantinople and Thessalonica. Despite all these pressures, Cydones remained in contact with the west for the rest of his life, visiting Venice (which was to play a pivotal role in ushering in the Renaissance) to plead for assistance in 1390. Constantinople so nearly fell during the next decade, being blockaded from 1394 to 1402, and it was during this dreadful time, in 1396, that Cydones – still under assault for his Catholic faith – escaped, aged 72, to Crete, where he died two years later. Apart from all his other great works, this tireless labourer for Christian unity will be forever remembered for his legacy of 450 letters, which are mainly concerned with Byzantium's relations with the west.

Manuel Chrysoloras (1355-1415)

Born in Constantinople, Chrysoloras was a budding statesman and protégé of Cydones, whom he accompanied on his diplomatic mission to Venice in 1390. The younger man made a great impression on two Florentines in particular, Robert Rossi and Coluccio Salutati (1331-1406). Although from the Byzantines' point of view the mission was an abject failure, back in Florence Rossi and Salutati raved about Chrysoloras's expertise in Classical Greek literature, so much so that their associate Jacomo Angeli de Scarpiera was inspired to brave the tightening Muslim stranglehold in 1395 so as to reach Constantinople, and have Chrysoloras teach him Greek.

Salutati himself then invited Chrysoloras to Florence, expressly to teach Greek grammar and literature. Inspired by Petrarch, Italian humanists dedicated themselves to recovering lost texts, mainly from monasteries, and it is only through Petrarch's quest that Salutati – chancellor of Florence since 1375 – was able to quote Cicero's words from his *Letters to Atticus*:

> 'Italy is invincible in war, Greece in culture. For our part, and we mean no offence, we firmly believe both Greeks and Latins have always taken learning to a higher level by extending it to each other's literature.'

It is worth noting that, for several years straddling the turn of the century, the enlightened republic of Florence, which espoused ancient Rome's concept of 'libertas', fought a desperate (and ultimately successful) struggle – inspired by Salutati – to avoid the clutches of tyrannical Milan.

Chrysoloras arrived in Florence on 2 February 1397, and it was a seminal moment when he started teaching straight away, since no formal study of Greek had taken place anywhere in Italy for more than 700 years!

What was so especially remarkable – in a milieu thirsting for this completely 'new' language, and effectively starting from scratch – was the way in which Chrysoloras rationalised the immensely complicated Byzantine Greek curriculum into a (comparatively) simple primer, under the title *Questions*. With this tool, his students were encouraged to translate so as to produce a Latin style that flowed, rather than the stilted alternative 'verbum ad verbum' – literally 'word for word'. So popular did his method become that *Questions* became one of the first printed works in Italy in 1484, and formed the basis for all Greek scholarship during the 15th century (the 'quattrocento') and well beyond.

It is perhaps difficult for us to appreciate the effect that the mid-15th-century printing press revolution had throughout Europe. Johanes Gutenberg's perfection of a speedy technique in 1440 at Maintz, Germany, enabled up to 3,600 pages to be produced in a single working day. A pertinent example is that both Thomas Linacre (1460-1524) and his then pupil at Oxford, Desiderius Erasmus (1466-1536), eagerly snapped up copies of *Erotemata Civas Questiones* as soon as the work reached England.

Apart from his energetic three-year teaching stint in Florence, Chrysoloras translated the works of Homer, and Plato's *Republic*, into Latin. Then, in 1400 – to the amazement of modern scholars, but not to his devoted students – he abruptly left Florence for (of all places!) Milan, while these two contrasting cities were in fierce conflict with each other. Only as recently as 1966 (according to Wells) did Ian Thomson offer an explanation for this seemingly irrational – indeed potentially treacherous – act. As Thomson puts it, the Florentines always knew that Chrysoloras had another (diplomatic) career, while he recognised that they were much more interested in the condition of Ancient Greece than ever they were in Constantinople's current travails. He had started his Italian experience in Venice, and was a friend of the current Byzantine emperor, Manuel II Paleologos, who – desperate to try and raise an army against the infidel – himself spent three years in Europe from 1400, visiting all the major centres of power, including London. The two celebrated their reunion in Milan that year, and Chrysoloras served the interests of his emperor in Rome and Paris, then in Germany in 1413. He was also much involved in repeated attempts to unify Christianity, and indeed was representing the Orthodox position at a conference in 1415 when he died at Constance in Switzerland.

Byzantium doomed

In the remorseless encirclement of Constantinople, an outside agency secured a short breathing space. This occurred when Tamerlane, or Timur – founder of the short-lived Timurid Empire – saw fit to invade

Ottoman-held Turkey, and secured a devastating victory over his Muslim brethren at Ankara in 1402. In the aftermath, the Ottoman Mehmed I eventually managed to regain control over his country by defeating his brother in 1413, but only with vital assistance from the wily Byzantine emperor Manuel II, who – a decade earlier – had spent three years trying to drum up support in Western Europe. Thereafter, Mehmed effectively pledged a certain 'loyalty' to the older adversary for his own lifetime – that is, he agreed not to try and encroach further into the shattered remnants of the once mighty Byzantine Empire.

Manuel realised that this was only a temporary relief, which he decided to use for fortifying the Peloponnese, one of Byzantium's remaining outposts of significance. Known as Morea by the Byzantines, he set about protecting this strategic peninsula by rebuilding the ancient wall that ran along the isthmus of Corinth, the Hexamilion, originally constructed by Theodosius II during the first half of the 5th century. The Morea was governed from Mistra, near the centre, a city close to ancient Sparta.

By 1430 both Mehmed and Manuel were gone, and Mehmed's son Murad II lost no time in renewing the Ottoman assault, first by the hammer blow of capturing Thessalonica, Byzantium's second city. With Pope Eugenius IV under pressure from dissidents in Italy, both wings of Christianity came to believe that their interests would be served by yet another attempt at reconciliation. Despite all the pressure to move quickly, the required council took years of painstaking negotiations to organise, the enormous retinues of all parties finally converging on Venice in February 1438. And in amongst all the religious worthies, there was a minor official – who was not even a Christian of any sort. Nevertheless this controversial man of over 80 electrified the esteemed audience with his rhetoric, his name being Pletho.

Pletho (Georgius Gemistus Plethon, c1355-c1452 or 1454)

Popular thinking is that, before the 20th century, people lived comparatively short lives. Perhaps so generally, which makes it all the more remarkable that Pletho and Cassiodorus – born exactly 870 years earlier – both lived to within a whisker of becoming centenarians!

Born George Gemisto in Constantinople, he lived and taught there (mainly in theology and philosophy, to the royal court) until he was over 50, at which stage he was expelled to Mistra by his long-suffering emperor because of his increasingly pagan beliefs, whereupon he immediately set up a school so as to continue proselytising his unique brand of philosophy. Essentially, Pletho's complex message became comprised of three main stands: a devoted adherence to Plato and debunking of Aristotle; a rejection of Christianity – in particular monasticism – in favour of reviving the ancient Greek gods; and a consequent identification with Greek patriotism.

Despite his contradictory and provocative nature, even devout Hesychasts within the rump of Byzantium admired him, mainly because he inspired so many who listened avidly to his promotion of Platonic ideals. It must have been because of the emperor's regard for him that Pletho was included in the vast delegation to Venice at all, since he was only required to attend the endless sessions intermittently. Indeed, he set up a temporary school in Florence, expressly so as to lecture (in Greek, with an interpreter, as he spoke no Latin) on the difference between Aristotle and Plato. In the High Middle Ages, Aristotle had come to be highly regarded by western students, whereas very little was known about Plato. Pletho set out to correct this imbalance, at this time pointedly adding 'Pletho' to his name, because the word was a synonym for 'Gemistos', meaning 'abundant', and sounded like 'Plato'!

Two vital consequences of Pletho so electrifying his audiences were, first, to stimulate a raging argument among Italian scholars over the respective merits of the pair of great philosophers, which ran for years, and, second, he so attracted the fascination of the influential Cosimo de Medici that this dominant Florentine immediately laid his plans for his Accademia Platonica, and subsequently commissioned his protégé Marsilio Ficino – who became the first director – to translate all Plato's works (and other neo-Platonic tracts) into Latin.

When Pletho finally returned to Mistra (aged about 90, and as blatantly controversial as ever), he continued teaching a clutch of dedicated students at his pagan academy while fanning the flames of the great philosopher dispute by summarising his lectures at Florence in a volume titled *On the differences of Aristotle and Plato* (*De Differentiis*). Bystanders were bewildered by the heat generated between the influx of Byzantine émigrés to Italy, who were mostly on the side of Plato, and the equally fervent defenders of his argumentative pupil Aristotle, two of the most notable of whom were Mark Eugenicos, Bishop of Ephesus (1392-1442), and George of

Trebizond (1395-c1472). Weighing in for Plato was the highly influential Basilios Bessarion.

Basilios (later Cardinal) Bessarion (1403-1472)

Bessarion was born at Trebizond, a strategic Byzantine port on the Anatolian side of the Black Sea. Educated in Constantinople, he travelled to the Peloponnese in 1423 to learn from Pletho, becoming a life-long adherent, though not so fanatically outspoken. Made Orthodox Bishop of Nicaea in 1437, he was a prominent delegate to the Ferrara (then Florence) ecumenical council from 1438. Bessarion enraged his more unbending Orthodox colleagues by asserting that he had no problem adopting Catholicism – so much so that he took up permanent residence in Italy, coincidental with Pope Eugenius IV investing him with the rank of cardinal. After years of debate, the positions of the parties were reconciled enough to lead to a crusade, wherein an army of 25,000 set out from Hungary to relieve beleaguered Constantinople, only to be overwhelmed by the Ottomans at Varna in Bulgaria in 1444.

For the rest of his life, Bessarion devoted himself to the collecting of Greek manuscripts, and their translation into Latin. Simultaneously, he turned his palazzo in Rome into a virtual academy for *humanistic learning*, and created there a haven for Byzantine émigré scholars. In between several stints as an ambassador, he wrote extensively – translating Aristotle's *Metaphysics* and Xenophon's *Memorabilia*. However, his most important work was his treatise directed at George of Trebizond, who had written most critically of Plato. Bessarion's masterpiece was *In Calumniatorem Platonis* (*Against the Slanderers of Plato*), which gained great fame for its moderate tone and made a significant contribution in the developing field of *theology*.

More than anything else, though, Bessarion will forever be lauded for donating (in 1468) his priceless collection of 600 Greek manuscripts to the city where he had first set foot on Italian soil – Venice. Today these works still form the nucleus of the Library of St Mark, the Biblioteca Marciana.

Byzantium's death, and the lingering afterglow

Centuries before its shoddy role in the Fourth Crusade, Venice had been a Byzantine province, and although the roles were now reversed

– with the former overlord now owing huge debts – Bessarion's generosity must also have been motivated by the cultural ties between the fast-fading empire and the burgeoning republic. Both immediately before the fall of Constantinople in 1453, and for decades afterwards, more Byzantine Greeks (perhaps 4,000) took refuge in Venice than in any other western city. Initially somewhat indifferent to the unique heritage being offered, it took until 1463 for a Greek seat of learning to be established at Padua. Very soon, Greek-orientated humanist schools were also flourishing in Florence, and at Venice itself – all headed by Greeks. And it was their good fortune that the printing press – first seen in Italy in 1465 – enabled dozens of texts to be circulated at bewildering speed. Printing in Venice itself started in 1480, and took off in 1495, when the Aldine Press specifically focussed on Greek works, rapidly turning the city into the printing capital of Europe.

It is remarkable to consider that the distribution of hundreds of books over vast distances by the end of the 'quattrocento' – representing hundreds of Ancient Greek writers in every subject – was taking place only 100 years after Barlaam's stuttering attempts to instil the language into the brilliant Petrarch's head! After their delight at studying Chrysoloras's *Questions* at Oxford, Linacre, Erasmus and another humanist, John Colet, all studied in Italy, as did Johannes Reuchlin from Germany. The Byzantine tide rolled on across the west well into the 16th century, with one John Lascaris (librarian to Lorenzo de Medici) scouring his – now Ottoman-held – homeland for more Greek texts, and later journeying to France to inspire that country's contribution to the fast-flourishing Renaissance.

Chapter 24

Into the Renaissance

The first issue to consider is when the Renaissance actually started. Unlike *single events* in history, this unsurpassed *phase* of Western development cannot be accurately dated. Though many have tried, it is pointless here to attempt to enter an arcane debate. Instead we will agree with most commentators that the 'quattrocento' (actually the 15th century) marks the pivotal transition from the end of the High Middle Ages to a state of full-blown Renaissance.

Before moving on it is interesting to ask why this period is always known by that title, signifying rebirth. One rather trite answer – though through the early decades, uncomfortably close to the truth – is that nothing genuinely *new* did take place or was discovered. Indeed, there is a case to be made that well into the 16th century the geniuses of old had ensured (at least, in certain fields) that there was nothing new to uncover – as the most learned Europeans of the age realised every time a great Classical work was revealed, after being apparently lost for a whole millennium. Another possible reason is that, in the early phase, the term was deliberately chosen to mark twin aspects, namely a longing to recapture the Classical Age, just at the time when Europe was 'feeling sorry for itself' after the traumas engendered by the Black Death.

In terms of the inferiority complex alluded to above, it is extremely important to separate the overwhelming *confidence* that Christian Europe had in the superiority of its *religion* from the sense of *wonder* felt as its greatest minds came to terms with a devastating realisation. This realisation was that almost everywhere else in the known world men had been continuously harbouring, interpreting and developing a fabulous body of knowledge and ideas from which – for at least 500 years to the dawn of the 2nd millennium AD – they and their antecedents, *alone in the West*, had been totally excluded.

And then – for another half-millennium – Europe, excluding only the southern half of Spain, had been spoon-fed a steadily increasing trickle of knowledge from this lost world – from before 1,000AD until the late 13th century from Arabic al-Andalus, and from the mid-14th to the late 15th centuries from Greek Constantinople.

Before we move on, here is what the eminent Richard Fletcher had to say at the beginning of his book *Moorish Spain*, on the occasion when the Hapsburg Holy Roman Emperor Charles V finally visited Cordoba in the middle of the 15th century, to see the massive works within the fabulous mosque, which had turned it into a cathedral:

'Charles's comment must rank as one of the most crushing royal rebukes on matters architectural ever delivered: You have built here what you, or anyone else, might have built anywhere; to do so you have destroyed what was unique in the world.'

Then, on his very last page, Fletcher writes:

'The traffic was all one way. Moorish Spain was the donor, western Christendom the eager recipient … [Muslim] geographers' accounts of Christian Spain tended to be cursory in the extreme: it was cold, the inhabitants were barbarians who ate pigs, you could get slaves there – that was about the sum of it.'

As mentioned at the outset of this book, we cannot attempt here to even summarise the Renaissance of the 15th and 16th centuries. What we will do, though, is describe the Arabic and Greek influences (together with that of long-silent Latin writers) on a selection of the great men who, sequentially, left a lasting legacy, and most of whom became 'household' names throughout the succeeding centuries – and who took up the baton from the great teachers who had been born in or near Constantinople, whose lives we covered in Chapter 23.

Arabic and Greek influences

Just before discussing these individuals, we should not overlook the use of the long 'dead' Latin language. Preserved in the west since the fall of Rome only in monasteries that clung on throughout the European 'peninsula', Latin enjoyed a great scholastic revival as the Church (together with papal supremacy) became paramount in Medieval society. In Chapter 21 we covered the energetic unearthing of Latin texts – untouched in many monasteries – that was initiated by Petrarch and Boccaccio. At the same time a flood of Greek works arrived from Constantinople, many of which were translations from the original Latin. We take for granted that these factors combined to ensure the use of Latin as the *technical* language from that day to this throughout the world, in all scientific applications, including medicine and botany, together with legal and philosophical terminology.

Filippo Brunelleschi (1377-1446)

Born in Florence, he trained as a goldsmith, but his fame rests on his becoming an architect, for which transition we have no records. We know that he studied the ancient buildings of Rome, and that the design of his first commission – the Foundling Hospital in Florence – made clear references to classical antiquity. Working almost solely in Florence, and influenced by Vitruvius (see below), Brunelleschi borrowed designs nearly 1,500 years old to devise the hoisting mechanism (which he patented) for his greatest work, the dome of the new cathedral of Santa Maria del Fiore. In a completely different field, he took up the researches of Euclid, which enabled him to invent linear perspective – initiating a revolution in painting that allowed for a *naturalised* style, as opposed to the Medieval *stylised* method.

Demetrius Chalcondyles (1424-1511)

A Greek born in Athens, he moved to Italy in 1447, and quickly secured Bessarion as his patron. His claim to fame is twofold. First, he was the last in the line of Greek humanists who taught Greek literature – over a 40-year period – in his case at Padua, Perugia, Milan and Florence. Second, he wrote copiously, his own great work being his handbooks of ancient Greek. Even more noteworthy are his translations of Homer's *Iliad* and *Odyssey* into Latin, followed by Galen's *Anatomy*.

From the previous chapter, we can also see that Chalcondyles lived towards the end of the crucial era when hundreds of texts covering Greek works of drama (including Demosthenes and Thucydides), which had been neglected by the Arabic world, were voraciously assimilated.

Leonardo da Vinci (1452-1519)

Leonardo was a polymath of such genius that he mastered at least a dozen completely different disciplines. Born the illegitimate son of a wealthy father, Leonardo was educated in Latin, mathematics and geometry, but gave no hint of the talents he later revealed. From 1466 he spent a decade apprenticed to the artist Verrocchio. The 16th-century biographer Vasari recounted how, in helping his master to paint *The Baptism of Christ*, young Leonardo's skill so outshone his tutor that Verrocchio vowed never to paint again. It would have been during this 10-year period that Leonardo first learned a range of technical skills.

A great influence on Leonardo was the 1st-century-BC architect and builder Vitruvius, whose *De Architectura* – known today as *The Ten Books on Architecture* – remains the only Latin work that describes in detail the breadth of Greek and Latin design, together with the associated engineering technology. Leonardo's famous 'Vitruvian Man' is thus based on specifications laid down 1,500 years earlier.

In Leonardo's paintings and sculpture, the desire to revert to Greek (and Roman) lifelike depiction – with technical and anatomical accuracy paramount – leapt to the fore. No better example can be given than in *Self-portrait in red chalk*, wherein his facial features (even eyebrows!) are of almost photographic definition.

Niccolo Machiavelli (1469-1527)

Born in Florence to a well-regarded family, his father was a lawyer. The young Machiavelli was educated in a wide range of subjects including Latin, but not Greek. Although notorious today for his convoluted political thinking and scheming, our interest in this multi-talented man is focussed on his education in *humanism*. By the 15th century, humanist education concentrated on the interpretation of ancient texts – 'Studia Humanitatis' – in the separate subjects of poetry, grammar, history, moral philosophy and rhetoric. The purpose was to 'recover, interpret and assimilate the language, literature, learning and values of ancient Greece and Rome'. In the turbulent – and very dangerous – milieu of Florentine politics, Machiavelli was one of the first to utilise his understanding of the ancients in his assessment of what was wrong with contemporary government, and how it should be conducted.

Of the whole body of ancient Greek and Roman thinkers – and

their later interpreters – modern-day students of Machiavelli's works deem him to have been most influenced by, on political philosophy, Xenophon (himself a student of Socrates), Polybius, Plutarch, Cicero and Averroes; on materialism, Democritus, Epicurus and Lucretius; on history, Thucydides; and on play-writing, Aristophanes.

Desiderius Erasmus (1466-1536)

Born out of wedlock, but to middle-class parents, in Rotterdam, Erasmus (from the Greek word 'erasmios', 'desire') led a peripatetic life, but had a good education, mainly through being attached to monastic schools. Although he became a Catholic priest, in effect he was allowed to take a permanent sabbatical once his masters realised his astonishing grasp of Latin, and his deep interest in the 'humanities'. By 1495 he was studying at Paris, and went on to live in England in the last years of the century, meeting a host of luminaries such as John Fisher, Thomas Linacre, Thomas More, and John Colet, whose 'fundamentalist' style of Bible teaching made Erasmus determined to master Greek.

By c1505 he had attained this goal, and then devoted a full decade to producing his translations of both the New and Old Testaments of the Bible – in both Greek and Latin. Moving to Leuven (Louvain) in Flemish Belgium in 1517, Erasmus was the prime mover in the founding of the Collegium Trilingue for the study of Hebrew, Latin and Greek, modelled on the curriculum at the University of Alcala, near Madrid.

A keen student of Greek philosophy – translating or annotating diverse works by Hesiod, Aristotle, Cicero and Augustine of Hippo – Erasmus stood as a towering figure of impartiality in the struggle for supremacy between emerging Protestantism and long-established Catholicism, earning the sobriquet of 'Prince of Humanists'. His outpouring of literary works was hugely popular, as he sought to promote man's 'free will', so much so that he was responsible for up to 20% of all book sales for many decades after his death. He also wrote *Education of a Christian Prince*, specifically as advice to the young King Charles V (Charles I of Spain), born in Ghent in 1500, the same man whose damning indictment of Catholic folly over the mosque at Cordoba we read earlier in this chapter.

Thomas More (1478-1535)

Born in London, he was the son of a successful lawyer. He had a good grounding, and spent two years at Oxford University studying Greek and Latin under – among others – Thomas Linacre. Returning to London, he became a lawyer himself, as well as a social philosopher, author and statesman. His talent soon drew him into a political career, with the rest of his (savagely curtailed) life still a controversial subject for countless authors.

As a keen student of antiquity, More utilised all his acquired learning in publishing his novel *Utopia* in 1516, written in Latin. The title itself is a Greek pun on the words 'ou-topos' ('no place') and 'eu-topos' ('good place') – a joke that many literate people at the beginning of the 16th century would have grasped. Drawing heavily on the works of Plato, Aristotle and Cicero, *Utopia* contrasted the contentious nature of contemporary European life/strife with an idealistically perfect society, wherein all land is communal; there is no private property; men and women are equally educated; and all religions are tolerated, but with no room for atheism.

Because of his fame throughout Europe, after his execution – religious issues apart – More was widely revered for his courage, steadfastness and dignity. Erasmus, in particular, defended his character, and the same King Charles V (Charles I of Spain), mentioned above, commented, 'Had we been master of such a servant, we would rather have lost the best city of our dominions than such a worthy councillor.'

Nicolaus Copernicus (1473-1543)

Born in Prussia (Kingdom of Poland), his everlasting fame derives from his being the first person to place the Sun (stationary) at the centre of the universe, with the Earth and other planets encircling it. This theory of heliocentric cosmology had first been proposed by Aristarchus of Samos in the 3rd century BC, but had been ignored then and ever since. The epoch-making book by Copernicus, *De Revolutionibus orbium coelestium* (*On the Revolutions of the Celestial Spheres*), was published just as he died, and is regarded as not only opening the age of modern astronomy itself, but also ushering in the scientific revolution.

One of the greatest polymaths of the Renaissance, Copernicus – who never married – mastered at least a dozen disciplines, regarding the field of astronomy as nothing more than a hobby! Among so many talents, he displayed a phenomenal grasp as a mathematician, classicist, translator and economist, as well as being a physician.

Copernicus spent four years at the University of Krakow, during which time (already familiar with Latin) he mastered Greek and covered every known aspect of mathematics in his studies. He read Aristotle's *De coelo* (*On the Heavens*) and *Metaphysics*; works of Euclid and Ptolemy; and tracts by Averroes that would be most influential in later shaping his astronomical theory. He was a humanist whose doubts about the accepted celestial order only deepened at the end of the 15th century, when living at Padua, then Bologna, as he read copiously the works of other ancients, including Pythagoras, Cicero, Pliny the Elder and Plutarch, as well as the great translator Bessarion (see Chapter 23).

Returning to Poland at the age of 30, Copernicus never left Eastern Europe again, first being retained as his uncle's secretary. During this time he displayed yet another facet of his genius by translating from Greek to Latin 85 poems of the 7th-century Greek historian Theophylact Simocatta. He also composed a Greek epigram of his own, and by the age of 40 had firmly sided with the humanist view (against a degree of Catholic antipathy) that, with the availability of mass printing, all classical Greek philosophical works should become circulated and widely studied.

As to his astronomical 'hobby', Copernicus was fully acquainted with the astrolabe, *The Almagest* and the armillary sphere, and utilised such primitive instruments as the quadrant and triquetrum in his research – both modelled on ancient devices.

Galileo Galilei (1564-1642)

Born in Pisa, he was the son of a famous musician, Vincenzo. The family soon moved to Florence and Galileo was sent to a nearby monastery for the usual all-round education. Eschewing the priesthood, his father urged him to take a medical degree at the university, but the young man chose mathematics instead. This decision may have emanated from his father's experiments in music, in that Vincenzo had followed the Pythagorean tradition (see Chapter 14) and had established what was possibly the oldest known non-linear relationship in physics: for a stretched string, the pitch varies as the square root of the tension.

In developing his mathematical theories, Galileo used Euclid's *Elements* as well as the works of Aristotle and Archimedes in his research into dynamics. In the field of astronomy, however, he followed the work of Copernicus, and – while being an adherent of Aristotle in his humanism – rejected his geocentric cosmology, as well as Ptolemy's theories, in proving the reality of a heliocentric universe. In doing so, he cited the Augustine view that not everything in the Bible had to be taken literally.

In 1616 he published his most famous work, *Dialogue Concerning the Two Chief World Systems*, which immediately led Galileo to be censured by the papal authorities – and eventually led to his being placed under house arrest for the rest of his life. In the book, an Aristotelian philosopher, Simplico, has his geocentric views (which Pope Urban VIII supported) demolished by the Copernican theory in a rather dismissive fashion – demonstrating Galileo's refusal to deny heliocentricism, which the previously supportive Pope had demanded.

René Descartes (1596-1650)

Born in the Loire valley, his mother died when he was one year old, and he was brought up by his father, a local politician. Sent to a nearby Jesuit college at the age of eight, Descartes then studied law at the University of Poitiers. In 1616, having refused to follow his father's chosen career, he travelled to Holland, where he became influenced by Isaac Beeckman, a noted philosopher and scientist. From that moment the budding genius was resolved to follow these twin interests for the rest of his life.

In his philosophical research he studied Aristotle, the Stoics and St Augustine, with his major work being *Meditations on First Philosophy*. Descartes became regarded as 'The Father of Modern Philosophy', and this text is still required reading in most university philosophical departments. In the arcane world of higher mathematics, Descartes's great contribution was in the field of algebra, building on the work of Fibonacci in the 13th century, and the earlier Islamic scholars. He 'filled out' the field of analytic geometry, the bridge between algebra and geometry, through the Cartesian coordinate system. He wrote extensively, his two most famous (mathematical) works being *Discours de la Methode* and *La Geometrie*.

We have covered above nine towering figures of the Renaissance, each of whose claim to fame is based on widely differing fields of activity. These men are but a small representation of the hundreds of individuals who set the course of European development for centuries to come. From Brunelleschi reaching adulthood in 1400 to Descartes dying in 1650, we have touched on the 250-year period that takes us to the edge of the Age of Enlightenment, which in turn led to the Industrial Revolution.

However, to show that the genius of Islamic learning and interpretation is still being felt in Western Europe, there is one more individual we must describe – in this case a man whose remarkable scholarship was entirely lost to the late Middle Ages and Renaissance, and whose record was only unearthed at the very end of the 17th century, for the inestimable benefit of historians and philosophers ever since.

Ibn Khaldun (27 May 1332-19 March 1406)

Of originally mixed Yemeni and Berber ethnicity, Ibn Khaldun was born in Tunis to parents who were of prominent Andalusian stock. They had returned to North Africa due to the febrile situation between Catholic and Muslim Spain, and much of Ibn Khaldun's life was spent oscillating between two volatile societies, with the success of his career ebbing and flowing at frequent intervals. We know all this because – most unusually – he wrote a meticulously detailed autobiography.

Even compared with thumbnail sketches of the dozens of historical figures in this book, Ibn Khaldun was the polymath of all polymaths, and it is worth listing each area in which he was expert. He was an astronomer and mathematician; master of Islamic law and theology, and 'hafiz' (guardian of the Quran); historian; military strategist; economist; philosopher; statesman; social scientist; and nutritionist. Today he is considered to have been a herald of academic disciplines we now see as commonplace: demography, cultural history, sociology, and economics.

In c1365, having held high office in Granada, Ibn Khaldun (always one to court controversy) made the wise decision to leave Spain for what turned out to be the last time. He spent the last 40 years of his life in North Africa, of which the final part was in Egypt. This is where he wrote his most famous work, the *Muqaddimah*, which is why publication took some 300 years to reach a European audience. In 1697 a biography of this most remarkable of men finally appeared in

Bibliotheque Orientale by Barthelemy d'Herbelot de Molainville. But Ibn Khaldun only began to attract serious attention in the first half of the 18th century, when Silvestre de Sacy began to publish extracts from the *Muqaddimah*, termed *Progelomena*, with a complete French translation not appearing finally until c1860.

The *Muqaddimah* was in fact the first section of a seven-volume work, with volumes 2 to 5 covering the history of mankind, and 6 and 7 a history of the Berbers, which has proved invaluable to modern researchers. In the *Muqaddimah*, Ibn Khaldun covers questions of economics, social conflict and social cohesion in great depth.

As an example of his outlook being far ahead of his time, would any reader believe that this extract on economics was written more than 600 years ago?

'When civilisation [population] increases, the available labour again increases. In turn, luxury again increases in correspondence with the increasing profit, and the customs and needs of luxury increase. Crafts are created to obtain luxury products. The value from them increases, and, as a result, profits are again multiplied in the town. Production there is thriving even more than before. And so it goes with the second and third increase. All the additional labour serves luxury and wealth, in contrast to the original labour that served the necessity of life.'

It is sobering to realise that the lifespan of this remarkable polymath almost exactly matched that of Geoffrey Chaucer, in that the output of each man occurred in the closing years of the 14th century. But with due respect to Chaucer's talents – and those of several other European figures at that time – it is inconceivable that any Western individual could have produced such a cogent summary of the surge that (under their feet) was just starting to take place in their own cities.

Ibn Khaldun also dwells on the circumstances (of hardship and common cause) that drive barbarians to create a great society; then the circumstances (of complacency and decay) that cause the now cultured society to be overrun by a fresh tribe of barbarians – a process that can (and does – as we know only too well!) lead to endless repetition over successive centuries and millennia.

In an incalculable legacy, comments on the *Muqaddimah* from modern writers include:

- Arnold J. Toynbee: 'a philosophy of history which is undoubtedly the greatest work of its kind that has ever yet been created by any mind in any time or place'
- Robert Flint: 'as a theorist on history he had no equal in any age… Plato, Aristotle and Augustine were not his peers'
- Ernest Gellner considered Ibn Khaldun's definition of government 'an institution which prevents injustice other than such as it commits itself' to be 'the best in the history of political theory'
- Arthur Laffer, after whom the Laffer Curve was named, noted that some of Ibn Khaldun's ideas preceded his own.

Finally, Spain – where until quite recently commentary on the wonders of Islamic al-Andalus and the country's Moorish (cultural and ethnic) inheritance had been somewhat diffident – made sure that the 600th anniversary of the death of this almost legendary figure in 2006 was properly commemorated.

Conclusion

Apart from the Preface, this whole book has been written in the third person. However, now that I am expressing my personal thoughts and opinions again – as opposed to setting out a largely factual record – I will revert to the first person.

Why such silence on the roles of Islamic Spain and Constantinople?

In the Preface I referred to the myth of the Renaissance being inspired in Italy and other European countries, and owing little or nothing to external factors. As I carried out research for Part III of the book, I increasingly realised that the influences on Medieval Europe from Islamic Spain, and from Constantinople, were far greater than I had previously thought – which again begs the question: Why are the extent of these influences, in making us Europeans who we are, not more widely promulgated?

In the Middle Ages, the unspoken excuse was mostly linked to the mounting of successive Crusades not being compatible with acknowledging any debt to the unspeakable infidel. During the Renaissance, the (Catholic) Church was determined not to have its authority undermined, as witness the ignominious treatment of Galileo. But what about the Age of Enlightenment, wherein – following the rigorous questioning of Papal Infallibility – great swathes of northern Europe had turned to Protestantism?

One would think that, from the death of Descartes in 1650, as the humanist movement gained ground, surely the history of access to our (by then) astonishing body of knowledge in all fields would be freely disseminated. My theory is that while the growing body of Academia knew how fortunate the West had been to be fed such a wide range of priceless information from not one, but two, key sources, there was no incentive to bring this news to the general public. After all, until at least the end the 19th century there was no universal education.

What then has been the excuse throughout the past 150 years or so? During this hectic modern era we have seen the Industrial Revolution achieve 'full throttle', wealth becoming widespread as never before, creating a genuine middle class, and a policy adopted of education for all, with progressive academic achievement marked (through examination) by the issue of ever more highly prized 'certificates'. I have started asking reasonably well-educated people, young and old (including the occasional academic), a standard question: Why does the mathematical branch known as 'algebra' carry this unusual sounding name? I am now approaching the 100 mark in my unofficial questionnaire, but have yet to elicit a correct answer (other than the occasional hint at the truth) from a single individual!

The answer is that algebra is derived from 'al-jabr', Arabic for 'the restoration' or 'the reckoning'. Nurtured in Baghdad from Greek (Hellenistic) origins, algebra owes part of its derivation to Indian mathematics. The breakthrough came via the genius of the Baghdad scholar al-Kwarizmi (c780-850), who, through his work *The Compendious Book on Calculation by Completion and Balancing*, established algebra as a separate mathematical discipline from arithmetic and geometry. What is more, through translation by Gerard of Cremona (see Chapter 22) it is the Latinised name for al-Khawarismi – Algoritmi – that gave us the term 'algorithm'.

Some of the people I have questioned (and, indeed, myself) studied algebra in their youth, at least for a period. Why, at the start of the academic year in question, did we not learn from our teachers the origins of the subject that we were to spend the next number of years struggling to understand? Perhaps such an explanation (exploration) would have grabbed the attention of this poor student! Perhaps part of the answer, between (say) 1850 and 1950, lies in the most powerful European nations vying to create their empires. With the attempts, now regarded as atrocious, to seize and hold territory in master/servant relationships, together with unfounded claims of the ethnic superiority of the rulers, maybe it would have been regarded as a sign of weakness to admit to increasingly well-educated populations at home, that – but for two strokes of outrageous luck, and 'the grace of God' – these empire-builders would never have become powerful enough to even dream of such expansionist ambitions.

A summary of Europe's outrageous luck

The first stroke

At the beginning of Chapter 17 we saw that, in c700AD, Western Europe was a shambles, as the result of wave after wave of massed insurgents sweeping in from Eastern Europe over the preceding 300 years – each wave in turn forcing its predecessors towards the 'Celtic fringes' in Britain and northern France, and otherwise into the Iberian or Italian peninsulas. At almost exactly the same time (see Chapter 20) Muslim armies had overrun the North African coastline, and these highly motivated invaders viewed with envy the vast lands of comparative fertility that lay only a short distance across the Strait of Gibraltar.

So the first stroke of good fortune for Western history arrives in *two parts*. First, the weak and divided Visigoths made the mistake of providing these militants with an even better insight into the potential of Andalusia by asking for their help to put down an insurrection in 710. And the Muslims seized their opportunity by returning to conquer Spain in 711.

Only 40 years later, in Syria (750) the Abbasids were totally ruthless in seeking to eliminate every member of the Umayyad dynasty. The young Abd al-Rahman only escaped by the skin of his teeth, eventually making his way along North Africa and taking his chance to cross into Spain with his small band of followers in 755.

The second part was subsequently put in place by Abd al-Rahman's arrival at Malaga – at least as momentous an event in Western history as William setting foot in England 300 years later. As Chapter 20 describes, during the next 30 years this remarkable young man oversaw the establishment of Europe's first 'medieval' style of government – centuries ahead of the rest of the West – with a massive infrastructure programme, buttressed by a professional army. And we have seen that, long before William reached England, both the standard and style of living, and cultural inheritance transferred from Baghdad, were beyond the wildest imaginings of the emerging 'barbarian' states north of the Pyrenees.

The second stroke

Now we move forward hundreds of years to the failing state of Byzantium. As we have seen in Chapter 23, Constantinople was under siege at various times in the 60 years before it finally fell in 1453.

371

So the second stroke of luck derives from a combination of two circumstances: that the intermittent blockade was porous, and the city did not fall in 'one fell swoop', with the conquering Ottoman troops wiping out the intelligentsia indiscriminately; and that the humanist philosophers and teachers felt more empathy for Catholic Italy than for their own harsher Hesychast-driven regime, and were intrigued by the possibilities that a new (and safer) life could give them.

It is appropriate to appreciate that limited knowledge clung on in the West after the fall of Rome (Chapter 17). Indeed, through the tireless searches of such men as Petrarch and Boccaccio (900 years later!) a wealth of priceless manuscripts that had lain dormant was eventually revealed. However, that apart, from 500 onwards the only *substantial* repositories of the classical knowledge that continued to be constantly studied and interpreted lay either in the shrinking Eastern Roman Empire, or (through the spread of Hellenism) in Syria and Iraq, in this case greatly augmented by the unbroken threads of original culture that had been passed down from Mesopotamia to the Sassanid (Persian) Empire, prior to the emergence of Islam.

It is clear, therefore, that – but for the two pieces of great fortune that so benefited Western Europe – this continent's development would have been drastically slowed, with all the wonderful features that so illuminated the Classical Age lost, or perhaps irretrievably buried.

For, although it could never be proven either way, if both the Middle East and Byzantium had been smothered by Ottoman militancy and bureaucracy *before* their miraculous transfer of priceless knowledge, the intellectual, scientific and cultural development of the West could have been set back a thousand years.

A final salutary point can be made at this juncture. As a contrast to every other corner of the Western World, the Middle East (for this purpose focussing on the fabled cities within the Fertile Crescent, and along the Tigris and Euphrates rivers) has been the only region in the western hemisphere that enjoyed a virtually unbroken sequence of scholarship from the dawn of civilisation until finally succumbing to Ottoman suffocation in c1550, an unparalleled span of some 5,000 years. Despite the sequence of empires, and damage inflicted by every marauder, our story of this cradle of civilisation shows that every conqueror absorbed and enhanced – almost without exception – the state of learning reached by his predecessors.

The West and the Middle East, 1950-2010

But what of the post-Second World War environment? The West has enjoyed a greater level of peace and prosperity than ever before; democracy has flourished in most of Europe, with the creation of the European Union; in c1975 the twin dictatorships of the Iberian peninsula were cast off; and in c1990 the Soviet Union collapsed, with most of its constituent states becoming fully democratic.

And yet, in the past 20 years the Western democracies have watched, with a growing degree of mutual hand-wringing, the steadily deteriorating situation in the Middle East (extending of course through Iran to Afghanistan). We have tried to help forcibly in Iraq and Afghanistan, only to be at best misunderstood, and – more realistically – hated for our bungled interventions. We have tried to cajole Israel into giving the Palestinians an independent homeland, a dream for that shattered and dispossessed people that is as far off as ever. Worst of all for our domestic security and sensibilities, we have seen fanatical terrorism (tragically in the name of Islam) reach the United States and Europe, even sucking in an unknown number of our own citizens.

The 'Arab' world today

As I write this conclusion – in the summer of 2011 – much of the so-called Arab world is in turmoil. Of course many members of the Arab League (of 22) do not have wholly ethnic Arab populations, nor is the Muslim faith as universal as is widely supposed, 10% of the population of both Egypt and Syria being Christian. And within most states there is a mixture of Sunni and Shia adherents, with (for example) 10-15% Shias in a Sunni-dominated Saudi Arabia.

While the 'West' envies the oil reserves in the Arab world, we should have enormous sympathy for some of their long-standing problems. After all, it was the UK and France that carved up most of the vast territory in an unholy scramble after the collapse of the Ottoman Empire during the First World War, and imposed artificial borders and rulers in one new country after another, without a proper form of legitimate process. (A new book by James Barr, A Line in the Sand, provides a scholarly and chilling account of this dreadful period of intrigue between these supposedly loyal allies.) If these factors did not create a deadly enough cocktail for instability and resentment, a further totally intractable problem was ensured through the well-meaning Balfour Declaration, in its ambiguously expressed desire to see the creation of a Jewish homeland.

But now we have the Global Economy. A majority of the population in each country in question is under the age of 30 and fully Internet-savvy. Their access to the World Wide Web has given them an insight into the freedoms enjoyed by most of the rest of the globe, of which their parents – just 20-30 years ago – were almost totally ignorant. Sooner or later, at whatever cost in bloodshed, these armies of young protesters will not be denied.

And now – with some rulers having purloined their country's assets over decades – there is talk of incentivising the incipient moves towards democracy by offering an updated version of the post-Second World War Marshall Plan. If ever actioned, this would offer *economic* support to buttress the series of democratic – or otherwise non-totalitarian – governments that will hopefully emerge. But, in my opinion, such a far-sighted move will not alone bring the West and the Arab world closer together in terms of the *empathy* required for long-term 'cohabitation'.

(As a contribution towards greater understanding, the three-part BBC2 programme in July 2011 fronted by Rageh Omaar, describing the life and work of the prophet Muhammad, can certainly be regarded as helpful. It is to be hoped that enlightened writers, historians and broadcasters – in the West – will maintain a steady flow of similarly meaningful output for years to come.)

Obviously, the largely Christian 'West' and the predominantly Muslim 'Greater Arabia' will continue to pursue their separate religions, but, in my view, if there is to be a programme of economic assistance this should be coupled with an equally dynamic programme to promote educational and cultural understanding. A prerequisite for this 'cement' that could fix the 'bricks' of a whole new relationship should be the mutual disavowal of religious zealotry. After all – as has been explained throughout Part III of this book – East and West share a common heritage from both a religious and a secular point of view, if only we are prepared to learn from the past. So we finish with my schedule of areas in which the 'West' should be proactive – ideally best promoted through various agencies of the United Nations.

We are at the crossroads. In our relationship with the nations of the

Arab League we have to seize the moment to link economic help and advice with a humble recognition of our own part in their tragic past – and offer genuine and original solutions so as to categorically safeguard the future of an 'Arab Spring'.

A programme of 'Truth and Reconciliation'

If, eventually, a version of the Marshall Plan is established, those rich countries that contribute to a UN-led fund should allow a proportion to be set a side for educational and cultural purposes. With funding from the Western democracies available to the poorer Arabic states, the following initiatives should be included in a sustained (say 20-year) programme of reconciliation:

1 The Western countries that bear the greatest responsibility for the colonisation and partition of many present-day countries within the Arab League (Britain, France and Italy) should issue a solemn declaration of their culpability in imposing such arbitrary decisions on the territories in question, mainly in the aftermath of the First World War.
2 Western and Arabic universities should initiate courses, involving the exchange of tutors and students, specifically to learn about their shared heritage of knowledge, and how the flow of original thinking made its way into Western consciousness.
3 Western countries should commit to including an introduction to each subject taught in schools – at each level of learning – that explains the origins and development of that subject, prior to it coming into the hands of European scholars.
4 The national museums of Western countries should enter into a programme of repatriation for ancient artefacts originating in the Middle East, where there is no record of a genuine arms-length acquisition.
5 A programme for the creation or expansion of museums in Arabic countries should be undertaken, so as to house the thousands of priceless treasures returned.

On 2 April 2011 *The Times* leader eloquently made the case for democratic institutions 'in societies with Muslim majorities'. I wholeheartedly agree with the sentiments expressed in that article, and believe that such a programme as outlined above would make the likelihood of a lasting outcome – along democratic lines – far more likely to materialise.

And what of Greece?

The country that absorbed the fragments of knowledge and skill that were extant from prehistory until c800BC, and then initiated such startling developments in every field, also deserves special treatment from the wealthy Western beneficiaries of ancient Greek genius.

The question of repatriation of works of art and artefacts – obtained by dubious methods, mostly in the 18th century – cannot be left at the discretion of museum authorities. The notorious case of the so-called 'Elgin Marbles' stands out, but is only one example of thousands, where the most famous repositories of some of the world's greatest wonders are holding on to these treasures quite indefensibly, on any independent assessment.

What makes the situation much worse is the revelation that – in Britain as a prime example – the British Museum is only able to display some 10% of its stock of treasures at any one time. Even at the Ashmolean Museum in Oxford, after the magnificent new extension had increased display space by 150%, only some 15-20% of artefacts held can now be shown simultaneously.

So my first plea is that a similar programme to that proposed under recommendation 4 above be initiated, without any further prevarication.

Another concern I have is the general lack of knowledge about our heritage from Classical Greece. Schoolchildren do not have to learn Greek to acquire even a basic understanding of the origins of many of the subjects they will be studying. Furthermore the cash-strapped British School of Athens and the Friends of same could become involved in promulgating the wonders of that ancient culture.

So my second plea is for a far greater awareness of Classical Greek history to be taught, coupled with encouragement to visit the most influential city in the ancient world. In an era where school trips abroad are commonplace, I would like to see Athens become a key destination. Even the most callow youth would be bowled over by a morning at the Parthenon, and another at the wondrously modernised Archaeological Museum.

I can finish by quoting the words of Horace, which shows my passion, and cannot be a surprising epilogue (from the Greek 'epilogos'!) to any reader who has managed to struggle through the whole of this book!

'Ille terrarum mihi praetor omnes angulus ridet.'

'This corner of the earth smiles for me more than any other.'

Bibliography

This section contains the books I have read since taking *The Bull of Minos* and *The End of Atlantis* to Crete on holiday in March 1977. All the others have been read in the subsequent 34 years, and have been quoted or referred to – with much appreciation – in the text of this book.

Quoted in the text
Aegean Bronze Age, The Oliver Dickinson (Cambridge University Press)
After the Ice Steven Mithen (Phoenix Books)
Ancient Egypt T. G. H. James (British Museum Concise Introduction)
Ancient History, The Penguin Dictionary of edited by Graham Speake (Penguin)
Archanes J. and E. Sakellarakis (Ekdotike Athenon)
Atlas of the Greek World Peter Levi (Facts on File, USA)
Babylon Joan Oates (Thames & Hudson)
Babylonians H. W. F. Saggs (British Museum Press)
Bull of Minos, The Leonard Cottrell (Efstathiadis, Athens)
Civilisation before Greece and Rome H. W. F. Saggs (B. T. Batsford)
Cyprus Before History Louise Steel (Gerald Duckworth)
Discovery of the Greek Bronze Age, The J. Lesley Fitton (British Museum Press)
End of Atlantis, The J. V. Luce (Thames & Hudson)
Engineering the Ancient World Dick Parry (Sutton Publishing)
Etruscans, The Graeme Barker and Tom Rasmussen (Blackwell Publishing)
Europe, a History Norman Davies (Pimlico)
Goddess and the Bull Michael Balter (Left Coast Press)
Greek Myths Robert Graves, introduction by Kenneth McLeish (Folio Society)
Greek and Roman Art Lucilla Burn (British Museum Press)
Hill of Kronos, The Peter Levi (Eland Publishing)

History of Knowledge, A Charles Van Doren (Ballantine Books)

Hittites, The J. G. Macqueen (Thames & Hudson)

Iceman Brenda Fowler (Pan Books)

Iliad, The translated by Robert Fagles (Penguin Books)

Iran, Empire of the Mind Michael Axworthy (Penguin Books)

Islam, a Short History Karen Armstrong (Phoenix Press)

Knossos (Mythology-History) Antonis Vassilakis (Adam Editions, Athens)

Knossos: Unearthing a Legend Alexandre Farnoux (Thames & Hudson)

Library of Alexandria, The edited by Roy Macleod (I. B. Tauris)

Mediterranean in the Ancient World, The Fernand Braudel (Penguin Books)

Mediterranean in History, The edited by David Abulafia (Thames & Hudson)

Minoans J. Lesley Fitton (British Museum Press)

Minotaur Alexander Macgillivray (Jonathan Cape)

Moorish Spain Richard Fletcher (Phoenix Press)

Motya: Unearthing a Lost Civilisation Gaia Servadio (Victor Gollancz/Orion Books)

Mycenaeans, The Louise Schofield (British Museum Press)

Phoenicians and the West, The Maria Eugenia Aubet (Cambridge University Press)

Pre-History of Europe, The Oxford Illustrated edited by Barry Cunliffe (OUP)

Punic Wars, The Nigel Bagnall (Hutchinson/Pimlico)

Odyssey, The translated by Robert Fagles (Penguin Books)

Odysseus Unbound Robert Bittlestone (Cambridge University Press)

Ornament of the World Maria Rosa Menocal (Little, Brown)

Otzi, the Iceman Angelika Fleckinger (South Tyrol Museum of Archaeology)

Rash Adventurer, The Imogen Grundon (Libri Publications)

Sailing from Byzantium Colin Wells (Bantam Dell)

Words of Mercury Patrick Leigh Fermor, edited by Artemis Cooper (John Murray)

Other reading referred to

Aegean, From Bronze Age to Iron Age Oliver Dickinson (Routledge)

Afghanistan: Crossroads of the Ancient World edited by Fredrik Hiebert and Pierre Cambon (British Museum Press)

After the Prophet Lesley Hazelton (Anchor Books)

Ancient Iraq (Eyewitness) edited by Clare Hibbert (Dorling Kindersley)

Byzantium, Oxford University History of edited by Cyril Mango (OUP)

Canaanites Jonathon N. Tubb (British Museum)

Flowering of the Renaissance Vincent Cronin (The Folio Society)

Freedom in the Ancient World Herbert J. Muller (Secker & Warburg)

Gibbon's Decline and Fall (abridged) edited by Rosemary Williams (Bison Books)

Great Adventures in Archaeology edited by Robert Silverberg (Robert Hale)

Great Civilisations (of the Ancient World) edited by Goran Burenhult (Fog City Press, USA)

Greeks and Romans, The Nathaniel Harris (Hamlyn Publishing)

Jerash, and the Decapolis Iain Browning (Chatto & Windus)

Homer's Landscapes J. V. Luce (Yale University)

Lost Civilisations of the Stone Age Richard Rudgley (Arrow Books)

Medieval Europe, Oxford University History of edited by George Holmes (OUP)

Much Have I Travelled (A book of quotations) compiled by Kirsty Crawford

Mycenae: Agamemnon's Capital Elizabeth French (Tempus Publishing)

Mycenaean World, The K. A. and Diana Wardle (Bristol Classical Press)

Petra Iain Browning (Chatto & Windus)

Phoenicians Glenn E. Markoe (British Museum Press)

Pompeii: The Living City Alex Butterworth and Ray Laurence (Orion Books)

Roman Italy T. W. Potter (British Museum Press)

Tomb of Agamemnon, The Cathy Gere (Profile Books)

Traces of Antiquity in the Greek Landscape texts by Maria Belogianni (Patakis Publishers)

Warfare in the Ancient World edited by General Sir John Hackett (Sidgwick & Jackson)

World of the Phoenicians, The Sabatino Moscati (Weidenfeld & Nicolson)

Museum and tourism guides, and other articles

Acropolis, The Manolis Andronicus (Ekdotike Athenon)

Alhambra and Generalife, The (printed in Spain)

Ancient Arabic Science pamphlet by Charles F. Horne (Kessinger Publishing)

Arthur Evans and the Palace of Minos Ann Brown (Ashmolean Museum)

Arthur Evans, Knossos and the Priest-King S. Sherratt (Ashmolean Museum)

Athens, History, Monuments, Museums (Ekdotike Athenon)

Heracles to Alexander the Great (Ashmolean Museum)

Heraklion Archaeological Museum Andonis Vasikalis (Adam Editions, Athens)

Herculaneum Vincenzo Carcavallo

Geoscientist (Volume 18): 'Testing classical enigmas', John Underhill

Mycenae–Epidaurus S. E. Iakovidis (Ekdotike Athenon)

National (Archaeological) Museum Dr Semni Karouzou (Ekdotike Athenon)

Paestum (Regione Campania)

Peloponnese, The E. Karpodini-Dimitriadi (Ekdotike Athenon)

Piazza Armerina Guiseppe Di Giovanni

Pompeii Falanga Edizione Pompeiani

Pompeii AD79 compiled by John Ward-Perkins and Amanda Claridge (Carlton Cleeve)

Pylos: A Journey through Space and Time G. & T. Papathanassopoulos (Athens)

Santorini (A Guide to the Island) Christos Doumas (Ekdotike Athenon)

Siracuse: History, Art and Legend (Ditto Italia Paola)

Story of the Roman Amphitheatre D. L. Bomgardner (Routledge)

Acknowledgements

The Times
On the recommendation of my Headmaster, I started reading this newspaper at around my 11th birthday, during the Korean War, when the Allies were (momentarily) hanging on in the Pusan Pocket in September 1950. More than 60 years later I am still reading the paper every day – and storing up copies at home, when we are abroad!

The wealth of information I have gleaned – on famous discoveries in particular, and on archaeology in general – is too numerous to mention, or even recall accurately, and is belied by only one of my many cuttings being quoted in this book, Marcus Binney's article, of 11 November 1992, on the restoration programme at the Parthenon.

Certainly it was 'The Thunderer' that caused me to buy Robert Bittlestone's book *Odysseus Unbound*, and follow this up by tramping around the Paliki peninsula of Cephallonia.

Wikipedia
After a very tentative start, I have referred to this amazing dictionary on many occasions, and am indebted to the genius of Jimmy Wales, the creator of this valuable medium.

Friends of the British School at Athens
Although my membership is quite recent, I have drawn inspiration from their dedication while writing this book.

Index